The Translation Zone

TRANSLATION | TRANSNATION

SERIES EDITOR **EMILY APTER**

Writing Outside the Nation   BY AZADE SEYHAN

The Literary Channel: The Inter-National Invention of the Novel
EDITED BY MARGARET COHEN AND CAROLYN DEVER

Ambassadors of Culture: The Transamerican Origins of Latino Writing
BY KIRSTEN SILVA GRUESZ

Experimental Nations: Or, the Invention of the Maghreb
BY RÉDA BENSMAÏA

What Is World Literature?   BY DAVID DAMROSCH

The Portable Bunyan: A Transnational History of The Pilgrim's Progress
BY ISABEL HOFMEYR

We the People of Europe? Reflections on Transnational Citizenship
BY ÉTIENNE BALIBAR

Nation, Language, and the Ethics of Translation
EDITED BY SANDRA BERMANN AND MICHAEL WOOD

Utopian Generations: The Political Horizon
of Twentieth-Century Literature
BY NICHOLAS BROWN

Guru English: South Asian Religion in a Cosmopolitan Language
BY SRINIVAS ARAVAMUDAN

Poetry of the Revolution: Marx, Manifestos, and Avant-Gardes
BY MARTIN PUCHNER

The Translation Zone: A New Comparative Literature
BY EMILY APTER

EMILY APTER

The Translation Zone
A New Comparative Literature

PRINCETON UNIVERSITY PRESS

PRINCETON AND OXFORD

Library of Congress Cataloging-in-Publication Data

Apter, Emily S.
The translation zone : a new comparative literature / Emily Apter.
p.   cm.   —(Translation/transnation)
Includes bibliographical references and index.
ISBN-13: 978–0-691–04996–0 (cloth : alk. paper) —
ISBN-13: 978–0-691–04997–7 (pbk. : alk. paper)
ISBN-10: 0-691–04996–3 (cloth : alk. paper) —
ISBN-10: 0-691–04997–1 (pbk. : alk. paper)
1. Translating and interpreting. I. Title. II. Series.
P306.A58 2006
418′.02—dc22   2005043382

British Library Cataloging-in-Publication Data is available
This book has been composed in Minion with Gill Sans Display
Printed on acid-free paper. ∞
pup.princeton.edu
Printed in the United States of America
10 9 8 7 6 5 4 3

CONTENTS

ACKNOWLEDGMENTS   vii

TWENTY THESES ON TRANSLATION   xi

INTRODUCTION   1
Introduction   3

1
Translation after 9/11: Mistranslating the Art of War   12

PART ONE
TRANSLATING HUMANISM   23

2
The Human in the Humanities   25

3
Global *Translatio*: The "Invention" of Comparative Literature,
Istanbul, 1933   41

4
Saidian Humanism   65

PART TWO
THE POLITICS OF UNTRANSLATABILITY   83

5
Nothing Is Translatable   85

6
"Untranslatable" Algeria: The Politics of Linguicide   94

7
Plurilingual Dogma: Translation by Numbers   *109*

PART THREE
LANGUAGE WARS   *127*

8
Balkan Babel: Language Zones, Military Zones   *129*

9
War and Speech   *139*

10
The Language of Damaged Experience   *149*

11
CNN Creole: Trademark Literacy and Global Language Travel   *160*

12
Condé's *Créolité* in Literary History   *178*

PART FOUR
TECHNOLOGIES OF TRANSLATION   *191*

13
Nature into Data   *193*

14
Translation with No Original: Scandals of Textual Reproduction   *210*

15
Everything Is Translatable   *226*

CONCLUSION   *241*

16
A New Comparative Literature   *243*

NOTES   *253*

INDEX   *287*

ACKNOWLEDGMENTS

The book was shaped by the traumatic experience of September 11, 2001, which occurred while I was a Rockefeller Fellow at the Institute for Research in African and Caribbean Cultures at the City University of New York. I am grateful to the circle of friends and colleagues at that time who bonded together in the surreal aftermath of that fateful day: James de Jongh, director of the Institute, and fellow members of the seminar were a mainstay, as were close friends: Rosalind Krauss, Denis Hollier, Nancy K. Miller, Sandy Petrey, Hal Foster, Tom Keenan, Margaret Cohen, and Anne Higonnet.

The book was begun in 1999 while I was teaching at UCLA. Support for research, writing, and sabbatical time was generously provided by the university. I was fortunate to have had occasion to work with inspiring colleagues, among them: Samuel Weber, Aamir Mufti, Efrain Kristal, Andrew Hewitt, Françoise Lionnet, Dominic Thomas, Kenneth Reinhard, Michael Heim, Michael North, Mary Kelly, and Pauline Yu.

For her invaluable assistance with interviews in Istanbul, as well as her discovery and translation of Leo Spitzer's essay "Learning Turkish," I offer profound thanks to Tülay Atak. Süheyla Bayrav offered hospitality and invaluable recollections of her experience as Leo Spitzer's student. I also thank Fredric Jameson for providing me with contacts at the University of Istanbul.

From 1997 to 1999 I had the good fortune of teaching at Cornell University and benefited from the unique spirit of intellectual exchange at the A. D. White House Society of the Humanities. It is with especial gratitude that I acknowledge the support of Jonathan Culler and Dominick LaCapra.

The award of a Guggenheim Fellowship in 2003 and a sabbatical leave from New York University enabled me to complete work on the book. I am indebted to these institutions for their support and to a number of colleagues at NYU who smoothed my transition back to New York:

Tom Bishop, Denis Hollier, Judith Miller, Richard Sieburth, Mary Louise Pratt, Virginia Jackson, and Martin Harries. I have also benefited from "uptown" collaborations with Gayatri Chakravorty Spivak (whose articulations of a "new comparative literature" inform the book's concerns throughout), Maryse Condé, Andreas Huyssen, David Damrosch, and the late Edward Said, who was kind enough to invite me to a commemorative conference on Orientalism at Columbia University in April 2003. My consideration of humanism owes much to Said's vision of *Welt-humanism* and is dedicated to his memory.

Many people provided crucial institutional opportunities to present phases of this work as it unfolded at New York University, UCLA, UC Riverside, Cornell University, Columbia University, Brown University, SUNY-Stonybrook, McGill University, Dartmouth College, Princeton University, Harvard University, Duke University, Stanford University, Yale University, the Getty Institute, the Institut Français in London, Fordham University, and the Whitney Program in Critical Studies, NYC. For their particularly generous hosting, I wish to thank Sandra Bermann, Réda Bensmaïa, Pierre Saint-Amand, Elizabeth Mudimbe Boyi, Michael Heim, Peter Gibian, Verena Conley, Jann Matlock, Emory Elliott, Ann Kaplan, Lawrence Kritzman, Margaret Cohen, Zaia Alexander, Charles Forsdick, David Murphy, Eva Hoffman, Pierre Force, Françoise Lionnet, Mary Kelly, and Ron Clark.

My research assistant at NYU, Jeppe Nielsen, provided invaluable assistance at all stages of manuscript preparation.

For permission to republish portions of this book, I gratefully acknowledge *October, Critical Inquiry, boundary 2, Parallax, Public Culture, Anglistica, Sites,* and *Romanic Review.* Muntadas kindly granted permission to use an installation image from his project *On Translation: The Games.*

A special word of thanks must be expressed to Mary Murrell, one of the great editors, with whom I enjoyed a wonderful intellectual collaboration on the Princeton University Press book series Translation/Transnation. Our exchanges about translation and comparative literary studies shaped the concerns of this book in countless ways. I am grateful to Princeton University Press for its recognition that books on and in translation are essential to the continuing vitality of the humanities, part of a university press's central mission. Hanne Winarsky, Mary's editorial successor at Princeton, has demonstrated professional integrity and vision in helping with the final stages of the book's production.

My family has been a constant source of personal sustenance: thanks to my parents David and Eleanor Apter, to my brother Andrew, to my spouse Anthony Vidler, whose knowledge, critical intelligence, and personal support have helped me beyond measure, and to my son Nicolas Apter-Vidler, whose commitment to translation in its many guises (music, French, Mandarin Chinese, computer language) represents inspiration for the future against the backdrop of political dark times.

TWENTY THESES ON TRANSLATION

- Nothing is translatable.

- Global translation is another name for comparative literature.

- Humanist *translatio* is critical secularism.

- The translation zone is a war zone.

- Contrary to what U.S. military strategy would suggest, Arabic is translatable.

- Translation is a *petit métier*, translators the literary proletariat.

- Mixed tongues contest the imperium of global English.

- Translation is an oedipal assault on the mother tongue.

- Translation is the traumatic loss of native language.

- Translation is plurilingual *and* postmedial expressionism.

- Translation is Babel, a universal language that is universally unintelligible.

- Translation is the language of planets and monsters.

- Translation is a technology.

- Translationese is the generic language of global markets.

- Translation is a universal language of *techne*.

- Translation is a feedback loop.

- Translation can transpose nature into data.

- Translation is the interface between language and genes.

- Translation is the system-subject.

- Everything is translatable.

INTRODUCTION

The urgent, political need for skilled translators became abundantly clear in the tragic wake of 9/11, as institutions charged with protecting national security scrambled to find linguistically proficient specialists to decode intercepts and documents. Translation and global diplomacy seemed never to have been so mutually implicated. As America's monolingualism was publicly criticized as part of renewed calls for shared information, mutual understanding across cultural and religious divides, and multilateral cooperation, translation moved to the fore as an issue of major political and cultural significance. No longer deemed a mere instrument of international relations, business, education, and culture, translation took on special relevance as a matter of war and peace.

It is in this political situation that *The Translation Zone: A New Comparative Literature* took shape. The book aims to rethink translation studies—a field traditionally defined by problems of linguistic and textual fidelity to the original—in a broad theoretical framework that emphasizes the role played by mistranslation in war, the influence of language and literature wars on canon formation and literary fields, the aesthetic significance of experiments with nonstandard language, and the status of the humanist tradition of *translatio studii* in an era of technological literacy.

Structuring my lines of inquiry has been an awareness of the contradictory process by which globally powerful languages such as English, Mandarin Chinese, Swahili, Spanish, Arabic, French simultaneously reduce linguistic diversity and spawn new forms of multilingual aesthetic practice. While it has become commonplace, for example, to bemoan the hegemony of global English as the lingua franca of technocracy, there has been insufficient attention paid to how other global languages are shifting the balance of power in the production of world culture. Chinese, for example, is now a major language of Internet literacy and is taking on English as never before.

An underlying premise of this book has been that language wars, great and small, shape the politics of translation in the spheres of media, literacy, literary markets, electronic information transfer, and codes of literariness. The field of translation studies has been accordingly expanded to include on the one hand, pragmatic, real world issues—intelligence-gathering in war, the embattlement of minority languages within official state cultures, controversies over "other Englishes"—and on the other, more conceptually abstract considerations such as the literary appropriation of pidgins and creoles, or multilingual experimentalism among historic avant-gardes, or translation across media.

Translation studies has always had to confront the problem of whether it best serves the ends of perpetuating cultural memory or advancing its effacement. A good translation, as Walter Benjamin famously argued, makes possible the afterlife of the original by jumping the line between the death of the source language and its futural transference to a target. This death/life aporia leads to split discourses in the field of translation studies: while translation is deemed essential to the dissemination and preservation of textual inheritance, it is also understood to be an agent of language extinction. For translation, especially in a world dominated by the languages of powerful economies and big populations, condemns minority tongues to obsolescence, even as it fosters access to the cultural heritage of "small" literatures, or guarantees a wider sphere of reception to selected, representative authors of minoritarian traditions. There is a Malthusian dimension to this ecology of endangered languages and literatures. In works like David Crystal's *Language Death* (2000) or Andrew Dalby's 2002 book, *Language in Danger: The Loss of Linguistic Diversity and the Threat to Our Future*, the analogy is drawn between the fragile survival prospects of animal and plant species in environmentally threatened habitats, and the prospects of threatened languages. In California alone, for example, of the ninety-eight Native American languages that were once spoken, not one is likely to survive. According to Dalby, "of those 98 languages, 45 or more have no fluent speakers left at all, 17 have only one to five speakers left, and the remaining 36 have only elderly speakers. Not a single California Indian language is being used now as the language of daily communication."[1] In the work of Dalby and Crystal, translation emerges as one of many enemies to the continued vitality of living languages, no matter how well it might preserve ethnic memory or mitigate cultural amnesia.

With their primary interest and expertise located in linguistic anthropology, Dalby and Crystal represent an ecological/environmentalist approach within translation studies, operating at the juncture of "fieldwork" on endangered language species and language politics (including the legitimacy struggles of dialects, the subversion of standard language usage by historic avant-gardes, the erosion of distinct literary traditions in the era of digital literacy). Where translation studies habitually concerned itself with questions of *adequatio*; that is to say, the measurement of semantic and stylistic infidelity to the original literary text, now it might emphasize language over literature, determining semantic loss and gain as a result of linguistic erosion or extinction.

I have real reservations about pushing translation studies in the direction of linguistic ecology even if this new direction offers potentially rich possibilities for interdisciplinary work between comparative literature and area studies. My worries are grounded in the concern that a translation studies overly indebted to linguistic ecology risks fetishizing heritage language as it devotes itself to curatorial salvage: exoticizing burrs, calques and idiomatic expressions as so many ornaments of linguistic local color, reinforcing linguistic cultural essentialism, and subjecting the natural flux and variation of dialect to a standard language model of grammatical fixity. I am personally more inclined toward a critical model of language politics that would continue to emphasize aesthetic and theoretical questions, while invigorating the investigation of linguistic nominalism, or what a language name really names when it refers to grammatical practices in linguistic territories.

Language wars have also remained a central theme in my conceptualization of translation zones. In fastening on the term "zone" as a theoretical mainstay, the intention has been to imagine a broad intellectual topography that is neither the property of a single nation, nor an amorphous condition associated with postnationalism, but rather a zone of critical engagement that connects the "l" and the "n" of transLation and transNation. The common root "trans" operates as a connecting port of translational transnationalism (a term I use to emphasize translation among small nations or minority language communities), as well as the point of debarkation to a cultural caesura—a trans——ation—where transmission failure is marked.

Guillaume Apollinaire's famous 1912 poem "Zone" defined a psychogeographical territory identified with the Paris periphery where bohemia, migrants, and marginals converged. But this idea of the zone has long since become topologically diffuse as distinctions between urban and rural, center and periphery, pre- and postindustrial, pre- and postcapitalist have melted away. Zones have been cast by the architect Rem Koolhaas as substitutes for planning, as limits on the capacity of space to change.[2] Extrapolating here, the idea of the translation zone corresponds in the terms of social engineering to regulated language parks, restricted areas of mixed use, demarcations of apartheid, *cordons sanitaires.* While the book focuses in several sections on how theories of semantic zoning (especially those of Willard Quine) have been used to keep languages separate, enclosed in their own worlds, and untranslatable, for the most part, the zone, in my ascription, has designated sites that are "in-translation," that is to say, belonging to no single, discrete language or single medium of communication. Broadly conceived in these terms, the translation zone applies to diasporic language communities, print and media public spheres, institutions of governmentality and language policy-making, theaters of war, and literary theories with particular relevance to the history and future of comparative literature. The translation zone defines the epistemological interstices of politics, poetics, logic, cybernetics, linguistics, genetics, media, and environment; its locomotion characterizes both psychic transference and the technology of information transfer.

Cast as an act of love, and as an act of disruption, translation becomes a means of repositioning the subject in the world and in history; a means of rendering self-knowledge foreign to itself; a way of denaturalizing citizens, taking them out of the comfort zone of national space, daily ritual, and pre-given domestic arrangements. It is a truism that the experience of becoming proficient in another tongue delivers a salubrious blow to narcissism, both national and individual. Translation failure demarcates intersubjective limits, even as it highlights that "eureka" spot where consciousness crosses over to a rough zone of equivalency or crystallizes around an idea that belongs to no one language or nation in particular. Translation is a significant medium of subject re-formation and political change.

Though I have translated professionally only rarely, and have never discovered a particular talent for it, the act of translation has proved to be vital to my thinking; a sobering corrective to the temptation to think too abstractly or figuratively about the topic. It is with a renewed respect for the *practicum* of translation that I finished this book, and I must herewith acknowledge pioneers in the field of translation studies, many of whom have also distinguished themselves as great translators: George Steiner, André Lefevere, Antoine Berman, Gregory Rabassa, Lawrence Venuti, Jill Levine, Michael Heim, Henri Meschonnic, Susan Sontag, Richard Howard, and Richard Sieburth. Equally important has been the work of Jacques Derrida, Paul de Man, Barbara Johnson, Philip Lewis, Samuel Weber, and Gayatri Chakravorty Spivak, all of whom defer to Walter Benjamin's unsurpassed essay on the "task of the translator," published originally in 1923 as the preface to Baudelaire's *Tableaux parisiens* under the German title: *Deutsche Ubertragung mit einem Vorwort über die Aufgabe des Ubersetzers, von Walter Benjamin.* My readings conflate "The Task of the Translator" with "The Work of Art in the Era of Its Reproducibility" in tracing a genetic interpretation of textual afterlife. Heuristically, I have also tried to read as an ensemble scattered writings on language and translation that Benjamin wrote at different stages of his life, some of them published only posthumously. "On Language as Such and on the Language of Man" (1916), "Language and Logic" (1920–21), "Problems in the Sociology of Language" (1934), and "Translation—For and Against" (1935 or 1936), when read alongside "The Task of the Translator," produced an array of theoretical problematics that resonated with contemporary debates around language as symbolic logic and digital literacy, the politics of sacred language, *techne* as a universal code-language, translation as an all-purpose, intermedial technology

> Translation attains its full meaning in the realization that every evolved language (with the exception of the word of God) can be considered a translation of all the others. By the fact that, as mentioned earlier, languages relate to one another as do media of varying densities, the translatability of languages into one another is established. Translation is removal from one language into another through a continuum of transformations. Translation passes through continua of transformation, not abstract areas of identity and similarity.[3]

In this passage from "On Language as Such," Benjamin effects an important shift in translation theory away from a "fidelity to the original" model (valorizing ideals of *adequatio*, commensurability, isomorphism, likeness, and same) and toward a transcoding model, in which everything is translatable and in a perpetual state of in-translation. The chronotype of Benjaminian translation is the *now-time* (*Jetztzeit*), the same time that Benjamin associated with revolutionary historicity in his theses on the concept of history (1940).

In addition to providing the field of translation studies with its most theoretically rich and enigmatic precepts, Benjamin forged an intriguing, yet undertheorized connection between philology and critical theory. Benjamin stands at a crucial intersection in the history of translation theory between philology and critical theory, between Erich Auerbach and the Frankfurt School, between historical materialism and psychotheology. Though he did not share the profound aversion to mass culture characteristic of the philologists and the Frankfurt school theorists, Benjamin forged an aesthetics of history that calibrated technological modernity's influence on the typology and standardization of style. His stylistics of industrial design—as a translational form that constructs a veritable philology of iron, steel, and glass in order to interpret the translation of production into culture—was not incompatible with Leo Spitzer's philological credo of "linguistics and literary history" or with Auerbach's understanding of *figura* as a representational construct of Western mimesis. Prescient in its conjugation of philology and Frankfurt School Marxism, Benjaminian translation theory overhangs the projection of future trajectories in comparative literature and motivates the passage from humanism to language technologies that structure the organization of this book.[4]

In the first section, "Translating Humanism," I discuss the origins of comparative literature as a postwar discipline in Leo Spitzer's Istanbul seminar of 1933. Erich Auerbach's eleven-year sojourn in Istanbul (where he was brought as Spitzer's designated successor) is also given its due, informing my speculation that many of the themes that preoccupied Auerbach—the future survival of Western civilization under conditions of "primal nationalism," the effect of linguistic (auto)-colonization on literary language and its public—grew out of parallels that Auerbach perceived among imperial Rome, Germany under the Third Reich, and Turkey after Attatürk's language reforms.

In focusing on the late Edward Said's preface to a new edition of Auerbach's *Mimesis*, I pick up the thread of Spitzerian humanism, itself dedicated to restoring the human (in the form of a neovitalist etymon) to the humanities. Saidian humanism became the logical place to consider how philology—so dependent on translation practice and on the kinship relations among languages—has returned in the guise of an ethics of ontogenesis and global *translatio*. Despite the problematic association of humanism with European universalism, humanism remains fast in Said's thought, integral to his program of a critical secularism that refuses to foreclose the possibility of a common world culture.

As this book unfolded, it became clear that two opposing principles—"Nothing is Translatable" and "Everything is translatable"—consistently emerge as poles of translation theory. As Barbara Johnson has observed: "The very obstacles to translation may point toward the 'pure language' that translation enables one to glimpse."[5] The fact that translation happens despite these very obstacles led me to the comparative poetics of Alain Badiou. Badiou's view of translation as a disaster that nonetheless enables a singular comparatism of the Idea afforded an interesting paradigm: one based not on shared philological word-histories, but on the limitless and irreducible bounds of *poesis.* In the permission it grants to translate from divergent periods and traditions, Badiou's philosophy of the Idea introduces an enhanced democracy of comparison.

Untranslatability was also a term that could describe the side effects of an international publishing industry that favors certain countries and specific kinds of writing. Here I focused on a number of interrelated problems: the marketing of national literature, the politics of publishing (with emphasis on the dominance of Anglophone or standard-language publishing houses), and the impact of an internationalized aesthetics that gives special treatment to translation-friendly prose and artistic genres. In assessing how works gain visibility, I took into account ideologies of reception and readability, material impediments to diffusion in economically beleaguered countries, and the impact of censorship (and the Rushdie effect) worldwide.

Part 1, on language wars, overlaps with Part 2 in its examination of responses to the effects of processed culture and the spread of global English. I interrogate the anomalous situation whereby authors writing in *patois,* vernacular, argot, creoles, pidgins and so on, gain international recognition *despite* the stylistic and rhetorical roadblocks thrown in the path of their reading publics, *despite* the special problems their use of language poses for translators, and *despite* the rejection they risk from native readers who may judge the literary display of their speech and dialect a form of betrayal, an exposure of private communication systems, an exoticization of their verbal culture. Though the provincialization of the internationalist canon, and the waning of translation may seem to be the inevitable outcomes of Anglophone dominance, there are significant instances of recalcitrance, ranging from Louis Wolfson's attack on English as the mother tongue in his 1974 novel *Le Schizo et les langues,* to Irvine Welsh's transcription (in *Trainspotting*) of a working-class Edinburgh vernacular that spits in the face of the British ruling class, to the "CNN Creole" of the Martinican francophone author Raphaël Confiant. Their writing demonstrates how the power of dominant languages can be subverted by the inventive creativity of the most disadvantaged peoples. It also provokes serious reflection on what constitutes the limits of a discrete language, not just in terms of original and target, or native and "foreign," but more precisely in terms of language as a border war conditioned by the clash between plurilingualism and corporate standardization. In a chapter on "Balkan Babel" I define the translation zone as a military zone, governed by the laws of hostility and hospitality, by semantic transfers and treaties.

In the fourth and final part, devoted to technologies of translation, I evaluate the impact of programming code and machine translation on the future of the humanities. Here I broach the question of how translation studies (and the humanities more generally) will or will not assimilate technological literacy and media theory. Digital technology, it would seem, is increasingly challenging the boundaries of what translation is, taking it out of the discourse of aesthetic original and copy and into the realm of technological reproducibility, linguistic and genetic. As everything (in theory at least) becomes translatable through the medium of digital code, translation embodies a systematicity or "will to System" that traces back to the "Earliest System-Programme of German Idealism" attributed by Philippe Lacoue-Labarthe and Jean-Luc Nancy to Hölderlin-Schelling-Hegel. Tangible as the "idea of a knowledge of the world as ideal knowledge," as "a greater physics," as a "programmatic" arrangement of exigency and desire, and as the "last task and the last work of humanity," this post-Kantian will to System describes the resurrected formalism and far-reaching epistemological aims of translation in the era of technological reproducibility.[6]

Leo Spitzer's philological credo of linguistics and literary history was crucial to defining the discipline of comparative literature in the postwar period and it continues to inspire new trajectories in comparative literary studies. Brought back from its distinguished past as the medium that permitted the Renaissance to invent itself through a recuperation of ancient learning and culture, translation became the pedagogical pivot of a curriculum established by Europeans in exile from Nazi Germany. This revaluation contributed to redressing the historic undervaluation of the translator's craft in the nineteenth and early twentieth century, during which the names of translators were frequently left off the books they translated. Members of the literary proletariat, classed among Grub street writers and the lowly ranks of copy editors, translators were often financially exploited and rendered anonymous unless they happened to be famous writers already. The same low status has frequently accrued to translation studies as an academic subdiscipline. Reversing this history of class injustice has been one of the objectives of this project.

A new comparative literature, with the revalued labor of the translator and theories of translation placed center stage, expands centripetally toward a genuinely planetary criticism, extending emphasis on the transference of texts from one language to another, to criticism of the processes of linguistic creolization, the multilingual practices of poets and novelists over a vast range of major and "minor" literatures, and the development of new languages by marginal groups all over the world.[7] A new comparative literature has prompted me to imagine a field in which philology is linked to globalization, to Guantánomo Bay, to war and peace, to the Internet and "Netlish," and to "other Englishes" spoken worldwide, not to mention the "languages" of cloning and computer simulation. Envisaged as the source of an ambitious mandate for literary and social analysis, translation becomes the name for the ways in which the humanities negotiates past and future technologies of communication, while shifting the parameters by which language itself is culturally and politically transformed. By insisting, too, on learning languages wholly distant from one's native philology, a new comparative literature based on translational pedagogies renews the psychic life of diplomacy, even as it forces an encounter with intractable alterity, with that which will not be subject to translation.

1

Translation after 9/11: Mistranslating the Art of War

In the wake of 9/11 translation became a hot issue when the United States realized that it had a dearth of Arabic translators. Suddenly transparent was the extent to which monolingualism, as a strut of unilateralism and mono-cultural U.S. foreign policy, infuriated the rest of the world. Though mono-lingual complacency evaporated along with public faith in the translation skills of State Department and intelligence operatives, the psychic and politi-cal danger posed by the Anglocentrism of coalition forces was never suffi-ciently confronted. The "terror" of mistranslation has yet to be fully diag-nosed, and the increasing turn to machine translation as a solution does little to assuage fear. Before the Iraq War began, MSNBC reported on Octo-ber 7, 2002: "If U.S. troops soon storm into Iraq, they'll be counting on computerized language translators to help with everything from interrogat-ing prisoners to locating chemical weapons caches. Besides converting or-ders like 'put your hands up' into spoken Arabic or Kurdish, [M]ilitary offi-cials hope to enable quick translations of time-sensitive intelligence from some of the world's most difficult tongues."[1] Reliance on hand-held MT devices developed by DARPA (Defense Advanced Research Projects Agency) for use "in the field" was especially popular during the Bosnian war. One of the favored programs bore the optimistic name "Diplomat." But the results proved to be unreliable, and in the worst cases fatally flawed. The stakes of mistranslation are deadly, for in the theater of war a machinic error can easily cause death by "friendly fire" or misguided enemy targets.

As this book's completion coincided with the U.S. invasion and occupation of Iraq, it became impossible to ignore the relevance of the daily news to my concerns, and I began compiling a running log of "translation and war" clippings from mainstream sources. Some salient examples included the following (ideally they would be presented in the format of a constantly self-updating disc):

Item: 7/25/03 Neil MacFarquahar in the *New York Times*: "Baghdad, Iraq, July 24—As soon as the photographs of Uday and Qusay Hussein appeared on the television screen tonight, arguments erupted in the Zein Barbershop downtown. Half the men present exulted that their former oppressors were dead, while the others dismissed the images as forgeries because the dictator's sons were elsewhere when the attack occurred."

Item: *Asia Times* 11/11/2003: "In terms of linguistic and cultural capacity the US today commands what may be the lowest-quality clandestine service of any great power in history."

Item: 11/22/03 *New York Times*: Judith Miller "A Battle of Words over War Intelligence." B9. Edward N. Luttwak (a maverick defense analyst at the Center for Strategic and International Studies) affirms that: "To be a case officer you have to be a poet. . . . You need to be able to learn Urdu in six months." Woefully short of language skills, many American intelligence officials, "can't even ask for a cup of coffee."

Item: 10/7/2003 *New York Times*: "Fear of Sabotage by Mistranslation at Guantánamo. American interpreters suspected of sabotage. Military investigators review interrogations involving Arabic-language interpreters. There is a fear of an infiltration conspiracy. 'The worst fear is that it's all one interrelated network that was inspired by Al Qaeda,' said a senior Air Force official."

Item: 10/8/03 *New York Times*: "Roadside Bombs Kill 3 Soldiers and a Translator in Iraq."

Item: www:thetalentshow.org/archives/000767 citing pages 70–72 of November 2003 report issued by the Joint Inquiry into Intelligence Community Activities before and after the Terrorist Attacks of September 11, 2001, and followed by commentary: Finding: Prior to September 11, The Intelligence Community was not prepared to handle the challenge it faced in translating the volumes of foreign language counterterrorism intelligence it collected. Agencies within the Intelligence Community experienced backlogs in material awaiting translation, a shortage of language specialists and language-qualified field officers, and a readiness level of only 30% in the most critical terrorism-related languages. The National Security Agency Senior Language Authority explained to the Joint Inquiry that the Language Readiness Index for NSA language personnel working in the counterterrorism campaign languages is currently around 30%. [...] The Director of the CIA Language School testified that, given the CIA's language requirements, the CIA Directorate of Operations is not fully prepared to fight a world-wide war on terrorism and at the same time carry out its traditional agent recruitment and intelligence collection mission. She also added that there is no strategic plan in place with regard to linguistic skills at the Agency.

... Nine soldiers being trained as translators at a military-run language school have been discharged for being gay despite a shortage of linguists for the US war against terror, officials and rights activists said Friday. The nine were discharged from the army's Defense Language Institute in Monterrey, California over the course of this year, said Lieutenant Colonel Wayne Shanks, a spokesman for the army's Training and Doctrine Command. They included six who were being trained as Arabic speakers, two in Korean and another in Chinese, he said. All the servicemembers had stellar service records and wanted to continue doing the important jobs they held, but they were fired because of their sexual orientation, said Steve Ralls of the Servicemen's Legal Defense Network.

Item: 12/14/2003 David Lipsky reviewing *I Am a Soldier Too: The Jessica Lynch Story* by Rick Bragg in the *New York Times*: "Some reviewers have questioned whether, without the exploits initially attributed to her, there could be any power in Lynch's narrative. (Though Bragg does not say so, the early error had a simple explanation. According to later news reports, the Army was intercepting Iraqi radio chatter, and overheard that a yellow-haired soldier from Lynch's unit had indeed fought bravely and fallen; that soldier turned out to be a sergeant named Donald Walters. Interpreters confused the Arabic pronouns for he and she, and thought it was Lynch.)"

Item: May 7, 2004, Brian Ross on the death of an Iraqi Baath Party official while imprisoned at Camp White Horse in southern Iraq ("Death in Detention: Marine Reservists Face Charges in Iraqi

Prisoner Death." ABCNEWS.com): "Lawyers say none of the Marines spoke Arabic, nor were there any translators assigned to the camp."

As each of the entries reveals, nontranslation, mistranslation, and the disputed translation of evidentiary visual information, have figured center stage throughout the Iraq War and its aftermath. The mythic story of Jessica Lynch's heroic resistance to her captors, fully exploited by the government and the media, risked fizzling away over a translation error, even as the most precious resource the CIA had in its possession—qualified translators engaged in counterterrorism operations—was squandered because of homophobic military policy. Over and over again, the pugnacious unilateralism of the Bush defense team found an outlet in championing monolingual jingoism, as when Donald Rumsfeld replied to questioning by a German reporter on being left out of the loop in the coordination of government agencies in Iraq with: "I said I don't know. Isn't that clear? You don't understand English?" Rumsfeld's English-only retort was symptomatic of a linguistic arrogance that flew in the face of American dependency on translators in Iraq, people who laid their bodies on the line as preferred human targets.[2] Translators in Guantánamo Bay became a different kind of target; as prime suspects in the eyes of the U.S. military, a substantial number were charged as Al Qaeda infiltrators. On the media war front, the "translation" of images became increasingly vexed. Images of the putative corpses of Hussein's sons, widely disseminated as "proof" of U.S. victory, aroused suspicion of image doctoring and faulty clues on the Iraqi street, as Morelli-like, people scrutinized ears and beards as insecure guarantors of documentary reality. The infamous medical-check video of Saddam Hussein, broadcast all over the world as proof in any language of the dictator's capture, did not convey the universal message that was hoped for by the administration. Instead, it inspired suspicion of image-manipulation. As John Milner has argued with respect to the rapidly produced paintings, prints, drawings, wood engravings, and photographs of the Franco-Prussian war (by artists such as Meissonier, Degas and Renoir), "realism, reportage, fact, fabrication and propaganda form[ed] a kind of spectrum."[3] No less subject to mistranslation than language, images remain untrustworthy documents of the event.

Mistranslation in the way I have conceived it is a concrete particular of the art of war, crucial to strategy and tactics, part and parcel of the way in which images of bodies are read, and constitutive of *matériel*—in its extended sense as the hard- and software of intelligence. It is also the name of diplomatic breakdown and paranoid misreading. Drawing on Carl von

Clausewitz's ever-serviceable dictum "War is a mere continuation of policy by other means," I would maintain that war is the continuation of extreme mistranslation or disagreement by other means.[4] War *is*, in other words, a condition of nontranslatability or translation failure at its most violent peak.

The so-called war on terror and the enhanced impact of translation on the way it is waged still awaits theorization, but as critics attempt to think through the role of translation as a weapon of war, they will undoubtedly defer, as have so many war theorists before them, to Clausewitz's classic 1832 treatise *Vom Kriege*, a combination bible and grammar of the art of war. Oskar Von Neumann, Anatol Rapoport, Michel Foucault, Gilles Deleuze, Paul Virilio, Manuel de Landa all took a pass through von Clausewitz even if only to stand him on his head. Rapoport, for example, criticized the way in which neo-realist Clausewitzians applied the indifferent moral calculus of game theory to military strategy, while Foucault inverted the famous Clausewitzian formula in arguing that "politics is a continuation of war by other means" (a principal theme of his 1976 Collège de France lectures, published under the English title *Society Must Be Defended*).[5] What interests me most about Clausewitz's theory is the way in which it formalized the art of war, casting it as a network or closed circuit that could be systematically modeled according to evolving phases of modernity.

In the second chapter of *Vom Kriege* Clausewitz traced the art of war to the coordination of combat during medieval sieges. As the conduct of war became gradually more systematic and self-conscious, there was a call for the explicit codification of rules and maxims. Material factors initially prevailed: superiority of numbers, the concept of the base (founded on the hypotenuse of length of armies to width of provision and communication center), and the idea of "interior lines." Von Clausewitz recomputed these features superadding emotional elements: courage, hostility, envy, generosity, pride, humility, fierceness, tenderness. These components of a military code of honor, when combined with the laws of strategy and tactics, gave rise to an eighteenth-century art of war defined along aesthetic lines, with emphasis on drills, formations, and the elegant and perfectly obedient execution of orders. War continued to be waged according to this model during the French Revolution, but with a substantive difference: the new class of soldier-patriot battled the enemy in the name of universal principles. Building cynically on the inspiration to fight "for France," Napoleon expended soldiers prodigally, using mass armies to annihilate rather than outmaneuver the enemy, and teaching the old Europe that "the universal currency of politics is power, and power resides in the ability to wreak physical destruction" (OW 21). In the estimation of many, Napoleon's abrogation of the fundamental rules of civilized warfare produced the great epistemic shift theorized by von Clausewitz: the passage from discrete standardized codes (typical of eighteenth-century warfare) to war as *Gesamtkunstwerk*, in which principles of morale, intuition, and nationalist purpose were fully activated. The Prussian invention of a citizens army, guided by von Clausewitz's "translation" of Napoleonic performatives into a philosophy of war, is arguably what secured Prussia's triumph over Napoleon in 1815, and its victory in the Franco-Prussian war.

In their eagerness to define modern war over and against eighteenth-century characterizations of it as a chess game or balletic choreography, von Clausewitz and his neo-realist followers seem to have underestimated the survival of *ancien régime* formalism in the nineteenth-century art of diplomacy. Diplomacy, along with the discursive approach to war analysis on which it historically relied, was considered by the neo-realists to be overly dependent on the Kantian view of war as the expression of psychological forces. This "soft" model compared unfavorably with "hard" rational-choice models that concentrated on power optimums, cost-benefit motive, and the maximization of military technology. In a bid to move beyond the hard-soft opposition, sociologist Philip Smith proposed a Durkheimian theory of war as social ritual and cultural *parole*.[6] Treating the language of diplomacy as "social fact," Smith gave a cultural assignation to the "inter-subjective basis for agreement and dissent," exploring the cultural grounding of diplomatic rhetoric, propaganda, and media coverage (PS 109). Instead of relying on a "popular understanding of the popular understanding of events," he interpreted the rituals of cultural mistranslation that lead to war as, "a festival of rationality, a celebration of modernity, and a rite of democracy." Patriotism, jingoistic rhetoric, and the like are for Smith part of the "civil religion" of culture, constitutive of its normative accounting system, culturally "rational" even when a nation's interests are not obviously served by going to war. Using a rational-choice approach to the cultural politics of war, Smith oddly enough returns us to old-fashioned diplomatic history with a renewed charge to take seriously the role of language—and by extension, the role of mistranslation—in fomenting preconditions for war.

Smith, in my view, proposes a semiological anthropology of diplomacy at the expense of psychoanalysis (dismissed as too reductive). I think it makes more sense to keep the psychoanalytic dimension of diplomacy in play, not so much because nations behave like individual human subjects (driven by common motivations and desires), but because diplomacy is the expression "by other means" of weaponized language and misfired signs. If war is a language of force, and diplomacy its cipher, then a psychoanalytic rational-choice theory of ballistic speech-acts could prove useful in dissecting historic cases of failed diplomacy.

In this context, the recent failure to find weapons of mass destruction in Iraq, and the subsequent questioning of the "dossier" prepared by Tony Blair and used by George Bush to justify the invasion, was appropriately compared to that earlier and celebrated fabrication by Bismarck that led to the outbreak of the Franco-Prussian War. Thus the *Daily Telegraph* reported a remark by the Labour MP Peter Tapsell to the effect that "Tony Blair's Iraq dossier was the most false publication in diplomacy since Bismarck falsified the 'Ems Telegram.' "[7] This tallies with a World Socialist Web site account of a meeting between George Bush and the German chancellor Gerhard Schröder in which the same analogy was drawn (occasioned by the story of how the ice was broken at their meeting by a "joke" Bush made when he referred to the pen that Schröder's translator had accidentally dropped in his lap, as "an attack with weapons of mass destruction").[8]

Given its renewed circulation in the press, the details of the Ems affair warrant rehearsal. In June of 1870, Spain and Prussia hatched a plan to put Prince Leopold of Hohenzollern-Sigmarinen on the Spanish throne, vacant after Queen Isabella II's abdication in the wake of the revolution of 1868. Leopold was a good choice from the Prussian point of view. Linked by blood to the Prussian king Wilhelm I, he would strengthen the hand of the German house in its bid to become an imperial European power. As a Catholic, with ties to the Murats and Beauharnais, he was in theory acceptable to the French. But this was not how the French saw the matter. Deeming the Hohenzollern candidacy an outrageous affront to their national honor and an illegitimate endeavor to upset the balance of power in Europe, the French cried foul, insisting that Wilhelm withdraw his support of the initiative on pain of war. The kaiser did not want war. Vacationing in the spa town of Ems (near Coblenz), the king arranged to meet with the ambassador of France, Vincent Benedetti, to inform him that his cousin's decision to renounce his claim to the Spanish throne would meet with his approval. In principle, the matter should have ended there, but the French sought further reparation. Goaded by the jingoistic Duc de Gramont, they insisted that the king meet again with Benedetti in order to extend a royal apology along with guarantees that no future claims would ever be made to the Spanish succession. Benedetti apparently stalked Wilhelm in the gardens of Ems, seeking an interview. At this provocation the king took umbrage and refused to meet with him. However, he indicated through the intermediary of his councillor of the legation, Heinrich Abeken, that he nonetheless intended to honor his commitment to the withdrawal of Leopold's candidacy. Abeken relayed this official position to the prime minister, Prince Otto von Bismarck in what came to be known as the Ems Dispatch. Wilhelm's text read

> I rejected this demand somewhat sternly as it is neither right nor possible to undertake engagements of this kind [for ever and ever]. . . .
> [The king, on the advice of one of his ministers] decided in view of the above-mentioned demands not to receive Count Benedetti any more, but to have him informed by an adjudant that His Majesty had now received from [Leopold] confirmation of the news which Benedetti had already had from Paris and had nothing further to say to the ambassador.[9]

When the telegram reached Bismark, he happened to be dining with General Helmet von Moltke, Prussia's paramount military officer. Their discussion focused on the state of the French army, weakened by aging troops, a lack of distinguished commanding officers, a disastrous expedition in Mexico, and the diversion of resources in Africa. Concerned to preempt a French plan for military reform, Bismarck and von Moltke decided the time was ripe to move against France. To guarantee a bellicose response, Bismarck "edited" the Ems telegram, turning its phrases so as to give greater offense. "His Majesty the King," Bismarck's version read, "thereupon refused to receive the Ambassador again and had the latter informed by the adjudant of the day that His Majesty had no further communication to make to the Ambassador." The effect was exactly what Bismarck had predicted when he noted that the dispatch would be "like a red rag to the Gallic bull." Although the changes may not seem hugely significant when examined up close, their import was great, for Bismarck implied that instead of just canceling a meeting, the king intended to cut off all further negotiations. Losing no time, Bismarck sent the telegram to the major European embassies and German newspapers. Here, one might note, the story of the dispatch reveals the increasingly determinative impact of information relay on the course of modern warfare. (The Zimmerman telegram, arguably the decisive factor in prompting the United States to enter World War I qualifies, perhaps, as the most flagrant case of all.) Clearly, as far as the Ems Dispatch is concerned, damage was done by its "straight to the media" path. The full text—a German translation of Bismarck's communiqué, which I believe was originally sent in French in accord with diplomatic custom—appeared that very night as a supplement of the *Nord Deutsche Allgemeine Zeitung* and was distributed free of charge in Berlin. When the French translation of the German translation appeared in the Parisian press, the reaction was one of hysteria. Not only had Bismarck "edited" the document to aggravate the affront to French pride, but the French translation of the German text contained a mistranslation of the word *adjudant*. It may be no great exaggeration to say that the entire Franco-Prussian war hinged on this single term. Adjudant in German signifies "aide de camp," and whichever paper translated the telegram from German to French simply transferred the same word to the French text. Unfortunately, the French term *adjudant* refers to a "warrant officer," or sergeant-major. The level of insult was profound, for it appeared that Wilhelm was treating the French ambassador with disrespect, sending an emissary of lowly rank to communicate his message rather than his ennobled aide de camp Prince Radziwell. Formal diplomatic reticence was thus "translated," with the help of the perfidious Bismarck, into an outrageous breech of protocol. Despite the upper hand gained by the peace party in Paris at just this moment, the Ems Dispatch was treated as direct provocation by the Prussians to Napoleon III, and cries could be heard everywhere of "La Guerre! A bas Bismarck! Au Rhin!" The momentum for war was impossible to curb even after the edited and unedited texts of the telegram had been compared and it was determined that France had obtained its most important concession. Thiers, joining Gambetta, Arago, and Jules Favre in opposing war argued plaintively: "Do you want all Europe to say that although the substance of the quarrel was settled, you have decided to pour out torrents of blood over a mere matter of form?" The answer was a resounding affirmative from the center and right; Guyot-Montpayroux retorted: "Prussia has forgotten the France of Jena and we must remind her," while Emile Ollivier made an unfortunate remark that he would never live down; that he would accept responsibility for war with "un coeur léger" hastily qualified as: "I mean a heart not weighed down with remorse, a confident heart."[10]

Viewed against the larger backdrop of two countries jockeying to become the continental superpower most challenging to Britain, the affair of the Ems Dispatch shows the outbreak of war turning on an act of mistranslation. In this particular case, it appears to have been the nontranslation of a word, what one often calls in the language business a *faux ami* (wherein a common word or root conveys a false synonym), that propelled the country to the brink. Had they checked the German word for warrant officer—*Feldwebel*—the French, one might speculate, could perhaps have avoided ensnarement in Bismarck's trap. And yet, even if one concurs with the historians in interpreting the Ems Dispatch as more a symptom than an outright cause of war, the whole affair points to the impossibility of dialogue constitutive of the "truth" of Franco-Prussian relations. As Jacques Lacan put it succinctly to the partisans of May 1968: "Il n'y a pas de dialogue, le dialogue est une duperie." ["There is no dialogue, dialogue is a sham"] Anticipating his more famous utterance: "Il n'y a pas de rapport sexuel," ["There is no sexual relation"] Lacan invokes a politics of nonrelation, in which monologues are arraigned side by side around a traumatic gap.[11]

Exposing the *duperie* of diplomatic dialogue, the Ems Dispatch, one could say, fulfilled a burgeoning French paranoia vis-à-vis the Prussians that shaped all of fin-de-siècle culture. Internal betrayal or treason was suspected as a way of blocking national self-criticism. Zola identified this attitude with the posture of denial in *La Débâcle* when Private Weiss is censored by his commanding officer after describing why Germany is a serious force to be reckoned with: "Then there was the system of compulsory military service, bringing an entire nation to its feet, bearing arms, trained and disciplined . . . and then there was this army's intelligence and strong generalissimo who seemed set to reinvent the art of battle." First reprimanded for demoralizing the troops, Weiss's clear-sighted view of the Prussian threat is greeted by a fellow soldier (a mercenary and veteran of the Algerian campaign) with incredulity: "What line are you spinning us there? What's all that rubbish meant to mean? . . . 'Beaten? France beaten? I'd like to see those Prussian swine try and beat us lot.'"[12] After the defeat, the delusional complex only worsens. As Freud noted in a paper addressed to Fliess in 1895, "The '*grande nation*' cannot face the idea that it can be defeated in war. *Ergo* it was not defeated; the victory does not count. It provides an example of mass paranoia and invents the delusion of betrayal."[13] One could argue that from the Ems Dispatch to the infamous *bordereau* used to convict Dreyfus, a line could be drawn connecting diplomatic *duperie* to cultural paranoia. Mistranslation in the art of diplomacy thus comes to signal an intractable nontranslatability between nations, a condition of catastrophic *blocage* that inspires paranoid projection and the moral calculus of the zero-sum game (in which whatever benefits one side is assumed to hurt the other).

Baron von Clausewitz was the quintessential theorist of the zero-sum game in the art of war, and it is no accident that postwar game theorists of nuclear deterrence relied on his work. And one could say that Clausewitzian principles are in full bloom in the contemporary notion of "war all around" in which the state of not-war is proved to be the exception. Diplomacy and the psychoanalytic reading of national desire in this new theater of war may seem increasingly irrelevant. And yet, as Freud knew well, exclusively realist, rationalist, and normalizing accounts of war foreclose a critical understanding of catastrophist causality and the operative force of diplomatic "black holes" in the psychic life of nations. In his late text "Warum Krieg?" Freud essentially shifted the paradigm from a Clausewitzian "vom" Krieg to a Freudian "warum." And what this transit from *vom* to *warum* ultimately entailed was the move from an ethically neutral philosophy of war—one based on converting Napoleonic performatives into a metaphysics of strategy and tactics—to a psychoanalysis of war, conceived as a failed "abreaction" of repression. When, in "Why War?" Freud asked Einstein, "Why do you and I and so many other people rebel so violently against war? Why do we not accept it as another of the many calamities of life? After all, it seems to be quite a natural thing, to have a good biological basis and in practice to be scarcely avoidable," he seemed to have been taking direct aim at the Clausewitzian position, which accepts war as the logical extension of politics, as integral to a naturalized status quo. By posing the question "Warum krieg?" Freud questioned blind adherence to a law of intellect that represses instinct, overrides the self-preservative erotic drive to life, and mis-recognizes the destructive persistence of the death instinct (SE 22 213–14). In hindsight, Freud's psychoanalytic attention to war's "reason" takes us not in the direction of a utopian politics that could be realized through the practice of expert diplomacy or "good" translation. Accepting mistransla-tion as a given, Freud opened the door to a pragmatist politics of *mésen-tente*—a rationality of disagreement model in Jacques Rancière's terms, or what Jonathan Schell (in *The Unconquerable World*) calls "civil non-cooper-ation." The aporia of nontranslatability would thus be factored into rethink-ing the art of war.[14]

Abstract though it may seem, the idea of war as a codified language, "translatable" according to fixed rules or laws, is hardly immaterial, for as we may ascertain just by scanning the newspapers after 9/11, there is no clean split between the theory of war and its consequences on the ground. As the "enemy" in the so-called war against terror increasingly diffuses its base of operations, and as battle zones remove themselves to Internet net-works and the arena of electronic diplomacy, war as such is increasingly defined as a translation war: its formal strategy determined by the ability to translate intelligence, its stated objectives increasingly subject to mistransla-tion, and its diplomatic *duperie* as a Great Game ever more crucial to the probability of global extinction or the prospect of global peace.

PART ONE

Translating Humanism

2

The Human in the Humanities

In 1948 the literary critic Leo Spitzer published his celebrated essay "Linguistics and Literary History." Originally titled "Thinking in the Humanities" when it was delivered as a lecture at Princeton to the Department of Modern Languages and Literatures, it became a foundational text and curricular staple in the burgeoning field of comparative literature and in the human sciences generally. From Spitzer to Paul de Man, etymological method fired debates around the postwar humanist legacy, structural semiotics and intertextuality. It informed deconstruction's rhetorical practice, and, in political terms, it gave substance to linguistic racial and national claims, or more precisely, to language wars around philological heritage, patrimony, and the origins of literary culture. The fact that the French term *racine* (with its accrued, overlapping associations around verbal roots and the roots of national culture) may have stirred Gilles Deleuze to invent the counternationalist, nomadological *rhizome* or anti-root only attests to the monumentality of philological thinking. In what follows, I look specifically at the role of what I am calling the "racial etymon" in Spitzer's concept of philology, testing a hypothesis that this etymon calibrates the shifting status of the human in the humanities, from philology to philosophy, and from philosophy to the genetics of language.

As the category of the subject suffers signs of fatigue in contemporary critical theory, the category of the "human" acquires new significance. First, because it speaks to an intellectual surround dominated by the genome project, and the ethical dilemmas attendant on breakthroughs in cloning, reproductive technology, and biological engineering. Second, because, as Thomas Keenan, has pointed out, the human, as a general category partnered uneasily with humanitarianism, serves, however problematically, "as the name of that which would precede geographical divisions and political articulations, of that which is by definition essentially unbordered."[1] And third, because the human represents a possible alternative to the subject, whose grip on critical discourse, both pre- and post-1968, has been relatively firm: the subject of ontology, signaled with the X-mark in Heidegger's "Question of Being," or by Jacques Derrida's rhetoric of difference; the Lacanian subject, linguistically spoken for, and rhetorically desired; the "death of the author" subject, decoded in social and linguistic mythologies; the Foucauldian subject, institutionally formalized within regimes of power and knowledge; the ethical subject, located within models of inoperative community, or hailed by Law; the screened subject of surveillance, cultural reproduction, and commodity fetishism; the proliferating subjects of minority claims and identities; the disremembered subject of historical trauma and repressed memory; the posthistorical subject, negotiating between the anxiety of lost origins and foreclosed teleologies.

In the wake of all this, the human is ushered in as an emergency measure, promising, however utopistically, to put nothing less than life itself back on the table without resubjectivizing it in a neoromantic or postmodern guise. The category of the human thus becomes a way of rethinking the terms of aliveness within the humanities at a time when the refrain "death of the humanities"is all too frequently intoned. And it becomes a way of reemphasizing how race has functioned historically as a constitutive, yet volatile category within postwar humanism: responsible for hoisting Jean-Paul Sartre's "existentialism is a humanism" on the petard of his concomitant essay "Anti-Semite and Jew"; resonating in Frantz Fanon's denunciation of racism within Marxist emancipatory humanism; and complicating paradigms of philological humanism from Spitzer to the present. Though Spitzer's work may not at first blush seem to be the most obvious point of departure for a discussion of the human, on closer inspection it provides a paradigmatic example of how postwar humanism negotiated its way—via the human—into important disciplinary formations of the humanities. Spitzer, if you will, was to literary theory, what Heidegger and Sartre were to philosophy.

An Austrian Jew who was something of a *juif d'état,* having worked during WWI as a military censor, Spitzer was the quintessential apologist for European civilization—a Euro-universalist in the grand manner, a cultural secularist with little use for ethnic affiliation or racial politics.[2] But race, inevitably, claimed him as Nazism gained its foothold in Germany and Austria.[3] In 1933 he emigrated to Istanbul, founding the Department of Latin Language and Literature that Erich Auerbach later joined in 1936. Though it appears that their time in Istanbul did not overlap, Auerbach took over seamlessly the institutional responsibilities that Spitzer had put in place. There were, however, significant differences between them. Spitzer was more open than Auerbach to engaging with Turkish culture, publishing an article, "Learning Turkish" ("Turkceyi Ogrenirken"), in the journal *Varlik* (*Being*) in 1934. The essay is at once a model of linguistic cosmopolitanism (a case for learning non-western languages), and an argument for the European etymon as hegemon (Spitzer takes issue with the emotionalism and excessive spirituality of the Turkish language, recommending corrective therapy that would bend Turkish into conformity with Romance languages).

If "Learning Turkish" shortchanged the possibility of a transnational philology by propounding linguistic universalism, an essay written in the same year as "Linguistics and Literary History" charted the pitfalls of universalism from a racial perspective. Titled "Ratio>Race," the piece would later form part of a study of historical semantics. Spitzer plotted the ominous turn from a Thomistic tradition of *ratio* or *reason* to Italian *razza* and German *rasse* both of which, in different registers, denote the submersion of the Logos in a biological, species-driven vision of the human. The noble tradition of etymological roots or *racines,* crucial to the hierarchical structures and generative grammars of the rational faculty, gradually deteriorate *in the very process of philological demonstration*, into the degraded substance of bestial inhumanity—exhibits in the *tiergarten* of Hitlerism.

Read together, "Ratio>Race" and "Linguistics and Literary History" appear to be part of an effort to rescue philology from Nazi race theory's application to language. When Spitzer speaks of placing his faith in what he calls "my etymon," one knows he is pinning the highest value on this possession. The Spitzerian etymon emerges as the DNA of humanist humanism, the kernel of universalistic *ratio*. Characterized in "Linguistics and Literary History" as "the radix of the soul," the etymon not only holds up the world of the literary work and serves as the connective tissue of theocratic unity, it also operates as the weapon of last resort in the war against cultural barbarism.[4]

On closer inspection, however, Spitzer's etymon seems to stumble into traps of its own making, performing acts of racial injury even as it affords incredible insight into the psycholinguistics of racism, and demonstrating the contagion of the racist spore even as it aims for a philological imperative that explicitly challenges the conservative default to a racialist *racine*. To get some perspective on this claim, let us go back to the essay "Linguistics and Literary History." For Spitzer, the etymon has a very particular character that can be teased out of the essay's autobiographical glimpses of his Austrian formation. The critic's infatuation with the sensuality of the French language is extinguished by the protocols of Germanic pedagogy, with its lifeless treatment of phonetic laws and grammatical history. "We saw incessant change working in language," Spitzer writes, "but why? We were never allowed to contemplate a phenomenon in its quiet being, to look into its face" (LLH 5). This personification of philology is no mere stylistic device; it symbolizes the rescue of linguistic life, of phenomenological experience ("Methode ist Erlebnis"), and what he and Auerbach called "reality," from the clutches of a "meaningless industriousness" that even his esteemed teacher Meyer-Lübke could not eschew. For Spitzer, the stakes of yoking linguistics to literary history amount to nothing less than the retrieval of "man" from the ravages of positivism.[5] "The humanities will be restored only when the humanists shed their agnostic attitudes, when they become human again, and share the Rabelaisian credo: 'sapience n'entre point un âme malivole; et science sans conscience n'est que ruine de l'âme.'" ("Wisdom enters not into the malicious heart, and knowledge without conscience is but the ruin of the soul") (LLH 33).

Similarly committed to humanist vitalism, Auerbach invented the *Ansatzpunkt*—"a handle, as it were by which the subject can be seized. . . . the election of . . . phenomena whose interpretation is a radiation out from them and which orders and interprets a greater region than they themselves occupy."[6] This initiatory *punctum* of linguistic life frees "existence in a standardized world" and triggers the drive to attain "reality," itself constitutive of the worldly humanist individual. Similarly Spitzer marshals etymological "clicks" and "clues" to establish the "living" connection between reality and language. In a protracted demonstration of how disparate etymological mysteries, when brought together, can solve each other, Spitzer shows how the equation *conundrum* and *quandary* = *calembredaine* is proved by their mutual relation to the Norman word *équilibourdie* of 1658. For Spitzer, what is remarkable is not the fact that deductive historical method led to this missing connection, but that the word *équilibourdie* "providentially . . . turns up!" (LLH 11). The "providential" nature of discovery is key here, because the transformation of arbitrary besidedness into relationality—of meaninglessness into meaningfulness—suggests that the humanist etymon is a God term aligning civilization, the national soul, and the psychology of national authors.

The "racing" of philology, or the problem of philological racism, would seem to have little bearing on this explication of language mysteries, but for the presence of an unsettling example that follows closely on its heels:

I am reminded here of the story of the Pullman porter to whom a passenger complained in the morning that he had got back one black shoe and one tan; the porter replied that, curiously enough, a similar discovery had been made by another passenger. In the field of language, the porter who has mixed up the shoes belonging together is language itself, and the linguist is the passenger who must bring together what was once a historical unit. (LLH 11–12)

The anecdote is curious on a number of levels, first, because the point Spitzer is glossing—that language jumbles and distorts etymological connections, while the linguist shows how "Romance languages form a unity going back to Vulgar Latin"—is fairly straightforward and hardly requires adumbration. Second, the story bears an unsettling resemblance to an allegory drawn from everyday experience, something between a Freudian dream or joke and Paul de Man's use of Archie Bunker's "What's the difference?" to underscore rhetorical differentialism. But whether dream alleogry or allegory of reading, what does the analogy between the Pullman porter and the mixed-up-ness of language tell us? Is Spitzer simply drawing on a master/slave parallel to affirm the superior power of the linguist? Or is he suggesting that language, personified as an indentured employee, is readying itself for revenge on the linguist/master?

The air of vaudeville jocularity—a black minstrel show to be precise—works against this reading. The story's so-called humor depends on the reader's recognition that the Pullman porter is too dim to figure out what it means when, "curiously enough," another set of mismatched shoes is discovered on the train. Not unlike Derrida's argument in *La Vérité en peinture*, which faults Heidegger's interpretation of van Gogh's painting of peasant shoes on the grounds that Heidegger fails to see that the shoes do not form a pair, Spitzer derives a critical insight from the example of blindness to "pairness." But what of his own blindness to the culture of Jim Crow on which this story relies? As any conventional source reminds us:

During the century spanning the years 1868–1968, the African-American railroad passenger train employee became a tradition within the American scene. These porters were as universally accepted as apple pie and baseball, yet these were not merely American men and women who just happened to be Negroes working on the railroad. . . .When George Pullman was ready to hire service personnel . . . in 1868, the most logical pool from which to draw was the ready-made work force of recently freed slaves. . . .

> For the price of a Pullman ticket, even the most common man
> could now be waited upon and pampered in the grand manner
> of the privileged Southern gentry.[7]

Spitzer neglects, almost inexplicably, to provide comment on the historical
and social context of his example. Cutting to the chase of "linguistics" he
blindsides the "literary history" half of his theoretical model. The same in-
souciant insensitivity to history would permit him, in discussing the
Friedrich Gundolf dictate *Methode ist Erlebnis* to write: "I would advise every
older scholar to tell his public the basic experiences underlying his methods,
his *Mein Kampf*, as it were—without dictatorial connotations, of course"
(LLH 4). Spitzer's choice of *Mein Kampf* as exemplum of the critic's credo—
an error of poor taste, or poor judgement, or both—leaves the contemporary reader nothing short of incredulous, and yet, it is unsettlingly consistent
with his exegetical practice. Beyond the obvious conclusion that Spitzer was
intermittently tone deaf to the racial and political connotations of his material, these rhetorical episodes reveal the imbrication of a racial unconscious
within humanist philology. Psychological etymology and racial psychology
seemingly chase each other around the same hermeneutic circle.

This intuition is borne out by Spitzer's treatment of Louis-Ferdinand Céline, whom he situates as one of the descendents of Rabelais in a
lineage passing through Balzac, Flaubert, Gautier, Hugo, Huysmans, and
Charles-Louis Philippe. In the latter's novel *Bubu de Montparnasse*, the expression *à cause de toi* becomes the key to understanding an entire symptomology of "pseudo-objective motivation," itself derivative of a demi-
monde vision of causality—"the fatalism weighing on the masses, the *hic*
and *nunc* of a historical phenomenon." Out of the "underworld of pimps
and prostitutes," he gleans "the radix of the soul" or what he later calls the
"psychogram" of the individual artist (LLH 16–18). Spitzer is fascinated by
the way in which dross is converted into gold. His interpretation complements Bakhtin's, in which "Rabelais and his world" are seen as the source
of a carnivalesque aesthetic turning marketplace language or billingsgate
into the currency of linguistic rejuvenation. Rabelais, according to Spitzer,
makes marvelous philology out of linguistic monsters: "He creates word-
families, representative of gruesome fantasy-beings, copulating and engendering before our eyes" (LLH 19).

Céline is important to Spitzer as the Rabelais of the twentieth century. Noting that he builds "a whole book out of invectives against the Jews,"
he emphasizes the hallucinatory, pseudo-Rabelaisian effect of its prose (LLH
19). The book in question, and from which he quotes, *Bagatelles pour un*

massacre, happens to be Céline's most virulent anti-semitic tract, routinely excluded from his complete works even today. Spitzer quotes a particularly offensive passage, though there are many of equal magnitude:

> Penser "sozial!" cela veut dire dans la pratique, en termes bien crus: "penser juif! pour les juifs! par les juifs, sous les juifs!" Rien d'autre! Tout le surplus immense des mots, le vrombissant verbiage socialitico-humanitaro-scientifique, tout le cosmique carafouillage de l'impératif despotique juif n'est que l'enrobage mirageux, le charabia fatras poussif, la sauce orientale pour ces encoulés d'aryens, la fricassée terminologique pour rire, pour l'adulation des "aveulis blancs," ivrognes rampants, intouchables, qui s'en foutrent, à bite que veux-tu, s'en mystifient, s'en baffrent à crever.

> To think "sozial!" It means, in practical, in real crude terms, "to think Jew! For the Jews! by the Jews, under the Jews!" Nothing else! All the immense surplus of words, the roaring socialitico-humanitaro-scientific verbiage, all the cosmic mumbo-jumbo of the imperative despotic Jew is nothing but the miragelike coating, the jumbled short-winded gibberish, the oriental sauce for these bloat-fucked Aryans, the terminological fricasee just for kicks, for the adulation of the "white blobs," crawling drunks, untouchables, who fuck themselves with it, with dicks or what have you, mystifying themselves with it, stuffing themselves to the bursting point. (LLH 30)

Spitzer's colloquial English translation conveys the madcap shock value of turns of phrase in the original French. The word "sozial," in the opening sentence is left the same in English, transcribing the Yiddish-inflected pronunciation of East European Jewish immigrants. The replacement of "c" by "z" introduces an eye dialect internationally recognized as "Kikespeak," or, in the French context, *youpin* language, familiar to European readers from the anti-semitic literature popularized at the turn of the century by anti-Dreyfus pundits such as Léon Daudet and Edouard Drumont. Spitzer's analysis studiously avoids any mention of the language politics infusing Céline's employment of racist graphemes. He passes over the Rabelaisian hybrid tropologies of race and cuisine in expressions such as "oriental sauce" or "terminological fricassee." Notably absent, too, is a discussion of what Dina Al-Kassim calls "the literary rant," referring to historic modes of hate speech. Spitzer goes on:

Here, evidently, the verbal creation, itself a *vrombissant verbiage* [roaring verbiage] (to use the alliterative coinage of Céline), has implications more eschatological than cosmic: the word-world is really only a world of noisy words, clanking sounds, like so many engines senselessly hammering away, covering with their noise the fear and rage of man lonely in the doomed modern world. (LLH 30)

Celebrated as a modernist sound machine, Céline's prose is virtually shorn of its racist sting. Spitzer's interpretation of the *enragé* as the lone man of history, universalized beyond recognition, a figure comparable to the wandering Jew who is the object of his hatred, now raised up as the heir to a new humanism, is astonishing. The vision of Everyman allows us to forget the speaker whose contagious words, in their historical moment, have the performative impact of death sentences. Preoccupied with matters of style, to the exclusion of any comment on the blatant anti-Semitism of the prose, or the historical circumstances of its articulation, Spitzer quite unselfconsciously minimizes, as he did with the Pullman porter, the *Realpolitik* of literary history. "This is really a 'voyage au bout du monde' " Spitzer writes, "not to the oracle of Bacbuc but to chaos, to the end of language as an expression of thought" (LLH 30).

And yet, a more sympathetic reading of Spitzer's suppressed racial etymon is possible if one interprets his emphasis on "the end of language as an expression of thought," as a euphemism for philological genocide and the death of reason. This interpretation gains support from the "Ratio > Race" essay mentioned earlier, which allows us to see how Spitzer's Céline is both the bearer of etymological riches and the carrier of philological nightmare. His abusive tongue provides a perfect example of how the etymon of race—identified with the truth of *ratio*—slips out of the sphere of the Logos and into the clutches of a "*geistverlassen* and God-forsaken modern racialism."[8] "For medieval man, Spitzer writes, the comprehensiveness of this word *ratio* was fertile: the intellect could pass from the nature of things to the idea of them as pre-existent in God's mind, from the content to the container of thought: this was the truth stored up for the believer in the word *ratio*, which seemed to contain an "etymon," a "truth." Probably the fact that the term *species*, also, covered the range from 'species' to 'example, form, idea' made it possible for *ratio* 'idea,' 'type,' to meet it halfway."[9] Reason meets racism halfway in their common cognate, *species*. It is this culprit that opens the door to a moral void, severing the German term *Rasse* from its connection to the "universalistic *ratio*," and anticipating

Peter Sloterdijk's location of humanism in the breeding ground of the "human zoo" (RR 156).

In July 2000 the German philosopher gave a lecture titled "Rules for a Human Park: Response to Heidegger's "Letter on Humanism" that ignited fierce debate in the German and French press. Sloterdijk sketches a brief history of *humanitas* as a literacy network—activated by a caste of philologists invested in reproducing the lettered fold to which they belong—as it evolves into a pedagogical platform for disseminating modern state ideology. This nation-state function of literature has in its turn become superannuated, giving way in our own time to a postliterary, posthumanist condition in which literature "only marginally influences modern megasocieties in the production of a political-cultural tie." The exception to this posthumanist rule, according to Sloterdijk, occurs briefly in 1945, the moment when Heidegger, seeking to exculpate himself from the taint of Nazi collaboration, responds to a question posed by his French disciple Jean Beaufret: "Comment redonner un sens au mot 'Humanisme' " ("How do we restore meaning to the word 'Humanism'?"). Heidegger's response involves questioning the centrality of the human in humanist thought, a centrality to which he attributes overvalued metaphysical explications of what it means to be human, and worse, acts of barbarism committed in its name. Heidegger proposes a custodial relation of man to Being. Pulling him off center and pushing him to the side, he positions Man as the guardian or, more benevolently, as the neighbor of Being. No longer reductively defined as a "thinking animal," overburdened by *ratio*, and locked into an agon with his bestial nature, the Heideggerian human accedes to ontology, a state defined as radical difference from the animal, where thought thinks itself without recourse to vitalist myths and metaphysical compromises. For Sloterdijk, the resulting ascesis of anthropocentrism opens the door to further radicalizing Heidegger's rejection of modern humanism. Rather than conceive of man as an "animal under the influence," that is to say, a creature who, rising above the tempting circus of blood sport, gives himself over to the stationary position of scholarly domestication, Sloterdijk envisages instead a technologized revamping of the biological human—what he calls an "anthropotechnology"—dedicated to the genetic reformation of the species. Nor does he stop there: Sloterdijk's future human seems to legitimize, at least inadvertently, the adoption of pseudo-eugenicist strategies for obtaining a Nietzschean *Uber*-species. With his use of historically freighted language—dressage, breeding, prenatal selectionism, characterological "planification" or personality-management—he opens himself to accusations of fascism by detractors such as Jürgen Habermas.[10] For Habermas, Sloterdijk's genetically inflected vision of community as a theme park of humans is nothing other than a breeding ground for the master-race.

Clearly Sloterdijk has willfully brooked scandal in exposing, with insufficient sobriety, the disturbingly suppressed, yet obviously visible affinity between the specter of Nazi eugenics and the hologram of a genetically engineered super-race hovering over current breakthroughs in the genome project. But for my purposes, what is most interesting about his argument is the way in which he implicates the tradition of philological humanism in a genetic model of the human, thereby entering into imaginary dialogue with Spitzer's bio-organicist vision of linguistic life. For though he never says so explicitly, Spitzer was clearly fascinated by the way in which Céline's offensive anti-Semitic utterances reveal the bio-racial, genetic character of language.

Spitzer's diagnosis of the way in which the word *Rasse* performs the double function of parasite and host to the racist biologism attached to animals, lower-class people, nonwhites, and Jews, is congenial to psychoanalytic paradigms of disavowal and identification. Céline unleashes the Jewish etymon on the native soil of French belles-lettres; he is a linguistic polluter profoundly cathected with what he despises, a practitioner of the rant: "an address, according to Dina Al-Kassim, that must construct the law it seeks to rebuke."[11] On one level, the rant, in *Bagatelles*, does indeed follow this logic, shoring up the law against racist defamation—as when one of the narrator's interlocutors says: "Mais t'es antisémite ma vache! C'est vilain! C'est un préjugé"—even as it prepares the way for repeating, over and over again, the classic anti-Semitic tropes (Jews manipulate world finance, Jews control the culture industries from Hollywood to French publishing, Jews use socialism as an alibi for their evil plots, etc., etc).[12] Introjecting what he loves to hate—the Jew as law of the father, the Jew as master of *jouissance*—the narrator demonstrates a complex that Daniel Sibony has characterized as "hate-desire" (*la haine du désir*). The racist "desires-racist," just as he "buys French," in an essentialist, knee-jerk, nationalistic way ("Il désire-raciste, comme on dit "Il achète français").[13] Citing Dominique de Roux, who argues that for Céline, the word "Juif" is not an ethnic or religious moniker, but rather a magic word for a locus of fear, Sibony suggests that the word "Juif" in Céline's writing functions as a place-marker for the psychodynamics of "loving hate," itself as crucial to the workings of racism as modern pathology.[14]

Using an expression—"l'affect 'ratial' " (which recalls the Célinian "sozial" or parody of Jewspeak)—to identify the hemorrhaging of language typical of Céline's anti-Semitic writings, Sibony shows how racial affect whips up a repression already simmering deep inside the subject. The hatred of Jews, in a familiar construct, thus becomes a mode of hating one's own repressions—specifically castration fear. When, in the beginning of *Bagatelles* the narrator loses a dancer to a Jewish rival, he retaliates threateningly: "you made me stuff my sexual satisfaction back in my pocket, you tore off my balls, you'll see what kind of revenge is in store, you're going to see some anti-Semitism!" (BM 41).

For Sibony, Céline's use of racist locutions such as "sale Juif" or "sale nègre" signify an "impasse in the symbolic, a place where concentrated affect resides, having no other place to go in the symbolic order." Describing *Bagatelles* as "a poetics bordered by insults, a dazzling form of verbal vomiting," Sibony reads Céline's use of oral invective, of sucking, biting, spitting, and so on, in terms of the *blocage* of affect in the esophagus (HD 45). Symptomatic of infant fury, blocked at the oral and anal stage, the childish rant subtends Céline's "anal avant-gardism." According to Sibony, Oedipal anti-Semitism, captured in the perverse semiosis of Célinean rhetoric, operates as a furious, if futile, effort to countermand the splitting of the genitive seme, in turn typecast as maternal and Jewish: "Le champ de la parole craque, s'ouvre." Attaching itself to and mimicking the differential object (the Jewish seme), Célinean hate speech tears language to bits, leaving broken etymological stems waving in the air. This vacillating motion is associated by Sibony with the vacillating character of Bloom, the Joycean Jew, who registers uncertainty, the "hole in knowledge," the Achilles heel of reason (HD 58–59).

Here the slide between reason and racism comes once again to the fore, with the errant "z" sounded out in Spitzer's philological dissection of *ratio* moving closer to Céline's castigation of *Sozial Denken* as the Jewish alibi for conspiratorial designs on world finance (BM 76). "Z" marks the zoomorphic or bestial dimension of *ratio*, the site of the racial etymon's susceptibility to conversion into inhumanism, its mutation into a bad gene. As the distinguished Céline biographer Henri Godard has noted, Céline, while a medical student, was "fascinated not only by the Pasteurean biology of microbes, but also by the first discoveries concerning the cancerous proliferation of cells, and the genetics of Mendel."[15] Godard confirms what is clearly in evidence, namely, that gene theory anchors Céline's philological anti-Semitism. The racial etymon—the Jewish seme—works its way like a secret agent or cancerous cell through the national body, reinforcing paranoid politics, erupting like a mutant genus that develops, full-blown into a rancorous language of contagion.[16] Céline's medical thesis on *The Life and Work of Ignaz Philip Semmelweis* is relevant here. This nineteenth-century Hungarian doctor, a precursor of Pasteur's, was the unsung hero of sterilization practices in obstetrics; he died in an insane asylum after contracting meningitis from a patient. Céline's description of his death throes—"he began to babble out with an endless verbal stream, one interminable reminiscence, in the course of which his cracked head seemed to empty itself of long dead phrases"—exemplifies the way in which disease enters the body and passes into language.[17] It is the model for the Jewish antibody coursing through the bloodstream and issuing into Céline's singularly rebarbative idiolect.

The question of a genetics of racism—taken out of the age-old theory of hereditary transference and into the realm of pathological humanism—is what, in hindsight, may guarantee "le cas Céline" special significance in the history of French racisms. This is not just a case whereby Céline goes on trial for anti-Semitism, nor is it merely a psychoanalytic case history of identification with the "other" one loves to hate, or with an "othering" perspective on oneself.[18] It is rather, a ritual desecration of philological humanism, a disabling of molecular etymology's stewardship of the human.

The human stakes become clearer if one looks again at the passage of Céline's *Bagatelles* cited by Spitzer. The attack on *Sozial denken* targets the Marxist tradition within Jewish thought, specifically the ideas of scientific socialism, ethical humanism, and a humanitarian vision of social welfare. Simone Weil, Hannah Arendt, Trotsky, Adorno, Horkheimer, all would go under the knife of Céline's condemnation of socialism with a Jewish face. Designated the prime culprit for the Russian Revolution, "Jewishthink" is portrayed as responsible for unleashing immigration waves of "Asiatic" undesirables on West European territory. From Dunkerque to the Côte d'Azur, the narrator imagines a human tide composed of dervishes, lepers, and drug dealers from the East, and riffraff from the Ukraine, Tel Aviv, and the United States, crushing native inhabitants in its path. As in *Mea Culpa*, his scathing and verbally scrofulous attack on the Soviet experiment, Céline's denunciation of socialist humanism paves the way for an unfocused rant against the brutalization of the human. Jewish "theory," with its exaltation of an abstract ideal of utopian humanism, comes, for Céline, at the expense of the person.

"Spitzer *avec* Céline" suggests not only that a buried problem with race lies at the heart of the philological tradition, but that the "racing of philology" converts into the broader problem of the human in the humanities, or the linguistic genome. With statements such as "The humanist believes in the power bestowed on the human mind of investigating the human mind" (LLH 33), or his definition of philology as that which "deals with the all-too-human, with the interrelated and the intertwined aspects of human affairs," he inadvertently predicts philology's future relevance to genetics (LLH 31). Spitzer's association of philology with the human mind's existential and neuroscientific self-decoding anticipates connections currently being established between biological evolution and linguistic diversification. In an astute study of "genes, peoples, and languages," for example, Luca Cavalli-Sforza examines the evolutionary synchronization of "linguistic families"and "genetic trees" making the case, it would seem, for imagining the intercalation of genetic and linguistic material, as if both were branching off from common strands of DNA.[19]

Extrapolating a genetics of the human from Spitzerian philology may not be the most obvious interpretive move, given that platitudes about humanism were the order of the day during the early years of his formation. Biographically disposed, Hans Ulrich Gumbrecht sees Spitzer's grandiose claims for the human as histrionic and cliché; pointing to a phrase "my motto is: first a human being, and only then a scholar"—used by Spitzer in a 1923 letter to his Marburg colleague Karl Vossler—as evidence of his "trivial presentation of self," his "enthusiasm for commonplaces," his "embarassing self-fashioning."[20] But if we reread Spitzer's motto in the light of his career-long commitment to rethinking the terms of aliveness within humanist practice, it begins to ring with consequence rather than triviality. It also acquires significance in the context of his acute awareness of the *deathliness* of academic humanism.

Let us recall that Spitzer's most famous essay, "Linguistics and Literary History," was written in a dyspeptic mode, describing the beleaguered status of the humanities in a way that eerily anticipates contemporary lamentations on the "death of literary studies." In retrospect the essay forms a bookend with the "university in ruins" phenomenon described by Bill Readings in his posthumously published book of that title. Spitzer bemoans the loss of close reading and the bankruptcy of literary interpretation attributable to the anti-aestheticists of his day: "It is paradoxical that professors of literature who are too superficial to immerse themselves in a text and who are satisfied with the stale phrases out of a manual are precisely those who contend that it is superfluous to teach the aesthetic value of a text of Racine or Hugo" (LLH 3), while Readings, in the early 1990s affirms nihilistically that "culture no longer matters to the powers that be in advanced capitalism."[21] Readings senses that the humanities has lost its raison d'être, its ability to defend its stakes and intellectual objectives. Tolerated as a luxury item within the elite walls of the university, its purchase has atrophied in the public sphere. Worse still, the ethics of the humanities has come to ape the legalistic, monetary logic of capitalism—victims' rights, compensation, damages—all pegged to a floating, spectral standard of value called excellence.

Both Spitzer and Readings have a revivified humanist project as part of their agenda; both are vitally concerned with the problem of cultural value in periods of ethical relativism. And both place enormous weight on the practice of philology qua tropology. Spitzer sets great store on a theory of metonymic relatedness anticipating deconstruction's heuristic, whereas Readings speaks of "working out how thoughts stand beside other thoughts," a theory, perhaps, of "besided-ness" that relies on metonymic contiguity while refusing a Spitzerian theology of etymological unity. Both are diagnosing the same crisis condition—the one anticipatory, the other retrospective—associated with structuralism's onslaught on the linguistic person. As Denis Hollier reminds us:

> Structuralists displayed a decided taste for texts that could be studied apart from any personal reference such as popular litera- ture and the products of mass culture, which, like myth, are not rooted in what Leo Spitzer called "these texts having psychologi- cal etymology." . . . Once the literarinesss of a text ceased to be defined by its "personalizing" vocation and to be centered on some sort of "psychological etymology," functionalism could be extended to literary works themselves, where it could continue its work of dissolution.[22]

Hollier prompts us to read the Spitzerian ideal of "psychological etymology" as a goad to the nuclear antihumanism of structuralism. I would argue, as a pendant to this interpretation, that the genetic vision of philology embed- ded in Céline's violently anti-Semitic rhetoric and transformed by Spitzer into a vision of philological humanity, reveals a tension between humanism and the human that has been carried forward in successive debates within literary criticism. It is a tension that haunted deconstruction in its final days, and that, one could say, continues to haunt us now as we attempt to define the human within the broader disciplinary rubrics of the humanities. Con- sider, for example, Paul de Man's discussion with Neil Hertz and M. H. Abrams shortly before de Man's death. Taking Walter Benjamin's idea of translation as the historic afterlife of the original as his point of departure, de Man made the argument that Benjamin's notion of the poetic measures the distance of *errance* or alienation from "the language one calls one own."[23] "It is this errancy of language, this illusion of a life that is only an afterlife, that Benjamin calls history," de Man writes. "As such, history is not human, because it pertains strictly to the order of language: it is not natural . . . it is not phenomenal, in the sense that no cognition, no knowledge about man, can be derived from a history which as such is purely a linguistic complication" (RT 92). Abrams retorts with Spitzerian *doxa*, contesting de Man's insistence on the "fundamental nonhuman character of language," with the assertion that "instead of being the nonhuman, language is the most human of all the things we find in the world. . . . That syntax, tropes, and all the other operations of language, are equally human" (RT 99). Cleverly, de Man shifts the debate from a discussion of humanist language theory to the problem of "the human," as the central problem of philosophy, claiming that "Philosophy originates in this difficulty about the nature of language which is as such . . . and which is a difficulty about the definition of the human, or a difficulty within the human as such. And I think there is no escape from that" (RT 101). In the ellipses in de Man's utterance, in what is left unanswered in Abrams's objections, there is a forced and as yet unresolved confrontation between philological humanism and the philosophical human leading back to Spitzer's essay on "Linguistics and Literary History." It is a problematic that besets the humanities anew, not in the form that we are used to recognizing—the loss of consensus around universal humanist values, the depersonalization of the poststructuralist subject, the crisis of ethical relativism in secular mass culture. It emerges, rather, as an anxiety stirred by the phantom menace of a philological genome project or language gene. Like Sloterdijk's anthropotechnological idea of the human, this phantom literacy machine implies programmable language technologies built up out of etymons, a managed philological inheritance conducive to digital literacy. The impact of this idea of "literacy in an age of intelligent machines,"[24] though difficult to imagine, prompts a number of important questions that scholars engaged in the humanities might well have to address: Will Spitzer's idea for a revived idea of the human within philological humanism be redefined to include genetics within humanistic pedagogies? Or was his fixation on what Littré called "verbal pathologies" in Rabelais, Louis-Charles Philippe, and Céline a symptom of philological decadence, the anticipation of a fin-de-siècle deterioration of *ratio* into the bestial dimension of *rasse* or species-being? Certainly two distinct problematics emerge from Spitzer's legacy: first, that race will continue to disturb philological ideals of *ratio*, pointing up the eugenicist agendas that implicitly reside in technologies of the human (and the race-neutral languages that such a future human will speak). And second (on a more futuristic note still), the etymon, as the smallest unit of linguistic aliveness, may well renew its vital connection to the history of humanism in an era of digital languages.

3

Global *Translatio*: The "Invention" of

Comparative Literature, Istanbul, 1933

> Any language is human prior to being national: Turkish, French, and
> German languages first belong to humanity and then to Turkish, French,
> and German peoples.
> —Leo Spitzer, "Learning Turkish" (1934)

In many ways, the rush to globalize the literary canon in recent years may
be viewed as the "comp-lit-ization" of national literatures throughout the
humanities. Comparative literature was in principle global from its incep-
tion, even if its institutional establishment in the postwar period assigned
Europe the lion's share of critical attention and shortchanged non-Western
literatures. As many have pointed out, the foundational figures of comparative literature—Leo Spitzer, Erich Auerbach—came as exiles and émigrés
from war-torn Europe with a shared suspicion of nationalism. Goethe's ideal
of *Weltliteratur*, associated with a commitment to expansive cultural secularism, became a disciplinary premiss that has endured, resonating today in,
say, Franco Moretti's essay "Conjectures on World Literature," in which he
argues that antinationalism is really the only raison d'être for risky forays
into "distant reading." "The point," he asserts, "is that there is no other
justification for the study of world literature (and for the existence of departments of comparative literature) but this: to be a thorn in the side, a permanent intellectual challenge to national literatures—especially the local literature. If comparative literature is not this, it's nothing."[1]

Anyone who has worked in comparative literature can appreciate
Moretti's emphasis on antinationalism. The *doxa* of national language de-

partments tend to be more apparent to those accustomed to working across or outside them, while critical tendencies and schools appear more obviously as extensions of national literatures to those committed self-consciously to combining or traducing them. National character ghosts theories and approaches even in an era of cultural anti-essentialism. English departments are identified with a heritage of pragmatism, from practical criticism to the New Historicism. Reception and discourse theory are naturalized within German studies. French is associated with deconstruction even after deconstruction's migration elsewhere. Slavic languages retain morphology and dialogism as their theoretical calling cards. "Third World Allegory" lingers as an *appellation contrôlée* in classifying third world literatures, and so on. Lacking a specific country, or single national identity, Comp Lit necessarily works toward a non-nationally defined disciplinary locus, pinning high stakes on successfully negotiating the pitfalls of *Weltliteratur* especially in an increasingly globalized economy governed by transnational exchanges and flows. But as we have seen, the more talk there has been of "worlding" the canon along lines established by Edward Said, the less consensus there is on how to accomplish the task. As Moretti puts it: "[T]he literature around us is now unmistakably a planetary system. The question is not really *what* we should do—the question is *how*. What does it mean, studying world literature? How do we do it? I work on West European narrative between 1790 and 1930, and already feel like a charlatan outside of Britain or France. World literature [CWL 54]?"

A number of rubrics have emerged in response to this how-to question even if they hardly qualify as full-fledged paradigms: "Global Lit" (inflected by Fredric Jameson and Masao Miyoshi), "Cosmopolitanism" (given its imprimatur by Bruce Robbins and Timothy Brennan), "World Lit" (revived by David Damrosch and Franco Moretti), "Literary Transnationalism" (indebted to the work of Gayatri Chakravorty Spivak), and Comparative Postcolonial and Diaspora Studies (indelibly marked by Edward Said, Homi Bhabha, Françoise Lionnet, and Rey Chow among others). While promising vital engagement with non-Western traditions, these categories offer few methodological solutions to the pragmatic issue of how to make credible comparisons among radically different languages and literatures. Moretti, once again, articulates the matter succinctly: "World literature is not an object, it's a *problem*, and a problem that asks for a new critical method; and no one has ever found a method by just reading more texts" (CWL 55). Does he himself propose a method? Well, yes and no. He introduces the promising idea of "distant reading" as the foundation of a new epistemology (echoing Benedict Anderson's notion of distant or e-nationalism), but it is an idea that potentially risks foundering in a city of bits, where micro— and macro—literary units are awash in a global system with no obvious sorting device. Distance, Moretti pronounces, "*is a condition of knowledge*: it allows you to focus on units that are much smaller or much larger than the text: devices, themes, tropes—or genres and systems. And if, between the very small and the very large, the text itself disappears, well, it is one of those cases when one can justifiably say, Less is more" (CWL 57).

If, in this formulation, distant reading seems scarcely distinct from the old tropes, themes, and genres emphasis familiar in the comparative literature of yesteryear, Moretti, to give him his due, is proselytizing for something more radical. Acknowledging the daunting prospect of what Margaret Cohen has called "the great unread," and frankly admitting that in his own area of expertise he has dealt only with literature's "canonical fraction," Moretti advocates a kind of Lit Crit heresy that dispenses with close reading, relies unabashedly on secondhand material, and subordinates intellectual energies to the achievement of a "day of synthesis." Following Immanuel Wallerstein, the champion of world-systems theory, Moretti sets his hopes on the synthetic flash of insight that produces a shape-shifting paradigm of global relevance. His examples emphasize a socially vested formalism—"forms as abstracts of social relationships"—ranging from Roberto Schwarz's formal reading of foreign debt in the Brazilian novel, to Henry Zhao's concept of "the uneasy narrator" as the congealed expression of East-West "interpretive diversification," to Ato Quayson's use of genre— Nigerian postrealism—as the narrative guise assumed by imperial interference (CWL 60–64).

Moretti's attempt to assign renewed importance to plot, character, voice, and genre as load-bearing units of global literature has much to recommend it, as does his political formalism in the expanded field of world-systems theory, which bluntly recognizes the uneven playing field of global symbolic capital. Like the work of Perry Anderson, and other affiliates of the *New Left Review*, his "macro" approach is clearly indebted to Jameson's *Marxism and Form*. But it is an approach that ignores the extent to which "High Theory," with its internationalist circulation, already functioned as a form of distant reading. It also favors narrative over linguistic engagement, and this, I would surmise, is ultimately the dangling participle of Moretti's revamped *Weltliteratur*.

The problem left unresolved by Moretti—the need for a full-throttle globalism that would valorize textual closeness while refusing to sacrifice distance—was confronted earlier in literary history by Leo Spitzer when he was charged by the Turkish government to devise a philological curriculum in Istanbul in 1933. In looking again not just at what Spitzer preached—a universal Eurocentrism—but more at what he practiced, a staged cacophony of multilingual encounters, one finds an example of comparatism that sustains at once global reach and textual closeness.

It is by now something of a commonplace in the history of comparative literary studies to cite Erich Auerbach's melancholy postscript in *Mimesis* in which he describes the circumstances of the book's preparation during the period of his exile in Turkey from 1933 to 1945.

> I may also mention that the book was written during the war and at Istanbul, where the libraries are not well equipped for European studies. International communications were impeded; I had to dispense with almost all periodicals, with almost all the more recent investigations, and in some cases with reliable critical editions of my texts. Hence it is possible and even probable that I overlooked things which I ought to have considered. . . . On the other hand it is quite possible that the book owes its existence to just this lack of a rich and specialized library. If it had been possible for me to acquaint myself with all the work that has been done on so many subjects, I might never have reached the point of writing.[2]

Equally famous is the use Edward Said made of this passage, making it not just the cornerstone of a critique of the Orientalist worm gnawing the internal organs of Eurocentric literary criticism, but also the foundation of his own particular brand of exilic humanism: "The book owed its very existence to the very fact of Oriental, non-Occidental exile and homelessness," he would write in *The World, the Text and the Critic*.[3] Auerbach, as many have remarked, remained a consistent *point de repère* for Said, starting with his translation (with Maire Said) of Auerbach's seminal essay "Philology and *Weltliteratur*" at the outset of his career in 1969, and continuing through to his 1999 PMLA presidential column titled "Humanism?" where he chastises Auerbach for being "mystified" by the "explosion" of "new" languages after World War II. But even in this critical sally, Said recuperates the Auerbachian project in his vision of humanism: "In any case, he concludes, I don't believe that humanism as a subject for us can be evaded."[4]

In his essay "Auerbach in Istanbul: Edward Said, Secular Criticism, and the Question of Minority Culture," Aamir Mufti uses the Auerbachian Said as a point of departure for rethinking comparative literature in a postcolonial world, by firmly grounding it in the experience of the minority.[5] Where Said, according to Mufti, took the condition of Auerbach's exile as a goad to "questioning received notions of 'nation, home, community and belonging,'" Mufti proposes moving from the politics of un-homing, to the politics of statelessness, with all that implies: the loss of human dignity, the stripping of rights, and the reduction of an ethnic identity to the faceless category of the minority (Mufti is borrowing here from Hannah Arendt's analysis of the Jews as paradigmatic minority in her *The Origins of Totalitarianism*) (AI 103).

> Said's insistence on the critical imperative of the secular can appear elitist and hence paradoxical only if we fail to recognize this minority and exilic thrust in his work, if we forget the haunting figure of Auerbach in Turkish exile that he repeatedly evokes. It is in this sense that we must read Said when he himself speaks of exile not as "privilege" but as permanent critique of "the mass institutions that dominate modern life." Saidian secular criticism points insistently to the dilemmas and the terrors, but also, above all, to the ethical possibilities, of minority existence in modernity. (AI 107)

Arguing against Ahjaz Ahmad, according to whom, Mufti maintains, Auerbach is shorthand for a High Humanist, "Tory orientation" locked into permanent battle with Foucauldian antihumanism, Mufti underscores parallels between Auerbach's "synthetic" critical practice and the holistic aspects of Saidian Orientalism. He discerns, in the Auerbach of Said's invention, an ethics of coexistence, an ethical ideal of *Weltliteratur* that acknowledges the fragility of worldliness and refuses to be threatened by the specter of "other" languages crowding the floor of European languages and literatures.

But what happens to this ethical paradigm of global comparatism if we are compelled to revise the foundation myth of exile? Does the picture change, does the way we read Auerbach's melancholy postscript and self-described intellectual isolation shift when we reckon fully with the fact that Spitzer had already been in Istanbul for several years by the time Auerbach got there? There are few traces of the Istanbul chapter of literary history in the annals of early comparative literature; there are scant references to the intellectual collaborations among émigré colleagues and Turkish teaching assistants at the University of Istanbul in the 1930s, and there are really no full accounts of what happened to European philological pedagogy when it was transplanted to Turkey.[6] I would like to suggest that the fact that Spitzer had established a lively philological school in Istanbul, and learned Turkish along the way, might have significant bearing on attempts to redefine Comp Lit today as a "worlded" minoritarian comparatism. My point is that in globalizing literary studies, there is a selective forgetting of ways in which early comparative literature was always and already globalized. Spitzer in Istanbul, *before Auerbach*, tells the story not just of exilic humanism, but of worldly linguistic exchanges containing the seeds of a transnational humanism or global *translatio*. As the status of European traditions within postcolonial studies continues to be negotiated, this transnational humanism may be construed as a critical practice that reckons with the uncertain status of European thought in the future global marketplace of culture. It questions the default to European models in hermeneutic practices, and yet recognizes, as Said so clearly does, that the legacy of philological humanism is not and never was a Western versus non-Western problematic; it was and remains, a history of intellectual import and export in which the provenance labels have been torn off. René Etiemble clearly intuited this legacy when in 1966 he called for recasting comparative literature to accommodate future demographics:

> one or two billion Chinese who will claim to be of the first rank among the great powers; Moslems in hundreds of millions who, after having asserted their will to independence, will re-assert (as indeed they are already doing) their religious imperialism; an India where hundreds of millions will speak, some Tamil, others Hindi, still others Bengali, others Marathi, etc.; in Latin America tens of millions of Indians who will clamor for the right to become men again, and men with full rights; at least one hundred and twenty million Japanese, besides the two present great powers, Russia and the United States, who perhaps will have become allies in order to counterbalance new ambitions; a huge Brazil, a Latin America perhaps at long last rid of United States imperialism; a Black Africa exalting or disputing *négritude*, etc. As for us Frenchmen, we are quite willing to create an *Agrégation* of Modern Letters, provided, however, that it does not include China or the Arab World.[7]

Etiemble's prescient vision of contemporary literary politics extends to his disciplinary reformation of comparative literature in the year 2050. The topics he came up with—"Contacts between Jews, Christians and Moslems in Andalusia; Western influences during the Meiji era; Role of the discovery of Japan on the formation of liberal ideas in the century of the Enlightenment; Evolution of racist ideas in Europe since the discovery of America and Black Africa; Bilingualism in colonized countries; the influence of bilingualism on literatures," and so on, are profoundly in step with the kind of work being done today in transnational and postcolonial literary studies.[8] If Etiemble fashioned a futuristic global comparatism for the 1960s relevant to 2005, he inherited a vision that had already been put into pedagogical practice in the 1930s by Leo Spitzer. The story of Spitzer's Istanbul seminar, and the model of global *translatio* that it affords, thus has special bearing on comparative literature today.

Most famous in the United States for a group of essays on stylistics published in 1967 under the title of the leading essay, *Linguistics and Literary History*, Leo Spitzer was rivaled only by Auerbach in his breadth of erudition and role in the academy as the teacher of multiple generations of comparatists. Paul de Man placed him squarely in an "outstanding group of Romanic scholars of German origin" that included Hugo Friedrich, Karl Vossler, Ernst Robert Curtius, and Auerbach.[9] In his introduction to the collection *Leo Spitzer: Representative Essays*, Spitzer's former student at Hopkins, John Freccero, acknowledged Spitzer as the premier founder of comparative literature in America.[10] Spitzer preferred hermeneutical demonstrations to books devoted to single authors. His oeuvre was sprawling and unsystematic, unified primarily by his consistent attention to heuristics, and by a preoccupation with select writers of the Spanish Golden Age, the Italian Renaissance, the French Enlightenment, and the Decadents (Cervantes, Gongora, Lope de Vega, Dante, Diderot, Baudelaire, Charles-Louis Philippe).

Spitzer was profoundly unprepared for the institutionalization of anti-Semitism in the Nazi years preceding World War II. Like Victor Klemperer, he assumed he would have immunity from political persecution as a result of his distinguished record of military service during World War I (his experience as a censor of Italian prisoners' letters formed the basis of an early publication on periphrasis and the multiple "words for hunger").[11] Unlike Klemperer, who stayed in Dresden throughout the war—somehow managing to survive and keeping himself from suicidal despair with the help of a "philologist's notebook" in which he documented the perversion of the German language by Nazi usage—Spitzer fled to Istanbul in 1933. On May 2, 1933, the Ministry of Education approved his replacement at the University of Cologne by Ernst Robert Curtius, and in July of that year he was denounced along with other Jewish faculty members in a report submitted to the university president authored by the head of a National-Socialist student group.[12] With the writing on the wall, Spitzer resigned shortly after receiving invitations to teach at the Universities of Manchester and Istanbul. As he sailed for Turkey, his entourage included his wife, his children, and his teaching assistant Rosemarie Burkart. Burkart and Spitzer enjoyed a passionate liaison in Istanbul.[13] By all accounts a gifted philologist in her own right, and judging from her photograph, a thoroughly "modern woman," with cropped hair, and a passion for sports, art, and music, Burkart helped alleviate the melancholy that one would expect to have accompanied Spitzer's expulsion. It is perhaps no accident that in his article "Learning Turkish," he employed the language of love when describing what it felt like to learn a foreign language late in life.

Spitzer's situation in 1933 was comparable to that of hundreds of Jewish academics dismissed from their posts at the time. Many emigrated to Palestine, others found asylum in unoccupied European capitals (the case of art historians Fritz Saxl, Nikolaus Pevsner, Gertrud Bing, and Otto Pächt in London), and quite a few landed in Latin America (especially Brazil, Peru, and Mexico). The United States was a destination of choice, but unless they were internationally renowned scholars like Einstein, Paul Oskar Kristeller, or Panofsky, many who fled to the United States discovered limited employment opportunities in their adoptive country, largely because of anti-Semitism in the American academy. As the recent documentary film *From Swastika to Jim Crow* effectively demonstrates, it was America's black colleges in the South that often extended a helping hand, creating a generation of black academics trained by Jewish émigrés who would later attest to a sense of shared history as persecuted minorities. One of the lucky few, Spitzer secured job offers easily and spent three years, 1933–36, at the University of Istanbul as the first professor of Latin languages and literature in the Faculty of Literature and as director of the School of Foreign Languages. Though they did not overlap since Spitzer left for the United States just before Auerbach arrived in early December 1936, it was at Spitzer's invitation that Auerbach joined the department, not quite the isolation from Europe that he would have us believe in the afterword to *Mimesis*. Auerbach's jaundiced depiction of his loneliness in the wilderness really appears to be a somewhat distorted picture of what it was like to live and work in Istanbul on closer investigation of the intellectual community congregated there in the twenties and thirties.[14]

When I interviewed Süheyla Bayrav, a distinguished eighty-six-year-old emeritus professor of literature at the University of Istanbul and a member of Spitzer's seminar in 1933, it became clear that a familial atmosphere prevailed.[15] Turkish students—Nesteren Dirvana, Mina Urgan, Sabahattin Eyüboğlu, Safinaz Duruman—joined in discussion with the émigrés Heinz Anstock, Eva Buck, Herbert and Lieselotte Dieckmann, Traugott Fuchs, Hans Marchand, Robert Anhegger, Ernst Engelburg, Kurt Laqueur, Andreas Tietze, and Karl Weiner. The teaching sessions frequently took place in Spitzer's apartment, which was equipped with an extensive personal library of literature and reference works. When the young Süheyla Bayrav (who did a thesis with Spitzer on the *Chanson de Roland*), solved an etymological mystery that Spitzer had been wrestling with for some years, he instantly confirmed that her intuition was accurate with the help of volumes on his shelf. From then on, she was anointed a serious philologist and eventually joined the ranks of Spitzer's department as a faculty member. Bayrav belonged to the first generation of Turkish women to attend university and pursue professional academic careers. Spitzer's seminar, though intimidating, professionally launched a number of women scholars: Rosemarie Burkart played an active and productive role as a Romance philology professor, Eva Buck, a translator of German origin brought up in China and educated by British nuns, used her comparative background in languages to compose an anthology of European literature in Turkish; Azra Ahat, a Belgian-educated humanist, edited a dictionary of Greek mythology and became a well-known translator; and Bayrav forged a transition between philology and structural semiotics through her work on linguistic literary criticism, in addition to becoming an intellectual magnet for Turkish writers and visiting intellectuals such as Barthes and Foucault.

Bayrav and her cohort carried on the tradition of East-West exchange and commitment to translation fostered by the Spitzer seminar well into the 1970s and 1980s. By contrast, Auerbach and his students, most of whom, like Walter Kranz or Herbert Dieckmann, hailed from Germany and concentrated on European languages and literatures, seem to have been relatively uninterested in the potential for an enlarged vision of World Lit presented by the conditions of their exile. On meeting Harry Levin in America for the first time, Auerbach discredited the scholarship of his Turkish colleagues, pointing to the case of a Turkish translator of Dante who admitted to working from a French translation chosen at random.[16] A more important cause of his intellectual dyspepsia was political. Auerbach bitterly opposed the climate of burgeoning nationalism in Turkey and remained highly suspicious of the strange attempt to marry it to European culture. In a letter to Walter Benjamin written in 1937, he repudiated the "fanatically anti-traditional nationalism" that came out of Atatürk's "struggle against the European democracies on the one hand and the old Mohammedan Pan-Islamic sultan's economy on the other." The émigrés, he conjectured (in an argument that has become familiar in the wake of 9/11) , were in Istanbul as part of the Turkish government's premeditated scheme to free itself from imperial hegemony; acquiring European technological know-how with the aim of turning it back on Europe:

... rejection of all existing Mohammedan cultural heritage, the establishment of a fantastic relation to a primal Turkish identity, technological modernization in the European sense, in order to triumph against a hated yet admired Europe with its own weapons: hence the preference for European-educated emigrants as teachers, from whom one can learn without the threat of foreign propaganda. Result: nationalism in the extreme accompanied by the simultaneous destruction of the historical national character.[17]

The new Turkish nationalism, and its repressive cultural arm, was certainly in evidence during Auerbach's eleven-year sojourn in Istanbul, but one could argue without really overstating the case that it was the volatile crossing of Turkish language politics with European philological humanism that produced the conditions conducive to the invention of comparative literature as a global discipline, at least in its early guise. A fascinating two-way collision occurred in Istanbul between a new-nations ideology dedicated to constructing a modern Turkish identity with the latest European pedagogies, and an ideology of European culture dedicated to preserving ideals of Western humanism against the ravages of nationalism.

Auerbach's self-portrait as a lonely European scholar seems increasingly questionable the more one takes into account the sizeable professional, artistic, and political European community that was well established in Istanbul (and Ankara) by the time he arrived in Turkey in 1936.[18] The mythographer Georges Dumézil worked in Istanbul between 1925 and 1931, having come at the invitation of Atatürk to help prepare the ground for alphabetization in 1928. Leon Trotsky found safe harbor there between 1931 and 1933, as did Gerhard Kessler, the German socialist political exile who helped found the Turkish Worker's Syndicate. Spitzer was preceded by the Romanist Traugott Fuchs, who taught at Roberts College and helped facilitate his appointment at the University of Istanbul (known, at this time, as the *Emigré Universität*).[19] Shortly after Spitzer's arrival, he was joined by a large number of German-speaking academics and creative artists including the distinguished philosopher of mind Hans Reichenbach (who taught at the University of Istanbul from 1933 to 1938; Fritz Neumark (economy and law, Istanbul University), Georg Rohde (a classical philologist based in Ankara in 1935, who studied Arabic influences on world literature and initiated a Translations from World Literature series), Wolfram Eberhard (Chinese language and literature in Ankara University), Paul Hindemith (1935–37), who founded the Ankara State Conservatory with Carl Ebert and brought Béla

Bartok in 1936, and a host of innovative architects and planners, among them Bruno Taut (who taught between 1936 and 1938 at Istanbul Technical University) and the French urban planner Henri Prost.[20] Later arrivals whose impact was equally significant (in more ways than one, since many of them were apparently engaged in espionage during the war) were the British historians Sir Ronald Syme (a specialist of Rome and Anatolia, appointed professor of Classical philology at the University of Istanbul from 1942 to 1945), the classical archaeologist George Bean (at Istanbul University starting in 1944, where he worked on *Aegean Turkey*, and *Turkey's Southern Shore*), and the famous historian of Byzantium and the Crusades, Sir Steven Runciman.[21] An essay by Runciman demonstrating the Eastern origins of Western tropes and poetic devices, published in 1959, anticipates many of Said's discussions in *Orientalism* of suppressed Muslim cultural influences.[22] In addition to the presence of these renowned British scholars, the American writer James Baldwin, and the structural linguists Émile Benveniste and A. J. Greimas also worked in Istanbul in the 1950s. According to Fredric Jameson's recollection, Greimas, Michel de Certeau, and Louis Marin claimed to have "invented semiotics" when they overlapped in Istanbul in the 1950s. These successive generations of scholars and critics appear as so many *couches* added to the city's historic role as a magnet for diaspora, migration, and cultural fusion, and as a capital of world-historical power, from the Holy Roman Empire to the Ottoman Empire.

Istanbul's tradition as a cultural crossroads, combined with the fact that it already had established Jewish and German enclaves (and had served as a way station for Jews immigrating to Palestine), made university posts there in the early thirties especially coveted by European exiles.[23] When financial hardship took a turn for the worse in July 1936, a year after his dismissal at the Dresden Technical University in 1935, Victor Klemperer recorded in his diaries the extent to which jobs at the University of Istanbul were jealously monitored. After noting that "Spitzer's post in Istanbul has finally been given to Auerbach," he confided with a touch of pique the story of how Auerbach had lobbied Benedetto Croce to secure the position, succeeding despite his inadequate fluency in French:

> This morning, with a recommendation from "Vosslaiir," I was visited by Edmondo Cione, a little librarian from Florence, *amico del Croce, anti-fascista*. Would like to be a lecturer in Germany, did not know that I had lost my post. I recommended him to Gelzer in Jena. He will see if he can be of assistance to me in Italy. He told me how Auerbach came to the Istanbul ap-

pointment. He had already been in Florence for a year, and Croce provided an opinion on him. [. . .] Now Auerbach is brushing up his French in Geneva. And Spitzer had been saying in Italy that only someone who could really speak French would get the appointment! If I go off to Geneva for a couple of months then I too could "really speak French" again.[24]

Istanbul was particularly popular because it *was* Europe as far as many of the Austrian and German émigrés were concerned. As Klemperer's friend, the physicist Harry Dember wrote in a letter of August 12, 1935, on learning he had been appointed at the university: "It is certainly right on the edge—you can see across to Asia—but it is still in Europe."[25]

The influx of émigrés to Istanbul grew as the dire need for employment by victims of Nazism who had been fired from their jobs in Germany and Austria converged with the opportunism of a young Turkish republic (1923–30) eager to Westernize by instituting "reforms" within the Academy (often at the expense of scholars already there). It is nothing short of historical irony that in many cases, a Turk's job lost was a German's job gained. Firings, at both ends, were crucial to the formation of this humanism at large. In hindsight, one wonders whether émigré professors in Turkey were aware of the Turkish government's manipulation of their circumstances. Did they know, for example, that in 1932 the government had commissioned a Swiss pedagogue named Albert Malche to write a report on the state of the Istanbul Darülfünun (as it was then called), used to justify mass dismissals of Turkish faculty in 1933?[26] Malche's scathing report recommended complete overhaul of the university, citing insufficient publications, inferior foreign language training, and inadequate scientific instruction. In his agenda for reform, Malche envisioned a cosmopolitan university with professors from "Berlin, Leipzig, Paris or Chicago." This cosmopolitan culture, he insisted, would be the only guarantor against single schools becoming dominant. Charged with a global recruitment mission, he received acceptances of his offers mainly from German or German-speaking professors.[27] It was Malche, working closely with an organization charged with placing German scholars abroad—"Notgemeinschaft deutscher Wissenschaftler in Ausland"—who helped bring Spitzer to Istanbul. Spitzer's initial mandate was daunting, "he was in charge of coordinating classes in four languages for several thousand students," "lectured to his classes—through an interpreter—in French and used a multitude of other languages to communicate with his teaching staff."[28]

As I have already intimated, Spitzer and Auerbach cut overlapping yet distinct paths through the disciplinary prehistory of comparative literature. Both were profoundly engaged with philology, translation, and Western humanism, but Spitzer adopted a linguistic cosmopolitanism, while Auerbach focused on the poetics of narrative realism. Spitzer allowed Turkey to shape his formation of a field of modern humanism, becoming, if you will, the forerunner of postcolonial humanism. Auerbach resisted Turkey. Though he spent over a decade in Istanbul,[29] he apparently never mastered the Turkish language, and there is little evidence to suggest seepage of his "foreign" surround into *Mimesis*, or into his textbook *Introduction to Romance Languages and Literatures*, the latter "written at Istanbul in 1943 in order to provide my Turkish students with a framework which would permit better to understand the origin and meaning of their studies."[30] One can readily appreciate how Herbert Dieckmann (one of the star German students formed by Auerbach in this period who later went on to a distinguished career as a literary critic, coauthoring the influential *Essays in Comparative Literature* with Harry Levin in 1961) could become an Enlightenment specialist in a purely European mold. Unless they went on to become Turcologists (like Robert Anhegger or Andreas Tietze, who founded Turkish studies at UCLA after working at Istanbul University from 1938 to 1958), the non-Turkish students and faculty in literature tended to hew to a standard European curriculum. On the one hand, Auerbach endorsed the enlarged cultural purview of his own generation of European philologists (Vossler, Curtius, and Spitzer), but on the other, he was concerned to maintain exclusive boundaries around European civilization, keeping it "from being engulfed in another, more comprehensive unity," a unity that in today's parlance might correspond to global comparatism.[31]

It comes as no surprise that Auerbach's *Introduction to Romance Languages and Literatures* packages the Romance syllabus with few concessions to his Turkish audience beyond the addition of a chapter on Christianity. And yet, on closer inspection, the attention paid in this work to Romanization and the long-term impact of Roman linguistic colonization on the history of European languages might well be attributed to the fact that Auerbach bore witness to the process of Romanization in Turkey.[32] Auerbach greeted the massive literacy campaign in which he himself was a participant with extreme pessimism (placing it in the wider context of a global standardization of culture—"an International of triviality and a culture of Esperanto"),[33] but the issue of literacy became a crucial theme in his 1958 masterwork *Literary Language and Its Public in Late Latin Antiquity and in the Middle Ages*. Here he showed how linguistic conservatism—the grammatical stability of literary Latin that resulted from efforts made during the late Roman republic to standardize spelling and grammar—helped form a literary public that in turn guaranteed the legacy of Western culture. Though it remains a matter of speculation as to whether or not the standardization of modern Turkish directly inspired Auerbach's *Literary Language and Its Public*, it seems safe to assume that Turkey's self-colonizing policy of *translatio imperii* afforded compelling parallels to imperial Rome.[34]

Varlik, the journal of art, literature, and politics in which Spitzer's "Learning Turkish" was published, can be seen as a direct outgrowth of the language reforms of 1928 instituted by the newly minted Turkish Republic. It is difficult to overestimate the impact of these reforms on Turkish politics and culture. Abolishing the Arabic alphabet used in Ottoman writing and abruptly introducing a phonetic, Romanized modern Turkish script, Atatürk effectively rendered the older educated classes illiterate, while ensuring that the next generation would be unable to access historical archives, legal documents, or the Ottoman literary tradition.[35] As Auerbach wrote to Benjamin shortly after arriving in Istanbul, literary traditions of the immediate past already struck him as "fantastical and ghostly." "There is hardly anyone who can understand Arabic or Persian and even Turkish texts of the last century," he observed, rendering "untranslatability" (the *unverständlich*) and "misunderstanding" (*missverständnissen*) the twin orders of the day.[36] Spitzer's article on "Learning Turkish," appearing as it did under a rubric called "language debates" that attracted contributions from Turkish intellectuals ranging from university professors to the minister of education, must thus be situated in the political maelstrom of this literacy revolution.

Spitzer and Auerbach published substantial essays on philology alongside the work of their students in the Istanbul university journal—*Publications de la faculté des lettres de l'Université d'Istanbul*, edited by Auerbach. The table of contents of the 1937 issue, which included Spitzer's Romanology seminar, attests to its cosmopolitan reach:

> Azra Ahat, "Üslup ilminde yeni bir usul"
> Eva Buck, "Die Fabel in 'Pointed Roofs' von Dorothy Richardson"
> Rosemarie Burkart, "Truchement"
> Herbert Dieckmann, "Diderots Naturempfinden und Lebensgefühl"
> Traugott Fuchs, "La première poésie de Rimbaud"
> Hans Marchand, "Indefinite Pronoun 'one' "
> Sabahattin Eyüboğlu, "Türk Halk Bilmeceleri"

Leo Spitzer, "Bemerkungen zu Dantes 'Vita Nuova' "
Süheyla Sabri, "Un passage de 'Barlaan y Josaiat' "
Erich Auerbach, "Uber die ernste Nachahmung des Alltäglichen"[37]

It is tempting to read this table of contents as the in vitro paradigm of a genuinely globalized comparative literature, as evidence of critical reading practices that bring the globe inside the text. Though merely a coda of working papers, it offers a glimpse into the way in which European humanism "Atatürk style" (that is, attuned to Turkey's modernizing agenda) played a key role in transforming German-based philology into a global discipline that came to be known as comparative literature when it assumed its institutional foothold in postwar humanities departments in the United States.[38] The contributions of young Turkish scholars to the seminar publications are particularly significant in this regard. Azra Ahat, whose essay treated Spitzer's methodology and word art, dedicated her career to the translation of Greek and Latin classics for a state-sponsored project to create a modern library for the newly minted Turkish Republic. The library formed part of a concerted mission to "Greekify" Turkey and thereby consolidate the state's efforts to establish non-Islamic, anti-Ottoman cultural foundations on which secular nationalism could be built. Initiatives as far-ranging as the "Blue Cruises" (boat trips featuring sites of Greco-Roman civilization along Turkish shores) or the government's investment in classical philology in the university system, were linked to the myth of Turkey as a new Greece. The appropriation of classicism for the purposes of cultural prestige and national identity is a familiar enough move since imperial Rome, but in the specific context of Atatürk's reforms, it took on new implications, forcing comparative literature, in its nascent form, to renegotiate its relation to nationalism (the émigré generation tended to be *anti*nationalist in reaction against the hypernationalist Nazi *Kulturkampf*), and opening up philological humanism to historic debates over "who claims Greece" in the Balkans, the countries bordering the Black Sea, and Asia Minor.[39]

If the complex relationship between classical philology and nationalism was represented in the Spitzer seminar through the work of Ahat and her associates, the seminar also acted as a laboratory for working through what a philological curriculum in literary studies should look like when applied to non-European languages and cultures. Spitzer's assistant Sabahattin Eyüboğlu, an editor of *Varlik* and a strong participant in the language debates, was a crucial player on this front, adapting Spitzer's methods to analyses of folktales, stories, and poems written in Turkish vernacular tongues. Eyüboğlu's predilection for linguistic and generic morphology, as well as Süheyla Bayrav's work on morphology, tilted old-school philology toward formalism.[40] With the arrival of Benveniste and Greimas (who introduced the structural linguistics of Roman Jakobson), Istanbul assumes renewed importance in literary history and theory, from philological humanism to semiotics and structuralism.

Spitzer's seminar in Istanbul was obviously not an inaugural or unique example of global comparatism. The idea is as old as that of culture itself, and extremely widespread, especially if one takes into account successive generations of avant-garde writers and intellectuals working on journals or political initiatives outside the academy and within transnational circuits of exchange. Nonetheless, Spitzer's seminar would seem to afford an example of global *translatio* with contemporary relevance insofar as it furnished the blueprint for departments of comparative literature established in the postwar period. I would like to suggest that Comp Lit continues to this day to carry traces of the city in which it took disciplinary form—a site where East-West boundaries were culturally blurry, and where layers of colonial history obfuscated the outlines of indigenous cultures. Edward Said was clearly aware of the importance of Auerbach's location in Istanbul when he chose him as a disciplinary figurehead of *Weltliteratur* in exile. Paul Bové maintains convincingly that Auerbach bequeathed to Said a "critical humanism," whose "progressive secular potential" Said would spend much of his career seeking to fulfill.[41] I would suggest here that Said might have made his case for retaining Auerbach as a precursor of his own brand of secular humanism even stronger had he been more familiar with the story of Spitzer in Istanbul.

It may seem forced to resurrect Spitzer as a figure of transnational humanism *avant la lettre*, but the stakes in construing this figure are high, since laying claim to comparatism's philological heritage is synonymous with securing symbolic capital in the humanities. Carrying the illustrious tradition of Renaissance humanism into modern scholarship, and having, so to speak, mapped the etymological genome, philology claims a long history of shaping literary institutions and national politics. As Bernard Cerquiglini has observed: "At the dawn of the nineteenth century, extremely diverse phenomena of order, nature, and evolution all seemed to converge, forming a coherent semantics connected with the practice and study of texts. Philology is the most significant expression of this coherence. Its history is the history of our spontaneous philosophy of the textual."[42] For Michael Holquist, philology and more broadly, the study of language, allowed Wilhelm von Humboldt, Johann Fichte, Friedrich Schleiermacher, and Friedrich

Schelling to "resolve the Kantian paradox of how to institutionalize autonomy" in the context of the newly formed Berlin University, itself, of course,
the template for the American academy.[43]

Even if one insists, as does Andreas Huyssen, that the Kantian ideal
of secular humanism embodied in German philology became irredeemably
tainted by the worst kind of German nationalism, philology's history contains distinguished counterexamples. Victor Klemperer kept his will to survive intact during World War II by devoting himself to his "philologist's
notebook"(referred to affectionately as his "SOS sent to myself," or "secret
formula"), a meticulous chronicle of the damages of Nazi diction to everyday life. Klemperer employed the Latin expression *lingua tertii imperii* (or
LTI for short) when designating the language of the Third Reich.[44] By re-
trieving the Roman legacy of *translatio imperii* and reconnecting it to the
lingua imperii of the Third Reich, Klemperer not only drew an analogy between Nazi and Roman linguistic imperialism, he also emphasized the very
particular contempt for original meaning that characterizes translation
under conditions of conquest. In this view, he seems to have subscribed to
the position of his fellow philologist Hugo Friedrich who drew on Saint
Jerome's assertion that: "The translator considers thought content a prisoner (*quasi captivos sensus*) which he transplants into his own language with
the prerogative of a conqueror (*iure victoris*)." "This," Friedrich concluded,
"is one of the most rigorous manifestations of Latin cultural and linguistic
imperialism, which despises the foreign word as something alien but appropriates the foreign meaning in order to dominate it through the translator's
own language."[45] For Klemperer, Nazi discourse provided a comparable
model of language domination. In examining the term *Strafexpedition* (pu-
nitive expedition), a word initially registered in the speech of a former family
friend and the first term recognized as being specifically National Socialist,
he noted: "[T]he embodiment of brutal arrogance and contempt for people
who are in any way different, it sounded so colonial, you could see the
encircled Negro village, you could hear the cracking of the hippopotamus
whip" (LTI 43). Klemperer discerned in Nazi language a similar pattern of
violent semantic usurpation to the one that Friedrich ascribes to Roman
translations, even though the language of the original in the Nazi case was
one and the same with the target. This *intralingual* or German-to-German
translation (in Jakobson's terms a "rewording," or "interpretation of verbal
signs by means of other signs in the same language")[46] covered a host of
travesties. There was what Klemperer called the "poisoning of the drinking
water of language," an expression applied to the casual adoption of Nazi-
sanctioned words by ordinary citizens as in the case of coworker who, with-

out apparent malice, falls into using words like *artfremd* (alien), *deutsch-blütig* (of German blood), *niederrassig* (of inferior race), or *Rassenschande* (racial defilement). There was semantic substitution, for example, the replacement of the word *Humanität* (with its "stench of Jewish liberalism") with the "manly" term *Menschlichkeit,* which went along with the program of Germanicizing lexical roots and stamping out "foreign" etymons. Klemperer also noted the Nazi technologization of language, the new privileging of a verb like *aufziehen,* meaning "to wind up a clock or mechanical toy" or "mount warp on a loom." In conjuring up automatic, robotic actions that are both comic and deadening, the verb mimicked the hollow, deanimating rhetoric of Nazi speeches or the goose-step march. And then there was the prevalence of pictograms capable of emitting subliminal psychological messages. Klemperer decodes the letters *SS* sported by the Nazi Storm Troopers as a rune based on the visual appropriation of a common symbol for "Danger! High Voltage!"[47]

Klemperer's powerful use of philology as a prophylactic against Nazi-think (complementing the strategic use made of philologically trained literary critics such as I. A. Richards and Leo Marx, both deployed as cryptographers during the war) bears directly on the politics behind Spitzer and Auerbach's philological practice during the war. It is a "resistance" philology with an impeccable ethical pedigree, which is perhaps one reason why the fight over "who claims philology" continues in the context of contemporary canon and culture wars. Charles Bernheimer's *Comparative Literature in the Age of Multiculturalism* (1995) may be read in this light as a turf battle with Lionel Gossman and Mihai Spariosu's *Building a Profession: Autobiographical Perspectives on the History of Comparative Literature in the United States* (1994). In the former essay collection the critics tend to frame postcolonial theory as the logical outcome of comparative literature's polyglot, international heritage, whereas in the latter, the postcolonial turn, if recognized at all, is positioned as a reductive politicization of comparative literature's distinguished European foundations.[48] Though the stakes involved in these most recent philology wars appear academic and parochial in comparison to those of Klemperer et al., they are linked to critical problems, ranging from the cultural implications of literary methodology, to rethinking World Lit beyond Anglocentric parameters of the "foreign" languages, to the question of whether European humanism will continue to have traction in the global marketplace of culture.

In the battle zone of Europe pro and con, Saidian humanism has remained a major flashpoint. Said's 1978 watershed book *Orientalism,* together with his notion of "contrapuntal reading," introduced in *Culture and*

Imperialism (which stressed "simultaneous awareness both of the metropolitan history that is narrated and of those other histories against which [and together with which] the dominating discourse acts"), have been assailed on the grounds that they shortchange aesthetic value by reducing texts to sociological example, while fostering "victim studies" and antihumanism.[49] But, as Herbert Lindenberger reminds us, when Auerbach's *Mimesis* was attacked on the left for its Eurocentrism in the early 1980s, it was none other than Edward Said who rescued it as a model work of broad cultural authority and *Welt-lit*, earning him, at least in Lindenberger's estimation, the Auerbachian mantle.[50]

Saidian humanism views Europe from outside Europe ("provincializing" it, to borrow Dipesh Chakrabarty's phrase), while roundly criticizing the habit of referring to traditions such as Islam in an impacted, monolithic way.[51] "It is very much the case today," Said would argue in *Representations of the Intellectual*, "that in dealing with the Islamic world—all one billion people in it, with dozens of different societies, half a dozen major languages including Arabic, Turkish, Iranian, all of them spread out over about a third of the globe—American or British academic intellectuals speak reductively and, in my view, irresponsibly of something called 'Islam.' "[52] Taking translingual perspectivism as an a priori, Saidian humanism pivots on the vision of the intellectual who refuses to see languages and cultures in isolation. What legitimates the intellectual's claim to knowledge and freedom is a sensitivity to the demography of Babel.[53] The radical side of Saidian humanism—its agitation of the status quo and refusal of congruence with the contoured, habituated environments called home—lies, I would suggest, not so much in its philological ecumenicalism (which could easily become watered-down linguistic multiculturalism), but rather, in its attachment to the shock value of cultural comparison.

If, instead of taking Auerbach for its *Ansatzpunkt* (and by extension, the fetish of "exile" since the record shows that Auerbach was in pretty good cosmopolitan company during his Istanbul sojourn), Saidian humanism had started with Spitzer, it might have gleaned from Spitzer's critique of Ernst Robert Curtius—the scholar who swooped in to take his job just as he was dispatched to Istanbul—its very own practice of a "lightened" philology, a philology that has shed its "solidity," "aridity," "asceticism," and "medieval garb."[54] Said's memoir *Out of Place* exemplifies this culturally lightened and globally expanded philology, placing Shakespeare with Shirley Temple, Kant *avec* Wonderwoman. The narrative mobilizes a lexicon in which American product labels are grafted onto Arabic and Anglophone expressions. The anomalous acoustic effect of words like Ping Pong and

Dinky Toy vie with Britishisms (BBC, Greenwich Mean Time) and local brand names ("Chabrawichi cologne") on a single page.[55] "Like the objects we carried around and traded, our collective language and thought were dominated by a small handful of perceptibly banal systems deriving from comics, film, serial fiction, advertising and popular lore that was essentially at street level," Said tells us, as if to dispel any temptation to make humanism the high serious preserve of an indigenous culture untouched by global capitalism and trademark literacy (OP 205). Said's sense of marvel at the way in which the coinage of popular culture interacts with the hard currency of European aesthetics recalls, perhaps not surprisingly, Spitzer's landmark 1949 essay, "American Advertising Explained as Popular Art" in which he analyzed the Sunkist orange juice logo as a modern-day equivalent of medieval heraldic insignia.

So, given this Spitzerian lineage, who, for Said, might embody Spitzer in transnational times? In *Out of Place* the author's family friend Charles Malik emerges as the most obvious choice, despite Said's political differences with him. A spokesman for Palestine in the 1940s and a former U.N. ambassador for Lebanon, he became a professor of philosophy at the American University of Beirut, having studied with Heidegger in Freiburg and Whitehead at Harvard (OP 264). With his "strong north Lebanese village (Kura) accent affixed to a sonorously European English," Malik becomes, in Said's ascription, a kind of Spitzer of the Middle East; demonstrating fluency in English, Arabic, German, Greek, and French, while ranging, in conversation, from Kant, Fichte, Russell, Plotinus, and Jesus Christ, to Gromyko, Dulles, Trygve Lie, Rockefeller, and Eisenhower (OP 266).

Said's own language proficiency together with his intellectual interests and accomplishments—in music, politics, and literary criticism—made him an equally compelling example of the secular humanist. As a "self-reader" he was mindful of the *translational* transnationalism of humanism, a condition that, I would surmise, is ultimately more significant for the future of humanism than the premium placed on exile throughout many of Said's writings. Reading the hyphenations of his identity as a "Palestinian-Arab-Christian-American," or the mutations of his own name at various stations of life, Said can be said to have been above all a self-translator. In Cairo, he is "Edward," a symbol of Arab Anglophilia. In his father's stationery store, he is "Mister Edward" or "Edward Wadie." And at Mount Herman boarding school, he is Americanized as "Ed Said,"which on the page begs to have the second name pronounced to rhyme with the first. "Ed Said" becomes a place-holder for the expectation of speech, as in: "Ed said . . . what?" What Said says, it turns out, is flush with the polyvalent associations around his name, now, in its own right, a transnationally circulating signifier of global comparatism, ethical militance, exilic humanism, and contrapuntal reading practices. But this over-reading of a name begs the question of defining transnational humanism; shifting the burden of definition to identity, and thereby evading the complex issue of how transnational humanism selects for culture—that is to say, how it excludes as well as culls a philological example from an unsorted jumble of texts. To give this problem its due, one must reflect more fully on the role played by philology in reaching for connections across languages, while at the same time respecting the recalcitrance of the original.

Looking again more closely at the table of contents of the Istanbul literary review, a paradigm of *translatio* emerges that emphasizes the critical role of multilingualism within transnational humanism. The juxtaposition of Turkish, German, and French attests to a policy of *non-translation* adopted without apology. Spitzer's own contributions are exemplary here; in each individual essay, one hears a cacophony of untranslated languages. And as a literary critic in command of French, German, Hebrew, Hungarian, Latin, Greek, Italian, English, Provençal, Spanish, Portuguese, Catalan, Rumanian, Gothic, Anglo-Saxon, Sanskrit, Lithuanian, Old Church Slavonic, Albanian, Neo-Greek (and now, we ascertain, Turkish as well), he had many languages to choose from. It was, of course, a common practice among highly educated European literary scholars to leave passages and phrases free-standing in a naked state of untranslation, for Spitzer nontranslation was a hallowed principle of his method, enunciated most famously in a starred passage of the famous 1948 essay "Linguistics and Literary History":

> *The frequent occurrence, in my text, of quotations in the original foreign language (or languages) may prove a difficulty for the English reader. But since it is my purpose to take the word (and the wording) of the poets seriously, and since the convincingness and rigor of my stylistic conclusions depends entirely upon the minute linguistic detail of the original texts, it was impossible to offer translations. [Since the linguistic range of readers of literary criticism is not always as great as Spitzer's, the editors of this volume decided to provide translations.][56]

The editors' remarks in brackets are literally beside the point. Their well-meaning pandering to Anglophone readers may well facilitate accessibility, but it renders moot Spitzer's explicit desire to disturb monolingual complacency. Spitzer inserted this note not just to admonish his readers to refer to the original, but to insist on their confrontation with linguistic strangeness.

In allowing the foreignness of the original to "shine through," he resembles the ideal Benjaminian translator for whom the model translation is a scriptural "interlinear" rewording, proximate to the original to the point of being, almost, no translation at all.[57]

Spitzer's practice of nontranslation is not an argument against translation per se, but rather, a bid to make language acquisition a categorical imperative of *translatio studii*. A profound respect for the foreignness of a foreign language—of foreignness as the sign of that which is beyond assimilation within language itself—motivated Spitzer's plurilingual dogma, allowing him to be linked, albeit somewhat anomalously, to Benjamin, Adorno, and Paul de Man. Adorno's paraphrase of how "Benjamin spoke of the author inserting the silver rib of the foreign word into the body of language" shows how important this idea of the foreign became to critical theory. The rib represents Hebbel's "schism of creation": in "sticking out," Adorno noted, it embodies "suffering in language" and "in reality as well."[58] Adorno's formulation echoes in Paul de Man's idea of translation as "the suffering of the original" ("die Wehen des eigenen"), by which he refers to the "bottomless depth of language, something essentially destructive, which is language itself."[59] Responding to questions posed after a lecture he gave on *The Task of the Translator* at the very end of his career, de Man contended that what was interesting about Benjamin's "language of historical pathos, language of the messianic, the pathos of exile and so forth" was the fact that it "really describes linguistic events which are by no means human" (RT 96). De Man then associates Benjamin's "pains of the original" with "structural deficiencies which are best analyzed in terms of the inhuman, dehumanized language of linguistics, rather than into the language of imagery, or tropes, of pathos, or drama, which he chooses to use in a very peculiar way" (RT 96). De Man dries out the residual humanism of Benjamin's sacred language (*reine Sprache*) and turns it into something technical, "purely linguistic." Though Spitzer's humanist credo of linguistic foreignness for its own sake and de Man's theory of linguistic inhumanism may seem very far apart, they come together in a common love for linguistic foreignness.

Spitzer's abiding respect for the integrity of individual languages resonated in the concluding remarks of his lecture on "Development of a Method," delivered four months prior to his death in 1960. Adopting a credo of linguistic serial monogamy, he posits that each and every language, at the time of the critic's engagement with it, lays claim absolutely to his or her unconditional love:

> [P]hilology is the *love* for works written in a particular *language*. And if the methods of a critic must be applicable to works in all languages in order that the criticism be convincing, the critic, at least at the moment when he is discussing the poem, must love *that* language and *that* poem more than anything else in the world. (RE 448, emphases in the original)

Now even if Spitzer failed to demonstrate the same degree of passion for Turkish as for classical, Germanic, and Romance languages, he placed Turkish on an equal footing, as a language worthy of love. And in his essay "Learning Turkish," he showed more affection for the language than one might expect; comparing the effort of a linguist in midcareer trying to learn Turkish to "the situation of an old person learning to ski," a figure of speech connoting, on the one hand *le démon de midi* (midlife crisis), and on the other, the pulse-quickening thrill of dangerous liaisons. Despite the fact that he is no expert in Turcology, and despite his rudimentary grasp of the language, the intrepid philologist throws himself willynilly into analyzing the word for "veil"—*Kaçgöç* (meaning "the flight of women when a man enters the house," "the necessity for women to hide and escape from men"). Focusing on its usage in a Turkish novel called *Casual Things*, Spitzer draws parallels with Roman carnival masks, and links the word to the expression "this is no laughing matter" in Balkan languages.

Below its philological surface, Spitzer's explication resembles a classic captivity narrative, in which the European gentleman rescues Turkish womanhood from the clutches of Muslim repression. And Spitzer's conclusion—that the spirit of the Turkish people inclines more toward emotionalism than logic—falls prey to familiar Eurocentric refrains. But the "love" of Turkish is manifest, evident in the author's admission of "inferiority" in the face of a language with so old and venerable a tradition, and discernible in the second part of the essay in which he searches in vain among the European languages for the spiritual equivalent of Turkish expressions of prudence and precaution. By the time we get to Part 3, Turkish has become a language uniquely blessed with a quality he names "symbolical hearing," or "psychophonics." This subtle parallelism between "real and phonetic resemblances" lends itself to fantastic abilities to represent the mood of reality, emerging, in this regard, as the non-Western correlary of the German *Stimmung* or "atmosphere," to which Spitzer devoted an entire book. Muting his earlier dismissal of Turkish "emotionalism," Spitzer, by the time he reaches the essay's third section, is extolling the calibration of abstraction and reality unique to the Turkish language. Though Spitzer never states the case in so many words, his reading challenges the shibboleth that Indo-European languages are superior because of their higher incidence of abstraction.

In disrespecting narrowly construed East-West dichotomies; in learning Turkish (in learning, even, to love a non-Romanic language), and in establishing a seminar in which Turkish assumed its place alongside European languages as a subject field of philological research and criticism, Spitzer forged a worldly paradigm of *translatio studii* with strong links to the history, both past and present, of *translatio imperii.* The strange parallelism of Latinization during the Middle Ages, Romanization under Atatürk in the 1920s, and the institutionalization of the language of the Third Reich under Nazism produced a heightened awareness of the political complexities of linguistic imperialism in the work of European émigré scholars, even when they defined their pedagogical mission around the preservation of High Latinity's cultural remains. Scanning the grammars of the world in search of connections that unlocked the secrets of a cultural unconscious, tracking, to paraphrase Geoffrey Hartman, "the sources and intentions that turn words into psychic etymologies, even at the risk of destroying the identity of the sign," Spitzer's seminar yielded a linguistically focused worldsystems theory that stands as a counterweight to Moretti's narrative-based paradigms of distant reading.[60] If distant reading privileges outsized categories of cultural comparison—national epic, the "planetary" laws of genre—philology affords its micrological counterpart as close reading with a world view: word histories as world histories; stylistics and metrics in diaspora. Where Auerbach, according to David Damrosch, established an ethics of textual autonomy in which texts discover order and relationality because they are "allowed to live freely," Spitzer created a similar ethics for the language of the original, whereby originals are not surrendered to translations, but instead find each other freely, attempting connection even at the risk of failure and shock.[61] The practice of global *translatio* as Spitzer defined it, is patterned after untranslatable affective gaps, the nub of intractable semantic difference, episodes of violent cultural transference and countertransference, and unexpected love affairs. In retrospect, Spitzer's invention of comparative literature in Istanbul transformed philology into something recognizable today as the psychic life of transnational humanism.

4

Saidian Humanism

The humanism of Leo Spitzer and Erich Auerbach found, as I have implied in the previous two chapters, its late-twentieth-century correlative in Edward Said's elaboration of what might be called *Welt*-humanism. In taking up the issue of Saidian humanism, I want to consider: what it is, why it was such a fixture of Said's intellectual trajectory, and how humanist interpretation was complicated by the critique of Orientalism. As is well known, the German philologist Erich Auerbach remained a consistent reference point in Said's oeuvre; a figure of secular criticism in exile, a defender of literary worldliness in an era of cultural standardization, an explicator of Dante who drew Christian ontology into concert with the representation of earthly realism. Drawing on Said's preface to a 2003 edition of Auerbach's *Mimesis*, I want to examine the question of why Said held on so tenaciously to humanist precepts and exegetical practices. In *Orientalism*, humanism and empire are revealed in mutual compact, but there are other humanisms that survive the compromise with imperialism: emancipatory humanism, the ethics of coexistence, figural paradigms of ontogenesis in world-historical forms of culture, and the ideal of *translatio* as portal to a universal or sacred language. Such a language may be seen as comparable if not equal to a linguistic monotheism whose very sound-values—as in the case of classical or Koranic Arabic—are thought to be tangible evidence of Paradise. Said's reading of divine language in the preface to Auerbach intimates—though not in any explicit way—that humanism provided a crucial way of dealing with the "God problem," allowing Said to negotiate his way around the categorical imperatives of Christian and Islamic tradition. And this, of course, has significant bearing on definitions of secular criticism indebted to Said's work. Saidian humanism emerges as a place at which a number of key theoretical moves occur: worldly *translatio* (grounded in philological vitalism) merges with secular criticism, and secular criticism weans the ideal of a sacred unity of culture from its underpinnings in theology.

Edward Said was always an accomplished literary critic in a humanist vein, interested in "great writers" even, as he noted in a 1993 interview cited by Jonathan Arac, when those writers are orientalists and/or imperialists.[1] Humanism was integral to his vision of cultural coexistence without coercion, as well as to his ascription of Goethean *Weltliteratur* which harks back to his translation in 1969 of Auerbach's "Philology and *Weltliteratur*" essay. The back jacket of *Edward Said and the Work of the Critic: Speaking Truth to Power*, an anthology of essays edited by Paul Bové, highlights the inseparability of humanism and politics in Said's work: "Perhaps more than any other person in the United States," we read, "Said has changed how the U.S. media and American intellectuals must think about and represent Palestinians, Islam and the Middle East. Most important, this change arises not as a result of political action but out of a potent humanism."[2] Said's fidelity to humanism's synthetic approach to diverse cultures (on the order of Goethe's "common world-council"), to philological credos of *translatio studii*, and to literature's ability to settle value on the human person allowed his work to remain congenial to the humanities mainstream even when his political and theoretical engagements aroused antagonism on the part of conservative critics. Said's adherence to emancipatory humanism was profoundly in step with that of Frantz Fanon insofar as it embraced values of individual freedom, universal human rights, anti-imperialism, release from economic dependency, and self-determination for disenfranchised peoples. In his posthumously published book, *Humanism and Democratic Criticism* (2003), Said amplified the philological prerogative within humanism by extolling "reception" and "resistance" in the practice of close reading.[3]

In *Orientalism* humanism was rarely directly indicted, but as the ballast of philological Euro-nationalism, and as the purveyor of Orientalist tropes and archetypes, its complicity with Orientalism became evident. Said's assessment of Dante's *Divine Comedy* was particularly illustrative in this regard. It focused on Dante's encounter with "Maometto" (Mohammed) in the eighth of the nine circles of Hell. Mohammed, he reminds us, is lower down than the lustful, the avaricious, the heretics, the suicidal, and the blasphemous. He is second only to Judas, Brutus, and Cassius on the absolute scale of iniquity. Cleft in two from his chin to his anus, his entrails and excrement extruding, Mohammed is punished for the sin of schism. Islam is also antagonized by the anachronistic and unfair placement of pre-

Christian luminaries in the same category of heathen damnation with post-Christian Muslims. Even though, as Said notes, the Koran recognizes Jesus as a prophet, Dante fails to acknowledge this important fact. Dante's "poetic grasp of Islam," Said avers, thus reveals "an instance of the schematic, almost cosmological inevitability with which Islam and its designated representatives are creatures of Western geographical, historical, and above all, moral apprehension. Empirical data about the Orient . . . count for very little. . . . Dante's powers as a poet intensify, make more rather than less representative, these perspectives on the Orient." Mohammed, Saladin, Averro, and Avicenna are fixed in a visionary cosmology—laid out, boxed in, imprisoned, without much regard for anything except their unction and the patterns they realize on the stage on which they appear.[4]

Said's interpretation of Dante prepared the way for a larger argument to the effect that the Orient of Orientalism was essentially a "laicized Christian supernaturalism" dressed to modern taste by philology (O 122). It was criticism in this vein that I expected, but did not find, in Said's preface to the new edition of Auerbach's *Mimesis*, the reissue of which, by Princeton University press, was scheduled to coincide with the first English-language publication of the book in 1953.

Said's introduction to *Mimesis* offered a moving account of Auerbachian humanism, capturing a sense of the vulnerability of subjectivity or "individuality" in Auerbach's magnum opus. Said was particularly appreciative of Auerbach's Vico-inspired historicism, his capacity for synthesis, holism, and the cosmic view, his sense of the inner mobility, the animation of inner forces, that endow great works of literature with vitality. Like Walter Benjamin, Said understood that Auerbach's hermeneutical philology was interesting because it threw into relief the places where humanism abuts materialist theology. Where Said noted how Auerbachian philology's "extraordinary attention to the minute, local details of other cultures and languages" (M xv) shores up the "spiritual energy of *veritas*" invested in the Christian *figura* (M xxi), Benjamin homed in on Auerbach's literary materialism, associated with his attention to the facticity and facture of esoteric poetry (including that of Mallarmé).[5] For Benjamin, the way in which craft value underpinned the aesthetic sign paralleled the hidden value of labor inside the commodity fetish.[6] "The philological approach," Benjamin wrote in a 1938 exchange with Adorno on "Paris of the Second Empire,"

> entails examining the text detail by detail, leading the reader to fixate magically on the text. . . . The appearance of self-contained facticity that emanates from philological study and casts

its spell on the scholar is dispelled according to the degree to which the object is constructed in historical perspective. The lines of perspective in this conclusion, receding to the vanishing point, converge in our own historical experience. In this way, the object is constituted as a monad. In the monad, the textual detail which was frozen in a mythical rigidity comes alive.[7]

The spell of the textual detail was broken by history, but history (or at least the history with which there is personal identification) also liberated the textual monad from the protocols of philological reification and the frozen bonds of myth. In seeming, once again, to come alive, the monad re-achieved the power of the fetish, retaining its materialist origin while acquiring a soul.

If Said, like Benjamin, often appeared drawn to the way in which Auerbach's practice of philology tested the limits of secularism within humanist historicism, he was also fascinated by the temporal modalities of *Mimesis*—the *longue durée* of the book's chronological span (Homer to Virginia Woolf) and extended afterlife in literary criticism. Where Auerbach himself tended to stress the circumstantial historical conditions inflecting the making of *Mimesis*—"*Mimesis*," he wrote in the 1953 Epilegomena, "is quite consciously a book that a particular person, in a particular situation, wrote at the beginning of the 1940s"—Said identified humanist value in the longevity of *Mimesis* (M 574). If centuries seem to be getting longer—in Giovanni Arrighi's sense—then Said, we might say, attended accordingly to temporal duration in coordination with the spatial reach of geographic, transnational relevance. In this, he seemed to echo his earlier book *The World, the Text and the Critic*, where he praised Auerbach and Spitzer for being "extraterritorial" critics "whose philological scholarship is mainly concerned not with reading but with describing the modes of persistence of texts."[8] Along with Georg Lukács, Auerbach and Spitzer were understood to be "the great intuitors of textual filiation" who made of the text "a locus of human effort," a "text-ile fertility gathering in cultural identity, disseminating human life everywhere in time and space" (WTC 250).

In the preface to *Mimesis*, Said was brilliant on Auerbach's signature theme—"the representation of reality"—showing how Auerbach's concern with the "transmutation of a coarse reality into language and new life" had its roots in Christ's *sermo humilis* (M xx). In literary terms, the "low style" produced a representation of the real that was essentially comedic and earthly (*irdisch* in the sense assigned to that word by Auerbach in his early study *Dante als Dichter der irdischen Welt*, and misleadingly translated as

Said noted as *Dante, Poet of the Secular World*). "What fascinates Auerbach," Said observed, "is the mounting tension in Dante's poem, as eternally condemned sinners press their cases and aspire to the realization of their ambitions even as they remain fixed in the place assigned to them by Divine Judgment. Hence, the sense of futility and sublimity exuded simultaneously by the Inferno's earthly historicity, which is always pointed in the end toward the white rose of the 'Paradiso' " (M xxvi). "Having established the systematic nature of Dante's universe (framed by Aquinas's theocratic cosmology)," Said continued, "Auerbach offers the thought that for all of its investment in the eternal and immutable, the *Divine Comedy* is even more successful in representing reality as basically human. In that vast work of art 'the image of man eclipses the image of God' " (M xxvi). Finally, Said contended that "Auerbach's choice of Dante for advancing the radically humanistic thesis carefully works through the great poet's Catholic ontology as a phase transcended by the Christian epic's realism, which is shown to be 'ontogenetic, that is,' " (and he is cited Auerbach), " 'we are given to see, in the realm of timeless being, the history of man's inner life and unfolding (M xxvi).

Said's eloquent reading of Auerbach's Dante chapter concentrated on the crucial association of the Incarnation with realism, a realism brimming over with such aliveness that it eclipses the divine. Reading his preface, I found myself stirred by Said's obvious passion for the great works of Western literature analyzed by Auerbach, as well as by his recuperation of Auerbach's typological model. But I also found myself perplexed by what seemed to be a noticeable *lack* of attention to Auerbach's Eurocentrism. In writing about Auerbach in *Culture and Imperialism*, for example, Said had alluded explicitly to the philologist's phobia of non-Western languages, his reluctance (in contrast to his Istanbul colleagues Leo Spitzer or Traugott Fuchs) to risk scholarly engagement with cultures falling outside of the Holy Roman Empire. As I have noted in the previous chapter, analogies beg to be drawn between Roman linguistic imperialism and the Turkish linguistic auto-colonization that Auerbach was witnessing firsthand. And yet, written in Istanbul between 1942 and 1945, *Mimesis* bears scant evidence of the site of its writing.

In Said's preface I expected the Turkish circumstances of the book's genesis to be woven into an account of how Auerbachian humanism fared in the late twentieth century viewed from a post-*Orientalism*, if not post-colonial vantage point. But to my surprise, there was nothing obviously "Saidian" about the preface, and if I had covered up the signature, I probably would never have guessed that it corresponded to that of the author of *Ori-*

entalism. Perhaps this was a text written in the spirit of confirming the critic's freedom to address his interests in any way he saw fit, an example of the pure intellectual pleasure Said always took in certain forms of traditional humanist scholarship. Or perhaps, submerged somewhere in this Auerbachian *homage*, there lay the makings of a theory of *Welt-humanism* that, once adumbrated, would suggest what humanism after *Orientalism* might be. In *Humanism and Democratic Criticism*, *Welt-humanism* emerges as synonymous with an ecumenical "human," indebted not so much to Auerbach as to Spitzer. Citing Spitzer's assertion in "Linguistics and Literary History" that "[t]he Humanist believes in the power of the human mind of investigating the human mind," Said underscored the point that "Spitzer does not say the European mind, or only the Western canon. He talks about the human mind *tout court*" (HD 26).

The centrality of humanism in Said's oeuvre may be partially understood as a means of preserving the secular foundations of his thought. Aamir Mufti has analyzed multiple ways in which Saidian secular criticism unfolds out of the "worlded" humanism associated by Said with the figure of Auerbach in exile. In Mufti's ascription, this "critical secularism" is associated with minority consciousness (dislocation, statelessness, psychic unhoming),[9] and the traumatic reckoning with "what it means for a group to become a minority" (a condition of becoming-minor, a state of being included but unrelated or misfitting in the national whole).[10] Mufti's ethics of transnational solidarity among minorities relies on a vector of comparison between Indian Muslims minoritized after Partition and Jewish refugees exiled during World War II. This ethic of relation, posed against unmediated claims of national membership, belongs to a secularist project that implies: a holding on to anti-imperialism and the ends of economic and social justice, a commitment to the tactical dejuridification of democratic legalism (which allows a superstate to suspend rights in a state of emergency), freedom from religious opiate, a transnational politics of the multitude built on revolutionary social formations and subjectivities, and not least, a theoretical disposition of critique that hews to the logical rigorism of the collective while challenging the call to arms embedded in sectarian casuistry.

Mufti offers a renewed appreciation of Said's Auerbach as a model of minority subjectivity running counter to identity politics. In an interview with Jacqueline Rose, Said confessed: "I have become very, very impatient with the idea of and the whole project of identity: the idea, which produced great interest in the United States in the sixties and which is also present in the return to Islam in the Arab world and elsewhere, that people should really focus on themselves and where they come from. . . . What is much more interesting is to try to reach out beyond identity to something else. It may be death. It may be an altered state of consciousness that puts you in touch with others more than one normally is."[11] This concern to move "beyond identity"—reprised in the opening of his memoir *Out of Place* in which he describes the sense that "there was always something wrong with how I was invented" in which he admits to feeling on some occasions "nearly devoid of any character at all"—recalls the intellectual disposition of an entire generation of humanists during World War II who, even at their peril, resisted the claims of identity in the name of an ontological something else.[12] Dismissed from his position as professor of Romance philology, and certain that he would be deported by the Nazis, Victor Klemperer, for example, confided in his diary that he would rather remain a German (because of his identification with the language and culture) than emigrate to Palestine: "Belonging to a nation," he maintained, depends less on blood than on language. "Language contains the totality of the intellectual." Like Walter Benjamin, exhorted by Gershom Scholem to emigrate to Palestine, Klemperer resisted emigration, remaining fast in his convictions: "We hear a lot about Palestine now; it does not appeal to us. Anyone who goes there exchanges nationalism and narrowness for nationalism and narrowness."[13] And in December 1944, on the eve of fleeing his Dresden home, he wrote: "Perhaps we Jews always want to be something else—some Zionists, the others Germans. But what are we really? I do not know. And that, too, is a question to which I shall never get an answer. And as a scholar that is my greatest fear of death: that in all probability it will give me no answer to all my questions."[14] For Klemperer, Jewishness *is* perforce the condition of "no-answer," a state of statelessness contoured by an abiding commitment to secular humanism.

Auerbach's national, religious, and cultural affinities were just as complex, a fact that helps explain why, for Said, he often seemed to function as a stand-in or alter-ego. We cannot fail to be struck by parallels between Said's ironic portrait of Auerbach, as "a non- Christian explaining Christianity's achievement" and his own predicament as a Palestinian with Christian roots, explaining the need for a nonmonolithic understanding of Islam (M xviii). The figure of the critic negotiating dissensual ideas and making his ecumenical filiations the very precondition of humanism mattered a great deal to Said, who wrote:

> In Auerbach's searingly powerful and strangely intimate characterization of the great Christian Thomist poet Dante—who emerges from the pages of *Mimesis* as *the* seminal figure in West-

ern literature—the reader is inevitably led to the paradox of a Prussian Jewish scholar in Turkish, Muslim, non-European exile handling (perhaps even juggling) charged, and in many ways irreconcilable, sets of antinomies that, though ordered more benignly than their mutual antagonism suggests, never lose their opposition to each other. (M xviii)

In comments like these, one recognizes the familiar compassion and intellectual respect that Said consistently demonstrated toward Auerbach, indicative of the special place he reserved for him as acknowledged precursor of his own version of worldly humanism in exile and "resolute secularism" (M xxii). When Said characterized Freud's Moses as a representative figure of non-exclusivist, nondiscriminatory religious origins in *Freud and the Non-European,* his Auerbach resembled this Freud: a secular Jew open to non-Jewish traditions, and keenly aware of how allegorical typology may be applied like powers of ten to the analysis of global humanity.[15]

Reading Said's preface a second time, I began to appreciate why it would have been uninteresting for Said to harp on the limitations of his Eurocentrist humanism. For Said was taking up the challenge of using Auerbachian humanism to fashion new humanisms, not merely because of a sober conviction that great books, on the grounds of their intrinsic merit, should continue to have traction in a global, increasingly mediatized culture industry, but more because of his belief that humanism provides futural parameters for defining secular criticism in a world increasingly governed by a sense of identitarian ethnic destiny and competing sacred tongues.

In the preface to *Mimesis* it was Goethe's humanist vision of *Weltliteratur* that opened the door to a humanism negotiating analogically between Christianity and Islam. In the decade after 1810, Said noted, Goethe

> became fascinated with Islam generally and with Persian poetry in particular. This was the period when he composed his finest and most intimate love poetry, the *West-Ostlicher Diwan* (1819), finding in the work of the great Persian poet Hafiz and in the verses of the Koran not only a new lyric inspiration allowing him to express a reawakened sense of physical love but . . . a discovery of how, in the absolute submission to God, he felt himself to be oscillating between two worlds, his own and that of the Muslim believer who was miles, even worlds away from European Weimar. (M xv)

Raised as a Christian, the great-grandson of the first native Evangelical minister in Lebanon, yet brought up habituated to Muslim culture in Palestine and Egypt, Said clearly forged his secularism in the midst of contesting world religions. One finds traces of their impression in the way in which Said evoked Auerbach's vision of the drama of earthly Incarnation. Auerbachian themes drawn from doctrinal Christianity—the mystery of the Logos, the Word made flesh, God made into a man, theological typology, the notion of *figura* as the name for the "intellectual and spiritual energy that does the actual connecting between past and present, history and Christian truth," and the magisterial demonstration of the "millennial effects of Christianity on literary representation"—build up to remind us of humanism's predication on theistic structure (M xxi—xxii). In his bracing account of Auerbach's reading of Dante's earthly Paradise, Said moved well beyond the commonplace of *Einfuhling* in the service of historicism. Almost seeming at times to be flirting with the temptations of Paradise himself, Said identified the godly within humanism with a logic of extension. Old Testament figures, "including God," are adduced to be "heavy with the implication of extending into the depths of time, space, and consciousness, hence of character, and therefore require a much more concentrated, intense act of attention from the reader" (M xix). It is this logic of extension (with its distant echo of a Spinozist ontology of common notions enabling the extension of the one to the many, of the social multiple to the fortified unicity of the multitude) that brings us to Saidian *Welt-humanism.*[16] This is a humanism foreshadowed in *Orientalism* in the "enlightened" pursuit of theological unity as a governing principle of a plurality of worlds, and in the "summational attitude" of the highly educated Orientalist, which carries over in Said's estimation to the non-Orientalist Western scholar, the philological humanists of the twenties and thirties: Dilthey, Curtius, Vossler, Gundolf, Hofmannsthal. Auerbach, Spitzer, and Freud, whose Egypto-Jewish cultural syncretism Said treats in his book *Freud and the Non-European.* Late bourgeois humanism, Said argued with neo-Hegelian fidelity in *Orientalism,* with its commitment to understanding culture "*as a whole,* antipositivistically, intuitively, sympathetically is what made possible the conversion of the discrete particular into a world-historical process" (O 258–59).

If at times in this preface it seemed as if Said minimized humanist Orientalism in order to salvage humanism *tout court,* or the universal human, it is perhaps because he believed that there was simply too much at stake within the humanist tradition to justify simplistic denunciations. At the late stage of his career during which he composed the new introduction to *Mimesis* and completed the series of lectures that would comprise the book *Humanism and Democratic Criticism*, Said was clearly committed to the future of humanism conceived as a world system that takes account of the vast traffic in international learnedness informing Greek-Arab-Judeo-Christian practices of cultural translation from the early Middle Ages to the present. I would submit further that Said seemed to have been urging humanism in its prospective guises to take on not only the history of *global translatio*, but also to build on its past tradition as instigator of intellectual fields that decompartmentalize established discourses and subjects. Following on from the range of questions addressed in Said's Auerbach preface, one could argue that it is now the mandate of humanism to define a critical secularism that seeks to reconcile the rival claims of theodicy, relativism, ontogenesis, and anti-imperialism.

In *Orientalism* critical secularism was identifiable with the exposure of Orientalism's crypto-religious heuristic practice. In tracing historic connections between Herder-inspired studies of the Orient, and philological secular humanism, Said described some of the infelicitous side effects of Herder's challenge to universalism. For even if Herder introduced a salubrious new awareness of world cultures that encouraged the beginnings of an enlightened cultural relativism and fostered secular modes of inquiry into cultures of the Orient (so that, for example, "Gibbon could treat Mohammed as a historical figure who influenced Europe and not as a diabolical miscreant hovering somewhere between magic and false prophecy," thus making possible "a selective identification with regions and cultures not one's own [that] wore down the obduracy of self and identity, which had been polarized into a community of embattled believers facing barbarian hordes"), this secularizing tendency hardly vaccinated against what Said termed "a reconstructed religious impulse" within Orientalist philology (O 120–21). According to this model, the Orientalist himself became the new God, creating "the Orient" as a culturally reified, historicized object of research and, in the process, legitimating the "modern" heuristics and doxologies of philology, history, and translation.

As an antidote to philology's inveterate practice of using Orientalism to "play God," Said, and many of the critics influenced by him, extended worldly humanism to critical secularism. Humanism, of course, has been a tradition shaped and structured historically by tensions between religion and secular culture, tensions that fracture multiply into differences among theology, dogma, popular belief, inner spirituality, individuality, reason, piety, religious telos, and ontology. Secularization arose, at least in part, out of disavowed references by the church fathers to classical authors and texts of antiquity, references in turn drawn on by the quattrocento humanists to legitimate their embrace of classical allusion. In the early fifteenth century, Petrarch swept aside doctrinal strictures against classicism inherited from medieval scholasticism to create a *studia humanitatis* that absorbed antiquity into a general, secular Italian culture, while Valla extended the reach of humanism to the domains of philosophy, religion, and legal theory. Dante's invention of what Auerbach calls "extreme subjectivity" in *The Divine Comedy* advanced secularization yet further, but this new emphasis on human subjective consciousness was hardly at odds with religious purpose because Dante's first concern was to transpose sacred, biblical knowledge into the modern form of textuality known as European literature.[17]

Tensions between religion and secularism remain anchored in humanism, inflecting even the most recent attempts to engender a humanist critical secularism. As a free-standing term, secularism carries problematic connotations as a code word to distinguish "fundamentalism" or theocratic states in the Middle East from (Israeli) "democracy." In this case, secularism becomes all too easily assimilated to the political export of hegemonic models of democracy. Moreover, it repeats and reinforces old Orientalist binarisms that have acquired new currency in Samuel Huntington's "clash of civilizations" paradigm. Critical secularism, by contrast, seeks to countervail such binarism by framing the venerable humanist concern "to connect the renewal of liberal disciplines with the subjective consciousness of such an undertaking," within the broader context of colonial history, imperialism, and the critique of nationalism.[18] Pointing to the theocratic dimension of nationalism, for example, Bruce Robbins defines "secular" not in opposition to the religious, but as a term for the critique of "nation and nationalism as belief system."[19] In a complementary vein, Stathis Gourgouris sees "[t]he motif of transformation against the grain of transcendence" in Said's work as reaching "beyond mere opposition of the secular to the religious to another configuration that strips away from the religious (and indeed from metaphysics itself) an assumed imperviousness to the political, so that perhaps we may speak of Said's work, rather dramatically, as an exfoliation of the repressed politics of transcendence."[20]

Saidian secular criticism may certainly be said to sublimate a repressed politics of transcendence while unmasking organized religion's pose of political impartiality. But one might also venture to say that Said's attentiveness to theological exegesis in the preface to *Mimesis* attests to an intellectual curiosity toward cultures of belief, a willingness to engage "religiously" with the matter of how philosophies of transcendence have shaped revolutionary ethical militance and subjective freedom. How, for example, should we interpret Paradise, defined as a language of revealed truth embodied in linguistic theism? This question becomes particularly urgent now: the lure of Paradise is often invoked in Western denunciations of Islam, especially when it is targeted for caricature as a motivation for suicide martyrdom. The politics of religion, and the very particular complexities attending the sacred status of Koranic Arabic (sometimes characterized as the instructions of God *en direct*), would be better appreciated if read contrapuntally in relation to the political cosmogony of Paradise in Christian humanism, specifically as it emerges in Dante's language of Paradise, in which, according to one commentator, "All heavenly phenomena are direct utterances of God and of His angels."[21]

Auerbach's Dante monograph, originally published in 1929, and deemed by Said to be possibly his best work, affords a relevant point of departure. Through his close reading of the *Divine Comedy* Auerbach set himself the task of describing how Dante made Paradise linguistically tangible. He began with the time-honored problem of theodicy confronted by Dante, namely, how to reconcile divine order and the actually lived experience on earth of supreme injustice. It was Augustine, according to Auerbach, who gave man something to hope for in the form of Christ's story, communicated as "the idea of a personal God," in such a way as to preserve "the fundamentally European determination not to abolish reality by speculation, not to take flight into transcendence, but to come to grips with the real world and master it"[22] (D 17). Augustine, maintained Auerbach (citing Harnack), was "able to endow Latin and the future tongues of Europe with a Christian soul and the language of the heart" (D 17). This language of the heart was fully mobilized by Dante in the *Inferno* and the *Purgatorio*. Preparing the way for his future arguments in *Mimesis*, Auerbach showed how crass vernacular inflections, concrete sound values, and metric monotony emerged as the linguistic equivalents of Christ's mortal and mortified body. Even the preferred verse form of *terza rima* (an homage to the sacred number three) was treated as essential to Dante's construction of what Auerbach called an "Other World," at once ethereal and *irdisch*, anthropocentric and referential to God.

When it came to the *Paradiso*, Auerbach acknowledged, Dante encountered greater difficulty in preserving the human character of the Christian afterlife. Subjective rapture and celestial radiance, he thought, threatened to disembody the subject, inducing radical depersonalization. And yet, despite what Auerbach argued, the language of the *Paradiso* is in fact far from dull. Yes, there is an abstract, radiant lexicon of beatitude and satisfaction that tends to numb the senses and distance the reader from earthly reality, but if we take Auerbach's reading of Dante seriously, we should also note a rhetoric of geometric metaphysics in Paradise that provided a truly "worlded" expressionism:

> In Paradise all the souls have undergone a transformation which the human eyes cannot penetrate; they are hidden by the radiance of their beatitude and Dante cannot recognize them; they themselves must say who they are, and they cannot express their emotions by human gestures; strictly speaking, personal emotion can only manifest itself here by an increase in radiance. The danger of depersonalization and repetition are evident, and many believe that Dante succumbed to it and that the *Paradiso* lacks the poetic power of the first two parts of the *Comedy*. But such a criticism of Dante's *ultimo lavoro* springs from the Romantic prejudice of which we have spoken above. . . . The great similarity between the luminous manifestations, resulting from their common beatitude, does not exclude a preservation of the individual personality; the man is almost if not entirely hidden from the eyes, but he is there and finds means of making himself known. (D 155)

The reference to "luminous manifestations" in this passage reveals Dante grappling with the theophanic dilemma of making God manifest in language.

Although the bodies are hidden, the luminous apparitions of the *Paradiso* have expressive gestures that accompany their memories of their former lives on earth; these are different modes and movements of light, which Dante illustrates with an abundance of metaphors; the feminine souls of the moon appear as pearls on a white forehead; the souls of the sphere of Mercury gather around Dante like fish in clear water, swimming toward food that has been cast to them (D 155–56). Auerbach savored these images of effulgent, ghostly bodies while cautioning the reader against interpreting them as decorative similitudes of "pure inspiration." They were allegoremes with a distinct purpose, he insisted, sensuous images placed before the reader not just to serve as delectable "food to catch the eyes and so possess the mind," but rather—and the distinction was crucial—as diaphanous traces of the real that signify rational thought: God as idea and absolute of justice. The only human shapes figured in Paradise are St. Thomas and St. Francis, but their physical forms are encased in veils of light. It is their sacral language that conserves the phantom of their former individuality as material for testing the suffering or enjoyment of divine justice. Reading the *Paradiso* in the "right" Auerbachian way thus entails reading linguistic theophany as *justicium*. Why was justice in Paradise so important to Dante? Perhaps because, as Auerbach reminds us, Dante was bent on obtaining it. As is well known, much of the polemical import of *The Divine Comedy* lies in redeeming the Christian faith from ecclesiastical corruption (and more specifically, the particularly egregious venality of the church in his home town of Florence).

Though justice emerged as the preeminent abstract ideal of Paradise, it was imbricated within a vision of imperial glory. Auerbach traced Dante's "imperialist" vision of Paradise in the typological *surcodage* of Roman military and Christian virtues (self-sacrifice, conquest, salvation). A clear example may be pinpointed in Canto 14 of the *Paradiso* where the phrase "Resurgi" e "Vinci" ("Arise" and "Conquer") that comes to the narrator in a flash of messianic imperial hope, prefigures the representation of all-out redemption as *Gloria Patri*, the union of church and empire in God in Canto 27. Consider, too, the place in Canto 28 where Dante plays on the Gothic capital form of the letter *M*. First the letter is shown to resemble the (the French-Guelph-Florentine) lily, then an eagle, the movement of the wings, upright and then down forming the last letter of the word TERRAM (earth, world), taken to stand for *Monarchia* (Empire).[23] It might strike the modern observer as strange, Auerbach said, but Dante introduces

> the idea of the special mission of Rome and the Roman Empire in history. From the very beginning Divine Providence elected Rome as the capital of the world. It gave the Roman people the heroism and the spirit of self-sacrifice necessary to conquer this world and possess it in peace; and when the work of conquest and pacification, the sacred mission announced to Aeneas, was accomplished after centuries of bitter battles and sacrifices and the inhabited world lay in the hands of Augustus, the time was fulfilled and the Saviour appeared. . . . Rome was the mirror of the divine world order. (D 122)

Dante's allegory focused subsequently on earthly Rome's fall from grace as it yielded to the greed-driven institutions of church and state, but the version of the Roman Empire that was, so to speak, made in Paradise represented the unity of all peoples in a just world order, an "empyreal" imperium as it were. This upper reach of the celestial spheres transcended dialectical striving; even the millennial desire to recover a new king was replaced by the will of a collection of souls forming a spirit of the multitude and held together in a space-time continuum commonly known as the Primum Mobile.[24]

If, in the 1920s, Dante's Paradise served Auerbach as a *figura* for a reconstituted humanism, in the present era the work of the Palestinian poet Mahmoud Darwish endows it with contemporary resonance. Dante and Darwish may seem initially to share little ground of comparison, but on closer reading Darwish's volume of poetry *Unfortunately, It Was Paradise* offers interesting parallels. In the poem "Like the Letter 'N' in the Qur'an," the letter *N* (referring to a chapter of the Koran that uses a dual rhyme scheme ending in *N*) renders God alphabetically perceptible, recalling Dante's designation of the imperial TERRAM, with its final *M* in Gothic script. In the work of both writers, Paradise emerges as a place holder for political utopia—a just world—that looks more like a perfected secular society than a holy land beyond representation. In Darwish's "Earth Presses against Us," much loved and oft-quoted by Said, Paradise—located somewhere "after the last sky"—is the name for the dream of a restituted homeland. "Earth is pressing against us, trapping us in the final passage. / To pass through, we pull off our limbs. / Earth is squeezing us. If only we were its wheat, we might die and yet live. . . . Where should we go after the last border? Where should birds fly after the last sky?"[25]

Christian and Islamic Paradise, in the work of Dante and Darwish respectively, resembles an Auerbachian *figura*—a term that Said, in his first book, *Beginnings*, credited Auerbach with finding in the course of his research on Dante. An *Ansatzpunkt* or key word, springing directly from historical context, *figura* functions as an *X* term, assuming an algorithmic function in the meaning-production of humanism. For Said, this *X* sign carries maximal significance since it allows epistemes to crystalize and enter history (B 68). "No longer mere words or unknown symbols," Said wrote in *Beginnings*, these *mots-thèses* in Auerbach's writing "enact the combination of past and future woven into the historical fabric of language. A mute term, relatively anonymous, has given rise to a special condition of mind and has evoked the poignancy of time" (B 69). For a term to become a piece of "reconstructed history," it must be fortunate to find—in the manner of Walter Benjamin's text of the original in search of the ideal translator—an interpreter capable of conferring an afterlife. For Said, the term *figura* became "incarnate" (that is to say a term of agency, ready to change and be changed) only by virtue of being discovered by Auerbach in the course of his scholarly research (B 69). One could say the same about the term "Orientalism," which lay dormant in Western philology until Edward Said plucked it from the fusty shelves and galvanized it as a critical episteme, a foundational *Ansatzpunkt* for an anti-imperialist understanding of world culture. And perhaps one could perform the same function on the word "Paradise," transforming it from a term connoting nonsecular utopias and the desire for self-sacrifice unto death, into an *Ansatzpunkt* defining future humanisms through the theory of possible worlds. Without relinquishing the commitment to exposing religion's threat to a politics of the here and now, or forgetting the need to hold steadfast against manipulative invocations of transcendentally authorized injunctions, humanism, informed by critical secularism, might be well advised to consider once more the temptations of "imparadising" oneself (to borrow Dante's phrase), that is to say, of attaining "God" for the love of justice. For though it may seem an antique dilemma, understanding the relationship between theophany and *justicium* would seem to be the political order of the day. In other terms, whether it is conceptualized as justice divined as the expressionism of sacred language, or as the transformation of an imperialist rhetoric of Christian salvation into a rhetoric of planetary utopianism, or as the space between physics and metaphysics that in contemporary theoretical parlance might be called "possible worlds" or "parallel universes," Paradise—as the signature expression of a politics of utopia—assumes new relevance to global humanism. Edward Said's legacy will unfurl into the future of comparative literary studies in ways that can not even be imagined. In paying tribute to Said as a reader of Erich Auerbach, the concern has not just been to confer the Auerbachian mantel on Said—he assumed that mantle quite naturally by refurbishing the Auerbachian project of "philology and *Weltliteratur*" for a late industrial, neo-imperialist age and by extending the political stakes of Jewish exile to Palestinian refugees. I have been interested, rather, in exploring specifically how Said's reception of (and oftentimes resistance to) Auerbach—particularly Auerbach the reader of Dante—defined a crucial set of questions and programmatic concerns for comparative literature, translation studies, and the humanities at large. Saidian humanism, as I have sought to define it, prompts an activist return to the "great works" of humanism, with the understanding that humanism itself should be rezoned to avoid misleading cartographic divisions between European and non-European culture. Like his lifelong exemplars, Vico, Dilthey, Hegel, and Auerbach, Said aspired to the flash of learned cultural synthesis in a historicist frame, and yet like Auerbach (or Benjamin), he remained chary of totalizing interpretations that lent themselves to hegemonic application. Auerbach said of *Mimesis* that "the book is no theoretical construct; it aims to offer a view, and the very elastic thoughts or ideas that hold it together cannot be grasped and proven wrong in single, isolated phrases," and Said, unlike many of Auerbach's critics, appreciated the lack of seamless narrative in *Mimesis*, seeing in its fragmentary structure and the quirky, very personal drift of literary analysis the mark of the human (M 562). Said in his own work never let the reader forget the human in the humanities. "Auerbach," he wrote, "is bringing us back to what is an essentially Christian doctrine for believers but also a crucial element of *human* intellectual power and will" (M xxii). The same of course could be said about Said's own work. Mining the humanist tradition for a utopian politics—despite the association of humanism with Eurocentrism and Orientalism—Said not only circumvented crude oppositions between cultures of belief and the critical secularism of technological modernity, he made palpable the effects of "*human* intellectual power and will" in the sacred narratives of divine ontogenesis.

PART TWO

The Politics of Untranslatability

5

Nothing Is Translatable

Over the last three decades, the French philosopher Alain Badiou (building on Gilles Deleuze) has reworked notions of singularity and poetic universalism for comparative poetics in an era that has often treated such principles as theoretically suspect. While I remain wary of attempts to resuscitate unipolar thinking at the expense of multiplicity, entropy, heterodoxy, and transversality, I find Badiou's refutation of easy relationality, along with his willingness to recognize the limits of cultural translation, an incentive to rethink translation studies from the standpoint of the presumption that "nothing is translatable." Construing a translation theory from Badiou is tantamount to playing devil's advocate with my own conviction (set out in the last section on humanism) that the translation zone is established on the basis of the philological relation.

In a chapter of his book of essays *Petit Manuel d'inesthétique* (1998) devoted to a comparison between the poets Labîd ben Rabi'a and Mallarmé, Badiou emphasizes the chasms and gulfs of untranslatability that make the enterprise of comparative literature so tenuous. The chapter's opening line—"Je ne crois pas beaucoup à la littérature comparée" ("I do not really believe in comparative literature")—prepares his case for disbelief in matters of literary comparatism, placing the onus of skepticism on the overdetermined failure of translations to transmit the genius of a source text. In Badiou's view, translation itself is tantamount to a writing of disaster, a kind of black hole or meaning-void; and yet, for all the obstacles posed by translation, "great poems" surmount the difficulty of being worlds apart and manage to achieve universal significance. This poetic singularity against all odds challenges the laws of linguistic territorialization that quarantine language groups in communities "of their own kind" (as in Romance or

East Asian languages) or enforce a condition in which monolingualisms coexist without relation.

Badiou's literary universalism, built on affinities of the Idea ("une proximité dans la pensée") rather than on philological connections or shared sociohistorical trajectories, defines a kind of *comparatisme quand même* that complements the militant credo of his political philosophy (indebted to Beckett's formula for existence—"I can't go on, I will go on"). It argues for the ability of art to release the revolutionary possibility of an Event by making manifest Truth, a truth that surges forth unexpectedly from art's most "inaesthetic" philosophical expressionism. Ultimately it is a text's singularity that confers universal value or truth. Identifiable as the form of what is unrepresentable in the situation—its void or empty set—singularity lines up in Badiou's political thought with the exception or exclusion on which a set is grounded. According to Badiou's mathematical ontology, indebted to Cantor's set theory, singularity qualifies as an "eventual site" guiding revolutionary truth to the historical situation. In aesthetic terms, singularity is what allows a given poetic masterwork to become the predicate of a shape-shifting poetic form, a carrier of universal truth insofar as it exceeds specificity or the boundaries of the relation.[1]

Badiou's account of this singular universalism has interesting ramifications for literary comparatism, as seen in the example of Labîd ben Rabi'a and Mallarmé. A comparison between two wildly divergent authors—one a nomad writing in classical Arabic in the pre-Islamic period, the other a bourgeois saloniste of Second Empire France—has just as much credence for Badiou as a comparison between authors hailing from a shared tradition. Indeed, it would often seem that the greater the arc of radical dissimilitude and incomparability, the truer the proof of poetic universalism. Badiou's *astuce*, which almost seems to insist that comparativity with the least relation guarantees the maximum of poetic universalism, challenges shibboleths of translation theory and comparative literature alike. Translation theory and Comp Lit have traditionally supported each other in arguing for enhanced conduits of linguistic and cultural exchange. The principle of *adequatio*, based on values of equivalence, commonality, and aesthetic measure, has led to the professional triage of literary fields, with comparisons favored among language groups with a shared philological heritage. Even newer forms of postcolonial comparatism have inadvertently perpetuated neocolonial geopolitics in carrying over the imperial carve-up of linguistic fields. So, for example, in the case of the Caribbean: Haiti, Martinique, and Guadeloupe are placed under the rubric of Francophone studies, Cuba falls under the purview of Spanish and Latin American studies, and

Jamaica remains sequestered in Anglophone fields. While there are obvious historical and pedagogical reasons for maintaining geopolitical relations between dominants and their former colonies, protectorates, and client states (one wouldn't want, for example, to encourage European literatures to erase the past of their colonial encounters or to relinquish commitments to postcolonial literatures), there are equally compelling arguments for abandoning postcolonial geography. Francophone might, then, no longer simply designate the transnational relations among metropolitan France and its former colonies, but linguistic contact zones all over the world in which French, or some kind of French, is one of many languages in play.

Badiou's comparatism could not be further from this location-conscious "translational transnationalism," a term I have relied on to anchor the rethinking of translation studies. If there is a transnational dimension to his reading practice, it is produced collaterally, that is to say, as an unintended side effect of tracking the Idea wherever it might lead him. Where postcolonial comparatists have imagined a "trans" to "trans" space-time of literary analysis, reciprocally arraigning minority languages while bypassing metropolitan vehicular tongues (as in the hypothetical translation of Moncton Joual into the Creole spoken in Mauritious, Tagalog into Ogoni, Hinglish into Spanglish), Badiou pays little heed to linguistic class struggle. Comparative literature—even when it relies on the imperfect vehicle of translation ("toujours presque désastrueuse")—rises to the political occasion precisely because it contributes to the unpredictable release of a revolutionary Truth-Event; this is what makes it an important "inaesthetic" praxis (with "inaesthetic" referring to the "strictly intraphilosophical effects produced by the independent existence of works of art").[2] Thus, Badiou's reading of Labîd ben Rabi'a and Mallarmé promises a comparative literature that seeks out rather than shies away from parallels between languages of great discrepancy. Though he himself is not interested per se in making an argument about comparative literature as a discipline, his provocative opening salvo "Je ne crois pas beaucoup à la littérature comparée" hitched to a tempering "Et pourtant" stakes its claim on a Comp Lit willing to embrace linguistic nonidentity. Like Walter Benjamin, in "The Task of the Translator," he accepts translation failure as an a priori condition (Benjamin argues that to translate mere content is simply to repeat, badly, the most inessential nature of the original), and like Benjamin, he turns this failure to advantage, transforming it into an enabling mechanism of poetic truth.

I must confess to having been initially disconcerted by Badiou's blanket rejection of the ethics of location. But on further reflection, his paradigm of *comparatisme quand même* seemed bracing, a way of confronting the bare truth of translational dysfunction while soldiering on. There was also theoretical significance accruing to the specific comparison between the Arabic ode (the *mu'allaqa*) of Labîd ben Rabi'a and Mallarmé's symbolist masterwork (*Un Coup de dés*). "We remain," Badiou insists, "between Mallarmé and the *mu'allaqa*" (PM 85). The choice to compare these particular Arabic and French texts is gradually revealed as far from arbitrary: questions of democracy and subjectivation, terrorism, despotism, the nature of mastery, the seduction of sacred language, the influence of clans (the "call" of the *tribu*), the intoxicating desire for collective destiny and a *vita communis*, the sacrifice of civilization to science and technology, the spiritual "desert" or empty set of subjectivity, decampment, exile, and the defection of place—these ideas of paramount mutual concern to Labîd ben Rabi'a and Mallarmé constitute an Event in Badiou's sense of that term, even as they announce a universalist poetics that allows for linguistic relations of radical dissimilitude.

Badiou's argument that "we remain between Mallarmé and the *mu'allaqa*" prompts examination of a *mu'allaqa* by Mahmoud Darwish, *A Rhyme for the Odes* (Mu'allaqat), published in 1995. Darwish triangulates the anomalous pairing of Labîd ben Rabi'a and Mallarmé with his meditation on exile and the autonomy of the word:

> No one guided me to myself. I am the guide. / Between desert and sea, I am my own guide to myself. . . . Who am I? This is a question that others ask, but has no answer. / I am my language, I am an ode, two odes, ten. This is my language. / I am my language. I am words' writ: *Be! Be my body!* / And I become an embodiment of their timbre. / I am what I have spoken to the words: *Be the place where / my body joins the eternity of the desert. / Be, so that I may become my words.*[3] (emphasis in the text)

Darwish chisels a subjective space from the desert sand, itself an expanse defined by temporal portage and forced emigration: "They emigrated. / They carried the place and emigrated, they carried time and emigrated." With a concluding line "So let there be prose," Darwish would seem to echo Mallarmé's famous phrase in *Crise de vers* "Je dis: une fleur!" ("I say: a flower") or the categorical infinitive "Écrire" of *Quant au Livre*.[4] In the face of disaster—defined by Mallarmé as the crisis brought on by Victor Hugo's overdetermination of modern verse—these simple declarative utterances induce a revolution in poetic language, licensing prose to become a purveyor of the universal poetic idea ("la notion pure"). The last line of Darwish's *mu'allaqa*, "There must be a divine prose for the Prophet to triumph," also parallels Mallarmé's finale in *Quant au Livre*: "L'air ou chant sous le texte, conduisant la divination d'ici là, y applique son motif en fleuron et cul-de-lampe invisibles" ("The tune or song beneath the text, inching our guess-work forward, applies its emblem to the text as an invisible fleuron and tallpiece").[5] Both poets accord the language of the everyday a prophetic, incantatory sway. Moreover, Darwish's writing, like that of Labîd ben Rabi'a and Mallarmé, builds on the void as the *Abgrund* of singular creation. The form of this singularity is discernible in Badiou's assertion that "the master of truth must traverse the place of defection for which, or from which, there is truth. He must bet on the poem as the shortest way to absolute revenge against the indifference of the universe. . . . To say it another way, the master must risk the poem exactly where the poem's resources seem to have disappeared" ("le maître de vérité doit traverser la défection du lieu pour lequel, ou à partir duquel, il y a vérité. . . . Il doit parier le poème au plus près d'une revanche absolue de l'indifférence de l'univers. . . . Autant dire que le maître doit risquer le poème exactement là où la ressource du poème semble avoir disparu") (PM 78). Singular poetic form, manipulated by the poet as a way of beating the odds against cosmological diffidence, and approximating pure creative expression, is thus built up out of evacuated points of origin. In establishing the albeit implausible colloquy between Labîd ben Rabi'a and Mallarmé, Badiou seems bent on conjugating the two writers in a single declension, and in so doing, reconciling two voids, or squaring two models of truth: the truth of the ode, founded on immanence (of deserted place), and the truth of Mallarméan verse, founded on authorial anonymity. "How," Badiou wants to know, "can one think the truth as simultaneously anonymous, or impersonal [Mallarmé], and yet immanent and terrestrial?" (PM 87). The answer lies in eliding philosophy and art by subjecting the subject to the "being" of place and positing a credo of militant fidelity to the sites of abandonment in and by the world, whether it is the isolated tree on a dust-swept dune in ben Rabi'a's text, or the furious, winged Abyss with which Mallarmé defines art, in Badiou's terms, "subtracted from the impasse of the master" (PM 88–89).

While the anomalous prospect of a "communist" Labîd ben Rabi'a, or of an "absolutely postcolonial" Mallarmé, or of a Mallarméan Darwish may disturb conventional paradigms of literary comparatism built on historical or philological relation, it also reactivates the aesthetic. "The realm of the aesthetic," according to Peter Hallward, "invariably solicits the exercise of a *thought-ful* freedom" (AP 334). To my knowledge, Hallward's book *Absolutely Postcolonial: Writing between the Singular and the Specific* is the sole experiment to date of a Badiou-inspired postcolonial comparatism. In recentering the aesthetic within postcolonial theory (displacing the field's preoccupation with what he castigates as a "deadened nativism"), Hallward harks back to an earlier era—the 1980s and early 1990s—before theory fatigue set in, and before cultural critics stigmatized colonial ontology as an elitist threat to materialist *Verstehen*. In practicing theory without apology, Hallward revisits the time when Anglophone and Francophone critics alike—among them Edward Said, Gayatri Spivak, Homi Bhabha, Ngũgĩ Wa Thiong'o, Paul Gilroy, and Robert Young on the Anglophone side, and Frantz Fanon, Albert Memmi, Edouard Glissant, Abdelkedir Khatibi, Abdelwahab Meddeb, Achille Mbembe, Françoise Vergès, and Réda Bensmaïa on the Francophone side—availed themselves unabashedly of continental theory, developing critical paradigms that engaged deeply with the work of Freud, Adorno, Lacan, Bakhtin, Benjamin, Althusser, Foucault, Derrida, Levinas, Deleuze, Irigaray, Cixous.

Hallward subscribes to Badiou's notion of singularity as a corrective to the postmodern relativism besetting postcolonial studies, its uncritical embrace of plural registers, its fetishization of the politics of difference, and its naive celebration of "the local." "The singular creates the medium of its own substantial existence or expression," he writes in an affirmation drafted from Deleuze's pronouncement that "the One expresses in a single meaning all of the multiple."[6] Edouard Glissant, Charles Johnson, Mohammed Dib, and Severo Sarduy are elected for analysis by virtue of their invention of a singular postcolonial subjectivity. Representative of Francophone, Anglophone, Hispanophone, Caribbean, Maghrebian, and Latin American trajectories, these writers, considered together, offer a model postcolonial comparatism. But rather than focus on grounds of comparison common to all, Hallward explores how each writer, in a free-standing way, engages with the philosophical idea of the "univocity of being."

Absolutely Postcolonial produces a chilly comparatism tilted toward logic, ontology, and ethics. In this picture, the old Comp Lit utopia of global *translatio* and humanist dialogue gives way to an ascetic model of individuation in which the transcendence of specificity and relationality yields poetic singularity and solitude. "To write," Hallward maintains, in a paraphrase of Blanchot,

> is to undergo a radical detachment, to become *absolutely* alone, impersonal, isolated within an im-mediate atemporality ("the time of the absence of time"). Like the Deleuze he inspires, Blanchot tends to absorb all "actual writers as so many echoes of a singular '*murmure anonyme*.'"

The "essential solitude" of the writer, then, is not that of an anguished isolation among others, but of a submersion within the aspecific or indifferent pure and simple, a space generally rendered in Blanchot's fiction as void, desert, snow, night or sea—spaces rediscovered, as we shall see, by the later novels of Mohammed Dib. Writing begins when the writer forgoes the "power to say I." (AP 17–18)

Hallward's idea of postcolonial worldliness is truly otherwordly, suturing itself to Islamic constructs of *Islam* (surrender to God) and *Shadâdah* ("the assertion that there is no God but God") and to Buddhist notions of *sunyata* (void) and *nirvana* (self-extinction, transcendence of desire) (AP 7, 9). These principles, allowed to shine through in their linguistic foreignness, inadvertently reveal the catastrophic state of untranslatability that has allowed the word "Islamic" to become a predicate of terrorism in Western parlance.[7]

The challenge of Comp Lit is to balance the singularity of untranslatable alterity against the need to translate *quand même*. For if translation failure is acceded to too readily, it becomes an all-purpose expedient for staying narrowly within one's own monolingual universe. A parochialism results, sanctioned by false pieties about not wanting to "mistranslate" the other. This parochialism is the flip side of a globalism that theorizes place and translates everything without ever traveling anywhere. Gayatri Spivak has taken direct aim at the way in which globalization theory treats real places like computer spaces "in which nobody actually lives."[8] In proposing "the planet to overwrite the globe," Spivak embraces a humbling view of the alterity of humans, cast as temporary occupants of a planet on loan.

Spivak remains, so to speak, firmly on the ground, in her commitment to a radical alterity defined by the politics of translation. By contrast, Hallward, like Badiou, casts literary theory as cosmology, jumping parallel universes that share no philological common culture. Hallward's efforts to articulate the singularity of being might be seen as analogous to efforts in quantum cosmology to explain the origins of the universe as a "zero-moment of infinite density—a so-called singularity."[9] In a chapter of *Absolutely Postcolonial* devoted to "the Buddhist path" in Sarduy, Hallward evokes *satori*, which he characterizes, quoting Daisetz Teitaroo Suzuki's *Essays in Zen Buddhism* as "the Zen version of enlightenment . . . a kind of instantaneous flash or explosion, 'a sort of mental catastrophe' " (AP 286). A controversial doctrine running counter to the quietest strain in Zen Buddhism, *satori* is characterized by Suzuki as having the characteristics of irrationality, intu-

itive insight, authoritativeness, affirmation, a sense of the beyond, impersonality, exaltation, and momentariness. Alternately described by Suzuki as sud-
den access to the unconscious, a "new world of personal experiences, which
we may designate 'leaping,' or 'throwing oneself down the precipice,' " and
a "one-pointed concentration . . . realized when the inner mechanism is ripe
for the final catastrophe," *satori* takes on a historical dimension when set
against the backdrop of the Hiroshima bombings.[10] As the first prong in a
new order of comparatism based on the Idea of catastrophism, *satori* invites
comparison with Heidegger's "zero-line [that] is suddenly emerging before
us in the form of a planetary catastrophe." (This 1955 text addressed to
Ernest Jünger, published as "Concerning 'The Line,' " responds to Jünger's
reference to the "zero meridian" or "zero point" as "the world-historical
moment of the planetary completion of nihilism."[11] Walter Benjamin's short
essay "The Railway Disaster at the Firth of Tay" may be read as the third
prong in this poetics of planatary catastrophism. Delivered as a 1932 radio
lecture, this prescient short history of technology leads us from the baseline
of small disasters (accidents) to an end point of mass destruction:

> [W]e may say that the most striking alterations to the globe in
> the course of the previous century were all in some way or an-
> other connected with the railway. I am going to tell you today
> about a railway disaster. Not so much to recount a horrifying
> story, but rather to put the event in the context of the history of
> technology and more particularly of railway construction. A
> bridge plays a role in this story. The bridge collapsed. This was
> without doubt a catastrophe for the two hundred people who
> lost their lives, for their relatives, and for many others. Neverthe-
> less, I wish to portray this disaster as no more than a minor epi-
> sode in a great struggle from which human beings have emerged
> victorious and shall remain victorious unless they themselves de-
> stroy the work of their own hands once more.[12]

Drawing Suzuki, Heidegger, and Benjamin into orbit, catastrophism begets
a planetary comparatism that demands theorization as a new form of poetic
singularity. This planetary paradigm, by turns nihilistic and enlightening, is
not necessarily restricted to an eschatological poetics of the Idea. Wai Chee
Dimock, Gayatri Spivak, and Edward Said have taken planetary criticism in
other directions, focusing not on imminent destruction, but rather, on using
planetarity to impede globalization's monolithic spread: its financialization
of the globe and proselytism of orthodoxies of likeness and selfsame. In
Spivak's usage, planetarity implies a critical politics of the Idea capable of

lending credence to comparisons among languages and cultures habitually located at an intractable remove from one other, or remotely seated in area studies. And in Said's work on humanism, an anti-imperialist reinvention of Goethean *Weltliteratur* comes into focus as part of an expanded worldliness. Though Spivak and Said hardly share Badiou's nondialectical notion of Truth, they too seem to be, to use Badiou's parlance, communists of the Idea, following *le grand écart* of cultural comparison in the name of militant principles of worldly dialectics and the transformative power of cognition in the historical process. The implications of a planetary criticism for the future of a comparative poetics thus place renewed emphasis on a unidimensional formalism—univocity, singularity, irreducibility, holism, quantum cosmology, the Event—while remaining constant to an earthly politics of translation and nontranslatability.

6

"Untranslatable" Algeria: The Politics

of Linguicide

In Juan Goytisolo's *Paisajes después de la batalla* (*Landscapes after the Battle*, 1982), a Parisian quartier overcome by immigrant taggers turns into a calvados-imbibing Frenchman's worst nightmare—Paris translated into Arabic. Stumbling toward his favorite bar, the man encounters a "strange script" scrawled over the entrance. "Dumbfounded, he quickly blinked his eyes: the incomprehensible inscription, in luminous characters, was still there."[1] Figuring the café has changed management, he steers himself toward another, only to confront the same phenomenon. Everything has been changed over to Arabic, including his favorite newspaper *L'Humanité* and the traffic signage:

> What invisible hand could have woven the threads of this terrible plot? Why hadn't they been forewarned? Whose purposes did this diabolical confusion serve? Countless drivers from the provinces stuck their heads out of the windows of their cars, trying to figure out the meaning of a street sign and its pointing arrows: it should at least be bilingual! What the hell did —— mean? Amid the deafening din of horns, a number of drivers jumped from their cars to question the group of smiling individuals comfortably installed on the terrace of the café: Arabs, Afghans or Pakistanis who, with a self-assurance bordering on insolence, answered the questions of the illiterate and con-descendingly pointed out which way to go. . . . The sirens of ambulances and patrol cars wailed vainly. Helicopters flew over the

hecatomb of scrap iron. Trying to hide his laughter, a swarthy-skinned youngster with kinky hair pridefully purveyed his services as guide to which helpless soul bid the highest. (LB 7)

Though Goytisolo employs a familiar carnivalesque conceit of the world gone topsy-turvy, this vignette of Arabized Paris is more than just a comic revenge fantasy of the *immigré* underclass; a *Gulliver's Travels* in the Lilliput of linguistic estrangement. As the foreign alphabet erupts on the page of Roman script, the non-Arabic-reading lector hits a semantic impasse. Is this a translation, or something else, a joke at the reader's expense? In "trysting dangerously with the untranslatable" (to paraphrase Homi Bhabha's allusion to the alienation of standard language within the migrant's hybrid speech), Goytisolo's narrative records the ambush of alterity; the threatening prospect of *seeing yourself in translation.*[2]

Goytisolo's parody of language fear grows out of the climate of early-1980s Paris, with its phobic response to the linguistic, cultural, and political claims of Maghrebian residents. But now, sadly and ironically, the novel is perhaps more relevant still to a Paris that has become refuge to Algerian writers and artists who have contracted language fear at home—the fear of speaking out in Arabic, Berber, or French; the fear of accusations of blasphemy and apostasy; the fear of *fatwa* unilaterally issued by hardline Islamists against those who would "liberally" interpret Koranic references; and finally, the fear of death. "Silence is also death," Tahar Djaout wrote shortly before being shot in the head outside his home in 1993, "If you speak, you die. If you keep quiet, you die. So speak and die."[3]

In the wake of decolonization in the 1960s and 1970s, Algeria was hardly a magnet of media attention, but it was not walled off the way it was after civil war among Islamists, secularists, and government forces erupted during the 1990s. In the wake of the aborted elections of 1992, the complex power politics of franchise, ethnic secessionism, embattled laicity, and *linguicide*—definable as a culturally suicidal self-censorship linked to *intellocide*, the murder of prominent Algerian intellectuals— seems to have immured Algeria in an untranslatability exacerbated by Western media coverage. Consider, for example, a typical *New York Times* article on a massacre in September 1997 in the outskirts of Algiers:

[C]asualty figures in the Algerian conflict, which has left tens of thousands dead since 1992, are often as *murky* as the identities of the killers.

The splintering of Islamic movements in Algeria, the paucity of official information, the reluctance of authorities to grant

visas to foreign journalists and fragmentary evidence that the
army or groups linked to it have sometimes encouraged violence
for the own ends have contributed to making the Algerian conflict one of the *murkiest* of wars. . . . In a statement on Sunday,
Prime Minister Ahmed Ouyahia did not say how the Government proposed to stop the deterioration and bring hope to the
millions of Algerians trapped between a *shadowy* oligarchy con-
trolling Algeria's oil wealth and an equally *shadowy* Islamic
movement.[4]

The "murk," and the "shadow" congeal in an epistemological black hole.
The *Times* reporter only reinforces this opacity when he emphasizes the
enduring political culture of secrecy, nurtured by "the revolutionary cells
that led the war against France" and persisting as "one of the defining traits
of the Government that grew out of those cells and has ruled since 1962."[5]
Regardless of whether or not there is truth in this observation, such articulations locate Algerian society beyond bounds. Throughout the nineties—a
period of extreme violence—virtually every fresh report of massacres in
Algeria came accompanied by a self-absolving reference to the barriers
against information access.

If Western depictions of Algeria have tended to emphasize blackout,
Algerian writers themselves have asserted a complementary whiteout; a
post-liberation condition of linguistic uncertainty, compounded by a post-
1992 condition of censorship (an Algerian version of the "Rushdie effect").
Réda Bensmaïa has diagnosed this first condition in *Experimental Nations*,
arguing that the literary Maghreb has yet to be invented; it exists in a geolin-
guistic, "virtual" space at once *françisant, arabisant,* and *anglisant,* oral and
written, national and sacred, traditional and futurist.[6] This condition is the
direct result of a dilemma faced by writers who, after decolonization, were
forced to make often impossible choices among Arabic, French, and vernacular languages. "For most of the writers concerned, the Gordian knot had
to be cut: some stopped writing altogether, others opted for one language
or the other; still others moved from one language to the other; but the
problem has never been solved. Above all, the internal and external conflicts
have never ceased to haunt Maghrebi consciousness" (EN 103). Transference
and linguistic displacement have fomented a unique "whiting out" of language according to Bensmaïa. When, with reference to the work of Abdelkedir Khatibi, he refers to "an atopical cipher" or "monogram" in the
target language that coincides with the trace in French of disappeared Arabic, Bensmaïa inscribes a Derridean logic of *blankness/whiteness* on Algerian

language politics (EN 114). This state of translating "without returning us to the same . . . alludes to that which *exceeds* any language" (EN 113–14, emphasis in the original).

For Assia Djebar, in *Le blanc de l'Algérie* (her requiem to the decimation of multiple generations of writers and intellectuals), there is no Algerian writing left to translate—there is a *blanc*, a gap occupied by a body-politic afflicted by suicidal anemia, a corpse wrapped in white linen. Djebar sees contemporary Algeria as a writing desert, or blank territory: "The white of writing, in an untranslated Algeria? For the moment, an Algeria of pain, without writing; for the moment, an Algeria without literature written in blood, (*sang-écriture*), alas."[7]

This "white death" of writers is a decease robbed of history. Djebar warns against the fate that her book attempts to ward off, namely the consignment of depublished books to the dustbin of cultural memory. In Djebar's text, the writers who used to be there—Kateb Yacine, Jean Sénac, Abdelkader Alloula, Mouloud Mammeri, Tahar Djaout—emerge as zeros exerting pressure on the censored public sphere of today. Though it is possible to argue that such conditions of censorship have helped spawn a new wave of exilic Algerian/*beur* writing (evidenced in the journal *Algérie Littérature/Action*, featuring *samizdat*, excerpts of plays and stories by young authors, interviews with established scholars or theorists working through their *pied noir* inheritance, human rights briefs), Djebar's vision of Algeria as a literature-less place is confirmed by its low visibility in the global market of translation. In what follows, I want to situate Algeria's real and perceived occultation in the broader context of global translation. Of course Algeria is far from being unique as a nation of literary exclusion, but it stands in for all those nations that, for a host of different reasons, face dire market siege.

The problem of translation markets and the "untranslatability" of certain national literatures fits into a larger framework of reflection on literary *mondialisation*, and the future of the "culture industry" a term borrowed from the *Dialectic of Enlightenment*'s famous fourth chapter, "Culture Industry, Enlightenment as Mass Deception." In applying the term "culture industry," however, one must shift the Horkheimer/Adorno emphasis on the supposedly corrosive influence of mass and popular culture, to a more open-ended inquiry into the conditions of cultural globalization, specifically as they apply to the commodification of foreign authors within a niche market subsuming ethnics, immigrants, elite cosmopolitans, and the formerly colonized in a "multiculti" hodgepodge. Whereas Adorno, Horkheimer, and the

Frankfurt School more generally focused their critique on how emergent capital logics were encoded in mass cultural forms, they paid little attention to questions of translatability across the complex cultural and social terrains of capital. The question of how one achieves a mass cultural object—a cultural object that can be translated across linguistic, cultural, and social contexts—still begs to be answered. When the problem of a globalizing mass culture and public culture is approached from the perspective of translatability, new and important questions of cultural commodification and thus ideology arise. How do some works gain international visibility while others do not?

These questions take on curricular and pedagogical urgency in the context of efforts to globalize the canon. The constraints imposed by what is available in translation become constitutive of a transnational canon, contributing another layer of complexity to the value-laden selection process of authors, and serving as partial explanation for why "global lit" courses tend to feature similar rosters of non-Western authors (such as Wole Soyinke, Salman Rushdie, Derek Wolcott, Tayeb Salih, Gabriel Garcia Márquez, Nadine Gordimer, Naguib Mahfouz, Assia Djebar, Ben Okri, Arundhati Roy). The most obvious explanation—that these and other writers among the "happy few" are selected because they are universally acclaimed, excellent writers—obviously fails to account fully for their predominance. The difficulty of book distribution in many economically beleaguered countries remains an insuperable impediment to transnational exchange (a point made by the distinguished author Mongo Beti when he spoke of the dire situation in Cameroon).[8] There are specialized niche markets within the "global" that contribute to fads and fashions (to wit, the current popularity of Anglo-Indian novelists and Irish playwrights), sorting writers into subcategories such as "international" (Milan Kundera, Julio Cortázar, Samuel Beckett, Ferdinand Pessoa, Octavio Paz, Orhan Pamuk, Danilo Kiš), "postcolonial" (Aimé Césaire, Albert Memmi, Anita Desai, Patrick Chamoiseau, Mariama Bâ,), "multiculti," "native," or "minority" (Toni Morrison, Theresa Hak Kyung Cha, Sherman Alexie, Jessica Hagedorn, Gloria Anzaldua, Haruki Murakami, Amitav Ghosh, Colm Tóibín). These labels, though they can help launch or spotlight world-class writers—pulling them out of ethnic area-studies ghettos on the bookstore shelves— also cling like barnacles to their reception and afford constrictive stereotypes of identity. The Australian case is interesting in this regard: a strong, institutionally well-connected Australian poet like John Kinsella fails to warrant inclusion in the global canon even though his poetry uses his native landscape to brilliant effect as the stage for futurist visitations by robots and psychics. Naturalized in the British and American literary market, his writing is not exotic enough, while a poet like Lionel Fogarty—whose dense, compelling verse incorporates Aboriginal language—fails to cross over because it remains too exotic for mainstream taste.

The increased motility of global culture—fostered by an art market system of international galleries, museum shows, and biennials that highlight select "star" artists all over the world—foretells a time when these labels will become obsolete. Even very locally grounded works are acknowledged to be readily consumable by international media. Web diffusion also contributes to a deregionalization that renders labeling and bracketing within a global frame incoherent. We can already observe a situation in which location has become somewhat meaningless as the work of artists, writers, and thinkers is dispatched simultaneously and instantly to electronic sites, or as artists themselves become conscious of living transiently in one city while exhibiting in others. Producing work directly in a non-native tongue (as in the case of the Haitian novelist Edwige Danticat, who lives in New York and writes in English), many artists seem to bypass the act of translation, subsuming it as a problematic within a larger project of cultural or self-representation. In this picture, "global" signifies not so much the conglomeration of world cultures arrayed side by side in their difference, but rather a problem-based monocultural aesthetic agenda that elicits transnational engagement.

This drive toward a transnationally translatable monoculture is supported by the fact that linguistic superpowers increasingly call the shots and turn once formidable competitors (European languages) into gladiators fighting among themselves for international market share. In French bookstores, for example, translations or even *un*translated books in English, have acquired more and more space on the shelves. This suggests that France, despite the polemics of its academies, is losing the battle against the encroachment of English, but on a more optimistic note, it indicates a return to cosmopolitan attitudes within French culture, abetted by post-Wall, pro-Europe sentiments and a greater responsiveness to the claims to hospitality, residency, and citizenship by non-nationals in the wake of tragic wars in Africa, the Balkans, and the Middle East. Most cynically perhaps, it implies that France no longer maintains its special hold on the market in "hot" fiction, philosophy, and theory—a novelty deficit that must be made up domestically by translations. Contemporary American fiction holds sway; the French edition of the latest Russell Banks can be found in the *vitrine* of many bookstores, and it bests British best sellers (though a valiant effort to translate the Edinburgh street slang of Irvine Welsh's *Trainspotting* into French attests to a French interest in Britpack fiction).[9]

Like its Anglophone counterparts, French publishing seems to have preserved neocolonial networks of metropole-periphery exchange (even as it fans its reputation as the beacon of world culture for the New Europe).[10] But looming on the horizon is a neo-imperialist situation that puts translation, especially from non-Western languages, in an especially precarious state. In this scheme nation-states become obsolete as publishing markets shrink the global literary market using laws of international copyright, regulation, book distribution, and marketing. One can envisage an era in which the appellations of a national literature are headed for extinction. If publishing businesses will have any incentive to preserve the tradition of nationally marked authors within systems of global interstate culture, it will only be because the classificatory device of national literatures enhances the marketability of cultural product. French Lit, British Lit, American Lit and so on, in lending coherence to retail, will survive as mega-units within supermega, transnational corporations, while non-Western cultural identities will be managed as subsidiaries. The "foreign lit" deemed most susceptible to profit-making will naturally receive preferential treatment.

In this Malthusian scheme, small presses will be increasingly controlled by or located outside the ken of the mega-houses, and writers taken on by these marginal publishers will gain paltry international attention. Publishing will become (indeed has already become) subject to stratified and specialized "niche" marketing, with strategically targeted communities of readers ghettoized according to nation, class, education, race, and gender. As the division between mass market and high culture erodes in the face of a frenzy for commercial solvency at all levels of the publishing business, the "niche" of foreign or translated writers turns into a multiculti hodge-podge—a place in which ethnics, minorities, immigrants, émigrés, elite cosmopolitans, and former colonials are indiscriminately thrown together.

In the marketing of Third World difference, what sells? A writer who appeals to universalism or nonsecular religious philosophy? A dissident author? A subcontinental writer who capitalizes on exoticism or one who explores postcolonial identity? A Pacific Rim writer who reinforces essentialist stereotypes of Asianness, or one who embraces Western literary conceits and avant-gardes? A traditional African writer or an Afro-futurist? Obviously the choices are largely dependent on the whimsy of fashion and politics, but one thing is clear, though the current World Lit market is volatile and unpredictable, an identifiable canon that one might call "in-translation" (dominated by PEN and UNESCO writers) crowds out competitors that remain stuck in anonymity.[11]

We might ask then, to what extent "foreign" writers of ambition are consciously or unconsciously writing for international markets; building translatability into their textuality. Though the notion of translatability is itself elusive (as Walter Benjamin understood so well when he idiosyncratically assessed what makes a work ripe for translation, its qualities of numinousness, redemptive potential, or "foreignness," disrupting and estranging the target language), clearly some originals qualify as better candidates for translation than do others.[12]

Though Anglophone publishing statistics reveal a virtual absence of translations on any bestseller lists, PEN estimates that less than 2 percent of literary market share is devoted to works in translation.[13] In America, Michael Crichton, John Grisham, Danielle Steele, and Tom Clancey remain the big sellers with movie tie-ins usually a must. The recent boom in Indo-Anglian novels has sent British and American editors scurrying for South Asian talent, though not necessarily on the subcontinent. Despite the fact that India is now the third largest English-language publisher after Britain and the United States, its fiction stars, often specializing in hot themes— "the partition, the Emergency, identity"—usually prevail on the international circuit only if they have first received backing from publishing houses in Europe and North America.[14]

Occasionally, popular non-Western authors are openly accused of pandering to the interests of commercialized internationalism, as when the scholar Stephen Owen alleged in a now famous article ("What Is World Poetry: The Anxiety of Global Influence") that the poetry of the Chinese writer Bei Dao was often translated because it offered a "version of Anglo-American or French modernism," embellished with judicious (and always translatable) dollops of "local color," and marketed to international audiences for its "cozy ethnicity."[15] Owen was criticized by Michele Yeh for a "flawed binarism," while Rey Chow read his implicit nostalgia for China's traditional heritage as perpetuating "a deeply ingrained Orientalism in the field of East Asian Studies."[16] Summarizing the debate, Andrew T. Jones argued that Owens's detractors ignored his emphasis on the neocolonial dynamics of Third World First World publishing: "If world literature is envisioned as international traffic, Jones queried, are there trade imbalances? Is there exploitation? Do certain nations supply certain kinds of products? Do developing nations supply raw materials to the advanced literary economies of the 'First World'? Finally, is it possible to posit a kind of dependency theory inhering in the transnational economy of literary production and trade?" (AJ 181). In addition to a dependency theory of production and trade in cultural capital, Jones also imputes a labor theory of value to the translated text, drawing an analogy between translations and outsourced piecework:

> In rendering a mute text intelligible to his compatriots, the translator single-handedly *creates* the text's "use-value" for the targeted readership. This "use-value," of course, is also the basis of the text's "exchange-value" on the world literary market. The translator, then, "finishes" the source text in much the same way that an industrial worker in an advanced economy assembles raw materials imported from developing countries into a product to be sold on the open market. (J 182)

The inference to be drawn here is that properly "finished" translations will aid and abet authors whose eyes are on the prize. And here, it is revealing to take stock rather literally of the wording of international prizes, many of them holdovers from imperial times. The Commonwealth Prize keeps alive a certain idea of the queen's English in lands of the Pacific. The Before Columbus Foundation American Book Awards, "for literary achievement by people of various ethnic backgrounds" (won recently by Sherman Alexie, *Reservation Blues*; Chita Bannerjee Divakaruni, *Arranged Marriage*; Chang-rae Lee, *Native Speaker*), misleadingly suggests an all-purpose historical watershed applicable to the cultural heritage of Native American, Indian, and Korean peoples. The Kiriyama Pacific Rim Book Prize, whose mission is "to contribute to greater understanding and increased cooperation among peoples of the nations of the Pacific Rim," bolsters the illusion of regional solidarity among highly disparate languages and cultures. If here the trend is toward simplified territorializations, elsewhere the prizes seem regionally rarefied, as in the Noma Award, which goes "for Japanese Literature in Translation published in Africa." The French Prix Méditerranée smacks of the colonial era by harking back to Camus's idealized vision of a common Mediterranean culture untroubled by the gross power imbalance between France and Algeria. Each of these prizes implicitly rewards a kind of writing compatible with the normative baggage of the award.

For Gayatri Chakravorty Spivak, the only way a translator can undermine the neocolonialism of translation-speak is by deploying a technique that she calls "fraying," a disrupting, yet "loving" rhetoricity that, instead of trawling for structures of equivalency between original and target, enters into the text's self-staging:

The task of the translator is to facilitate love between original and its shadow, a love that permits fraying, holds the agency of the translator and the demands of her imagined or actual audience at bay. The politics of the non-European woman's text too often suppresses this possibility because the translator cannot engage with, or cares insufficiently for, the rhetoricity of the original. . . . Without a sense of the rhetoricity of language, a species of neo-colonialist construction of the non-western scene is afoot.[17]

In the arena of unfrayed, prize-friendly, translation-happy World Lit success stories, Algeria fares poorly. Indeed, Algeria's untranslatability seems to have acquired the status of a given in the global market. Few works by Algerian writers (in French or Arabic) have internationalist distribution or standing; few are available in English translation. A popular anthology boasting a representative potpourri of non-Western authors—Elisabeth Young-Bruehl's *Global Cultures: A Transnational Short Fiction Reader*—contains not a single entry by an Algerian author.[18] In the French publishing industry, where one expects a stronger ethic of Maghrebian representation, celebrated Algerian writers are frequently confined to a series, only to be routinely featured for a time, and then dropped (as in the case of Nabile Farès, abandoned by Le Seuil). Small presses, such as Sinbad or Marsa, occasionally come to the rescue, but circulation remains marginal. Moreover, when a "classic" of Algerian fiction finally does make it into English, it is often condescendingly framed. The Braziller edition of Kateb Yacine's *Nedjma* is a case in point; the editors mitigate the Western reader's anticipated hostility to the text by resorting to formulas of cultural essentialism:

The narrative techniques Kateb Yacine uses are occasionally disconcerting to the western reader. The latter, as a last resort, will take refuge in the subtleties of comparative literature to exorcise the mystery: apropos of *Nedjma*, some readers will undoubtedly cite Faulkner. It seems to us that the explanation of the novel's singularities are to be found elsewhere. The narrative's rhythm and construction, if they indisputably owe something to certain western experiments in fiction, result in chief from a purely Arab notion of *man in time*. Western thought moves in *linear* duration, whereas Arab thought develops in a *circular* duration, each turn a *return*, mingling a future and past in the eternity of the moment. This confusion of tenses—which a hasty observer will ascribe to a love of a genius for synthesis—corresponds to so constant a feature of the Arab character, so natural an orientation of Arab thought, that Arab grammar itself is marked by it.[19] (Emphasis in the original)

Part of the problem clearly lies in the West's reactive politicization of all things Arab. Edward Said addressed this dilemma in reviewing the obstacles to his own role as "broker" for Naguib Mahfouz:

> Eight years before Naguib Mahfouz won the Nobel Prize in Literature, a major New York commercial publisher known for his liberal and unprovincial views asked me to suggest some Third World novels for translation and inclusion in a series he was planning. The list I gave him was headed by two or three of Mahfouz's works, none of which was then in circulation in the United States. . . . Several weeks after I submitted my list I inquired which novels had been chosen, only to be informed that the Mahfouz translations would not be undertaken. When I asked why, I was given an answer that has haunted me ever since. "The problem," I was told, "is that Arabic is a controversial language."
>
> What, exactly, the publisher meant is still a little vague to me—but that Arabs and their language were somehow not respectable, and consequently dangerous, *louche*, unapproachable, was perfectly evident to me then and, alas, now. For of all the major world literatures, Arabic remains relatively unknown and unread in the West, for reasons that are unique, even remarkable, at a time when tastes here for the non-European are more developed than ever before and, even more compelling, contemporary Arabic literature is at a particularly interesting juncture.[20]

Said also charts the extra disadvantage borne by Arabic texts judged translation-resistant because of their rebarbative stylistics. The difficult formalism of Adonis's *An Introduction to Arab Poetics* (Al-Saqi), the Coptic Egyptian author Edwar al-Kharrat's *City of Saffron*, and the Lebanese feminist novelist Hanan al-Shaykh's *Women of Sand and Myrrh* is posed against the content-oriented prose of "the overexposed and overcited Nawal el-Saadawi."[21] Thus, formalism emerges as an obstacle to translatability, along with "subjective geographies" (Aimé Césaire's Martinique or the Peru of Mario Vargas Llosa's *The Green House*).

While stylistic opacity can alienate a mainstream reading public, the "difficulty" yardstick is not wholly reliable since an aura of arcana can often enhance a book's attractiveness to readers in search of an exoticist *frisson* (in the fin de siècle, writers such as Théophile Gautier, Pierre Loti, and Isabelle Eberhardt discovered the trick of dousing their prose with foreign loan words to impart local color and induce *dépaysment*). More recently, a vogue for intralingual vernaculars and interlingual creoles (replete with glossaries) has made its mark.

In attempting to account for Algeria's untranslatability, one must look not only at stylistic complexity, anti-Arab prejudice, or conditions of local censorship, but also at the fraught postcolonial legacy of what Hélène Cixous has dubbed *Algériance*. A Jewish *pied noir* feminist theorist and woman of letters professionally based in France, Cixous, in attempting to define Algerianness, returns to the atmosphere of bad class and ethnic relations reigning among French, Jews, Berbers, and working-class Arabs in the postwar, pre-Independence Algeria of her childhood. The progressive ending "ance" connotes the thwarted project of pass*ance* or "passing" (as French if you are Jewish, Algerian, *harki*, or *beur*; as Algerian if you are *pied noir* or Jewish) and the acceptance of a perpetual err*ance*, or homelessness, which Cixous takes as the condition of postcolonial Algeria—left twisting in the wind after the French departure, internally riven by its own violent sectarianism, antifeminism, intolerance, *ressentiment*, and ambivalence toward the West. For Cixous, Algériance is not only this kernel of hate carried by a jaundiced, disaffiliated generation ("we were together in hostility, . . . the hate that united us, was also made of hope and despair"), it also carries the seeds of a renewed world-feminism proffered as a gift from her newly discovered "Algerian sisters," activists whose lives are marked by clandestinity and persecution.[22] Cixous raises the question of whether Algériance, with its redemptive, ineffable air of promise, will fall into the trap of reinforcing Algerian untranslatability or whether it will activate the untranslatable, turning it into a historical probe.

Abdelkedir Khatibi, whose ground-breaking text *Amour bilingue* (1983), translated as *Love in Two Languages* and published in English in 1990, defines untranslatability as a layered forgetting associated with traumatic memory sequences, erotic fantasies, and intimations of mortality that are unexpectedly triggered by the bilingual unconscious:

> And in French—his foreign language—the word for "word,"
> *mot*, is close to the one for "death," *la mort*; only one letter is

missing: the succinctness of the impression, a syllable, the ec-
stasy of a stifled sob. Why did he believe that language is more
beautiful, more terrible, for a foreigner?

He calmed down when an Arabic word, *kalma*, appeared,
kalma and its scholarly equivalent, *kalima*, and the whole string
of its diminutives which had been the riddles of his childhood:
klima. . . . The diglossal *kal(i)ma* appeared again without *mot*'s
having faded away or disappeared. Within him now both words
were observing each other, preceding what had now become
the rapid emergence of memories, fragments of words, ono-
mato-poeias, garlands of phrases, intertwined to the death: un-
decipherable. And when he speaks, he will wear himself out in
amnesia, dragged down by a prodigious weakness, forgetting
even the words that are most often used in one or the other of
his languages.[23]

Khatibi enacts a seizure of language fear mollified only by amnesia. The
"garlands of phrases, intertwined with death" decorate the tomb of forgetting and exhaustion, which is the bilingual's only hope for peace.

Where Khatibi emphasizes psychic history in recording linguistic
breakdown, Rachid Boudjedra evokes the "real" history of the Algerian War
when he speaks of his linguistic inheritance as a "form of war and hell." "As
an Algerian, I did not choose French. It chose me, or rather, imposed itself
on me through centuries of blood and tears, and through the painful history
of the long colonial night."[24] For a writer like Boudjedra, whose native languages are Arabic and Berber, but whose elected literary tongue is often
French, there is a translational violence seething inside the act of writing.
The writer's consciousness resembles a theater of war in which words are
accused of betrayal, squatting, spying, fraying sense, or performing as "iras-
cible intermediaries between the object and its image" (B 95). Worst of all,
words engage in pitched battle over untranslatable remainders that spill out
of their literary containers: French is "too voluble," while Arabic is "excessive." The latter has 600 words for lion, and 99 respectively for male and
female sex. This frustrated "plethora," with nowhere to go, exerts its pressure of the extra on the chosen utterance; lending it a "passional" explosive
charge; battering the walls of "the house of being," (Heidegger's character-
ization of language) (B 96). As the walls of the house give, yielding to a
new Babel or *charabia* (buyers and sellers market), languages achieve a new
reciprocity (B 95–97). But lest one think that Boudjedra is heralding a happy
world order of linguistic interchange, a cynical volley is lobbed at global

culture. Boudjedra heaps scorn on the prize-chasing "Maghrébins de service" who have been rewarded by the West for pronouncing Arabic a dead language. Fueling anti-Western *intégrisme* among young Algerians concerned to redeem Arabic as a sacred, living language of world culture, these careerist Francophone stars, in his view, have "damaged" the cause of Algerian writers who, like Boudjedra, remain passionate writers of French. Here, the menace of commericalism joins the menace of Arabocentric intolerance, casting a deathly pall on the fate of the Franco-Algerian writer.

Though hailing from a very different political position, Assia Djebar sees the French language as a similarly fraught and complex carrier of pain for the Franco-Algerian writer, not just because of its association with a former colonial power, but because it has become a sign of Algeria's loss of the secular. No paean to Algeria's francophone past, Djebar's novel, *La disparition de la langue française* (The Disappearance of the French Language) directs nostalgia as much to the recollection of Arabic sayings and expressions spoken in childhood in the period shortly after Independence as it does to the recall of a time when Algerian writers and artists animated the cultural scene with work written in French. The double-headed legacy of French is fully in evidence. It is shown to ignite revolutionary passion, as when Alaoua, a young man in 1960, is spurred to activism by a radio announcer's specious declaration in French that calm has returned to the Casbah. But in an ironic twist of fate, French returns as a language of protest against Islamism and government corruption for the generation of 1993. The term "les francophones" in Djebar's novel is used to designate Algerian professionals and intellectuals of both sexes forced to "flee, in disorder, their country, for France and Quebec, much like the Spanish Moors and the Jews from Grenada, after 1492. . . . just as Arabic then disappeared in the Spain of the very Catholic Kings (vigorously helped by the Inquisition), is it now suddenly the case that the French language will disappear from over there?"[25] One of the central characters, Marise, is an actress exiled in France who mourns the loss of her former lover Berkane, an Algerian poet who wrote in French and who has disappeared. It suddenly dawns on Marise that the mere fact that Berkane chose to write in French may be the cause of his downfall.

Somewhere in the interstices among Cixous's *Algériance* in perpetual *errance*, Khatibi's atopic bilingualism, Boudjedra's pugilistic fatalism, and Djebar's elegies of language loss, lies the tomb of Tahar Djaout, who refused to allow language fear to vanquish his voice. Djaout's last novel *Les Vigiles* can be read as an allegory about prizes, Third World authors, and the particular situation of Algeria in the market of world literature. The story of a post-Independence inventor of a special loom who garners the contempt of his compatriots and the suspicion of Islamists convinced that Allah alone is sanctioned to invent, it recounts his reversal of fortune once the device wins an international prize in Germany. If we extend the symbolism of the "invention" to works of literary creation, then the story reads as an admonition to Algerian writers who risk incurring Muslim wrath. Even when an opportunistic government appropriates them as world-class, national authors after their legitimation by the West, these writers will at home remain vulnerable to becoming targets of censorship, and in the worst cases, assassination.

Tahar Djaout's death stands as a testimonial to the dangers of becoming translatable, but it also stands as a tragic injunction to the West not to collude in walling off Algeria behind a fortress of untranslatability. Despite the questionable stakes of a publishing industry ever poised, piranha-like, to exploit the embattled situation of the dissident writer, and despite the homogenized, commercialized flavor of translationese afflicting many prize-winning works of foreign fiction, efforts must be made to keep Algeria, and the many countries that find themselves in comparable situations, from being blacked-out or whited-over in the international public sphere of letters.

7

Plurilingual Dogma: Translation by Numbers

The Celebration (Festen), a Danish film directed by Thomas Vinterberg, ranks high as a harrowing cinematic experience. Part *Buddenbrooks*, part send-up of schlock reenactments of recovered-memory-syndrome, the story, such as it is, devolves around a son's revelation of his father's sexual abuse in the public forum of a paternal birthday celebration. Friends and relatives have gathered from far and wide to toast the patriarch on his impressive estate. Everyone, from the cooks and kitchenmaids, to the errant sons and daughters, have been commandeered to assemble and remain on best behavior. But the camera is doing strange things in recording the festival's preparations, lurching and rolling, hatching light and shadow, tumbling the eye, as if in a washer-dryer, so as to give the spectator dry heaves. This use of jagged camera motion and searing slices of light, is somehow crucial to the narrative, whose catalyst is the moment when the tousle-haired golden boy of the family taps his champagne glass and stands up to give a speech. He offers the guests a choice between two texts, thus setting the terms of a game of chance that leaves the spectator projecting the movie that might have been, had the other piece of paper been chosen. After the guests select a text, a look of malicious satisfaction steals across the son's face: "good choice" he compliments them, as he calmly proceeds to narrate, in the tone of a mock children's hour, a tale of parental sodomy, sibling suicide, and maternal complicity in crime. What is being filmed here is not just cinema verité's encounter with the plots of familial dysfunction (as some critics would have it), but more significantly, an exercise in aesthetic dogma. Taking a "vow of chastity," the adherents of "Dogme '95" agree to proscribe the technical crutches of illusionism, to ban genre and style, and to bar displays of *auteur*ship:

Furthermore, I swear as a director to refrain from personal taste!
I am no longer an artist. I swear to refrain from creating a
"work," as I regard the instant as more important than the
whole. My supreme goal is to force the truth out of my characters and settings. I swear to do so by all the means available and
at the cost of any good taste and any aesthetic considerations.
Thus I make my vow OF CHASTITY.
Your Location/Your Date,
Your name here.[1]

Now the relevance of this cinematic dogma to contemporary translation
theory may not be obvious, but I would suggest that it lies in the appeal to
rule-based systems and procedures in the face of cultural relativism. The
turn to dogma means exchanging a baggy model of translation—identified
with easy transfers of identity and willy-nilly notions of cultural transposition, hybridity, or *métissage*—for militant formalism. Dogma captures the
sovereign imperiousness of linguistic worlds that whimsically decree the
laws and constraints of literary license, or that produce subjects living by
numbers. "Dogma" is another name for linguistic essentialism; it is the su-
perstructural expression of base structure in the mother tongue.

The terms of linguistic essentialism were clearly set by Baron Wilhelm von Humboldt. Von Humboldt's belief in *Natursprache*—in language
as the connection between nature and idea, and as the means by which man
is identified as human—fostered a linguistic model of speech and national
culture. In his text on *Linguistic Variability and Intellectual Development*, he
maintained:

> Each tongue draws a circle about the people to whom it belongs,
> and it is possible to leave this circle only by simultaneously enter-
> ing that of another people. Learning a foreign language ought
> hence to be the conquest of a new standpoint in the previously
> prevailing cosmic attitude of the individual. In fact, it is so to a
> certain extent, inasmuch as every language contains the entire
> fabric of concepts and the conceptual approach of a portion of
> humanity. But this achievement is not complete, because one al-
> ways carries over into a foreign tongue to a greater or lesser de-
> gree one's own cosmic viewpoint—indeed one's personal linguis-
> tic pattern.[2]

In the twentieth century, the analytic philosopher Willard Van Orman
Quine would strip out the culturalism of the discrete language world, yet

endorse a similar skepticism toward the possibility of traversing language borders, basing his theory, in *Word and Object*, on the tectonics of analogy:

> In the case of some of the terms that refer or purport to refer to physical objects, the value of analogy is more limited still than in the molecular instance. Thus in the physics of light, with its notoriously mixed metaphor of wave and particle, the physicist's understanding of what he is talking about must depend almost wholly on context: on knowing when to use various sentences which speak jointly of photons and of observed phenomena of light. Such sentences are like cantilever constructions, anchored in what they say of familiar objects at the near end and support-ing the recondite objects at the far end. Explanation becomes oddly reciprocal: photons are posited to help explain the phe-nomena, and it is those phenomena and the theory concerning them that explains what the physicist is driving at in his talk of photons.[3]

The cantilever describes a reciprocity of theory and referent and is the closest Quine comes to the possibility of translation. The cantilever describes a jutting out from the language wall into an extended space of theoretical abstraction. It is language at its farthest remove from the referent before it breaks off and ceases being meaningful.

The cantilever can extend the range of reference within a single language, but it cannot support the weight of passage to another language. In defining the limits of what Quine calls "interlinguistic synonymy," the cantilever describes semantic extension that falls short of translation. Statements such as "Neutrinos lack mass," "the law of entropy," or "the constancy of the speed of light" depend wholly on the language they are in; they simply will not transfer. Bordering language with the *cordon sanitaire* of referential logic, Quine's translation zone returns us to the Greek sense of zone, meaning belt, a belting in of language. Insisting on non-identity between even the most scientifically compatible languages, Quine takes Wittgenstein's dictum, "Understanding a sentence means understanding a language" to be an article of faith (WO 76–77). As a dogma theorist, he updates in the terms of analytical philosophy von Humboldt's thesis that each language carries a world peculiarly its own ("so liegt in jeder Sprache eine eigenthümlich Weltansicht").[4]

Immured in a fortress of untranslatability, the Quinean language-user is caught in the vise of linguistic essentialism. The only recourse, under these circumstances, may be to try to "game the system," embracing its rules-based character, "loving" its dogma, miming the delirium of its logical formalism, and reducing translation to the play of semiotic substitutions within a univocal language world.[5] This seems to have been the gambit adopted by a series of eccentric literary figures through literary history, notable among them: J-P Brisset, Raymond Roussel, Eugene Jolas, Louis Wolfson, Georges Perec, and Perec's fellow Oulipo members Raymond Queneau, Harry Mathews, Jacques Roubaud, and Paul Fournel. What these writers have in common is the willingness to treat language as *Sprachspiel* (rules of the game). Writing algorithms with philology, they generated literary *logiciel* (the French term for programming or software), reproducing the closed circuitry of natural languages in artificial languages of their own making.

Eugene Jolas, James Joyce's editor, and the founder of the Paris-based avant-garde journal *transitions* has never been given his due as a premier dogma theorist of self-enclosed language worlds. Jolas's forays into polyglottal poetry—written in "Atlantica" and "Astralingua"—represent an attempt to scale the walls of untranslatatability between languages, by "Babelizing" the mother tongue. Like Louis Wolfson, Deleuze's favorite "language schizo," Jolas both submitted to and fought against the confines of language through a practice that might be thought of as recombinant philology.

Born in America of Franco-German parentage, Jolas was raised primarily in Lorraine. His mother spoke "a peculiar amalgam of the speech of her Rhineland youth and Lorraine and Alsatian locutions intertwisted with American phrases," and his subsequent commitment to "non-ideological regionalism" has been attributed by the editors of his memoir to his disgust at the Germans' efforts to impose a monolingual culture on multilingual Alsace. Rather than be drafted into the German army during World War I, he went to America, enlisted, and was stationed in the South, where he became familiar with a vast variety of American dialects and class inflections:

> They were profane words, crude words, voluptuous words, occult words, concrete words. There were turns of speech I had not heard before, a scintillating assemblage of phonetic novelties that enlarged my vision. At the camp we lived in barracks, and I heard my buddies use the fermenting American speech devoid of literary ornamentation. I heard the vocabulary of the bunkhouse, the steamer, the construction camp, the brothel, the machine shop, the steel mill. I heard the lexicon of the farmhouse and the mountain cabin. I heard the words of sissies, fairies,

homos, pretty boys, pimps. I heard the talk of salesmen, newspa-
permen, photographers, railroad clerks, truck drivers, saloon
keepers, postal clerks, detectives, working stiffs. I listened to the
different shadings in the speech of soldiers from the Southwest,
the deep South, the industrial cities of Pennsylvania, the East.[6]

This idiomatic exposure led Jolas to become a theorist of American immigrant English. In an opening statement to *Words from the Deluge* (with surre-
alist cover art by Yves Tanguy), published in a series called *Poets' Messages*,
which also published W. H. Auden, William Carlos Williams, and Boris
Pasternak, he forged a connection between the "inter-racial philology" inherent in American English, and the future language of Babel that he dubbed
"Atlantica."

> A new language is developing in the United States. It has no
> name as yet. It is never used by writers of prose and verse, yet its
> existence is very real, especially in the urban centers of the coun-
> try. Nor is it H. L. Mencken's *American Language*, but rather an
> intensification and expansion of it. It is a superoccidental form
> of expression. It has polyglot dimensions. Millions speak it
> throughout America. It is the embryonic language of the future.
>
> I call it the *Atlantic*, or *Crucible Language*. It is the result of
> the inter-racial synthesis that is going on in the United States.[7]

In propounding plurilingual dogma, Jolas foregrounded the poetics of migration. *Words from the Deluge* records the arrival of immigrants to the mill
towns of America at the dawn of industrial modernization. It captures the
melancholy of factory city-scapes, the loneliness of uprooted workers, and
the polyvocalism of an immigrant labor force:

> La grande migration is not yet over in our time
> Here in the milltown crucible je regarde les étrangers
> Die dunklen stunden der einsamkeit kommen zurueck
> And I remember a blizzard wept itself to death
> On the roof of the typewriter-clattering city-room
> C'était il y a si longtemps I was still an immigrant lad
> Ero americáno and all my friends were the aliens
> Dont les yeux regardaient tristement les usines fumantes
> Dans les aubes sales de las horas electro-mécanicas
> Tutto il mundo de las macinas era disgraziato
> Metallic parrots chattered odes to a dark age
> Travailing stickfuls danced on the city editor's desk

The mergenthalers roared a dirge from the composing room
And the strike of the alien laborers was a battle
Nous étions tous ensemble dans le creuset des races
We were in the wild melting pot of the fekterjas
Nous étions dans un vertige à perte de vue
The languages floated together into a sad chant

· ·

We are always amerigrating on a long journey
The columbian land of the shimmering universe beckons
In the malady of Europe I thought of the hard reality
I thought of the huge and borderless cosmos of brothers
That I always carried with me from childhood days[8]

Jolas's trilingual poetics unmoor national location. "America" ceases to be a static nation-marker and becomes instead the active gerundive "amerigrating," an expression of linguistic migration. Ralph Ellison would perform a similar operation on the city of Detroit when he used "detroiting" in his unfinished novel *Juneteenth* (1999):

> And how do they feel, still detroiting my mother who called me Goodrich Hugh Cuddyear in the light of tent flares then running away and them making black bucks into millejungs and fraud pieces in spetacularmythics on assembly lines? . . . O.K., so they can go fighting the war but soon the down will rise up and break the niggonography and those ghosts who created themselves in the old image won't know why they are screaming black babel and white connednation! Who, who, who, boo, are we? Daddy, I say where in the dead place between the shadow where does mothermatermanny—mover so moving on? Where is all the world pile hides?[9]

The evocation of factory life in an automobile-driven company town recalls the proletarian topography of Jolas's early verse, the hardships of the immigrant worker. But where Jolas sets great store for language renewal on the fusions of immigrant speech, Ellison eschews utopianism and develops an ebonics of black power ("black babel") as an idiom of protest.

Jolas's appropriation of dialect-inflected American speech places him in a group of prominent literary figures of the time that included Gertrude Stein, James Joyce, Ezra Pound, T. S. Eliot, Mina Loy, Langston Hughes, and Nora Zeale Hurston. Michael North's astute study, *The Dialect of Modernism: Race, Language and Twentieth-Century Literature*, has examined the seminal place of what he calls "racial masquerade" within the poetic practice of transatlantic modernism. In the correspondence between Eliot and Pound he unearths an unsettling use of black dialect and code names drawn from Uncle Remus, which he interprets in terms of a complex identification with the verbal stigmas of Americanness that Eliot, and to some extent Pound, were trying to efface from their literary reputations. Dialect, he maintains, was taken up as the secret alter ego of high modernism during the very period in which the Society for Pure English was establishing sway over institutional usage. North sees references to black speech in poems like Eliot's "Sweeney Agonistes" (originally titled "Fragment of a Comic Minstrelsy") or Pound's "Pisan Cantos" (a mélange of American, Irish, Catalan, African American, and "Japanerican" speech patterns) as traces of the authors' subversion of standard language. Hybrid speech, especially black English, promised linguistic regeneration, but these regenerative possibilities lay submerged under layers of racist parody or aesthetic stylization. Even Harlem Renaissance writers such as Hughes and Hurston were conflicted over whether to use black vernacular English. Their unfinished coauthored play in dialect, *Mule Bone*, may have foundered on this issue, possibly prompting Hurston to abandon "porch speech" in her later fiction.[10]

Jolas it would seem, was more interested than his contemporaries in honing an avant-garde aesthetic inside American English, one that would cut to the edge of intelligibility. Immigrant English became his passkey to a programmatic "revolution of the word." In a manifesto of that title published in *transition* 16/17 (1929) he laid down his dogma:

We hereby declare that:

1. The Revolution in the English Language is an accomplished fact.
2. The imagination in search of a fabulous world is autonomous and unconfined.
3. Pure poetry is a lyrical absolute that seeks an a priori reality within ourselves alone.
4. Narrative is not mere anecdote, but the projection of a metamorphosis of reality.
5. The expression of these concepts can be achieved only through the rhythmic "hallucination of words."
6. The literary creator has the right to disintegrate the primal matter of words imposed on him by text-books and dictionaries.
7. He has the right to use words of his own fashioning and to disregard existing grammatical and syntactical laws.

8. The "litany of words" is admitted as an independent unit.

9. We are not concerned with the propagation of sociological ideas, except to emancipate the creative elements from the present ideology.

10. Time is a tyranny to be abolished.

11. The writer expresses. He does not communicate.

12. The plain reader be damned.

The call for syntactic revolution was clearly indebted to the doctrine of *parole in libertà* promulgated by the Italian futurists (Marinetti, Carrà) and taken up elsewhere on the continent by Dadaists (Tristan Tzara, Richard Huelsenbeck, Hugo Ball) and proto-Surrealists (Guillaume Apollinaire and Blaise Cendrars) or writers fascinated with subaltern speech from Ezra Pound to Mina Loy. Mina Loy's *Anglo-Mongrels and the Rose* (1923–25) was particularly close in its language politics to Jolas's early poetry. The poem restages Exodus, substituting Moses with a Mitteleuropaische Jewish emigrant, "Lord Israel," fluent in German, Magyar, biblical Hebrew and "business English." His outsider status is confirmed by British imperial attitudes to exiles living on its shores and colonial subjects abroad. The "rose" of the poem's title refers to "other Englishes":

> Its petals hung
> with tongues
> that under supervision
> of the Board of Education
> may never sing in concert—
> for some
> singing h
> flat and some
> h sharp "The Arch
> angels sing H"
> There reigns a disporportionate
> dis'armony
> in the English Hanthem[11]

Loy focused on the impact of class and culture on the Queen's English, whereas other avant-garde writers were more interested in using plurilingualism to define the acoustic modernism of urban cosmopolitanism. Apollinaire wrote calligrams such as the 1914 concrete poem "Lettre Océan" (Ocean-Letter) in which Babel is visually patterned as a vortex of sound-meanings. Emitted like primal screams, these sounds spiral out from their nucleus in the Eiffel-Tower-of-Babel. A word circumference is formed out of the imperative command "to create"—"cré, cré, cré"—and extruding from the circle, like bicycle spokes or radial legs, are the languages of the world. The legs are composed of speech fragments in Spanish, French, and Italian. Anticipating Dada sound-poems such as Tzara's "L'Amiral cherche une maison à louer" or Huelsenbeck's *Phantastische Gebete* and *Schalaben Shalamai Shalamezomai*, Apollinaire syncretized language and street noise.

Jolas, too, treated the city as the logical place for experiments in linguistic and acoustic "marriages," especially in this untitled, undated text:

> We listened to the choral voices of Manhattan
> All the languages were melting one into the other
> Toutes les langues fêtaient des épousailles
> We saw the dance of the words of corbyantic names
> A storm of words organed catitatas over the city
> Antique rune-words wed French syllables
> Anglo-Saxon sounds mingled with Yiddish vocables
> Dutch vowels embraced the Spanish verbs
> A Flemish word fled into Italian nouns
> The lexicon of Hell's Kitchen melted into Portuguese
> White Chapel cockney united with Broadway double talk
> A Luxembourg dialect fused into Louisiana French
> Paris argot joined the slanguage of the Rialto
> All the vers of the world flowed gently into each other
> In a miraculous music of incantations[12]

This text reveals a progression in Jolas's procedure. In the earlier poems he alternated languages from line to line, but in the later poems he started to intersperse foreign elements within a single line. In a later phase, he fabricated glossaries of compound words eliding elements of English, Swedish, Dutch, Danish, Italian, Spanish, Portuguese, Polish, Czech, Russian. A list of "Vocabulary for the Superoccident" in his unpublished papers includes portmanteau constructions such as "skyv verheven" (english-dutch) skyhigh, "sublime," or "dieufome" (french-portuguese) = godhunger.[13] Harking back to the *Klanggedichtung* of Hugo Ball, foreshadowing the acoustic experiments of Alan Ginsberg and John Cage in the fifties and sixties, and approximating Jorge Luis Borges's language of Babel (described in his famous short story "The Library of Babel" as a "Samoyedic Lithuanian dialect of Guarani, with classical Arabian inflections"), Jolas gave full sway to lexical syncretism and fabulation.[14] "Babel 1940," a poem contributed to James Laughlin's anthology *New Directions*, illustrates how far Jolas was willing to go with "clashing vocabulary":

Clasta allagrona sil boala alamata
Cloa drim lister agrastoo
Cling aratoor
Es knistert es klappert es klirrt
On tonne on mugit on meugle
Toutes les ballades sont mortes
And we wonder in our deepest dream
Will the vocabularies never cease clashing
Werden die Woerterbuecher immer streiten
Will the bickerwords ever grow silent
In the elegy of a great love (MB 192)

Jolas's plurilingual idiolect occasionally verged on the ridiculous. *Silvalogue*, for example, reads like Wordsworth transposed by Lewis Carroll; a kind of pastoral doggerel: "In funkling stemwhorl mutes the postnoon dripling grou. Loney I slike over stilettoes of pine. The loobatinkala glucks soft. Oaks maulk under the shliffknives of the fallers. A grayard moods before a flame rooling the huss-hiss of charring. Beeses bly through gelb-leaves."[15] Perhaps Joyce was the only one to carry off the plurilingual method with true panache, and this because he never strayed too far from the speech rhythms of Anglo-Irish vernacular. Semantic intelligibility was preserved even when meaning was obscure. In hurling language into trilingual limbo, severing its ties to nation and region, Jolas may have been the more rigorous international modernist, and he may have come closer to breaking out of the monolingual prison-house, but his dogma was at greater risk of going poetically nowhere. It is no surprise that a poem like "Babel: Across Frontiers" was among his more successful poems, because the battle-scarred war zones of Europe contextualized his staging of language wars:

All the words are brawling
All the words are sick
Todas las palabras tienen pena
In the savage nights of the cosmopolis
The radios blast janglesounds
Les postes de T.S.F. sont déchaînés
The landscapes of grammar are covered with mildew
Zie zeitworte brausen sturm
It is verb against verb
It is syntax against syntax[16]

Jolas's desire to release words from the chains of the "millennial curse" of Babel (the separatist, sickened condition of language use in the balkanized territories of Europe) prompted him to construct an "astral" poetics based on the dogma of "vertigralism." "The vertical language," he wrote in an essay of that title, " is the true international language." Vertigralism placed faith in "winged wordes" to assuage an apocalyptic apprehension of "cosmic fear."[17] Proposing interracial fraternity as the means of righting the toppled tower of Babel, extolling the miracle of modern aeronautics in the conquest of gravitation, Jolas set great hopes on Vertigralism: "Vertical aimed to be an astro-mental vision of a pluralistic universe. I believed in the existence of other worlds, of beings living on planets, of a cosmological conception" (V 157). Confirming, perhaps, that fusion of "irrational elements" and "pseudo-rationality" that Adorno diagnosed in the *Los Angeles Times* astrology column as a sign of the occult in modern life,[18] Jolas depicted an explorer in the space of artificial languages, a traveler, who, in *Planets and Angels*, fords the banks of Babel and the Atlantic lip to reach the planet Astralingua.[19] Here, the migrant of his earlier poetry, scouring the byways of vernacular America, is replaced by a space nomad, dodging asteroids and comets, discovering new dimensions of the universe, and conversing in astral tongues. "Our words leap-tumbled into new words, into new dimensions of words. . . . We talked with interplanetary beings in a language that was music and balm."[20] In another book, *Secession in Astropolis*, Jolas experimented with science fiction language, inventing forms of *alienspeak*. The cast of characters ranges from "beings" who are "half root half man" gathered around a campfire reciting sagas, to races of "women-men" inscribing the temples of Astropolis with "baffling ideographs."[21] Unlike "Atlantica," Jolas's semi-decipherable private Esperanto, these astral languages resemble the Mayan and Egyptian hieroglyphs—they are *beyond* translation, beyond Babel. As such, they represent an ideal of universal utterance that can only be realized through futuristic fantasy.

In his monomaniacal commitment to making an extraterrestrial language world, Jolas may be classed as an important precursor of Louis Wolfson, another obscure American writer (now rumored to be living as a recluse in Puerto Rico), who, in his 1970 novel *Le Schizo et les langues ou La Phonétique chez le psychotique (Esquisses d'un étudiant de langues schizophrénique)* (The Schizo and Languages or the Psychotic's Phonetics [Notes of a Schizophrenic Language Student]) invented a homonymic French that transliterates German, Hebrew, Russian, and English word-sounds. Wolfson unhorses the mother tongue not just by inventing a substitute philology, but, more pointedly still, by mounting a strategic campaign against the *muttersprache* with an eye to occupying the linguistic field of his choosing. Convinced by his editor, the psychoanalyst J-P Pontalis, not to publish his novel in its deviant orthographic state, Wolfson preserved a fragment of what he wanted his text to look and sound like in an appendix. Here, even more than in the main text, a dizzying plurilingualism assaults the maternal linguistic body, miming on a formal level the book's narrative of oedipal aggression.

Le Schizo et les langues is something of a textual curiosity much like Georges Perec's *La Disparition* (A Void), a narrative published one year earlier in France that had observed the set dogma of excluding the letter *e* in both the original and the English translation. In *Le Schizo*, the main character is a "student"—a language-maker cum language-learner—who occupies the scarred battlefield of the translation zone as he attempts to unlearn his mother tongue. The writing embodies mental breakdown in clinically unstable phrases, utterances that founder on internal puns and phonetic abnormalities. Here, for example, is the author's self-description:

- L'étudiant malade mentalement
- L'étudiant d'idiomes dément
- le jeune Öme sqizofrène

Those familiar with Jacques Lacan's earliest case studies in "schizography," published as an appendix to his thesis on paranoia, or with the experiments of Oulipo, the sixties language game group headed by Raymond Queneau (famous for *Zazi dans le métro* and *Exercices de Style*), or with Perec's *A Void* (containing a chapter, titled in Shandyesque fashion "Which, notwithstanding a kind of McGuffin, has no ambition to rival Hitchcock") might be tempted to read Wolfson as a kind of linguicidal psycho. But what interests me specifically is the way dogma is used, quite treacherously, to "kill" monolingual orders of meaning and, by extension, the linguistic ballast of social orders.

The counterhegemony of Wolfson's "tour de babil" relies on a rule-based technique that leads the text to a form of serial polysemy, performed as rapid-fire tactical operations.

d to *t*
p to *b*

Where? becomes *Woher?. Tree = Tere* or *Dere. Milk* (mother's milk of course) is dragged along a translation path to the objective of phonetic deformation. Danish *maelk* to German *Milch* to Polish *mleko* to Russian *moloko.* The *i* in

English *milk* moves toward French *é*. The distance between the sounds is compared to the length between the back of the tongue and the roof of the palate. The soft *ch* of *Milch* is measured in intensity against the Polish *e* and *o*, in its turn pulled in the direction of the Russian *o* and *a* sounds. *Ch* comes back later in the text as the abbreviation of a prostitute's name, itself derived from *call-girl*, in turn transliterated as *kò:l ghe:l* or *ghe(r)l*, as if skidding between a Yiddish and Scottish pronunciation. Perhaps this circle of sounds describes the circulation of fluids from mother's milk to sperm.

In the physical thrashing of labial thrusts and parries, the tongue becomes an erotic animal swimming around in the bocal cavity. This emphasis on the materiality of *langue* and the linguistic medium in general, is also associated with eating disorders. The narrator's bulimic binges on tins, which he is trying to avoid looking at because of their English labels, mirror his obsessive need to derail Anglophone cognates. A word to which he has a strange attachment in English—*vegetable oil*—is orthographically rendered so as to capture pronunciation with a thick Russian accent: *vèdjtebel oïl*. The variant *vegetable shortening* proves harder to distort, but by spelling it *chortni(gn)*, the student eventually discovers with delight the "monstrosity" *shshshortening*, which allows him to "dismember" and "annihilate" the "hideous English vocable." Extracting the sound *ch*, he submerges the remainder inside the Hebrew word *chèmnn* (oil or grease) and the German word *Schmalz* (*chmalts*), another word for liquid lard or sickly sweetness. From *schmal*, to *chétif*, to *short*, the painful mutations continue until the last remnants of the original are broken up and redistributed. The rule, according to Deleuze, is to "unite languages in disorder" in order to conserve the same meanings and sounds, thus unleashing a "pathogene" or void that roves between words that are converted and words that are about to be converted.[22] For Wolfson, this is a melting pot gone sour, with migrant vowels and "foreign"-sounding immigrant sounds, exploding all over the territory of orthodox French or American English. One can see why for a philosopher like Deleuze, Wolfson must have seemed like a wish come true, a truly rhizomatic syntactician, who enabled elementary particles of language to roam the linguistic field, transforming roots into tumbleweeds that nomadically set up camp where they please, unafraid of combustive, combinatory language games. In Deleuze's view, Wolfson's phonetic decompositions turn translation into a supreme act of violence. The multilingual magma, instead of sorting itself into discrete target languages, reunites all languages *against* the mother tongue, "deboning" it of its consonantal substructure. Translation's linguistic arsenal is thus mobilized for the ritual murder of English—a parricidal death wish, as it turns out, since the father in *Le Schizo et les langues* is the most ardent defender of "English only" throughout the world. ("You're wasting your time," he tells his son, "English is the only language you need to go anywhere in the world. English is understood everywhere."[23]

Both Wolfson and his avatar Georges Perec have been classified as quirky torture-artists of the word who rely on the scientific impersonality of technique—*le procédé*—to reveal the libidinal surprises of free-form declensions and phonic flows. In his afterword to *A Void*, Perec makes light of these linguistic exercises, passing them off as mere games with himself:

> Offhand, with hindsight, I can think of many factors bubbling about in my brain, but I ought to admit right away that its origin was totally haphazard, touch and go, a flip of a coin. It all got out of hand with a companion calling my bluff (I said I could do it, this companion said I could not). . . .
>
> So was born, word by word, and paragraph by paragraph, a book caught within a formalist grid doubly arduous in that it would risk striking as insignificant anybody ignorant of its solution, a book that, crankily idiosyncratic as it no doubt is, I instantly found thoroughly satisfying.[24]

Perec's game with the grid of linguistic deep structure may have been only a game, but his text reveals just how easily such *Spielmeistering* falls in with the terrorism of *Realpolitik.* If Wolfson's fractured psychobabble carries a deadly serious attack on native language and identity, Perec's *A Void* is deeply in sync with the revolutionary impulses of French *gauchisme* of the sixties: Regis Debray's forays into guerilla warfare, Daniel Cohn-Bendit's choreography for May '68, Ben Bella's fatal aim at De Gaulle's oxymoron of "French Algeria." In this light, it is perhaps no accident that Perec's novel opens in a Parisian landscape as treacherous as a minefield, a premonition in 1970 of the terrorist wave of the 1980s, the racist attacks on North Africans by Le Pen's supporters in the 1990s, and the global climate of fear after 9/11:

> Arabs, blacks and, as you might say, non-goyim fall victim to racist attacks, with pogroms forming in such outlying Parisian suburbs as Drancy, Livry-Gargan, Saint-Paul, Villacoublay and Clignancourt. And stray acts of brutality abound: an anonymous tramp has his brains blown out just for a bit of moronic fun, and a sacristan is callously spat upon—in public, too—whilst giv-

ing absolution to a CRS man cut in half by a blow from a yata-
ghan (a Hungarian slicing tool, if you must know). (V vii–viii)

The pedantic, dictionary note ("a Hungarian slicing tool, if you must
know"), like the device of e-suppression, reminds us that there is a profound
connection here between language dogma and the *déclic* of social violence.
In *A Void* the cacophonous revolution of a newly minted postcolonial order
is translated by numbers. Where Wolfson computes his threat to society
according to chemical formulas and linguistic calorie counts (thus inducing
anorexia in the linguistic-social body), Perec counts down world leadership
like a Partridge in a Pear Tree:

> To cap it all, this particular May is proving a scorchingly hot and
> sunny month: in Passy an omnibus combusts without warning;
> and practically 60% of our population go down with sunburn.
>   . . . the nation has had, in turn, a Frankish king, a hospador, a
> maharajah, 3 Romuli, 8 Alarics, 6 Ataturks, 8 Mata-Haris, a
> Caius Gracchus, a Fabius Maximus Rullianus, a Danton, a Saint-
> Just, a Pompidou, a Johnson (Lyndon B.), a lot of Adolfs, a trio
> of Mussolinis, 5 Caroli Magni, a Washington, an Othon in oppo-
> sition to a Hapsburg and a Timur Ling, who, for his own part,
> got rid of 18 Pasionarias, 20 Maos and 28 Marxists (1 Chicist, 3
> Karlists, 6 Grouchists and 18 Harpists). (V ix–x)

The companion "lipogrammatic" text to *A Void*, *Les Revenentes* (whose title
evokes the ghostly return of the formerly banished *e*'s) carries the volatile
conjugation of language dogma and antiauthoritarianism even further.
Translated as *The Exeter Text: Jewels, Secrets, Sex* by Ian Monk, who, in defer-
ence to the *e*-only stipulation, calls himself a renderer rather than a translator and spells his name E. N. Menk, its dogma is ostensibly apolitical, with
rules qualified by rules:

> 1. The word "and" may be spelt "n."
> 2. The letter *y* when consonantal (e.g. "yes") will be permitted, as
> will the semi-vowel *y* in digraphs such as "they"; only the full
> vowel (e.g. "gypsy") will be disallowed.
> 3. Various distortions will be gradually accepted as the text pro-
> gresses; no list of them can possibly be given here.[25]

Though in appearance only a formalist exercise, the text's stringent system
of vowel restraints produces an idiom in which political resentments are
embedded. The English translation conveys this dormant explosiveness

in its pronounced resemblance to the language Anthony Burgess invented in *A Clockwork Orange*—a kind of blasphemous High Church cockney, or Old English vernacular containing scatological puns and violent subcultural innuendos.

> René led the men between the Berbers' entrenchments. He yelled:
> "Mehmet! Set Thérèse free then cede!"
> "Berbers never cede! They defend the men they esteem!"
> Then the rebels wrestled the rented henchmen. The sleek Berbers enmeshed René's men. Nevertheless, he lept between the tents, where heedless wenches fled pell-mell. [. . .]
> "Wretch," heckled René. "Sheep's excrement! Leper's feces! Geese crèpe! Serpents' engenderment! The hempen serf the desert ferret breeds!" (ET 65)

As in *A Void*, *The Exeter Text* encrypts explicit references to France's colonial wars: General Leclerc, the great French World War II hero, surfaces in his less glorious historical role as protagonist of "the dirty war" in Algeria. Here, all references to desert operations throughout the Middle East are enmeshed in puns on desertion and just deserts:

> René deserted then rented seventeen fez-dressed henchmen. Between the jebels, the deserts, the ergs where the steppes' breezes seeded then delete defenceless weeds, here erred these henchmen, needless brens, spent stens, nerveless épées, depleted steeds, kneeless gee-gees, bereft jennets. (ET 64)

Desert (the stronghold of Berber rebels) plus defection (of mercenary soldiers) adds up to military chaos. Leclerc's only buffer is a lawless pack of contraband "deelers" from around the world:

> Nettled, Leclerc re-expelled René then reflected where best he'd repel the well-mettled Mehmet Ben Berek, lest the rebels' relentlessness ended the French presence. The Czechs, the Swedes, the Engles, the Serbs, the Medes, the Tedesche 'n' the Greeks respected the French: the presence preserved peece settlements between Brest 'n' Temenressett—they let deelers peddle free-wheel.
> Leclerc, nevertheless, rejected heedlessness. He delved deep:
> "Eject Mehmet? Wrestle the rebels between these jebels then skewer them? Yet we'd never be serene then, never! These Berbers resemble sleek serpents. We'll never net them. The

desert dwellers defend them. The deepest secrets enshell them.
Whenever we seek them, we're checked! We'd best wheedle
them, then. Detect the pretext where they'll detest Ben Berek!
(ET 66–67)

The word "jebel" (perhaps a transliteration of the Arabic word *djebel*—pre-served in the original French—meaning mountain, and connoting the re-gion of Kabylia in which Berber resistance to the French was particularly fierce) contains a pun on stolen "jewels" that are integral to the story's con-struction around a heist involving the clergy and an ecclesiastic orgy. It also possibly alludes to the way in which the French always referred to Algeria as the "crown jewel" of their colonial possessions, as well as to their ultimate inability to reconquer the "djebels" during the course of the war. And the name Ben Berek recalls the name of Ben Barka, Morocco's antimonarchist rebel leader, assassinated in Paris in 1965. Though there is no way to distill any clear political "message" from these allusions, they percolate into the political unconscious, commemorating historical revolt in North Africa and demonstrating how colonial locutions can explode in the face of the French language like terrorist bombs.

Citing a "cybernetically-minded philologist," Norbert Wiener asserted that "speech is a joint game by the talker and the listener against the forces of confusion," and one could say that what allows us to bracket Jolas, Wolfson, and Perec—beyond their status as dogma theorists—was their dedication to language games that played fast and loose with such "forces of confusion."[26] It was as if, in matching the systematicity of linguistic deep structure, they were hoping to trigger devolution toward the roiling untranslatability inher-ent in all language. Jolas, Wolfson, and Perec can be book-ended chronologi-cally by J-P Brisset and Oulipo. A pioneer in the field of delirious linguistics, J-P Brisset was a retired officer who, in 1878, wrote a "grammar of logic or theory of a new mathematical analysis resolving the most difficult ques-tions," in which he attempted to recode semantics according to laws of hom-onymic resemblance. Brisset treated French as a sui generis primal lan-guage—untranslatable, self-referential, universal, and self-replicating. Not averse to playing God, he built up this language world by numbers. Decon-structed *Wortbildung* yielded genesis: a word was treated like a small miracle; it returned atavistically through time on account of chance repetition, like the roll of the dice that falls repeatedly on the same number. Brisset elabo-rated rules of phonetic decomposition and remixing guided by such random repetitions.[27] So, for example, he fabricated word waves full of internal puns:

Voici *les salauds pris*, ils sont dans *la sale eau pris*, dans *la salle aux prix*. Les pris étaient les prisonniers que l'on devait égorger. En attendant le jour des pris, qui était aussi celui des prix, on les enfermait dans une *salle*, une *eau sale*, où on leur jetait des *saloperies*. Là on les insultait, on les appelait *salauds*. Le pris avait du prix. On le dévorait, et, pour tendre un piège, on offrait du pris et du prix: c'est du prix. C'est duperie, répondait le sage, n'accepte pas de prix, ô homme, c'est duperie.[28] (emphasis in the original)

As Foucault has observed in his analysis of this passage, semblance affirms difference: the verb *prendre*, and its past participle "pris," are used not to draw out semantic equivalences between like-sounding phonemes (the "pri" of prisoner, the French word for price, or the term for "being taken" by a con artist), but to reveal the gulfs of untranslatability at the heart of every language.

Brisset's mad, mad world comes back in the age of cybernetics masterminded by the Oulipo collective. As *informatique* made its way into French culture in the 1960s, Oulipo set up a "laboratory" for mathematics and computer-assisted literature (foreshadowing by many years current work in hypertext and codework). By the 1970s the lab was sponsoring projects like USFAL (the acronym for A Formal System for the Literary Algorithm) that "calqued" literary formalism on the language of programming,[29] or that invented games, like the one called "cellular prosody," modeled after Conway's "game of life," itself inspired by the laws of cellular metabolism and robotic intelligence established by Von Neumann and Ulam.[30] Just as cybernetics was defining the living organism as a message that could be decoded like a language, so the Oulipo dogma theorists experimented with the recombinant DNA of language and literary forms, as if answering to Roman Jakobson's speculation that genetic code and language were of the same order.[31] Looping the loop in a continuum, the body and language would be conceived as a single system, immured in a closed world, and translatable only by numbers.

PART THREE

Language Wars

8

Balkan Babel: Translation Zones, Military Zones

Wars between languages are no less fateful than wars between men
—Ismail Kadare, *The Three-Arched Bridge*

A subset of politics at large, with particular agendas and strategic interests, language politics defines its theater of war in the space where a military zone may be superimposed on a linguistic hot spot or "translation zone." The expression "translation zone" could well refer to the demarcation of a community of speakers who achieve an ideal threshold of communication (the utopia of Leibniz, von Humboldt, and Habermas). But when war is at issue, it makes more sense to define it as a translation no-fly zone, an area of border trouble where the lines dividing discrete languages are muddy and disputatious, where linguistic separatism is enforced by high-surveillance missions or, where misfired, off-kilter semantic missiles are beached or disabled. Construed in terms of border patrols and military operations, the paradigm of a translation zone at war may be applied beyond the Balkans to the way in which monolingual nations police their internal linguistic borders, and to revolts against the computer as a machinic labor force in the economy of global translation. From the market in pocket translators to the onslaught of universal standards of technological literacy and the rise of comprador computer dialects that aggressively squeeze out weak competitors, a language war of the information age is taking shape with a distinctly bellicose rhetoric. Recent reports of attacks on internet sites (Yahoo, Buy.com, eBay) consistently rely on the language of ballistics—"assault," "barrage," "fortification," "seige," "bombardment"—and the loss of public safety. In this context, the affirmation cited above that "[w]ars between languages are as fateful as wars between men" is truly premonitory, indicative of a present condition in which *la guerre de Troyes* will not, indeed, take place, without computer-assisted violence and defense strategy.

In the Albanian author Ismail Kadare's 1976–78 novel *The Three-Arched Bridge*, this phrase is pronounced by a European monk, returning from a diplomatic visit to Byzantium, in conversation with the novel's main character, a translator, who is negotiating the terms of the construction of a bridge that would span rivalrous Balkan and Ottoman territories. Set in 1377, Kadare's novel uncannily anticipates the most recent Balkan conflagrations, specifically the way in which the Mitrovica Bridge on the Ibar River in northern Kosovo, flanked by self-appointed Serbian "bridge keepers," Albanian militants, and NATO peacekeeping forces, has made the question of partition and permanent secession the order of the day. Kadare's searing portrayal of mountain country vendettas in *Broken April* (1978) is equally prescient; the erasure of Tito's Yugoslavia and the collapse of Soviet hegemony have introduced a wild-card politics of East-West realignment enabling ancient ethnic, religious, and cultural feuds to reignite in the guise of modern mafia warfare.

Balkanism is a term wielded by Maria Todorova, in her book *Imagining the Balkans* as a self-conscious counterpoint to Saidian Orientalism.[1] Todorova and other scholars of Balkanism caution judiciously against regional stereotyping that equates "Balkan" with ethnic cleansing; bloodletting; a perpetual underground; mongrel regionalism; "semi-developed, semi-colonial" Europe; "an incomplete self of the West."[2] There is nonetheless, in representative literary works from southeastern Europe, a pronounced thematic focus on border wars and fractious linguistic copopulation. It is from these works that I take my cue in treating "Balkan" as a synonym for what occurs semiotically and socially when dialects or marginal world languages are in a war of maneuver unmediated by a major language of position.

The Three-Arched Bridge traces how language wars fit into the larger picture of political misalliance, blood feuds, and border trauma. Balkan babble—a condition of failed semantic transmission—obtains an isomorphic fit with Balkan Babel, a tower of Babel turned on its side to form a hapless bridge intended to ford the unbridgeable gulf between Europe and the so-called East. In the tense negotiations around the erection of the bridge, multilingualism asserts its importance at the bargaining table, raising stakes in what is already a lethal game of diplomatic and cultural one-upmanship. The politics, for example, of laying claim to linguistic superiority, is paramount, as when the narrator, a professional translator in the employ of an impoverished Albanian count, heaps contempt on the "foreigners [Turks]" by derogating their speech ("it is easier to interpret for woodpeckers").[3]

> The new arrivals did indeed speak the most horrible tongue. My ears had never heard such a babble. Slowly I began to untangle the sounds. I noticed that their numbers were Latin and their verbs generally Greek or Slav, while they used Albanian for the names of things, and now and then a word of German. They used no adjectives. (TAB 10–11)

This confusion issuing from strangers' mouths is transliterated as broken English:

> *This road bad because non maintain, mess complete. Water smooth itself, road non, routen need work, we has no tales, has instruct, we fast money, give, take. Water different, boat move itself graciosus, but vdrug many drown, bye-bye, sto dhjavolos. Funebrum, he, he, road no, road sehr guten but need gut repair.* (TAB 13, emphasis in original)

The translation implies a corrupt original language—Slavo-Germanic pidgin—whose broken grammar and encrypted allusions to bad roads, vengeful waters, and drowning men, foretells the contested construction of the bridge and the ensuing cycle of violent retribution that culminates in the encasement of a living man in its rampart.

If it is true, as the saying goes, that "language is a dialect protected by an army," then the novel may be read as a study of what happens when the security forces protecting the reigning tongue start to lose their strategic advantage and become vulnerable to the invading force of multilingual language users whose polyglot idiolect has yet to select a dominant dialect for standardization. Here this situation relates specifically to the Albanian claim to "first language" status, a claim that remains active even today in the politics of regional chauvinism. "I told him," says the narrator, "that we are the descendants of the Illyrians and that the Latins call our country Arbanum or Albanum or Regnum Albaniae" (TAB 69). After informing his listener that Albanians, together with the ancient Greeks, are the oldest people in the Balkans, with roots in the region "since time immemorial," and with a tradition that has embittered the "newcomers" (the Slavs), the narrator makes the familiar argument that the Albanian language "is contemporary with if not older than Greek, and that this, the monks say, was proved by the words that Greek had borrowed from our tongue"—and he then adds, they are "not just any words, but the names of gods and heroes" (TAB 70).

This linguistic patrimony is now under threat from the Ottoman language ("casting its shadow over both our languages, Greek and Albanian, like a black cloud") (TAB 70). The -*luk*' suffix, he laments, is pounding the originary tongue like "some dreadful hammer blow," and "nobody understands the danger." It is in the context of these observations that the sympathetic interlocutor makes the remark about wars between languages and wars between men.

Kadare's novel poses the proverbial question: What's in a name? The insidious beginning of an embattled condition, is the answer, when it comes to the word *Balkan* itself. To the narrator's amazement, the term passes from the Turkish language virtually unnoticed into the vocabulary of the Albanians after the count sells the Turks a stretch of highway: "More than by the desire of the Ottomans to cover under one name the countries and peoples of the peninsula, as if subsequently to devour them more easily, I was amazed by our readiness to accept the new name. I always thought that this was a bad sign, and now I am convinced that it is worse than that" (TAB 25). The seeding of conflict in the very name "Balkan" repeats a prior history of Germanic self-appellation: According to legend, passed along to the narrator by the old woman Ajkuna, the bedraggled Knights of the Teutonic Order, last of the crusaders, were heralded as the "'Jermans,' or people who talk as if in *jerm*, in delirium. Yet many people seem to have liked this name, since they say it is now used everywhere. According to our old men, these people have even begun to call their own country Jermani, which means the place where people gabble in delirium, or land of *jerm*" (TAB 27). This embedding of a story of Babel within ethnic and regional nomination acts as a secret weapon—a Trojan horse conceit—deployed by Albania's invaders. Smuggled across the border in the guise of a commercially motivated translation operation, the Turkish language behaves like germ warfare—impossible to contain, yet capable of spreading linguistic chaos once released into the atmosphere. Polyglot chatter breaks out at the bridge—Europe's symbolic weak link and the physical site of blood sacrifice—spreading confusion and narrative disorientation. As the Albanian locals lose their ability to distinguish legend from fact, or beginnings from endings, the "Ottoman hordes" advance upon them, subjecting their "majestic language" to the "terrible '*luk*,'" which strikes their native tongue like "a reptile's tail" (TAB 183). Here one must caution against a neutral reading of Kadare's political orientation. A dissident exile living in Paris since 1990, he is known for his pronounced pro-Europe, anti-Turkish, and anti-Islamic stance, as evinced in a polemical pamphlet on the "anatomy of tyranny" in which he refers derisively to the "baggage of the Ottoman overlords" while longingly prognosticating "a great rectification of [Albania's] history that will hasten its union with the mother continent—Europe."[4]

Kadare's professed commitment to removing traces of Turkish language and cultural influence on a future Albania surely render his texts problematic as exemplars of language politics, if one is committed to warding off the latest iterations of Orientalism. But it is also in their denunciations of the East that these texts function effectively as symptoms of what they diagnose—a condition of Balkan Babel defined by the acute anxieties that surround possession of a discrete language in territories of intense linguistic variegation and border conflict. Though not unique to the Balkans, this anxiety is aggravated by East-West barriers of untranslatability;[5] by the sameness between languages (such as Serbian and Croatian) that have been declared separate by official decree; by the physical proximity of differential language groups (with a language shift occurring at virtually every train stop); by the historic failure of nationalist linguistic policy to eliminate discrepancies; and by the proliferation of hybrid dialects that fall short of qualifying as standard languages. In the Balkans, the vindication of a language, or even a word, may be a lethal affair, and many writers have fastened on this problematic as key to understanding not only regional factionalism, but also the broadly applicable symptomology carried by the term *Balkanization.*

The Nobel prize—winning Serbian author Ivo Andrìc, whose 1945 novel *The Bridge on the Drina* clearly served as inspiration, if not as the occasion for rewriting *The Three-Arched Bridge*, gives special focus to the responsibility language bears for making Balkanization a synonym of profound regional dysfunction. Set in Bosnia, *Bridge on the Drina* spans several centuries, replaying the smoldering tensions between Orthodox Serbs and Islamic converts. The fateful construction of a bridge excites the wrath of the boatmen, who destroy by night what has been built by day, and who, as in *Three-Arched Bridge*, must forfeit the life of one of their own as punishment. As the novel moves forward to the end of the nineteenth century and the outbreak of civil war, the politics of blood tribute evolve seamlessly into the politics of occupation, with local militias doubling as military troops and vice versa. Violence, as in the Kadare novel, erupts on the occasion of a diplomatic translation: an old man from the Turkish side, thought to be a dervish, wanders unsuspectingly into the Serbian camp and is subjected to interrogation through the intermediary of a translator with "poor knowledge of the Turkish language." Intentionally performing a shoddy job, the translator puts "the worst possible construction on the old man's exalted phrases" such that they seem to "smell of politics and seditious intent."[6]

And so the old man is marked for execution, setting in motion the tit-for-tat engine of a language war. Turkish soldiers find their opportunity for retribution when they happen upon a mill attendant in a remote forest area giving full throat to a ballad of ancient Serbia normally reserved for "closed houses" (BD 87). The verse that speaks of a maiden whose lover hopes to carry a standard for her into battle is particularly offensive to the Turks, convinced that the words *maiden* and *standard* have been subversively purloined from their language. The narrator explains: "In that great and strange struggle, which had been waged in Bosnia for centuries between two faiths, for land and power and their own conception of life and order, the adversaries had taken from each other not only women, horses and arms but also songs. Many a verse passed from one to the other as the most precious of booty" (BD 87–88). In the fictional worlds of Andrić and Kadare, linguistic border-crossing (from the adoption of loan words to the appropriation of a rival country's verse) triggers paranoia and murderous hostility. Each side hears the theft of its patrimony in the other's language. Tracked like illegal transients, words become subject to military patrol, their border infractions punishable by death.

In Kadare's novels the Balkans become a microcosm of a state of civil society driven by what Manuel de Landa calls "intelligent machines." Only here, de Landa's vision of smart bombs and robotic channelers of human will are replaced in the Balkan context by age-old linguistic technologies, propelling themselves through maneuvers independent of individual agents.[7] From this perspective, consider specific moments in *The Three-Arched Bridge*. As East and West, Christendom and Islam, proceed full tilt into battle, the war machine is set in motion by a "commination," a gestural speech-act or ritual curse (from *comminari*, to threaten punishment or vengeance). Formally launched by the Turks against Europe, the commination resembles a machinic technology, built according to strict rules and safety measures culled from archival manuals. The commination has the power of first strike, embodying the terrible seriousness of cursing in Balkan lands. The curse activates a code of honor exacting blood payment for the redemption of good name and committing future generations to unrequited warfare. Evidence of how this fatal heritage gets passed on to future generations crops up in *The Palace of Dreams*, a sequel novel to *The Three-Arched Bridge*, in which the protagonist discovers that his family name is a cursed patronymic because an ancestor had adopted the name of the "bridge with three arches in central Albania . . . built with a man walled up in its foundations," thus dooming, for ever after, his descendants to an association with the "stigma of murder."[8] With its grammar of threats and punishments, vengeful cycles and blood sacrifice, the commination reveals how war is structured like a language.

In *Broken April*, perhaps Kadare's most harrowing novel, this structuralist vision of tribal peoples bound together in community by a common language of perpetual war is exemplified to the extreme. Recalling Pierre Clastres's theory of "the archaeology of war," specifically the case of the Tupi-Guarani Indians, whom he claims participated in the same cultural model without ever constituting a nation, since they remained in a permanent state of war.[9] Operating according to strict rules of linguistic and social contract, there is zero-sum ambiguity in the moves each side makes. Each infraction of the laws of hospitality triggers ritual killing, economized in the currency of truce periods and funeral tithes, debt wound paid off by human life, or the right to "own a death" redeemed by taking X number of family hits. The war machine, though reduced to local scale, nonetheless exhibits the key structural functions attributed by Bataille to military subcultures in his notes on "The Structure and Function of the Army": the psychic economy of the sacrificial victim, mystical corporatism, fealty to the autonomous engine of destruction, with its power to transform humans into a caste of fabricated beings called "men at war."[10]

Over and over, Kadare depicts war as language—that is, as a transparent accounting of death's score, charting wins and losses without affect, or with the precision and dryness of mathematical notation. This "dead" language—something on the order of what George Steiner would identify as the "postlinguistic" condition of inhumanism—describes language as pure linguistic technology geared up for militaristic use. This description is reminiscent, certainly, of Carl von Clausewitz's intimation of "combat no longer guided by the 'will of a guiding intelligence,'" of war that would "drive policy out of office and rule by the laws of its own nature."[11] Unlike the messy border wars that prevail in *The Three-Arched Bridge*, pitching Ottoman polyglottalism against European monolingualism in a fight that can only end in Balkan Babel, *Broken April* constructs its paradigm around a technocratic language of almost digital simplicity: strokes and naughts, hits and misses, minimal margins of error. In this paradigm, dialects and standard languages alike are flattened into an Esperanto of intelligent machines, an Esperanto close to what the linguist Randalph Quirk termed "nuclear English."

Nuclear English designates a language akin to C. K. Ogden's Basic English (BASIC)—that is, a language, in his words, that would be as "culture-free as calculus."

Culture-free as calculus, with no literary, aesthetic or emotional aspirations, it is correspondingly more free than the "national Englishes" of any suspicion that it smacks of linguistic imperialism or even (since native speakers of English would have to be trained to use it) that it puts some countries at an advantage over others in international communication. Since it is not (but is merely related to) a natural language, it would not be in competition for educational resources with foreign languages proper but rather with that other fundamental interdisciplinary subject, mathematics. Nor, by the same token, could its teachers be accused of wasting resources (as sometimes happens, distressingly, with foreign languages and literatures) on an elitist disciplinary ornament for the few. The relations of Nuclear English are less with the ivory tower than with public convenience.[12]

Nuclear English advertises itself politically as a force of democracy, but a democracy aimed at the boardrooms of multinationals. In execution, it seems to boil down to "restricting modalities," that is, reducing the incidence of polysemy wherever possible, constraining unconventional or pidgin grammar, and maximizing semantic intentionality. Nuclear English seems to promote a denationalized, Taylorized literacy in which signs do not misfire, but rather hit their mark with mathematical precision. Carried to its logical end, Nuclear English is, of course, tantamount to a prescription for total war on linguistic diversity and cultural inflection—nothing short of a nuclear attack on the language of humans. But the obvious humanist rebuttal may be all too easy. What makes the idea of Nuclear English rather interesting, it would seem, is that it updates the old dream of a perfectly standardized, universal language for an age of intelligent machines.

For what is Nuclear English if not the culmination of intertwining strands of imperial politics and utopian language philosophy—the former going back to revolutionary and colonial histories, the latter to the explosion of lingua francas at the turn of the twentieth century? As regards the revolutionary heritage, Renée Balibar (*L'Institution du français*), Pierre Clastres, and the Jesuit linguist Louis-Jean Calvet have traced how, particularly during the Terror, language squadrons were billeted to rural areas in a campaign to bring dialect into line with newly established codifications of French standard language.[13] Calvet shows how this French linguistic colonization of itself was extended to the colonies, documenting the application of French language policies *outre mer*, and the consequent consolidation of a dominant French culture in territories outside the Hexagon. He also examines the lack of tolerance for minority languages in Russia—both before and after the Revolution. The doctrine of "One Tsar, one religion, one language" is transformed by the Soviet regime into the mandate of a society without frontiers or nations. This "unique culture" was supposed to evolve in stages, from "rastvet" (the flowering of different cultures), to "sblizheniye" (their coming together), to "sliyaniye" (the emergence of harmonious unity in a single world language).[14]

In addition to spelling out causal connections between the rise of universal language ideology and imperialism, Calvet interprets the rise of Esperanto as a response to the growing divisionism of Europe on the eve of World War I. Nineteenth-century "logothèthes," he notes, invented around five hundred schemes for artificial languages that would transcend the imperfections of natural languages. "Cosmoglossa" (1858), "Universalglot" (1868), Volapük (1879), Weltsprache (1883), Esperanto (1887), Mundolingue (1890), Dil (1903), Simplo (1911), and Europeo (1914) were among the most popularly disseminated. Volapük, for example, sustained twenty-five journals, 283 societies, and an academy.

The idea of Nuclear English reveals the reductive drive inherent in Leibnizian schemes for a scientific language that were famously castigated by Ernest Renan in *De l'origine du language* (1859) as "mangled, tortured, artificial, painfully constructed, and inharmonious," in short, "plus barbare que l'iroquois" (more barbaric than Iroquois). Even worse than their infelicitous form, he argued, was their specious pretense to logic: "Premeditated linguistic reforms . . . are often less logical than humble patois."[15] If Nuclear English derives on the one hand from Leibniz, or from revolutionary standardizations of language, state-sponsored single-language policies, and lingua franca movements in turn-of-the-century Europe, on the other hand it has also been traced (by Alistair Pennycook among others), to British philosophical traditions of pragmatism, positivism, and utilitarianism that influenced Ogden's development, in 1930, of BASIC (an acronym for British American Scientific International Commercial). Comprising a vocabulary of only 850 words, boosted by Winston Churchill in the 1940s as part of a meliorist colonial platform, Basic English aspired to technological rationalism and mathematical simplicity. BASIC set a precedent for future wars against linguistic proliferation and prepared the way for future fetishizations of a supersimplified English vulgate or technological Globalspeak.

Of course, one can argue, it is precisely at the moment when Globalspeak becomes feasible in the age of intelligent machines that Balkan Babel breaks out on the borders. In Japan, for example, Babel can be identified in the teenage pidgins used to "evade parental surveillance." This code language draws on the transliteration of English words pronounced with a Japanese accent ("wonchu" for "I want you"); pig latin mixing product names with Japanese verbs ("deniru" for "let's go to a Denny's restaurant," "hageru" for "let's get a Haagen-Dazs ice cream"; and various forms of technobabble (as in "daburu-kurikku mausu" for "double click the mouse").[16] Here it would seem, the greater the reach of English, the greater the production of "other Englishes" that both undermine and reinforce monolingual orders.

For English to maintain and enhance its growing grip on international communication, it seeks to contain Balkanization by patrolling linguistic break-away groups, supporting linguicide or the stamping out of "useless" endangered language species, and routinely "cleansing" the language of rebarbative localisms or mongrel incursions. But already this task is complicated by the latest side effects of technological literacy, whereby hackers—enabled by the Internet—break in and disable the languages and codes by which computers protect themselves.[17] In an era of Internet attacks, the future theater of war, the future translation zone, is removed to electronic turf, and the crucial question becomes: how do we wage war, make peace, or control the enemy, when we do not even know who or where the enemy is?

9

War and Speech

Shifting notions of readability are crucial to the determination of major and minor languages and literatures. Harold Bloom's popular book *How to Read and Why*, with its breezy normative agenda aimed at delivering the right reading list to an educated public, confirms the degree to which the pedigree of great books is linked to critical edicts of readability.[1] The French sense of *lisible* (which hews to conservative standards of literateness) builds in the exclusionary function of readability tests, especially constrictive of authors working outside the pale of what Pascale Casanova has called the "Anglo-saxon model of modernity," and its opposite, the more Germanic "depth model" of subjective character-formation or *Bildung*.[2] Here, Casanova seems willing to desert the critic's most sacrosanct vocational mandate—the judgment call or designation of quality. "The critics do not create the works, but they do create the value of the works," Casanova asserts, calling, if not for blanket ecumenicalism in the business of literary criticism, then, at the very least, for a planetary redistribution of literary capital weighted more equably toward the minor.[3] Casanova's *La République mondiale des lettres* (The Global Republic of Letters) clarifies how the map of world literature has been defined by the Western tilt of international aesthetic criteria, but its treatment of "small literatures" accords insufficient attention to the intersection between "reading wars" and "language wars."[4] Reading wars—debates over the constitution of an international canon, conflicts over thresholds of literacy and readability—tend to take place in the confines of the academy or the literary public sphere. By contrast, language wars—national and ethnic linguistic rivalries, or the struggle of minority languages to survive the globalization of English—tend to be relegated to the domain of linguistics and sociology. But, I would surmise, it is precisely where these two fields of discussion come together that we can begin to define non-Western expression in a global context in terms other than those of a binarized cartography (major-minor/metropole-periperhy/global-local, etc.).

Jackie Kay's collection of poetry, *Off Colour*—particularly the poem *Virus****—compels just this sort of complication of binary models, exemplifying, as it does, the meeting of two forms of minority speech, Scots and West Indian English. The poems engage the politics of reading and speaking simultaneously, since many of the words need to be sounded out or read aloud in order to be understood. Virtually every line tests the limits of the reader's familiarity with a broad array of accents produced under historically and culturally disparate phases of British cultural hegemony. *Virus**** uses the contamination of standard English by minority accents to communicate the mother nation's paranoid fantasy of being poisoned by a foreign (immigrant) spore:

> *Virus* * * *
> No that Am saying Am no grateful.
> Am aye grateful tae ma hosts,
> awratime, and if by ony chance
> ma host the rat snuffs it,
> A kin a ways switch tack.
> Big man, wee wuman, wean:
> it's awrasame tae me.
> Don't get me wrang,
> Am no aw that choosy,
> as lang as the flesh
> is guid and juicy.
> One bite and Am in,
> one bite and they're mine,
> in the neck, the groin.
> Whit! Ma success rate
> is naebody's bisness.
> Wey ma canny disguise
> A make sure human hosts
> drap like flies.
> Bubo! It's all go.
> O sweet Christ.
> Sweet blood bodies.
> Somebody's dochter. Somebody's Maw.[5]

The slippage between "Am" (for "I'm"), "aye" (a sound of assent and affirmation as well as pain), and "A" (as in "A kin a ways switch tack") takes the impersonal, lyrical "I" of high modernism out of the purely literary realm and into the performative sphere of class- and race-inflected speech. This is language with bite, well serving a poem about a parasite biting and killing its host. It is full of orthographically transmitted double-entendres: "One bite and Am in," carries the subliminal "Amen" of last rights. Similarly, "Am no aw that choosy" sounds out the word "gnaw," conjuring the rat bite or worms eating away at a corpse. The word "dochter" slides between the English word "doctor" and the German "tochter" or daughter, blurring the boundaries between healer and sick person. Is the doctor infecting the daughter? Or is he felled by the plague himself? These ambiguities carry over to the word "Maw," signifying both "Mother" and the jaws of Death.

Kay's translingualism pays its due respects to Sam Selvon's introduction of West Indian immigrant English into landmark works of fiction such as *The Lonely Londoners* (1956) or to Linton Kwesi Johnson's book of poetry *Inglan Is a Bitch* (1980). Both texts are commonly referred to as examples of rotten English, but they also qualify in more theoretical terms as examples of how the violent stigmas and stakes carried by "other Englishes" form the bedrock of critical paradigms of minority literature.[6] Despite the fact that colonial histories are embedded in majority languages, they can sometimes offer the means of averting language wars between rival ethnic and linguistic groups. The writings of the late Nigerian writer Ken Saro-wiwa provide an opportunity to assess the apparent anomaly of a majority tongue becoming the vehicle of expression for a micro-minority linguistic group. His 1985 novel, *Sozaboy: A Novel in Rotten English* uses pidgin English rather than Khana, the language of his native Ogoniland, to capture linguistic minority politics, and the reason for this, according to Michael North, is that the choice "to write in one of Nigeria's major languages (Hausa-Fulani, Yoruba, and Igbo) would be just as oppressive to three hundred other ethnic groups."[7]

In his prefatory note to *Sozaboy*, Saro-wiwa acknowledges the use made of Nigerian pidgin and conversational exchanges.[8] He quotes the editor who anthologized his short story "High Life" in a Penguin African Library edition of 1969 as saying: " 'the piece is not in true "Pidgin" which would have made it practically incomprehensible to the European reader. The language is that of a barely educated primary school boy exulting in the new words he is discovering and the new world he is beginning to know.' Mr. Dathorne goes on to describe the style in the story as 'an uninhibited gamble with language,' and 'an exercise in an odd style' " (S Author's Note).

Though it is hard to ascertain with certainty whether Saro-wiwa is citing Mr. Dathorne's analysis of his prose approvingly or not, he clearly endorses the classification of his style among New Englishes that stridently and unapologetically lay claim to broken or rotten Europhonic usage. And insofar as rotten English, like Black Vernacular English (sometimes also referred to as Ebonics) can also be read as an assault on the Basic English of universal capital, it has been interpreted in the broader context of Saro-wiwa's later career as an environmental activist. From this perspective, the novel's treatment of linguistic auto-colonization—specifically the protagonist's aspiration to what he calls "big grammar"—may be aligned with the kind of indigenous colonialism or recolonization that has resulted from the Nigerian military junta's complicity in the devastation of Ogoniland by the unobstructed mining practices of the Royal/Dutch Shell Group.[9] Saro-wiwa paid dearly for his role as celebrity champion of the Ogoni people's rights as a micro-minority. He was condemned to death in a show trial and executed by the Abacha regime in 1995.[10]

In the short story "High Life," the predecessor text to *Sozaboy* in which Saro-wiwa first experimented with his distinctive brand of Nigerian Ebonics, rotten English coincides with what Philip Lewis has called "abusive translation." It experiments with what Lewis characterizes as "the translatability that emerges in the movement of difference as a fundamental property of languages . . . a risk to be assumed: that of a strong, forceful translation that values experimentation, tampers with usage, seeks to match polyvalencies or plurivocities or expressive stress of the original by producing its own."[11] Narratively driven by a kind of *Crying Game* conceit, whereby the narrator discovers that the prostitute he has taken home is a male transvestite, *High Life* introduces neologisms such as "prouding" and "shaming" to lend tropic force to states of affect:

> I undressed very quickly because I wanted to make romantica
> with the woman. But all the time, she refused to pull her dress. I
> thought she was shaming because of the light. So I quenched the
> electric. Then I went to the bed where she was sitting and re-
> moved her blouse. No breast. Ah-ah. What type of woman is
> this? Only artificial breast. Anyway that did not surprise me too
> much because I have heard that many women are using it. Then
> I began to remove the woman's loincloth. Although by this time
> I was feeling very hot inside and I was impatient, I took time to
> remove that loincloth. The next thing I found was that the
> woman was wearing short knicker. Ah-ah. What type of woman
> is this? is what I asked myself. Then I tried to remove the

knicker. All this time, the woman said nothing at all. She was very very silent like church on Monday. Then the woman-man picked up all his-her things and gave me three sound slaps on the face and ran away.[12]

While the short story deploys the theme of sex change to deflate the cult of hypermasculinity, *Sozaboy* ups the ante by internalizing sexual ambiguity within grammar itself:

> So that night, I was in the Upwine Bar. No plenty people at first. I order one bottle of palmy from the service. This service is young girl. Him bottom shake dey shake as she walk. Him breast na proper J.J.C, Johnny Just Come—dey stand like hill. As I look am, my man begin to stand small small. I beg am make 'e no disgrace me especially as I no wear pant that night. I begin to drink my palmy. The service sit near my table dey look me from the corner of him eye. Me I dey look am too with the corner of my eye. I want to see how him breast dey. As I dey look, the baby catch me.
> "What are you looking at?" is what she asked.
> "I am not looking at anything," was my answer.
> "But why are you looking at me with corner-corner eye?" she asked again.
> "Look you for corner-corner eye? Why I go look for corner-corner eye?" was my answer.
> "You dey look my breast, *yeye* man. Make you see am now."
> Before I could twinkle my eye, lo and behold she have moved her dress and I see her two breasts like calabash. God in Heaven. What kain thing be this? *Abi*, the girl no dey shame? (S 14)

Using a gender-inverted dative case—in which possessive pronouns designating parts of the female body are masculinized, "him bottom shake," "the corner of him eye"—Saro-wiwa depersonalizes the body, imaging it as a field of disparate, wildly associative, erogenous part-objects. A phrase like "I dey look am too" or "my man begin to stand small," or acronyms such as J.J.C ("Johnny-Just-Come"), maps a dispersed, biomorphic erotic animus that dissolves boundaries of subject and object. A compilation he-woman, she-man emerges from the gender-scrambled grammar, suggesting a phobic image of "queer Africa" strategically deployed to flush out homophobia and political anxiety around "Big-Manism" in Nigerian society.

Big-manism, a term generally used for tribal autocracy and what Achille Mbembe calls "the prosaics of the vulgar," is associated in Saro-wiwa's novel with Big Brotherism, specifically a ritual order of *commandement* that Mbembe ascribes to the mobilized system of state fetishes through which the state extends the psychic reach of its power:[13]

> Before, before, the grammar was not plenty and everybody was happy. But now grammar begin to plenty and people were not happy. As grammar plenty, na no trouble plenty. And as trouble plenty, na so plenty people were dying.
>
> . . . The radio continue to blow big, big grammar, talking big talk. We continue to make big money, my master and myself.
>
> . . . When I passed the elementary six exam, I wanted to go to secondary school but my mama told me that she cannot pay the fees. The thing pained me bad because I wanted to be big man like lawyer or doctor riding car and talking big big English.[14]

Where Mbembe stresses the relationship between power and the aesthetics of the vulgar (travestied body parts, sexual taboos, defecation, and fornication), Saro-wiwa invents a *vulgate*—a debased version of standard English—to demonstrate the way in which language submits to power, the dictates of "big grammar," even as it harbors an insurgent intent. Big English is to rotten English what the Nigerian state is to impoverished civilians, an ideal of empowerment that appeals to the ranks of "barely educated primary school boys," boys whose dreams of upward mobility make them ripe for mercenary recruitment. In this way, *Sozaboy* literalizes what Paul de Man, citing Nietzsche, referred to as a "mobile army of tropes."[15] The army becomes a kind of tropological boot camp in this narrative of the Biafran war, inducting country boys into a new order of language, warping their aspirations to fit a psychic economy materially directed toward guns, cars, big houses, and big grammar itself, the currency of *commandement*—the power to coerce and subject others in turn.

> After we have marched small and stood in line, then one big man came and gave us command, left right, and solope arms and udad arms and hopen udad mas and qua shun and ajuwaya. Very very tough man. He was shouting plenty. Tall man. Speaking fine fine English. "You boys must be smart. Salute properly. Behave like soldiers. Season soldiers." To tell the truth I cannot understand everything he was saying. But as i see 'am, I am pround to be soza with gun. I think that one day I will be like that soza with spectacle, tall and fine speaking with brass band voice, enjoying myself inside fine car and fine house, giving command to small boys who are just entering new into soza life. (S 77)

The phrase "Udad arms" (meaning "order arms," but phonetically conveying the signifier "you-dad" or the goal of becoming a "big Daddy") joins other phrases such as "Solope arms" (slope arms, arms down), "qua shun" (a transliteration of "Attention"), and "ajuwaya" (a transliteration of "as you were") is Saro-wiwa's appropriation of the militarized pidgin that was used by the British in training and conscripting Nigerian soldiers for service in World War I. This colloquial *soza* tongue is set off in the passage against the quotation of "fine fine English," as if to emphasize that now, instead of using pidgin to induct recruits into a colonial order of violence, the weapon of "fine fine English" will be used like a bludgeon to bring future troops to heel. In its code-switching between rotten English and standard English, *Sozaboy* demonstrates the extent to which "fine English" in Nigeria has traditionally functioned as a weapon of terror, keeping the linguistically impoverished underclass in line, while bending their desires toward colonial speech as a sign of power and riches.

Saro-wiwa's use of rotten English calibrates the psychic motivations for the militarization of culture in Nigeria, much like Amos Tutuola's use of "unpolished" English diction dramatizes violence in the bush.[16] In *My Life in the Bush of Ghosts* published in 1954, Tutuola mixes gods, guns, and technology in hybrid tropes (X-ray-making ghosts, the "Television-handed Ghostess," the "flash-eyed mother" ghost, who takes the form of a power station). Saro-wiwa, by contrast, mobilizes the swerves and deviations of rotten English into a rhetorical army dedicated to transposing war into speech. *Sozaboy* gives us a paradigm of war *as* speech, or *speech as a theater of war*. A name like "Hitler," for example, becomes "Hitla," an Africanized place-holder for the enemy or hit-man in a war that never seems to end. As a language that transliterates the psychic damage of war, rotten English becomes the carrier of the stress marks and psychic cavities of stymied hopes, starvation, violence, humiliation, and paralysis. The phrase "Tan Papa dere" (translated as "stand properly there") is an immobilizing command, marking the enduring partnership between colonial paternalism and military psychology in postcolonial Nigeria. Or take the word "porson," the substitute for person, in which the subject is effectively transliterated as a "poor-son," that is, an average soldier forced into war by poverty and fear of death, or as "poor sun," communicating the darkness of life at a time of unmourned death, when bodies are replaced as soon as they fall by the next round of human fodder. Even the book's structure participates in this ghostly chain of associations, its chapter divisions enumerated as "Lomber One, Two," and so on. Though "lomber" does not exist as the pidgin equivalent of "number," it sounds like it might, and this element of masquerade tricks the reader into projecting a spectral country or land of ghosts, what

Theresa Hak Cha calls a "phantomnation." The homophony with the French "l'ombre" reinforces this line of interpretation by suggesting a textual haunting or shadow book that makes its thematic apparition via the novel's representation of war. It falls once again to grammar to convey the disorienting prospect of war's physical theater: "Na just few of us remain. . . . And we no know what is bomb or that aeroplane dey shit bomb wey dey kill. And just that morning we see death. We all confuse. We no know wetin to do" (S 112). In the slippage between no and knowing, between confusing and being confused, between waiting and wetting (as in wetting yourself with fear), the psychosis of war takes shape. War is personified in a figure of speech—a personage called "Manmuswak," whose name is a contraction of the phrase "a man must live or eat by whatever means" (in a word, "shoot or be shot"). When the wounded narrator regains consciousness in a hospital, his spirit is possessed by this protean specter: "Manmuswak is here again. Oh, I cannot tell you how my heart just cut when I see this Manmuswak in the hospital. He is now nurse and chooking people with needle. What does all this mean? Am I prisoner of war? What happened to me in that bush? And why must I always see this Manmuswak man?" (S 118). Saro-wiwa's rotten English speaker is indeed a prisoner of war, a figure of reduced bellicosity—shivering, famished, sick, not sure whether he is alive or dead. Indeed he has become little more than the signifier "man," dangling tautologically on the end "this Manmuswak man," a ghosted presence at the end of a line.

Rotten English in *Sozaboy* defines the minor within a transethnic, translinguistic national context as a ghosted idiolect, at once a language of colonial mimicry ("big grammar") addressed to the specter of the vanished British colonial elite, and a conflation of war and speech, in which rhetorical aporias function as placeholders for the dead. This interpretation confirms Michael North's reading of rotten English, as "an alternative medium of national expression, one rotten with the untranslatable experiences of those the oil wealth had left behind" (PC 112). For North, rotten English holds out the utopian promise of cross-ethnic African *communitas* in a land riven by ethnic and linguistic divisionism:

> Rotten English is the language used between people who are
> away from their homelands, speaking to those with whom
> they have no close ties of culture or ethnic heritage. To propose
> brotherhood and sisterhood within that language is to propose
> a Nigeria that is not divided along ethnic and linguistic lines. As
> a hybridized, syncretic language, then, rotten English allows

Sozaboy to contradict, to speak against, the civil war at the level of form, while it is exposing the horrors of war in its content. (PC 108–109)

Where North's interpretation emphasizes the differential equation of rotten English in terms of its form (ethnic unity) and content (antiwar message), I would stress how rotten English figures death and spectrality within the rhetoric of grammatical incorrectness. The lapse of good grammar becomes a mechanism for representing ghostly aporias, double-entendres, and mimetic effects. Rotten English, in this sense, is English in a minor key— strange and sad—an off-kilter English that "translates" political trauma into linguistic mourning. Saro-wiwa's stigmatized, déclassé English may thus be read, as both a stand-in for Khanna—a micro-minority language globally restricted to Ogoni speakers—and as the memorial function of its ungrammaticality. This is English riddled with holes and bumps: the potholes where native languages have been expunged, and the poorly fitting manhole covers of "big grammar" thrown hastily on top of the gaps where native languages used to be.

Rotten English, in Saro-wiwa's inventive, idiosyncratic version of it, yields a spell-binding aesthetics of the minor not just because it is used to militate on behalf of oppressed and impoverished citizens, and not just because the minority tongue of its *soza* speaker substitutes for a micro-minority language such as Khana, inaccessible to world readership, but also because it invents a form of nonstandard English expressive of traumatized speech. Defective grammar leads to parapraxes (slips of the tongue) that encrypt the spectral presence of the dead, function as signage for unspeakable acts, and limn the outlines of historical tragedy, past and future: colonial wars of independence, civil war, and most recently, ecology wars—environmental, cultural, and linguistic—in which the oil-invested interests of the Nigerian state are pitched against the barest survival of ethnic minorities.

A comparable use of nonstandard language as the expression of traumatic survival can be found in Amadou Kourouma's *Allah n'est pas obligé*, a novel published in 2000 about kid armies in war-torn Liberia. As in Saro-wiwa's novel, the *soza* establishes identity in a rotten tongue: "M'appelle Birahima. Suis p'tit nègre. Pas parce suis black et gosse. Non! Mais suis p'tit nègre parce que je parle mal le français"[17] ("Call myself Birahima. I'm a blackboy. Not because I'm black and a kid. No! I'm black 'cause I speak broken French"). As in *Sozaboy*, translation in *Allah n'est pas obligé* is at the heart of the literary project: "Il faut expliquer parce que mon blablabla est à lire par toute sorte de gens: des toubabs (toubab signifie blanc) colons, des noirs indigènes sauvages d'Afrique et des francophones de tout gabarit (gabarit signifie genre)" ("Have to explain because my blablabla must be read by all kinds of people: toubabs (toubab means white), colonizers, black African savages, and French speakers of every mold (mold in the sense of genre)."[18] Moving among the languages and dialects of Malinké, English, pidgin, colonial French, standard French, and Parisian argot with a kind of mock pedantry (the narrator is constantly showing off his lexical erudition), the novel is an exercise in word-trafficking. Like arms, diamonds, or contraband, words are valued, exchanged, and fought over; the more you can stockpile the currency, the more power you wield. And as in *Sozaboy*, multilingual collisions within speech have the same casual, yet explosive shock value as the acts they so often describe, be it rape, pillage, abandonment, dismemberment, massacre, or ethnocide.

Saro-wiwa's rotten English and Kourouma's rotten French convey the parallel universe of war as linguistic realism. Both texts bring to mind James Baldwin's essay "If Black English Isn't a Language, Then Tell Me What Is?"[19] In arguing that Black English articulates the "reality" of racial and ethnic oppression, and in maintaining that modern American usage owes its language of jazz and blues to the sorry history of slavery embedded in Black English, Baldwin makes his case for seeing Black English as its own language, wearing its stigmas of ungrammaticality like a proud badge, and refusing classification by white grammarians as "Black Vernacular English": a term implicitly casting Black English as a deficient version of the vehicular tongue. Following Baldwin, we might define rotten English as the fount of an order of literateness that negotiates on its own terms with conventional standards of literary "excellence" or readability, and which affords literature written in nonstandard language the same kind of deconstructive intensity routinely assigned to canonical literary works. In redrawing the cartography of the global literature, it will no longer suffice to plot the coordinates of minor and micro-minority literatures according to their national, ethnic, or linguistic location on the periphery. The challenge will be to show how language wars and reading wars have revolutionized the protocols of readability and transformed the terms of response to Sartre's famous question "What is Literature?"

10

The Language of Damaged Experience

"Rotten" language converges with "damaged" language just as postcolonial theory converges with Frankfurt school thought in new forms of literary comparatism.[1] Theodor Adorno's *Minima Moralia* subtitled *Reflexionen aus dem beschädigten Leben* (Reflections from Damaged Life), published in 1951, emerges as a fulcrum for such comparatism. Though Adorno's life-world, shattered as it was by his conviction that Hitler had wrought the death of culture, was of course distinctly different from that of a postcolonial critic (the phobia of American mass culture, for a start, was a unique theoretical impetus for Adorno and his colleagues, while the same could not be said of many postcolonial theorists), I would argue nonetheless that the mix of Marxism and diasporic consciousness filtering both critical tendencies abuts in a keen sense of the "damage" to the human caused by capitalism, or, to borrow Adorno's phrase precisely, "the withering of experience" ("als Erfahrungskern überlebt"), itself the result of extreme capitalism, labor wastage, and technological functionalism:

> The new human type [Adorno wrote] cannot be properly under-
> stood without awareness of what he is continuously exposed to
> from the world of things about him, even in his most secret in-
> nervations. What does it mean for the subject that there are no
> more casement windows to open, but only sliding frames to
> shove, no gentle latches but turnable handles, no forecourt, no
> doorstep before the street, no wall around the garden? . . . Not
> least to blame for the withering of experience is the fact that
> things under the law of pure functionality, assume a form that

limits contact with them to mere operation, and tolerates no surplus, either in freedom of conduct or in autonomy of things, which would survive as the core of experience, because it is not consumed by the moment of action.[2]

This is not just nostalgia for the lost artisanal status of things. At the end of the century, in the era of what Benedict Anderson characterizes as "late nationalism," in twin-set with late capitalism, the idea of subjective damage, or the withering human, becomes a way of talking once again about class—specifically, the class that has been globally downsized, packed up and moved out, micro-minoritized, or managed like an exilic community within national borders. The case I will be discussing in most detail concerns white colonialism in proletarian Scotland.

But before I address Irvine Welsh's novel *Trainspotting*, and the Danny Boyle film that gave it celebrity currency on the global literary market, a few more words are in order about Adorno's notion of damaged or withered experience in *Minima Moralia*. Influenced throughout the 1930s by Max Horkheimer's sense that, in Susan Buck-Morss's words, "cognition had to acknowledge the reality of human suffering but also that the act of cognition itself had a somatic character," Adorno's thought was also profoundly indebted to Walter Benjamin's writing, in which: "thought presses close to its object, as if through touching, smelling, tasting, it wanted to transform itself" (Adorno, "A Portrait of Walter Benjamin," in *Prisms*).[3]

Language is the subaltern carrier of cognition's soma. In a section of an essay on Brecht's *Threepenny Opera*, Benjamin distilled a category called "crude thinking," referring to the "speeches and maxims, confessions and pleas" that stand apart in Macheathe's monologues. Created by the masses, according to Benjamin, crude thinking is epitomized by proverbs such as: "There's no smoke without fire" or "You can't make an omelette without eggs." These lead-weight utterances belong to "the household of dialectical thinking," because they enable action; indeed, "thought must be crude in order to come into its own in action."[4] For Benjamin, the raw, prole commonplace typical of "crude thought," operates as the engine of Brechtian satire, which pivots on expressions that "lay bare the fellow citizen," peeling back life's "legal drapery" to the point where "human content emerges . . . naked" (UB 83).

Just as Benjamin would look to Brechtian *lumpen* dialect for the inflections of a raw humanity, so Adorno would turn, interestingly enough, to North Berlin and Cockney speech for one of the keys to understanding subjective damage. In a section of *Minima Moralia* called "Not half hungry" (a British expression meaning "starving," that correlates to the German *kohldampf*—"steamed cabbage," or "poor man's food"), Adorno interprets workers' dialect as the bitter taste of class self-hatred:

> To play off workers' dialects against the written language is reactionary. Leisure, even pride and arrogance, have given the language of the upper classes a certain independence and self-discipline. It is thus brought into opposition to its own social sphere. It turns against the masters, who misuse it to command, by seeking to command them, and refuses to serve their interests. The language of the subjected, on the other hand, domination alone has stamped, so robbing them further of the justice promised by the unmutilated, autonomous word to all those free enough to pronounce it without rancour. Proletarian language is dictated by hunger. The poor chew words to fill their bellies. From the objective spirit of language they expect the sustenance refused them by society; those whose mouths are full of words have nothing else between their teeth. So they take revenge on language. Being forbidden to love it, they maim the body of language, and so repeat in impotent strength the disfigurement inflicted on them. Even the best qualities of the North Berlin or Cockney dialects, the ready repartee, the mother wit, are marred by the need, in order to endure desperate situations without despair, to mock themselves along with the enemy, and so to acknowledge the way of the world.

And this is the really strange part:

> If the written language codifies the estrangement of classes [due Entfremdung der Klassen], redress cannot lie in regression to the spoken, but only in the consistent exercise of strictest linguistic objectivity. Only a speaking that transcends writing by absorbing it, can deliver human speech from the lie that it is already human. (MM 102)

Though on one level Adorno seems to be fingering working-class dialect as a resource of *ressentiment* capable of turning against the master from within his own house, on another level he seems bent on militating in favor of the "literarification" of all human speech, such that, purged of barbarism, it realizes historical objectivity, and thus feeds itself no longer on the junk food of infelicitous grammar. The phrase calling for the "deliverance of human speech from the lie that it is already human" echoes the Benjaminian notion of humanity bared by satire, taken down to the bone of a harrowing, yet mesmerizing language of expletives and downbeat social realism—a "crude thought" lying in wait to feed its hunger on the defiles of standard language.

The linguistic construal of damaged life as a scrip conjoining class and cognition is directly relevant to the political aesthetic embedded in Irvine Welsh's low-life 1993 novel *Trainspotting*. The title is already in idiolect, for it is a slang term designating a favorite British pastime in the era of steam engines that consisted of collecting train-car numbers and their appointed station destinations. The trainspotter, as Randolph Stow reminds us, was the synonym of the preminent Nerd, preoccupied "with making his fellow citizens live like battery hens. He loves regimented living quarters, dining facilities and child-care arrangements. He adores interfering in other people's sex lives. He frequently shows an obsession with the trivia of decor: one of the ways in which the genes betray the Nerdish nature."[5] As in the way of all good appropriationism, the term's usage has moved off its "regimental" course and come to refer to the broader category of the loser, whiling away dead time, or doing drugs. The vocabulary of trains—"mainlining," "tracks," "spotting the vein," "getting a rush," a "hit," "crashing," or "getting wrecked"—is also the argot of smack addiction. Trainspotters, even if they are sympathetic dossers or vagabonds, and especially if they are junkies, are the lowest of the low.

In the Danny Boyle film, these associations may be cued to the scene where four junkies are sitting in a field, reflecting on the dead end of the Scots prole. He's the lowest of the low, so low in fact, that a nation of wankers (the English) lords it over him, relegating him to a state of neo-citizenship completely off the map of franchise. Both the movie and the book explore this peculiar strain of internal colonization as a kind of linguistic depressant, mired in the bog of poverty, class claustrophobia, addiction, and national self-cancellation.

Welsh belongs to a group of contemporary writers, including Iain Banks, James Kelman, and Duncan McLean who have created a fashion for Scottish "minor literature" by inventing an edgy, contemporary idiom orthographically transposed into what often seems to be another language, or at the very least a pseudo- or intralingual (English to English) translation. Now there has always been a folkloric tradition of regional accents in the British novel, well exemplified, say, by George Eliot's *Adam Bede*. Here, interestingly enough, it is a droll Scotsman who is introduced to play the "accent card":

I think it was his pedigree only that had the advantage of being Scotch, and not his "bringing up"; for except that he had a stronger burr in his accent, his speech differed little from that of the Loamshire people about him. But a gardener is Scotch, as a French teacher is Parisian.

"Well, Mr Poyser," he said, before the good farmer had time to speak, "ye'll not be carrying your hay to-morrow, I'm thinking: the glass sticks at 'change,' and ye may rely upo' my word as we'll ha' more downfall afore twenty-four hours is past. Ye see that darkish-blue cloud there upo' the 'rizon—you know what I mean by the 'rizon, where the land and sky seems to meet."

"Ay, ay, I see the cloud," said Mr Poyser, "'rizon or no 'rizon. It's right ov'er Mike Holdworth's fallow, and a foul fallow it is."[6]

The "translation" of the Scotsman's 'rizon into the Loamshire farmer's "fallow" (with its nasty pun on "foul fellow"directed at a neighbor) suggests that property disputes between local landowners (Mr. Poyser and Mr. Holdworth) outstrip the potential class and regional tensions between Mr. Poyser and his gardener. The accent differential, insofar as it is treated as no impediment to communication between Scots gardener and British employer, confirms an idealized picture of solidarity between landed classes and immigrant workers. Accent is thus politically neutralized as an additive of local color, providing ethnographic density to tableaus of rural life. Insofar as it also opens a portal into the regional consciousness of the Scots gardener working in Loamshire, this consciousness remains as closely bounded by the conventions of British realist fiction as the enclosed land parcel on which the gardener labors.

By contrast, the "New Scotologists," as they have been dubbed, use accent to situate the reader directly in the mental basin of urban regional consciousness. Typically, how the narrators see the world is filtered through how the narrators speak the world, that is, through orally inflected interior monologue. In James Kelman's Booker prize–winning novel *How Late It Was, How Late* (1994) language becomes the measure of extreme physical violence as a homeless man is nearly bludgeoned to death and blinded by the police. The fate of his stumbling frame, drifting through the serpentine pathways of the "system," becomes the story of a body so fearful that it muffles the subject's articulation of a legitimate claim to compensation in dialectal frustration: "But he wouldnay get his fucking Dysfuckingfunctional

Benefit man he would be lucky to get fucking re-registered christ almighty, and the actual compen was a joke."⁷

If Kelman specializes in linguistic splicing and deformities of utterance associative of the hand-to-mouth survival of the disabled vagrant, Duncan McLean unleashes an outward-directed, equally abusive orality. His short story collection *Bucket of Tongues* is described on the book jacket by Janice Galloway as "detailing the casual cruelty and absurdity, the daftness and awfulness of what passes for physical and verbal communication between folk. . . . This is lean, maggoty writing."⁸ McClean's novel *Bunker Man* (1992) rivals *Trainspotting* in its reliance on scatological nastiness. The story of a recently married school "jannie," the prose starts off relatively clean of Scottish burrs or swear words, but as the janitor becomes progressively ashamed of his profession as master of the "bothy," his speech becomes increasingly freighted with foul slang. A turning point occurs in the course of an argument with his wife Karen over a "translation" problem. Karen objects to his vernacular (and racist) use of "cunt" as an all-purpose word for "weirdo."

> You know me Karen, he said. You know I know the score. You don't have to be black to be a cunt, I know that. I mean, look at the fucking playground pervert, he's not black. But he is a cunt. He's a weirdo. Nothing to do with the colour of his skin, he's just a sick cunt. . . .
>
> Karen shook her head, then turned and started walking slowly along the road. Rob fell into step beside her.
>
> Even that, she said quietly. Even there, you see, you've changed. Saying things like that.
>
> Like what?
>
> Like . . . like calling people cunts. You never used to do that.
>
> What!
>
> You shouldn't do it, it's not fine.
>
> I've always talked about cunts!
>
> No you haven't. Not to me.
>
> But . . .
>
> You've talked about my cunt. You've talked sexy and talked about your cock and my cunt. Okay. That's alright. That's using the word properly.
>
> So?
>
> So you shouldn't start calling folk you hate after a part of me!

They can't hear.

Robbie! It's not them who mind. It's me. It hurts my feelings.[9]

Rob's use of "cunt" is presented as tantamount to conjugal betrayal, thereby anticipating one of the novel's most lurid scenes in which Rob arranges to have Karen raped by Bunker Man in retribution for an imagined infidelity.

The New Scotologists may be been classed among the white postcolonials of the British Isles who have given enhanced notoriety to "minor literature." David Lloyd has applied the term "minor literature" to writing by Britain's Irish cultural nationalists,[10] borrowing the term somewhat problematically from Gilles Deleuze and Félix Guattari's book on Kafka.[11] In a seminal chapter entitled "What Is Minor Literature?" Deleuze and Guattari analyzed Kafka's German as a pastiche of the "vehicular" tongue—meaning in this case the impoverished bureaucratese, the hollow state language imposed on Czechoslovakia by the Prussian state. According to their reading, Kafka subverted the vehicular by freighting it with unwelcome baggage, from Yiddish inflections to scraps of Czech vernacular. Now, even if the newly edited and translated Malcolm Pasley/Mark Harman editions of Kafka reveal a very differently textured use of the German language from the one characterized by Deleuze and Guattari, their argument is still valid insofar as it attempts to rescue the immanent, "becoming-animal" Kafka from the postwar, "Darkness at Noon" grip of spiritual anti–Iron Curtain allegory.

Kafka's German may be compared to Irvine Welsh's minoritarian English in the way in which it allows the animality of language to shine through; whether it is in accent transliteration (the "goatiness" of the word "goat," the Scots pronunciation of "got") or in similes of embodied animation and ingestion. A smack-injected phallus writhes like an ugly sea-snake; steak-mince and vomit stick in the craw; and the junkie beats his meat or vein, aiming for a hit. Language is the needle that pricks the reader into awareness of the deathliness of humanness, its proximity to meat or matter. Whether or not one interprets this raw immanence as part of a strategy to reveal hypocrisy festering within the humanist welfare-state, what Welsh and the New Scotologists seem to have in common is the use of invective, honed to the bone of explosive regional utterance.

Welsh's Scottish vernacular is not so much a transposition of accent and slang, but a subcultural *Sprache* that has the effect of wounding Standard English with the slings and arrows of warped speech, at least for a Brit or Anglophone reader outside of Scotland. Though some critics may argue that this warping effect is simply a matter of "eye dialect"—the use of nonstandard spelling to identify colloquial pronunciation—I would venture that Welsh's orthography contains a multigrained political aesthetic, a postcolonial politics of class. Even if one acknowledges the justified concern that reading too much into Welsh's rendering of "just the way people talk" risks exoticizing Scots working-class culture in a neocolonial way, I would argue with David Lloyd, in his chapter of *Anomalous States: Irish Writing and the Postcolonial Moment*, that "writing in the shit," or as Welsh puts it, listening to "gadges talkin through their erses" (T 126) lends a new ear to "damaged life" as the aural incision of capitalism on experience.

At first glance the obstacles to reading a page of *Trainspotting* create a shock to the system; there is such a disjunction between eye and ear, such a preponderance of what Deleuze and Guattari call "tensors" or nodes of pain. The "incorrect use of prepositions; the abuse of the pronominal; the employment of malleable verbs . . . the multiplication and succession of adverbs; the use of pain-filled connotations; the importance of accent as a tension internal to the word; and the distribution of consonants and vowels as part of an internal discordance," these were the traits of the tensor, by which Deleuze and Guattari, following Wagenbach, distinguished Kafka's Prague German. Along these lines, Welsh's Edinburgh dialect can be seen as a tensored language deeply indebted to Joycean linguistic play.[12]

It was of course Joyce who most famously mined Irish brogue for its cache of puns and double-entendres. *Finnegan's Wake*, in particular, fabricates a verbal fantastic out of vernacular expression, as in:

> His howd feeled heavy, his hoddit did shake. (There was a wall of course in erection) Dimb! He stottored from the latter. Damb! He was dud. Dumb! Mastabatoom, mastabadtomm, when a mon merries his lute is all long. For whole the world to see.
>
> Shize? I should shee! Macool, Macool, orra whyi deed ye diie? of a trying thirstay mournin? Sobs they sighdid at Fillagain's chrissormiss wake, all the hoolivans of the nation, prostrated in their consternation and their duodismally profusive plethora of ululation.[13]

In this scene of maudlin drunks fantasizing the erection of a corpse, Joyce embeds the image of a randy, impotent, moribund Irish nation that anticipates Welsh's semi-ironic chapter title "Scotland Takes Drugs in Psychic Defense." The word "duodismally," with its spin on duodecimal (systems of accounts payable), the saddest twelve days of Christmas (duodecimal signifies twelfths), and stomach trouble (duodenum is the medical term for intestine), generates a psychic economy of dyspepsia and national melancholia.

The play on "thirstay mournin," and on "Shize" and "shee," kneading together themes of inebriation and excretion, also underscores the image of a body-politic overwhelmed by bodily functions, wallowing self-pityingly in its own shit. On this score, *Trainspotting*'s descriptions of "pungent showers" of "skittery shite, thin alcohol sick, and vile pish," of characters diving into toilets or complaining of flooded tampons, may be read as a nineties echo of Joycean billingsgate, though Welsh's language is less poetic and more faithful to everyday speech:[14]

> We're drinking on a balcony bar, and our attention is caught by a squad of nutters entering the crowded pub below. They swagger in, noisy and intimidating.
>
> Ah hate cunts like that. Cunts like Begbie. Cunts that are intae baseball-batting every fucker that's different; pakis, poofs, n what huv ye. Fuckin failures in a country ay failures. It's nae good blamin it oan the English fir colonising us. Ah don't hate the English. They're just wankers. We are colonised by wankers. We can't even pick a decent, vibrant, healthy culture to be colonised by. No. We're ruled by effete arseholes. What does that make us? The lowest of the fuckin low, the scum of the earth. The most wretched, servile, miserable, pathetic trash that was ever shat intae creation. Ah don't hate the English. They just git oan we the shite thuv goat. Ah hate the Scots. (T 78)

The trope of being "wanked by wankers" figures white colonization as a state of political domination *en abyme* (Scots colonized by Scots colonized by Brits colonized by the global economy), compounded by abject servility, a psychic dependency correlative with the narrator's dependency on heroin. The English are the Big Smack, assuming the guise of the bad mother, aka Mother Superior, the street name for the local dealer, Johnny Swan.

> Ah went tae take a shot. It took us ages to find a good vein. Ma boys don't live as close tae the surface as maist people's. When it came, ah savoured the hit. Ali was right. Take yir best orgasm, multiply the feeling by twenty, and you're still fuckin miles off the pace. Ma dry, cracking bones are soothed and liquefied by ma beautiful heroine's tender caresses. The earth moved, and it's still moving. (T 11)

The maternal leitmotif comes to the ear through the pronunciation of "my" as "ma," and through reference to the "heroine's tender caresses," an image of the social body seduced by a soporific matriarchal embrace. Lulled by "the lady," depressed Scotland returns to a preoedipal state of libidinal depletion and ego loss. Internal colonization is thus represented through a subcultural language of addiction and class oppression. This amalgamation of prolespeak, drug argot, and pop-cultural lingo is also used to draw attention to the neo-imperialism of American global culture throughout Europe, as in a scene where Sick Boy tries to humiliate two Asian tourists:

> —Can I help you? Where are you headed? ah ask. *Good old-fashioned Scoattish hoshpitality, aye, ye cannae beat it, shays the young Sean Connery, the new Bond, cause girls, this is the new bondage . . .*
> —We're looking for the Royal Mile, a posh, English-colonial voice answers back in ma face. What a fucking we pump-up-the-knickers n aw. *Simple Simon sais, put your hands on your feet . . .*
> Of course, the Rent Boy is looking like a flaccid prick in a barrel-load of fannies. Sometimes ah really think the gadge still believes that an erection is for pishing over high walls. (T 29, emphasis in text)

The "Sh" sound signifies unhappy Scottishness. It may be read as a verbal tic of class resentment—smarmy, sarcastic and malevolent—erupting violently inside the words "hosh*pitality," and "pi*sh." The fear of impotence swirls through Sick Boy's speech; even the evocation of Scotland's only genuine action hero, James Bond, spirals self-defeatingly out of control in the form of a pun on girls in bondage. The schoolyard refrain "Simple Simon says, put your hands on your feet" becomes the pathetic jingle of losers reduced to compensatory rape-fantasy. Sick Boy's free-associating parapraxes articulate Scotland's servile relation to the United Kingdom and the United States, with James Bond(age) serving in the role of Scotland's prostitute-ambassador, the country's premier global export, alongside salmon and single malt. Ultimately *Trainspotting* itself, both the novel and the "fab-four" movie, can be placed on this continuum of cultural products that "capitalize" exploitation. In simplest terms, the dole-and-dope social formation characterized as "wanked by wankers" is converted via language politics into "wanking the wankers" on a world stage.

Though "wanking the wankers" goes nowhere politically, it encapsulates the end-game of late capitalism, somatizing its most useless citizens, sloughing them off into dark rooms with tourniquets, needles, spoons, and small flames.

Suddenly it's cauld; very fuckin cauld. The candle's nearly melted doon. The only real light's comin fae the telly. Something black and white's on . . . but the telly's a black and white set so it was bound tae be something black and white . . . wi a colour telly, it wid be different . . . perhaps.

It's freezing, but movement only makes ye caulder; by making ye more aware that there's fuck all you can do, fuck all you can really do, tae get warm. At least if ah stey still ah can pretend to masel ah have the power tae make masel warm, by just moving around or switching the fire oan. The trick is tae be as still as possible. It's easier than dragging yourself across the flair tae switch that fuckin fire oan.

Somebody else is in the room wi us. It's Spud, ah think. It's hard tae tell in the dark.

—Spud . . . Spud . . .

He sais nothing.

—It's really fuckin cauld man.

Spud, if indeed it is the cunt, still says nothing. He could be deid, but probably no, because ah think his eyes are open. But that means fuck all. (T 95)

In Junk Dilemma 65, OD'ing becomes a metaphor for the benumbed body-politic caught in the state of becoming-corpse. The flickering black and white TV screen, hovering at the on/off button like life itself, marks the loss of "living color," the freezing of volition, and the withering away of experience.

11

CNN Creole: Trademark Literacy and

Global Language Travel

Translational language, loosely defined as language in transit, has enjoyed a long association with genres of travel-writing charged with covering the life of linguistic contact zones. At its best, the travelogue gave us Alexis de Tocqueville in America, Théophile Gautier in Algeria, Washington Irving in Spain, Edith Wharton in Morocco, Ernestine Hill in Australia, and more recently, the contemporary picaresque of Bruce Chatwin and V. S. Naipaul. But now, increasingly, it seems to be a discredited, outmoded kind of writing. Defined in its stock form by the dictates of local color (from the virtuoso description of landscape and monuments to sketches of exotic customs and the sounds of foreign tongues), the travelogue, like its cousin, the anthropological brief, has been tainted as the preserve of neocolonial mentalities, and as the camouflage of a leisure industry that reinforces the class and race inequities of local economies. More significant still, as commercial monocultures extend their geopolitical reach, and nationality, ethnic affiliation, and heritage start to lose their distinctiveness in the welter of international media markets, the travelogue becomes obsolete. People, news, and money transfer physically and virtually with enhanced acceleration; hotel chains and Web sites offer increasingly packaged, generic accommodation; and pocket translators promise instant (if rudimentary) communication. Accordingly, the idea of travel erodes as an experience of cultural shape-shifting, replaced by a market model of import and export, by an image of world culture in the thrall of a traveling media circus, and by an emergent micro-genre of terrorism reportage featuring tourists or embedded journalists as targets of violence. This last generic shift can be charted in Michel

Houellebecq's 2001 novel *Plateforme*. With its scene of an attack on French sex tourists in Thailand, the novel ghoulishly predicted both 9/11 and the massacre of holiday makers in Bali.

Houellebecq's characters, cosseted in air-conditioned bubbles of monolingual sex and sociability, spell the replacement of the travelogue with the tourist novel permeated by the media-speak of global capitalism. But this culturally leveling mode of product placement and popular culture is hardly confined to Euro-American fiction. We find it cropping up in postcolonial fiction too, assuming the guise of what I will call "CNN Creole." Here, brand names build up into a new kind of language as they intersect with the languages of their reception. In this sense, conventional notions of travel should be adjusted to include the problem of global media diffusion, specifically the worldwide roving of consumer product names within regional languages, idiolects, and hybrid or creolized tongues. This involves assessing what happens when the names for commodities—what the philologist Leo Spitzer called "nonce-words"—are entered into literary expression.

Spitzer was particularly interested in how brand names functioning as corporate logos constitute a particular kind of neologism, breaking down the normal barriers of resistance to language change to gain universal linguistic currency. The Eastman firm, Spitzer pointed out, "created the new word *Kodak*, but would never have thought of replacing *taught* by *teached*, however logical or practical the latter may be, or of changing the pronunciation of English!" Individuals, he affirmed, have little chance of imposing comparable linguistic innovation:

> With the word *Kodak* we have given an example of a relatively recent individual innovation in word-formation ratified by a community (indeed by a world-community). This case stands for thousands of modern words in our languages designating objects in the commercial, industrial, scientific, technological, social and political areas of our civilization which did not exist before: indeed, the number of these new words (corresponding to the number of new objects) is a startling phenomenon in our modern times—in whichever period of world history have individuals (like the Eastman Kodak firm) enjoyed the power of disseminating new, arbitrarily coined terms in such number and over such large areas? How rarely has an individual in the past been able thus to influence linguistically the whole world?[1]

The Kodak case in his essay on "The Individual Factor in Linguistic Innovations" recalls, of course, Spitzer's more famous analysis of the Sunkist orange-juice label in his 1949 piece "American Advertising as Popular Art," where he famously applied his philological method to mass culture. While mining the symbolism of the brand name, Spitzer presciently stumbled on a useful way of describing the phenomenon of global language travel.

> In the drugstores throughout our country, the brand of oranges known as *Sunkist* was advertised some years ago by the following picture-with-text: on a high mountain range, covered with snow that glistens in the bright sunshine, furrowed by vertical gullies, towering over a white village with its neat, straight rows of orange trees, there rests a huge orange-colored sun, inscribed with the word "Sunkist."[2]

An accompanying note situates the orange juice ad in the genealogy of sixteenth- and seventeenth-century emblem literature. *Sunkist* becomes a heraldic device whereby the product is enframed in a scene of California pastoral before the incursion of Man, an Edenic concentrate of freshness "kissed by the sun." Marveling at how this feat of commercial expression erases awareness of "selling and profit-making," Spitzer takes the explication round again, returning the "modern advertisement to a medieval form" as he links the temptation of forbidden fruit to the apples on "the eleventh-century portal of the Hildesheim cathedral, in a bas-relief representing the scene of the Fall of Man" (AA 335). In another pass, the distortedly grand scale of the orange, portrayed on a par with its mountain surround, conjures up the " 'naive' technique of the medieval paintings, in which Christ is presented taller than his disciples." From here, Spitzer free-associates to "the Nuremberg tin soldiers, whose captain is twice as tall as the common soldier," and then on to the grandiose size of the juice glass, read as a "concession of realism to the beholder," a counterweight of the "critical attitude" to "the naive." Ultimately the orange is set off as a *mise en abyme* of business itself:

> That glass of orange-juice as tall as the mountains of California is a clear testimonial to the businessman's subjective estimation of the comparative importance of business interests. Indeed, when we view the violence done to Nature in our picture (displacement of proportions, surrealistic use of a motif, change of the natural color of objects), we see how, in a very artistic manner, this procedure has served to illustrate, in a spirit, ultimately, of candid self-criticism, the very nature of business which, while

associating itself with Nature, subordinates her to its purpose—
and to ours. Our picture has used all the attractions of living Nature in order to advertize her commercialized form. (AA 339)

Echoing Theodor Adorno and Max Horkheimer's profound disaffection
with American commercialism, Spitzer, in line with Heidegger, seized on
the important relation of language to technology; particularly postwar language's object love (introjection) for the names of things, gadgets, and products. In "The Individual Factor in Linguistic Innovations," he measured the
potential power accruing to this industrial-strength version of trademark
literacy in quantitative terms, noting that the sum total of neologisms
spawned by modern business far surpassed those coined by "all the rulers
of the world, the Alexanders, the Caesars, Augustuses, Napoléons, taken
together" (IF 66).

Treating name-brand monikers with pronounced paranoia ("it is
only the fanatical desire of the commercial world to make appear their products as totally new and unheard of that encourages them to create words that
we would otherwise only expect from victims of hallucinations"), Spitzer
nevertheless dignified their construction with his etymological attentions
(IF 66). He observed "the systematic abbreviation of long words that no
longer correspond to the accelerated tempo of hasty civilization (*bus-omni-
bus, métro/politain*)." He ennobled acronym words (CGT, GOP, URSS), by
comparing them to "the *nomina sacra* of the Middle Ages of the *Inri* type."
He evoked artistry to describe "the free handling of word formation (*klee-
nex, lastex*) with a commercial suffix," and evinced awe at "the indulgence
in foreign word-elements freely introduced, the puns, the colloquialisms
introduced into the written text, the juggling with spelling." Finally, he
crowned the word *Kodak* with the supreme honor of moving "beyond the
limits of language" (IF 66). Undercutting his own posture of dismay, Spitzer's analysis afforded a perfect test case for just how well this language of
the logo travels, taking up space in the philologist's repertory, insinuating
itself into the most subliminal recesses of diction. This is traveling language
at its carpetbagging best.

Of course the idea of language travel is a given of historical and
cultural linguistics, particularly in the study of how loan words signify as
colporteurs, defining trade routes and contact zones, and indexing migration
patterns on the ground. But what happens in a global economy when information and linguistic usage travel above ground, via the airways of media
and internet channels? Global idiom and slang penetrate language commu-

nities ever more rapidly and pervasively, sidestepping the traditional carriers of linguistic cosmopolitanism—newspapers and books—which depend on more traditional literacy networks. The question becomes, how will the global incursion of media-speak affect contemporary literature that seeks to write about the present, especially in postcolonial contexts in which the politics of indigenousness has been rightfully suspicious of globalism, posing it as a threat to native language and cultural integrity?

The novelist and critic Maryse Condé faced this issue when she took on the *créolité* movement in the Antilles, arguing that the culture of the islands laid no more claim to authenticity than its diaspora cousins. For years, she points out, the islands themselves have been melting pots, destinations of immigrants from Haiti and the Dominican Republic who threw their linguistic and cultural inflections into the mix. On the other side, half a million Guadeloupians and Martinicans live permanently in France. "Ils s'expriment de la même manière que les petits Hexagonaux, leurs camarades de classse. Pour eux, cet accent antillais, avaleur de *r*, dont parle Frantz Fanon, n'est plus Dieu merci qu'un souvenir. Ils lisent rarement, mais regardent énormément de dessins animés japonais ou américains à la télévision."[3] (They express themselves in the same way as the little Hexagonals, their classmates. For them, this Antillean accent, swallowing the *r* which Frantz Fanon spoke of, is no more, thank God, than a memory. They rarely read, but watch enormous amounts of Japanese and American cartoons on television.) These emigrant Caribbeans, according to Condé, are generally regarded with contempt by those who stayed at home. "Their accent is parodied, as is their inability to function well in Creole. . . . their culture is rejected or marginalized because it fails to correspond to a defined norm of authenticity. . . . they are derided as 'Negropolitains' or 'Neg'zagonals' " (PC 307). Underscoring the need to launch a new kind of *créolité* discussion that would take stock of the transnational, media-saturated nature of contemporary Caribbean culture, while moving beyond outmoded oppositions between Creole and French, Condé admonishes the eminent Martinican author Raphaël Confiant, who, in his strident Creoleophone days, reproached Aimé Césaire for writing in French. Césaire, Condé contends, should not be held accountable to nativism. Championing the writer's right to commit to a tongue of his or her own choosing, she extols Césaire's invention of "une parole césairienne," a "Césaire language" (a double-entendre, if one reads this as a verbal cesarean section, an incision below the belly of the mother tongue). Condé identifies contemporary Caribbeanness with the confluence of old and new forms of popular expression: rap alongside gwoka, boulevard theater next to the traditional vigil, root-poetry

(Max Rippon, Césaire, Derek Walcott) conjugated with border culture (Gloria Anzaldua) (PC 309). Significantly, Condé ends her critique of essentialist language politics by quoting not from a fellow Francophone Creole, but from an Anglophone counterpart, the Guyanese writer Wilson Harris: "When one dreams, one dreams alone. When one writes a book, one is alone" (PC 310). The language quoted is as important as the message contained in the citation, for the fact that Condé insists on stepping outside the parochialism of a Francophone *créolilté* debate into the larger sphere of Caribbean discourses that articulate themselves beyond the archipelago, is in itself a cosmopolitan stand, an implicit decision to scrutinize language politics through a transnational lens.

Condé's defense of the chosen tongue comes into focus as a response to the more hegemonic dicta of the famous *Éloge de la créolité*, coauthored in 1989 by Confiant, Patrick Chamoiseau, and Jean Bernabé. Though the manifesto defines Creole and Caribbeanness in inclusive terms, stressing the transnational geopolitical sweep from the Americas to Guyana, as well as the explosive fusion of cultures, it does in fact mandate certain prohibitions. French slang, for example, is decreed as *verboten* to writers of Creole: "Caribbean writers' use of French slang, slang which is already in itself an identity established in the language, is, it seems to us, a powerful cultural alienation. With the use of slang one goes outside the neutral field of language and enters a particular dimension: one adopts both a vision of the world and a vision of the language itself."[4] Confiant shifted position on this from the time he collaborated on the *Éloge* to when he began writing the collection of novellas *Bassin des ouragans* and its sequel, *La Savane des pétrifications* in the mid-nineties. In 1994 he told an interviewer:

> I had a shock this year. The Italian editors of the Thousand and One Nights series—which launched the ten-franc book—decided to publish modern authors. And when they asked me to contribute to the series, they stipulated that I write about the present. . . . It was the first time in my life that I wrote the word *television* in a text! This word, exactly like *computer* or *AIDS*, was absolutely foreign to my imagination. I was born in the fifties, my universe inhabited by sugar plantations, smoking distilleries, Hindu ceremonies. . . . I'm infused with the Martinican society of that time. It was extremely difficult for me to write about the present.[5]

In the early phase of his career, Confiant devoted himself to an orthodox Creolophone agenda. The fiction he wrote in Creole (*Jik dèyè do Bondyé,*

Jou Baré, Bitako-a, Marisosé self-translated into French as *Mamzelle Libellule*) and Kod Yamn (translated into French by Gerry L'Etang as *Le Gouverneur des dés*) effectively walled him off from reception by a wide reading public, and his *Lettres créoles* (1991) fetishized the Creole language as a repository of history, the living record of slavery and the abuses of plantation culture. So it is safe to surmise that the switch to CNN Creole in *Bassin* and *La Savane* (the latter has on its title page the letters *CNN* pictorially emblazoned, like an escutcheon against the backdrop of a TV screen) was a sea change of major proportions, an act of dramatic time travel, as radical, in terms of its impact on the writer's language politics, as the transplantation of literary habitus from one country to another.

In *La Savane* Confiant uses a Creole-inflected French, awash in commercial colloquialisms, to collapse distance and time, locating the postplantation culture of Martinique in the here-and-now of TV news.[6] He also uses narrative chronotypes to destabilize the historical present, as when, in *Bassin*, he makes Creole culture the subject of a mock archaeological excavation, examined as a specimen of a civilization long dead. The jaw bones of *Homo martinicensis* are seen to have evolved their morphology to fit the self-negating rote phrases beaten into speech by the colonizer: "La France est le plus beau pays du monde," "Les Nègres sont une sacrée race de fainéants," "Le créole est un vulgaire patois d'esclaves" (B 37). (France is the most beautiful country in the world, Negroes are a lazy race, Creole is a vulgar slave patois). In a perverse twist, this very "slave patois" is what attracts the interest of Western linguists sent by "la Johns Hopkins University ou la Carnegie Mellon University ou n'importe quelle université de merde des Etats-Unis" ("Hopkins, Carnegie Mellon or any other shit American university").[7] Such are the ironies of history, that scholars will expend great energy to conserve what their colonial predecessors sought to destroy.

Confiant consistently defines postcolonial modernity as linguistic modernity. When *Bassin*'s narrator fancifully imagines how Martinique will look to future archaeologists, he does so by archiving brand names. Used Tampax, a plastic Monoprix bag, an empty pack of Camel cigarettes, a telephone card with a picture of Jeanne Moreau from a fifties movie, a column from the newspaper *Minute* recounting a lurid *fait divers*, this effluvia, is seen as the anachronistic evidence of a vanished era, dominated by corporate megafirms, with its singular arsenal of logos and labels (B 36). The noncewords *Tampax* and *Monoprix* also testify to the irrefutable appeal of Spitzer's *Kodak* or *Sunkist*, not so much because they exemplify lexical innovation, but because they shock the ear attuned to French literariness. After Céline, Boris Vian, and Serge Gainsbourg, the old codes of *bienséance* may have sufficiently broken down in French letters to admit obscenities and argot, but trademark language is perhaps the last taboo, ushering in what is strictly speaking profoundly exogamous to literature.

Confiant's narrator revels in rubbing high literature's face in this linguistically biodegradable material, as when, in his pastiche of Proust's veiled descriptions of bathroom masturbation rituals associated with the scent of lilac, he pays homage to Marguerite Duras as a genie of the water closet:

> Il est vrai que, de guerre lasse, j'avais abandonné le ton élégiaque et lamartinien qui m'était naturel pour un style plus proche de celui de Mme Marguerite Duras dont les posters décoraient les quatre murs de mes W.-C. Souffrant de constipation chronique et, par moments, d'hémerroïdes, il m'arrivait de passer des heures merveilleuses en cet endroit grâce à la prose de cette charmante vieille dame et souvent, il suffisait que je m'esclaffe pour que le foutu étron qui éternisait sa descente dans mon intestin grêle tombât avec un grand plouf dans l'eau javellisée et parfumée presque rituellement à la pétale de rose par ma très chère Nanotte qui s'inquiétait avec une attention de mère poule de mes évacuations matinales. (B 65–66)

> It is true that, war weary, I'd abandoned the elegiac, Lamartinian tone that came naturally, for a style closer to that of Marguerite Duras, whose poster decorated the four walls of my W.C. Suffering from chronic constipation, and sometimes from hemorrhoids too, it was my wont to spend marvelous hours there, thanks to the prose of this charming old lady and often, a guffaw would suffice to make that slow-moving turd inside my small intestine fall with a big plop into the water, Javelized and perfumed almost ritually with rose petal freshener by my cherished Nanotte who fussed, with the concern of a mother hen, over my morning evacuations.

Miming the preciosity of Proust ("je proustifie un peu trop"), Confiant could not be further from the minimalist prose style of Marguerite Duras in this passage. Far from being an influence, Duras is rudely instrumentalized as an emetic, all traces of which disappear with a flush. But perhaps this is unfair, for Duras is not just evacuated, she is "javellisée," that is, subjected to the operation of neologism, as Confiant transforms the French toilet cleaner "Eau Javel" into a verb. "Javelization" emerges as the antidote to "Proustification," with Duras serving as the flush-pull of trademark literacy. In this way, product neologisim seems to function much like Creole in Confiant's earlier writings as a sign of an alien linguistic presence requiring patrol and containment. CNN Creole, in this sense, aligns normally opposed camps—the lingua franca of global capital and the oral culture of Caribbean countries—in a common struggle for access to literature. And lest one think that Creole ever had easy entry, it suffices to look again at Spitzer's "The Individual Factor in Linguistic Innovations," which takes great pains to distinguish Creole, stigmatized as nonlanguage, from *Sprachmischung*, the term for mixing "in the great cultural languages"[8] (IF 65).

In generating CNN Creole, Confiant does not simply substitute CNN for Creole, but instead treats CNN as a form of Creole that must be added to the "aggregate of Caribbean, European, African, Asian, and Levantine cultural elements" that define *créolité* (E 87). Creoleness, to paraphrase the notes of the *Éloge*, "is not just a network of cultures, it is the concrete expression of a civilization in the making" (E 121). This emphasis on "in the making" opens the door to Confiant's presentism, a presentism prompting him to record the most recent impact of high-speed language travel on creolized French. Typically, he experiments with a kind of postcolonial macaronics that truly defies the limits of translatability. If creolized French tests the limits of translatability at the best of times (I am thinking here of Rose-Myriam Réjouis and Val Vinokurov's unapologetic confession to having "overtranslated" Chamoiseau's language in their English version of *Texaco*), Confiant's *La Savane*, published in 1995 in the popular *Mille et une nuit* series, pushes the limit that much further.[9] In *La Savane*, the language of the news media is inserted as a tertiary linguistic *couche* between francophone in-jokes and exported Parisianisms, producing ironic double-entendres such as, "OMO-lave-plus-blanc," in which the French laundry detergent OMO sounds out the gay-baiting pronunciation of "homo" in French, and where the whole phrase alludes to bleaching products targeted at nonwhites. Allusions to Infomercials, American politics, sitcoms, and products abound: an island "negro" is "vacciné-scolarisé and CD-Romisé; a jumble of media brand names highlight the global relativism of a worldview filtered through CNN: Bill Clinton, Mother Teresa, Whoopy Goldberg, Claudia Schiffer, Hussein of Jordan, Bernard Tapie, Mobutu Sésé Séko Wa Ndongo and Madonna."[10] Confiant also applies his technique to the macabre: rapes in Bosnia are euphemized through rhetorical preciosity, as "fornicatory dilations" ("écartèlements fornicatoires"). Tin Tin pokes his childlike head into a scene of atrocities: "I guarantee you, it made a racket like the thunder of Brest over there" ("ce fera un raffut du tonnerre de Brest là-bas, je t'assure") (SP 9). Turning the value system of the micro-colony on its head, television provokes what the local sociologist diagnoses as an "onto-logical heart condition" ("l'infarctus ontologique") (SP 37).

Auto-pastiche anchors the narrative's satire of the *créolité* language movement in which Confiant himself figured so prominently. In *La Savane* an "éloge du fax" accompanies a withering portrait of a "hexagonal ne-grologue" specializing in *créolité*, Dr. Jérôme Garnier de l'université de Trif-fouilis-les-Oies (rendered by one translator as the "Université de Bumble-fuck"). We catch up with Professor Garnier in the midst of a futile interroga-tion of a native informant, who answers him contemptuously in language-lab English:

> "Cher ami, pou . . . pourriez-vous me. . . . Me . . . con . . . con-firmez que l'i . . . imaginaire créole ins . . . insuffle . . .", répétait-il pour la vingtième fois.
>
> "*What are you saying? You're nuts!*" répliquait le djobeur recy-clé (grâce au laboratoire de langues de la chambre de commerce de la Martinique).
>
> Accablé l'Hexagonal, qui avait bâti toute sa carrière universi-taire sur l'étude de ce qu'il appellait, ses confrères et lui, la "lit-térature nègre" ou "négro-africaine" (comme s'il existait une "lit-térature blanco-européenne!," bande de rigolos, va!) et ne trouvait plus rien à pondre sur la négritude, fouinait depuis quel-que temps dans les mangroves déroutantes de la créolité. Quand les nègres se proclamaient nègres, écrivaient nègres, en un mot se réclamaient d'une écriture noire épidermiquement, noire sty-listiquement, noire sémantiquement et tout le bazar, Garnier na-geait dans le bonheur le plus parfait. Mais tout cessa d'aller pour le mieux dans le meilleur des mondes lorsqu'une bande d'hurlu-burlus à peine quadragénaires décréta qu'en plus d'être nègres, ils étaient blancs, amérindiens, indous, chinois et levantins. Non mais? A-t-on idée d'inventer pareille idéologie macaronique, ar-lequinesque et patchworkienne? (SP 41–42)

"Dear friend, c-c-could you confirm for m-me that the Creole i-im-imaginary i-in-inspires . . . ," he was repeating for the twenti-eth time.

"*What are you saying? You're nuts!*" the recycled odd-jobber re-plied—in English, thanks to the language labs of the Martinican Chamber of Commerce.

The demoralized Hexagonal, who had built his whole aca-demic career on the study of what he and his colleagues called "Black" or "Black African literature" (as if there was a "White European" literature, the fools!), was running out of things to say about Negritude. He had been nosing around the disconcerting mangroves of Créolité for a while now. As long as Negroes proclaimed themselves to be Negroes, wrote Negro—that is, as long as they took inspiration from a writing that was epidermically Black, stylistically Black, semantically Black (and all that jazz), then Professor Garnier was in seventh heaven. But it stopped going so well in this best of all worlds when a band of lunatics barely in their forties decreed that they were White, Amerindian, Hindu, Chinese, and Levantine, as well as Negro. What the hell? Where do they get off, inventing some jumbled, hodgepodge, mingle-mangle ideology?[11]

Foiling the white academic's obsession with the blackness of Afro-Caribbean languages, Confiant vents his spleen against racial essentialism and Europe's infatuation with hackneyed discourses of the Other. To Garnier's consternation, blackness disintegrates into a dizzyingly variegated spectacle of hybridity in this not quite "best of all possible worlds."

As a bold-faced send-up of hybridity theory that nonetheless relies on the linguistic patchworkism that it parodies for its effect, Confiant's *La Savane* offers a strategic translingualism revealing the collisions and collusions between postcolonial history and multicultural identity politics. Unlike linguistic anti-imperialists such as Ngũgĩ wa Thiong'o, who vowed (at least provisionally) to give up writing in English in favor of his native Gikuyu, Confiant places European and non-Western languages in abrasive contact, thereby cutting target and source along the bias to ensure their mutual contamination. Africanizing metropolitan usage with the help of ironic exoticisms, unpronounceable loan words, verbal calques, and warped grammaticalities, Confiant both departs from and carries over certain traditions initiated by the Negritude poets of making the colonizer's language strange to itself. Though by now this "empire strikes back" paradigm is no longer radical, it is perhaps still underestimated as a tactic of contemporary language wars, those covertly being waged over the resignification of Francophonia and Creolization. No longer pinned to the right side of the metropole-periphery model, CNN Creole announces the globalization of the microcolony, and the relocation of hexagonal French in the linguistic carnival of an idiom that might be dubbed "postcolonial Rabelais." In this sense, Confiant's CNN Creole overturns the pieties of linguistic regionalism, with its historic "memories of underdevelopment" and "doudouist" poetics.

If Confiant effectively deterritorializes *créolité* in *Bassin des ouragans* and *La Savane des pétrifications* by submerging it in the language of big business and world news, it is perhaps logical that his next move would involve transporting his fictional world to Paris, to the milieu of the Antillean diaspora in the housing projects of Belleville. In a detective novel, *La Dernière Java de Mama Josepha* (1999), Confiant seems to have finally answered Maryse Condé's call to recognize the "Neg'zagonal" in the larger sphere of Caribbean discourse.

Mama Josepha has been brutally murdered, discovered stuffed between two overflowing garbage cans behind a Vietnamese restaurant, her body mangled like the dismantled carcass of a stolen Kawasaki that has also been stashed there. The manager of an HLM, known for taking in strays in exchange for sex, Josepha has many possible suspects in her entourage. But as Inspector Dorval interviews them—Mohammed Assedic, the bitter son of an Algerian Harki; Jean-Paul le Gaulois, "un séropo de merde" ("an HIV-positive shit"); Sissoko, a Malian *sans-papiers* who works for the Chirac government; Pham Dong, "le Viet" who lives above her; and Ti Mano, "l'Antillais bavardeur, flagorneur, menteur, proxo sur les bords, catho au milieu, DJ des boîtes techno-branchées, tagueur impénitent" ("the garrulous Antillean, flatterer, liar, pimp on the side, Catholic, DJ in the hippest techno clubs, impenitent tagger")—he becomes increasingly enmeshed in a case with no real conclusion, since it quickly fans out into an investigation of the place of immigrant culture in the *quartiers chauds* of Paris. Certainly it is no accident that Inspector Dorval is a Martinican Creole trying to understand the new breed of street-wise Antilleans who seem to have forgotten their culture. This culture clash adds piquancy to the narrative, complicating the terms of black solidarity. When Ti Mano compares Dorval to the incorruptible Sydney Poitier, hoping to play on black solidarity ("faire jouer la solidarité blackos"), Dorval rebuffs him: "If you prefer we can speak Creole," he tells Ti Mano. "I've forgotten Creole, Ti Mano," replies. "Great, O.K., so you've forgotten your mother tongue, I believe it," says Dorval, "but you're not going to try to tell me you've forgotten where you were yesterday evening, are you?"[12]

While the search for a solution to a crime clearly serves as an ingenious narrative foil for the search for missing origins, it also provides a perfect context for Confiant's continued exploration of linguistic *créolité* in an urban matrix. Ti Mano may have forgotten his native language, but this does not preclude using his speech to showcase creolized French. Still trying to make common cause with Dorval, Ti Mano speaks to him as best he can in island code language:

Avant de m'engouffrer entre ses cuisses, je n'avais jamais vraiment connu ce qui s'appelle la doucine. Pas la douceur, inspecteur, mais la doucine! Vous, vous êtes créole, vous pouvez comprendre ce que je veux dire. La doucine c'est une douceur sauvage et tendre à la fois, un migan de senteurs de prune-mouben et de pluie fifine. Dans la touffeur de son sexe, j'ai retrouvé d'un seul coup le souvenir de mes cinq premières années d'enfance à la Martinique que je croyais effacées à jamais. (MJ 72)

Before burying myself between her thighs, I never knew what was meant by "la doucine." Not "douceur" (sweetness), inspector, but "la doucine"! You, being Creole Inspector, you can understand what I mean. "La doucine" is a sweetness that is savage and tender at the same time, a mixture of smells, of exotic fruit and fine rain. In the tuft of her sex, I suddenly recovered the memory of my first five years of childhood in Martinique which I thought had been lost forever.

Doucine is a sixteenth-century architectural term describing the molding on a curvilinear arch. Here the architectural referent is incorporated into Creole pillow talk, with the wavy lines of the arch ascribed to the undulating motion of sexual gyration. The passage has the air of a vocabulary lesson as the speaker didactically insists on the fine distinction between *douceur* (a banal, ordinary pleasure) and *doucine*, a rarefied bliss that ignites powerful childhood memories and brings back pungent, long-forgotten Creole words like "migan" (mixture) and "prune-mouben" (exotic fruit).

Though Confiant rarely introduces Creole expressions directly into the Parisian dialect spoken by the characters, there is nonetheless a transference effect of *créolité* in the sheer orality of the text. *La Dernière Java* in this regard approximates in French what Africanists call *orature*, a term signaling the profound influence of oral traditions on written African literature (the transcription of oral epics and poetry, the re-creation of speech rhythms in writing), and more broadly still, the way in which literacy has historically functioned in colonial history to determine what qualifies as literary expression.[13] *La Dernière Java* tests the limits of the literary, giving full throat to Parisian *gouaille*, larding phrases with argot, and drawing heavily, as we have seen in previous works, on brand and celebrity icons of pop culture. Macdo (the shortened form of MacDonalds), Big Mac, Chicken Mac Nuggets, Lazer Techno Vision Prod., Chanel No. 5, Benson and Hedges, Charles Bronson, Spielberg, Lady Di, B.H.V. ("the philosopher of the *Pri-*

sunic"), Bernard Tapie, Magic Johnson, Salman Rushdie, and Jackie Kennedy—they all create a jarring effect when they appear on a page of French text. Confiant gradually naturalizes these foreign names within a rush of orality, fusing slang and commodity culture. In a phrase such as: "je devais m'envoler pour une clinique de Los Angeles afin de suivre le dernier cri en matière de traitement du sida. Hollywood Medical Hospital ça s'appelle et je vous prie de croire que là-bas, c'est pas les potes à Saint-François d'Assises qu'ils reçoivent, c'est les stars et rien d'autre," the words "Los Angeles," "Hollywood Medical Hospital," and "star" are conjoined to French expressions—"le dernier cri" and "Saint Francis of Assisi" (an allusion to the poor) in a seamless flow of language (MJ 75). Often *Franglais* is piled on top of Anglophone loan words to enhance the fluency of media-speak as in "Je vous disais donc que François-Dutrou de Mesdeux avait cliqué sur notre site Web et qu'il avait flashé pour ma chatte" where "cliqué" and "flashé" complement "Web site" in the lingo of virtual sex (MJ 103). In "Suis capable d'embarquer clando dans la soute d'un 747, de retraverser l'Atlantique dare-dare," the shortened form "clando" for "clandestine" also functions as a culture capsule of immigrant life, offering in condensed form, an image of the stowaway, stashed in airplane holds, jumping highway barriers, ducking coast guard radar (MJ 13). This use of truncation to say a lot with a little carries over into the way names are used as shorthand. Rivalries among minorities are communicated, for example, through the cipher of celebrity names when the Algerian Mohammed Assedic complains that the Arabs (who have Omar Sharif and Saddam Hussein) fail to compete with blacks (who have Eddy Murphy and Michael Jordan) in the international market of leading men (MJ 17–18). This shorthand also shows how celebrity names can flatten difference, reducing race and nationality to irrelevance, as when Dorval berates the Malien human rights worker Sissoko, for confusing Salman Rushdie with the Algerian writer Kateb Yacine. For Sissoko, any big name with sufficient intellectual capital will suffice; Rushdie and Yacine are, globally speaking, interchangeable counterparts. For the exasperated inspector, it is precisely this kind of facile conversion that accounts for cultural amnesia, generating spurious cultural equivalencies: Rushdie = Yacine, Omar Sharif = Michael Jordan, and so on. For the homeboys Dorval is interrogating, the equal sign is legitimate since the names have equal value in their purchase on the fantasy of fame.

Fueled by consumer desire, the engine of CNN Creole (like Rap) devours the latest product or label by converting it into a trope. Even President Bill Clinton's sex scandal becomes grist for the latest innovations in patois:

j'ai jamais réussi à la faire jouir, inspecteur. Et ça, une meuf, elle vous l'pardonne pas!—Une clintonne quoi, tu dis, Ti Mano?—Ben, suite aux cours d'éducation sexuelle que mister Clinton nous a donnés l'aut'jour sur le C.N.N., j'ai fini par comprendre la cause de mes malheurs avec Chatounette.—C'est-à-dire?—Ben, c'est-à-dire, que j'ai réalisé qu'à part les vaginales qui font semblant pour dorer la pilule à leur régulier, y'a deux types de femmes dans ce bas monde, inspecteur: les clitoridiennes et les clintoniennes. (MJ 69)

I never succeeded in making her come, Inspector. And that's something a cunt won't pardon you for!—A Clintonne what, was that what you said Ti Mano?—Well, after the sex education that Mister Clinton gave us the other day on CNN, I finally understood the troubles I was having with Chatounette.—Which means?—Which means that I realized that apart from the "vaginals," who fake it to justify the pill given to them by their regulars, there are two types of women in this lowly world, inspector, the clitoriennes, and the clintoniennes.

The lewd play between "clitoriennes" and "clintoniennes," together with the neologism "a Clintonne" recalls the "titim" and "sirandanes"—the Creole riddles and wordplays—collected by Confiant in his *Dictionnaire*. Both take foreign words and subject them to deformation and appropriation: "Dé nonm kouché lopital, yo ka palé de an péyi? (Deux hommes sont couchés à l'hôpital, ils parlent d'un pays, de quel pays s'agit-il?" / Two men are in bed in the hospital, they speak of a country, which one?) The answer is "L'Italie," which in Creole becomes "litali" or "lit à lit," "bed to bed." Another example given by Confiant: "Konmen fimèl ki ka viv ansanm nan an kay?" (Combien de femelles vivent ensemble dans la même maison? / How many females live together in the same house?) The answer: "Twa: lapot, laklé, séri" (Trois: la porte, la clef, la serrure. / Three: The door, the key and the lock). Here, as Confiant explains, there is a jibe at the fact that most speakers of Creole ignore the gender of French nouns. This wordplay works only if you know that door, key, and lock, in addition to having vulgar sexual connotations, are gendered feminine in French grammar.[14] Confiant is well aware of this "mi-français," "mi-creole" zone, where language becomes particularly inventive precisely because it is neither/nor. He fully exploits *slurvian*, the accented slurring of words (as in *fuggedaboutit* for "forget about it," "don't bother me with that") that allows an expression to break away from its original reference and take on an independent life of its own.[15] In one of the Creole riddles: "Baton dan deryer, louroun lo latet? Zannannan" (Bâton dans le derrière, couronne sur la tête? L'ananas. / Bayonet up the behind, crown on head. A pineapple), the z sound of the plural is conflated with the word pineapple to make "Zannanan," an emblem of divine sodomy.[16] The same effect is transferred to *La Dernière Java* when the z grapheme in the racist rant "Mort aux z'Arabes!" migrates from the expression of otherness ("vous 'aut,") to form a new compound of xenophobia, the word "Zarab." The slurred z crops up again as a sign of racist hate in an imitation of the speech of French paratroopers in the Algerian War who punctuate acts of torture with "Vive la Frrance, mon ziniral!" (MJ 16).

Though they occupy opposite sides of the political spectrum, the one postcolonial, the other corporate, Creole idioms and trademark nominatives share the fact that they are "foreign" phonemes that have forced their way into the host language, interrupting the course of its lexical flow. Leo Spitzer understood *why* these verbal imports could be allowed in. Citing Hans Sperber's notion of *Bedeutungslehre*, the "fixing factors" of coinage, Spitzer argued that new words come into fixity because they fulfill a cultural need, or more exactly, they respond to an overdetermined *hunger* in the culture that only a new word can satisfy. Spitzer came to this theory of hunger in a sinister way, while working as a censor for the Austrian military:

> I was able to study the whole phenomenon of the stylistic neologisms, its artistic-expressive and its conservative-limited side, its emotional creation by individuals and its acceptance and trivialization by a community, under particularly favorable circumstances, when I was an Austrian censor of the correspondence of Italian prisoners in the first world war (cf. my book *Die Umschreibungen des Begriffes "Hunger"* . . . published in 1919). The poor prisoners had been forbidden to write to their Italian relatives that they were suffering hunger, but attempted all possible ways of linguistic subterfuge to make this fact known to them in order to receive food packages. And surely enough, the less imaginative prisoners (perhaps also the most pitifully suffering ones) hid the blunt statement *ho fame* in a corner of their letters, but others, more detached from their dire fate and more artistically gifted, found ingenious stylistic, in this case periphrastic, ways to circumvent *la Signora Censura*. The simplest device was to have

recourse to idiomatic synonyms known to their relatives (but supposedly not to the censors) such as *la spazzola* (originally: "[we may as well use]"), the brush [because the meal is finished, because there is nothing to eat]' [*sic*]). (LI 71)

Though Spitzer skirts any discussion of the moral circumstances of his linguistic discovery, *la spazzola* is clearly, for him, a case of language as human survival, an example of *die Sprachschöpfer*, a phenomenon "of independent speakers who dig up latent language material in a situation which calls for it" (LI 71). For Spitzer, the artistic word formation of the Italian prisoners of war is far superior to Kodak's utilitarian neologism; however, both demonstrate the ability to bring a *new thing* into the world, a new product into being, "*thanks to the word*" (LI 72). Spitzer's emphasis on hunger, whether it was the chance result of his wartime duties or an intuition about the way in which trademark neologisms like *Kodak* or *Sunkist* seem to be gobbled up by everyday usage, points, significantly, to the way in which the desire for commodities is internalized within language. This hunger for what he calls "the irreality of a world of words" accounts for how corporate icons are branded into language, how commodities are burned into linguistic consciousness, how the trademark name becomes a kind of linguistic fast food that feeds ideologies of mass consumption as it becomes affixed to speech (LI 72).

It is this hunger for what the media sells, ingested in the form of trademark literacy, that Inspector Dorval discovers while attempting to solve his crime. And for his suspects, his willingness to speak their language means that he has essentially been won over to their side:

> Vous avez fini par adopter notre langage, inspecteur, c'est touchant comme pas possible. Minouchette, cette intello de merde, elle prétend que le banlieusard sera le français de demain et que les Chirac et Jospin de l'an 2050, ils ouvriront leur campagne electorale à la télé en disant "Salut, les potes!"
>
> . . . Digresse pas, tu veux, Sissoko, si y'a un truc dans lequel z'êtes fortiches, vous les Franchouillards de l'an 2050 machin, c'est bien le détournement de conversation. Z'êtes de vrais Palestiniens du langage, pour vous les mots, c'est comme des avions prosionistes. (MJ 84)
>
> You've ended up adopting our language, inspector, it's incredibly touching. Minouchette, that intellectual piece of shit, has said that the language of the *banlieu* will be the official French of

tomorrow, and that the Chiracs and Jospins of the year 2050 will open their electoral campaigns on TV saying "Hey guys!"

... Don't digress, if you will Sissoko, if there's one thing you guys are good at, you pseudo-Frenchies of the year 2050 whatever, it's changing the subject. You're like true Palestinians of language, for you, words are like Zionist airplanes.

Despite Dorval's stated intent to send Sissoko to the electric chair ("you can go ahead and call S.O.S. Racisme, they'll never believe that a Black would martyr another of his own race"), he realizes that he is in the midst of a language war (as intractable as the Middle East war), which he can never win. CNN Creole has taken hold, sending down roots in the banlieus of Paris and the streets of Martinique, and taking over the rest of the world in the language everyone speaks (MJ 85).

12

Condé's *Créolité* in Literary History

Though "Creole" increasingly works as a term for media-inflected hybrid speech, it is also entering the lexicon as a paradigm of literary history. Drawing on a wide range of theories of literary history and geography, I want to consider how *créolité* challenges paradigms of literary evolution, narrative markets, and comparative genre. In focusing on Maryse Condé's relationship to the British novel (with special attention to her rewriting of Emily Brontë's *Wuthering Heights* in her *La migration des coeurs* [trans. *Windward Heights*]), the intent is to emphasize the implications of Condé's decision to exchange a French literary genealogy for a British one (that, in addition to Brontë, also includes Jane Austen, Jean Rhys, James Joyce, and Virginia Woolf). An attempt will be made to develop a framework for thinking about genre translation and transmission that links *créolité* to "Caribbean Gothic" (countering the Orientalist "Imperial Gothic" readily apparent in British colonial fiction). Ghosts, telepathic communication, the channeling of spirits and voices emerge as important themes in *Wuthering Heights*, and their reappearance in *Windward Heights* brings into focus issues around communication and literacy that were as important to Emily Brontë as they are to Condé: questions around "whose tongue is chosen," and "how literature happens" under conditions of tenuous literacy and literateness. These questions advance reflection on how *créolité* translates time-honored models of literary history, while providing new ascriptions of literary genesis, genealogy, and genetic criticism.

There are myriad serviceable models of literary history still in use, many of them overlapping. One thinks of the encyclical structuralism of Vico-inspired models; of Lansonist histories of style informed by Taine's emphasis on *milieu*, genre, and social class; of transhistorical time lines of intellectual history—Arthur Lovejoy's history of ideas unfolding as a great chain of being or Leo Spitzer's adaptation of the philological circle, used to construe a national soul evolving through the ages. One thinks of Georg Lukács's Hegelian concept of *Geisteswissenschaft* based on a presumed match between the mind of the writer and the historical mind, which points to a supra-empirical vision of the totality of world history and to historically based universal dialectics of genre.[1] One thinks of Erich Auerbach's literary history with holes, his jagged genealogy of comedic realism, lurching back to Plato's *Republic* where "mimesis ranks third after truth"[2] and forward to Dante's *Commedia*, presented as "true reality." One thinks of Walter Jackson Bate's postwar update of the "ancients and moderns" quarrel to "the burden of the past," supplanted in turn by Harold Bloom's agonistic "anxiety of influence" theory of psychic poetic engendering and literary father-killing. One thinks of Mikhail Bakhtin's chronotypes, which introduced synchrony into the heavily diachronic tradition of literary history. These chronotypes become lengthened as temporal measures of periodicity under the guiding influence of Ferdinand Braudel, Michel Foucault, and Giovanni Arrighi, with their introduction, respectively, of *la longue durée*, epistemological break, and the long century. One thinks of how, from Elisée Reclus to David Harvey, the spatial conditions of long-distance narrative have come into historical focus, fostering cartographic literary histories and mappings of literary territory that compete with linear time. These geopolitical models urge literary history to take on imperial conquest and the rise of capitalism through renewed attention to epic genres: *le roman d'aventure,* the national ballad, travel chronicles, exoticism, the war novel, *la littérature coloniale.* One thinks of Sandra Gilbert and Susan Gubar's invention of feminist literary history focusing on women authors and female characters. Along the lines of canonical redress, one thinks of the monumental project of Henry Louis Gates to build African American literary history from the ground up. And finally, one thinks of a number of critics committed to global literary historiography: the Brazilian critic Roberto Schwarz's theory of "misplaced ideas," which complicates the story of Latin America's supposed dependency on European mimesis, or Franco Moretti's world systems approach to world literature.

Moretti's polemical essay "Conjectures on World Literature" is particularly availing to the problem of assessing the place of *créolité* in literary history first, to borrow a formulation from Paul de Man, because it diagnoses the present, forcing interrogation of the relationship between literary modernity and literary history, and second because it thinks big, imagining a world geography of literary fields in which major and minor, or metropolitan and periphery are given their due in determining reception.[3] Moretti shows how economism vies with evolutionism in the "two basic cognitive metaphors" that have dominated literary historiography: the philological tree ("the phylogenetic tree derived from Darwin, the tool of comparative philology") and the market wave (adapted from Schmidt's "wave hypothesis," which explained certain overlaps among languages).

> The tree describes the passage from unity to diversity: one tree, with many branches: from Indo-European, to dozens of different languages. The wave is the opposite: it observes uniformity engulfing an initial diversity: Hollywood films conquering one market after another (or English swallowing language after language). Trees need geographical *discontinuity* (in order to branch off from each other, languages must first be separated in space, just like animal species); waves dislike barriers, and thrive on geographical *continuity* (from the viewpoint of a wave, the ideal world is a pond). Trees and branches are what nation-states cling to; waves are what markets do.[4]

Moretti underscores how nations line up on the side of trees while world systems line up on the side of waves. This makes sense if we think of how the tree image informs myths of national roots. The rootedness of a culture has traditionally been a test of its strength, robustness, and the health of its imperial prospects. Philology, that disciplinary anchor of territorial and extraterritorial nationalism, also relied on the linguistic tree, building up from the *racine* or etymon a genealogy of word families that, in their turn, "branch out" into heritage culture, patrimony, and national history. The wave, by contrast, is associated with international economism; it relies on the analogy between the roiling motion of the high seas and the market flows of financial and symbolic capital. Genres provide an aesthetic currency of choice in plotting transnational wave theory: from Greek allegory to national epic, revenge tragedy to lyric poetry, social realism to melodrama, gothic horror to haiku, the global market of literary genres yields a cartography of cultural capital in transit.

How does the *créolité* novel sit in relation to these paradigms of the tree and the wave? To ask this question is to consider more generally how Caribbean fiction assumes its place in literary genealogy, plumbing the resources of its ecology for extensions of the tree metaphor into a spirit-driven *genius loci* manifest in land forms and mysterious weather: the mangrove, the *razyés* (a Creole equivalency term for heath or cliff), the hurricanes, cyclones and monsoons. The "tree" or evolutionary model of literary history allows *créolité* literature to be placed in a continuum stretching back to the vernacularization of Latin literature, to Renaissance macaronics and Rabelaisian billingsgate. Profoundly associated with what it means to, in Patrick Chamoiseau's words, "écrire en pays dominé," and anchored historically by the cataclysmic advent of slavery and the shift from plantation culture to tourism, *créolité* also extends the avant-garde revolution in poetics promulgated by Joyce, Pound, and Céline, all of whom grafted argot, dialect, and vernacular onto high literature.[5] From this perspective, one could say, the tree does well by *créolité*, crediting its lexical novelties and commitment to "new grammar" as a culminating moment in the grammaticalization of literature that took place in France between 1890 and 1940.[6]

By contrast, the "wave" points to conditions that impede *créolité*'s access to literary history, conditions that relate specifically to Caribbean literature's struggle to gain a place at the table in the global market of letters. Pascale Casanova's book *La République mondiale des lettres* addresses problems of reception faced by what she calls "les petites littératures" (borrowing from Kafka's *kleines literaturs*), referring to literatures that come in small bulk, hail from tiny countries or emergent nations, are produced under conditions of impoverishment and imperial adversity, and suffer from being badly translated or poorly marketed. Translation, which permits a wider sphere of reception, is considered by Casanova to be a sign of "consecration and accumulation of literary capital," shoring up the market economy of global literature.[7] In this scheme, minor literature in translation is placed in the uncomfortable bind of either being barred access to international circulation or accused of selling out once it enters the mainstream market.

Add to these obstacles the fact that a movement based in local language politics hardly lends itself to global application, and we can assume that *créolité* must of necessity struggle hard to become a free-standing category of literary history. And yet, taking a cue from curator Okwui Enwezor's use of the term as an organizing concept of *Documenta* XI (an international biennial exhibited in Kassel, Germany, in 2002), there are signs that *créolité* is gaining autonomous stature as a term of critique. Enwezor borrows from *Éloge de la créolité* in basing his definition of Creoleness on the "scissions and agglutinations forged in the contact zone of its historical transmission."[8] But he also generalizes the term as a synonym for world culture, "a critical theory of creole language, literary form, and mode of producing locality" that extends its "geographical character beyond the Caribbean."[9] Here Enwezor seems to echo both Casanova's dislocation of *créolité* when she speaks of "la créolité Suisse" (with respect to C-F Ramuz's call for a Vaudois linguistic populism as early as 1914) or Maryse Condé's insistence on taking stock of the transnational, media-saturated nature of contemporary Caribbean culture.[10]

Condé's refusal of linguistic separatism, her affirmation of transcultural fusion and her narrative engagement with Anglophone writers, reconciles, if you will, the tree and the wave, or nature and market. English allows her to bypass both the burden of the French literary tradition, weighing down on her own formation as a Francophone writer, *and* the strictures of nativist dogma adhered to by certain of her *créolité* cohort. The use of English also draws attention to the prevalence of British narrative models in her fiction. Unlike her forebears Césaire, Albert Memmi, Octave Mannoni, and Fernando Rétamar, all of whom fashioned postcolonial Calibans out of Shakespeare's *Tempest*, Condé's rewriting of *Wuthering Heights* has as much to do with establishing a new kind of literary inheritance, as it does with political *détournement* and appropriationism. By inheritance I do not mean to suggest that her imitation of the classics is an expedient way of gaining literary pedigree. Nor am I suggesting that her appropriationism squares with avant-garde and postmodern techniques of pastiche, cut-up, and plagiarism designed to kill the authorial subject (as exemplified by Kathy Acker who "authors" *Great Expectations* and borrows from *Wuthering Heights*). Condé's creolization of narrative form fits uncomfortably into hybridity models that stress an intertextual weave of disparate traditions and structures. Intertextuality in the service of an ethics of reversal is what generally reigns in narrative crossings. Consider Jean Rhys's *Wide Sargasso Sea* (1966), which depends on switching the roles of major and minor characters. Mister Rochester's hapless and insane Creole wife, Bertha Mason, is elevated by Rhys, who once wrote, "She seemed such a poor ghost I thought I'd like to write her life." Rochester, meanwhile changes places with Bertha in being assigned a background, subordinate role. In opting for an introjective rather than a purely intertextual model of literary transference, Condé's fiction downplays the ethics of reversal in favor of a preoccupation with the transmission of literary voice. This transfer of voice becomes a strategy for inserting oneself into a genealogy of "women writers of genius" that includes Jane Austen, the Brontës, and Virginia Woolf. When Condé dedicates *Windward Heights*—"À Emily Brontë, qui, j'espère, agréera cette lecture de son chef-d'oeuvre. Honneur et respect"—she is resurrecting Brontë from the dead, as if "making contact" with her spirit. It is as if Cathy's famous line in *Wuthering Heights*, "I *am* Heathcliff," typically read as testimony to the breakdown of the autonomy of the sovereign subject, or as an instance of pathological overidentification, could be translated as Condé saying "I *am* Brontë." Addressing Emily Brontë writer to writer, so to speak, across the divide of culture, language, and even death, Condé suggests a telepathic identification with her Victorian predecessor, characterized by Freud and Derrida as "thought transference."[11] Analogies between Western and African trance culture come to mind, with Greek oracles and European mediums compared to the *behiques* and *babalawos* of the Caribbean. In each case, the anthropology of ghosts, with its emphasis on the channeling of messages across vast distances of time and place, provides a framework for interpreting the transfer of literary genius from a nineteenth-century woman from Yorkshire to a twentieth-century Martiniquaise.

If it seems far-fetched to allow that the ghost of Brontë comes to inhabit the work of Condé, one might at the very least admit the analogy, drawn by Marina Warner, between the supernaturalism of British Gothic, and the cult of ancestor worship in stories of *vaudou* passed along by shamans and tellers-of-tales. Condé's homage to Brontë's voice merges with her respect for the African literary tradition of *orature*. In using Creole narrators of humble social station, Condé follows Emily Brontë's example of using the Earnshaw housekeeper Nelly Dean to recount large portions of the tragic love story between Heathcliff and Catherine Earnshaw, but she also brings storytelling itself back in touch with popular origins. In terms of genre transference, one could argue that Condé's *Windward Heights* deserves to be classified as both an exercise in and critique of "Caribbean Gothic." Marina Warner defines "Imperial Gothic," as the use of specters to embody "the collapse of the distant into the proximate brought about by empire."[12]

The haunting of the British drawing room or family foyer by ghosts of the oppressed from exotic lands, recalls Edward Said's analysis in *Culture and Imperialism* of Jane Austen's *Mansfield Park*. In Said's view, the distant economy of Sir Thomas's sugar plantation in Antigua links the heroine's cosseted world to the toil of indentured slaves. Said suggests that Sir Thomas's imposition of protocols of a measured existence—ordered landscape, fixed schedules—on daily life in *Mansfield Park* bespeaks anxiety about incipient rebellion far away. In Said's reading, small rituals of social control on a British estate become the telltale signs of colonialism at home. Though ostensibly a far cry from offering a big canvas of early British imperialism in the Caribbean, *Mansfield Park* shows how Austen's moral universe is shaped by the slave economy. The idea of distant worlds joined at the hip also informs Said's evaluation of Charlotte Brontë's Bertha Mason in *Jane Eyre*. The madwoman who haunts Mr. Rochester's upper floor is from the West Indies, thus setting Caribbean ghosts loose in the British domestic sphere. Said writes:

> As a reference point of definition, as an easily assumed place of travel, wealth and service, the empire functions for much of the European nineteenth century as a codified, if only marginally visible, presence in fiction, very much like the servants in grand households and in novels, whose work is taken for granted but scarcely ever more than named. . . . To cite another intriguing analogue, imperial possessions are as usefully *there*, anonymous and collective, as the outcast populations (analyzed by Gareth Stedman Jones) of transient workers, part-time employees, seasonal artisans; their existence always counts, though their names and identities do not, they are profitable without being fully there.[13]

In *Windward Heights* the theme of the colonially haunted house is affixed to the genre of dysfunctional family romance. As in Brontë's original, genetic repetitions of family cycles of violence mime political cycles of revolt and repression. When the Heathcliff figure, Razyé, sets fire to the estate of his brother-in-law Aymeric de Linnseul (an enlightened *colon*), we see glimmers of Toussaint L'Ouverture bringing principles of the French Revolution home to roost in Haiti, but we also see how Creole families, with their painful social splits around shades of white and black, and their dirty little secrets of rape, illegitimacy, and racially fractured kinship, are beset by phantoms of bad blood. The revenge of ancestors on future generations—specifically, the burden placed by Cathy and Heathcliff's unrequited love on posterity—allows us to see why Brontë's family melodrama lent itself to being creolized by Condé. "Caribbean Gothic," a foretaste of which we find in Faulkner, is built up around intergenerational race wars within the family. The ethics of character in Condé's version hinge on the idea that eternal love transcends the denial of African blood in mixed-race subjects. The Cathy of *Windward Heights* is the daughter of a "tallow-coloured mulatto" by the name of Hubert Gagneur, himself the son of a white Creole. She stands to whiten herself in forming an alliance with the rich Linnseul clan, but the rejection of her true love, Rayzé—the Heathcliff counterpart, described as black or Indian half-caste—costs her her happiness and ultimately her life. Razyé, meanwhile, is condemned to trying to escape the fate "mapped out for him in advance," of *embourgeoisement*, which only marriage to a girl "white enough to lighten the race" can assure. His son Razyé II is also destined to share the family curse. Haunted by the strange power exerted by the graveyard in L'Engoulvent, containing a tomb with "letters intertwined in stone—CATHY DE LINSSEUIL—RAZYE" (WWH 347), the junior Razyé lets himself go to ruin, tortured by the fear that his own daughter may be the fruit of an incestuous union. Genetic destiny is thus virtually mapped out like a genome, spelled out beyond the grave.

Telling the future by spelling the names draws attention to the way in which literacy and narration are as crucial to the plot of *Windward Heights* as they were to Brontë's *Wuthering Heights*. Condé effectively brings African oral traditions—the circulation of local knowledge by official tellers of tales or marketplace gossipmongers into alignment with the culture of *commérage* in Britain's rural backwaters. As class, gender, and region are to *Wuthering Height*'s linguistic world, so class, gender, and race are to *Windward Heights*—the coordinates of an uneasy entry into literate language. Emily Brontë's personal insecurities about presenting her own "monstrous" voice of female genius to the reading public of her time, parallel Condé's negotiation of the difficulty in promoting Creolophone French as a language of international literature. These biographical details add substance to the drama of alphabetization, reinforcing thematic connections between the problem of choosing a tongue or a literary language, and the problem of remaining faithful, in the language of narration, to a regional setting in which the grasp on literacy is tenuous.

In *Wuthering Heights* Catherine Earnshaw's old books and scrawled, diaristic notations discovered by Heathcliff's hapless tenant afford a spiritual channeling scene in which Catherine's ghost is summoned from the beyond. And yet, it would seem that Catherine is brought back not just as Heathcliff's lover, but also as a narrative pretext for Brontë to introduce—in the form of ghost-writing—the specter of female literateness:

> The ledge, where I placed my candle, had a few mildewed books
> piled up in one corner; and it was covered with writing
> scratched on the paint. This writing, however, was nothing but a
> name repeated in all kinds of characters, large and small—*Catherine Earnshaw*, here and there varied to *Catherine Heathcliff*,
> and then again to *Catherine Linton*.
>
> In vapid listlessness I leant my head against the window, and
> continued spelling over Catherine Earnshaw—Heathcliff—Lin-

ton, til my eyes closed; but they had not rested five minutes when a glare of white letters started from the dark, as vivid as spectres—the air swarmed with Catherines.[14]

For Harold Bloom the perdurability of Brontë's literary style, well-exemplified in this passage, can be traced to its occult quality, its ability to convey her "private gnosis."[15] "Though she was a clergyman's daughter," he writes, "there is not an iota of Christianity in Emily Brontë, and the gap between ghostly visions and natural realities is never closed ... she is a knower, though not to be subsumed under the rubric of any historical Gnostic sect" (G 321). "Emily in her poetry," he continues, "salutes the 'God within [her] breast' ... 'affirming the heroism of her own soul' " (G 324). Bloom's association of genius in Brontë's language with religiosity should not preclude an awe-inspired appreciation of the way in which Brontë's unconventional way of writing instantiated *écriture féminine.* Just how anomalous her inscription of feminine literateness was can be gleaned from Charolotte Brontë's preface to the posthumous republication of her sister's novel. In what amounts to a kind of preemptive strike, she alerts sophisticated readers to the barbarisms, orthographic infelicities, and shock of Yorkshire dialect that they will encounter in *Wuthering Heights* (infelicities that she apparently had no qualms about trying to edit out of Emily's poetry when preparing an edition after her death, and which may even have led her, according to the speculation of one biographer, to burn the manuscript of an unfinished novel abandoned when Emily became too ill to complete it).[16] To those unacquainted with the West-Riding setting of the novel, Charlotte wrote, "Men and women who ... having been trained from their cradle to observe the utmost evenness of manner and guardedness of language, will hardly know what to make of the rough, strong utterance, the harshly manifested passions, the unbridled aversions, and headlong partialities of unlettered moorland hinds and rugged moorland squires, who have grown up untaught and unchecked, except by mentors as harsh as themselves."[17] The warning against uncouth diction serves to divert readers from the more controversial issue of Emily's questionable taste in portraying moral monsters such as Heathcliff, but regardless of its purpose, this excuse for wild writing draws attention to the liminality of Emily Brontë's manipulation of the English language. Literature "happens" in and through her prose much like ghosts make their appearance—that is, as something frightening and incendiary erupting out of nowhere and disturbing the social order. Many have wondered how a woman writer of Emily's regional isolation, limited life experience, and uneven education could have mastered the English language to the extent that she did. Her invention of an idiom of Yorkshire Gothic was borderline—a language of genius hovering on the edge of madness and pushing the envelope of acceptable literateness—but it also resembles Creole *avant la lettre*, a meld of the Gondal fantasy language of her childhood in which she wrote tales and sagas along with her siblings, and the Yorkshire pidgin of her surround. As Charlotte noted, though her sister remained remote from the rural laboring classes and "*with* them, she rarely exchanged a word," nonetheless "she knew them: knew their ways, their language, their family histories; she could hear of them with interest and talk of them with detail, minute, graphic, and accurate" (WH xliv—xlv).

Far from being a study in linguistic folklore however, *Wuthering Heights* explores the depths of social stigma attached to speaking badly and growing up unlettered. Catherine's daughter Cathy reaps bitter scorn on her cousin Hareton, just as her mother had faulted Heathcliff for his degradation of character, directly attributable to lack of education. Heathcliff, we learn, never reads, and, as if in defiance of social norms or in defense of his own class complexes, he rears his nephew Hareton with the help of the boorish family retainer to scorn "book-larning." When Hareton confesses, "It's some damnable writing, I cannot read it," Cathy replies, "Can't read it? . . . I can read it. . . . It's English," trouncing him with the help of her snobbish cousin as a deuce (WH 218). Hoping to earn Cathy's respect, Hareton tries in secret to teach himself to read only to be ridiculed for his stumbling results. Illiteracy sets off a cycle of shame, revenge, and self-destruction that is impossible to break in the first generation.[18] In the second, the same cycle seems about to repeat itself as Hareton withdraws into the nebula of wounded pride. But Cathy listens to the reproof of her housekeeper ("he is not *envious* but *emulous* of your attainments," Nelly Dean tells Cathy) and resolves to win back his trust, despite fearing that her beloved books will be "debased and profaned in his mouth" (WH 298). Hareton initially remains suspicious of her motives, destroying her offerings in a shocking book-burning scene. But eventually he succumbs to the charms of a sentimental education, and as the two gradually form a reading couple, their hair and features mingling as he reads aloud and she corrects him, their physiognomic similarities appear—the ghostly resurgence of their forgotten kinship bond in the person of Catherine Earnshaw, Cathy's mother and Hareton's aunt.

> They lifted their eyes together, to encounter Mr. Heathcliff—perhaps, you have never remarked that their eyes are precisely similar, and they are those of Catherine Earnshaw. The present Catherine has no other likeness to her, except a breadth of forehead,

and a certain arch of the nostril that makes her appear rather haughty, whether she will, or not. With Hareton the resemblance is carried farther: it is singular, at all times—then it was particularly striking, because his senses were alert, and his mental faculties wakened to unwonted activity. (WH 319)

Reading faces, forming a composite portrait out of two distinct sets of facial signs, mimics the act of learning to read itself in which visual cues suddenly coalesce into a unit of semiotic recognition and intelligibility. Perhaps for this reason, Heathcliff is tormented when the spectacle of these two lovers side by side becomes focused into one obsessive visage of the lover he could never possess. Forced to spell out the visual characters that form a picture of Cathy's ghostly face, Heathcliff starts to hallucinate her image everywhere: "And what does not recall her?" Heathcliff cries, "I cannot look down to this floor, but her features are shaped on the flags. In every cloud, in every tree—filling the air at night, and caught by glimpses in every object, by day I am surrounded with her image. The most ordinary faces of men, and women—my own features—mock me with a resemblance. The entire world is a dreadful collection of memoranda that she did exist, and that I have lost her" (WH 320–21). Paranoid vision, certainly, but more interesting for my purposes, an indirect representation of the telepathic nature of reading as well. Heathcliff's interiorization of Catherine Earnshaw as a "collection of memoranda" that may be read out as ghostly resemblances bouncing off the visible world are like books that take over subjective consciousness.[19] In a more stable mental framework, Catherine's daughter Cathy is shaped as who she is by virtue of having committed her treasure trove of books to memory: "I've most of them written on my brain and printed in my heart" (WH 298). Literacy thus emerges as the agent of spiritual transference and touchstone of identity, even if it risks evacuating individuality in favor of a transubstantiated soul.

In Condé's *Windward Heights* literacy is used to thematize the "raced" history of language as a fixture of the Caribbean novel. When Razyé comes back to visit Cathy after she is married to Aymeric de Linsseul, and turns the head of her sister-in-law, Cathy tries to ward off her rival's attraction by alluding to his illiteracy: "Mais ne te fie pas à sa mine ni à son français. C'est une personne sans éducation ni culture. Une sorte de *Soubarou*, de *nèg-mawon*. De toute sa vie, il n'a pas dû ouvrir un livre, et, s'il sait compter, il sait à peine signer son nom."[20] ("But don't go by his looks or fancy French. A kind of *soubarou*, a wild man of the forest, a runaway slave. I'm sure he's never opened a book in his entire life, and though he knows how to count, he can hardly sign his name.")[21] Cathy's suspicions are confirmed when we see Razyé trying to decipher a letter from his sickly son Justin Marie: "Razyé read the short letter over and over again. It inscribed his defeat in writing" (WWH 148). The illiteracy stigma is passed from father to second son, Razyé II, the "remnants" of whose education, we learn, are virtually nonexistent. Seeking to remedy the situation in order to bolster his standing as a political activist, Razyé II comes to the schoolroom of Cathy II, daughter of his father's great love, and a trained schoolmistress no longer comfortable speaking Creole herself. When Cathy asks the crude yet alluring Razyé why he has bothered to come to school, he replies sarcastically with a reference to Schoelcher, champion of colonial education: "To make your dear Monsieur Schoelcher happy . . . 'Educate yourselves, savage Africans, and shame your detractors.' Isn't that what he said?" (WWH 234). The novel plays literacy both ways, exposing it as an instrument of colonial paternalism and "enlightened" racial oppression, while recognizing it as the conduit to emancipation. Refusal to speak Creole, on the other hand, becomes tantamount to denying blackness, and by extension, denying the subliminal colonial history of rape and miscegenation.

Maryse Condé fastens onto the literacy theme, much like her predecessor did, because it problematizes issues of readability that govern the reception of anomalous voices, whether it be the vernacular-inflected voice of female genius that exploded onto the scene of Britain's mid-nineteenth-century literary public after the gender unmasking of the pseudonymous Ellis Bell, or Condé's stalwart late-twentieth-century endeavor to define a nonsectarian creolized language of literature that (to paraphrase Paul de Man) "restores the link between literary theory and praxis while historicizing new forms of literary modernity."[22] Brontë and Condé surmount enormous obstacles to entering literary history with what Lukács, commenting on Sir Walter Scott, called "triumphing prose." In assessing how the British historical novel got to be historical, Lukács wrote: "Scott's works are in no way modern attempts to galvanize the old epic artificially into new life, they are real and genuine novels. Even if his themes are very often drawn from the 'age of heroes,' from the infancy of mankind, the spirit of his writing is nevertheless that of man's maturity, the age of triumphing 'prose.' "[23] It is prose, or as I have suggested more pointedly, new orders of literateness that bind *Wuthering Heights* to *Windward Heights*, a literacy revolution, if you will, that reinforces the revolutionary undercurrents rippling through the historical settings of both novels. It seems no great stretch to see the Luddite revolts in Yorkshire that unsettled the landscape of Emily Brontë's childhood and materialized in her fiction in the form of a treacherous natural world, as analogous to the antiplantation rebellion led by Razyé, who stands in favor of a countereconomy or radical ruralism comparable to today's anti-globalization protests in subsistence-farming regions of the world. In this context, *créolité* refers to a language soldered to a counterhegemonic politics of insurgency, a galvanization of the base that turns literary history on its head. Character, plot, narrative voice, genre, markets, chronotypes, cartography, geography, to be sure all these terms remain in place as fundamental categories of narratology and literary history, but to this lexicon, I would insist on adding a term not normally used historically or in relation to the novel—that of *créolité*. *Créolité* used not as a synonym of narrative hybridity (which implies, problematically, that African and European elements of the novel happily meet, or are equitably distributed), but rather, as a transhistorical denomination referring to the way in which Creole fiction reveals literature "happening" as a narrative event or plot dimension. Literacy as a shaping force of character *Bildung*, the passage of common or marginalized speech into the domains of *lisibilité* and *littérarité*, and the transcoding of language politics into narrative structure—these aspects of the novel hold out the promise of a creolized world-historical turn.

PART FOUR

Technologies of Translation

I3

Nature into Data

"The rural," Gayatri Chakravorty Spivak has asserted, "is not trees and fields anymore. It is on the way to data."[1] If, following Spivak, media and environment are conceived as capable of mutual translation, then the idea of critical habitat could be "located," so to speak, as a margin of critique inserted in the space where this translation process occurs. As such, the term owes a clear debt to the intellectual zone of criticality developed in continental theory by the Frankfurt School and must also fully acknowledge Kenneth Frampton's precursory paradigm of "critical regionalism," which takes its stand against the megalopolis on architectural forms of resistance—specifically, on an "unsentimental" tectonics of localism capable of sustaining a "dialectal relation with nature."[2] In addition to being an expression grafted from the lexicon of environmentalists who use it to refer to the minimal conditions necessary to sustain the life of endangered species, I am defining "critical habitat" as a translational medium that links territorial habitat and intellectual *habitus*, physical place and ideological force-field, economy and ecology.

The South African artist William Kentridge has, since the mid-eighties, been working to transform the traditional genre of landscape painting into a medium of geopolitical critique. In a series of charcoal drawings from 1988 entitled *Landscape in a State of Siege*, he describes how landscape—the background music of painting or the filler between plot and character in a novel—"takes over" the privileged space of the interior, much like an act of territorial reclamation by the dispossessed:

> For about a year I have been drawing landscapes. They started off as incidental details in other drawings. A window behind a

couple dancing, an open space behind a portrait. Gradually the landscape took over and flooded the interiors. Few of the people in the pictures managed to retain their place in them. . . . A few of the drawings are of specific places but most are constructed from elements of the countryside around Johannesburg.[3]

Kentridge pastiches South African landscape painting, typified, in the 1920s and 1930s by the work of Jan Ernst Abraham Volschenk and J. H. Pierneef:

> The Volshenks and the Pierneefs are empty of tribal images but are not unrelated. The landscape is arranged into a vision of pure nature, majestic primal forces of rock and sky. A kloof and escarpment, a tree is celebrated. A particular fact is isolated and all idea of process or history is abandoned. These paintings, of landscape in a state of grace, are documents of disremembering. (WK 109)

Kentridge combats "the plague of the picturesque" through acts of close reading, coaxing the suppressed history of South Africa's violent past out of geological formations. Celebrated landscape singularities—the kloof, the escarpment, the tree—are supplanted by randomly chosen pieces of turf on which industrial incidents are plotted. What interests Kentridge are "pieces of civil engineering, the lines of pipes, culverts, fences" (WK 110).

> It has become clear that the variety of ephemera of human intervention on the landscape is far greater than anything the land itself has to offer. The varieties of high mast lighting, crash barriers, culverts, the transitions from cutting, to fence, to road, to verge, to fields are as great as any geological shifts. . . . There are other traces there too. A never-ending chronicle of disasters or almost disasters in the sets of skid marks that punctuate the road. (WK 110)

The slashed turf and zigzags of tire tracks establish the warp and woof of environmental violence, even as they point Kentridge, in Rosalind Krauss's virtuoso interpretation, toward a reinvestment of drawing, graphic trace, and medium in an era of postmedia.[4] For Krauss, this aesthetic commitment to medium is in and of itself a strategy of anti-globalization; a refusal of complicity "with a globalization of the image in the service of capital."[5] In my own reading, Krauss's marshaling of medium against the global market is only further strengthened by the manifest dimension of eco-critique within Kentridge's approach to nature.

Colonial Landscapes—a series of charcoal and pastels on paper of 1995–96—is an exercise in the art of doing South African pastoral otherwise. Despoliation and the ransacking of land make for what Kentridge calls "a desperate sort of naturalism," a dark-side version of the geography textbook's approach to habitat, which presents the trope of "land and peoples" as natural extensions of each other. Kentridge blasts the bucolic myth of harmony between man and nature; the interdependency of ecosystems gives way to visual narratives of forced labor and enslavement. Kentridge's bid for empirical banality in his "naturalistic drawings" of the South African veld prove that land "holds within it things other than pure nature" (WK 111).

J. M. Coetzee has observed that in Kentridge's films, "it is nature, for a change, that is vulnerable to man. The landscape of his films in particular is the devastated area south of Johannesburg: mine-dumps and slime dams; pylons and power cables; roads and tracks that lead from nowhere to nowhere" (WK 84). What is so fascinating in this work is the "figure in the carpet" leitmotif; the way in which landscape, upon closer scrutiny, reveals the signs of ecological travesty. Red pointers and circles appear on these bleak scapes, as if to ID sites of pollution and illegal dumping. Carolyn Christov-Bakargiev, in dialogue with Kentridge, remarks: "The red pastel surveyor's marks on your black charcoal drawings indicate how the colonial images were like projections onto the land. By observing the landscape itself you discover things you wouldn't normally notice: for example that a hill is really an artificial mound left over from a mining dump" (WK 22). The scenery, in other words, is composed of optical illusions that in closeup bear witness to environmental damage. According to Dan Cameron, "Not only is Kentridge signaling that this ruined vista is as much his cultural inheritance as the idyllic Eden was to his forebears, but in his refusal to ascribe any ideological position to nature he is also pointing out *the inherent connections between ecology and civil rights*" (WK 49, my emphasis).

In a nod to Bertolt Brecht's *Threepenny Opera*, Kentridge employs stock characters—the plutocrat, the capitalist—to dramatize the conversion of human ashes into gold. The 1991 film *Mine* features the capitalist Soho Eckstein: "Seated at his desk in the customary pose of the patriarch, Soho punches adding machines and cash registers, while the fruits of his efforts spill forth in the form of gold bars, exhausted miners, blasted landscapes and blocks of uniform housing" (WK 60). Coetzee claims that the film finds "pictorial means to link the notions of underground and repressed memory" (WK 84). The landscape as archive of human history and memory is an old idea, of course, compatible with the Freudian analogy between the unconscious and the dark continent. But in Kentridge's drawings there is generally an avoidance of subjectivism. Pastoral furnishes no inscape of the soul, but, rather, is deployed to build a brainscape, a CAT-scanned landfill, or mental environment: "Building off the geological metaphor deployed in *Mine*," Dan Cameron writes of the work *Weighing . . . and Wanting* (1997–98), "the scanned brain transforms into a kind of porous rock. . . . Embedded within the rock . . . are memory layers, fossilized like primordial records of long extinguished species" (WK 71).

The allusion to "extinguished" rather than "extinct" species points me to a poem called "Dispossession" by the contemporary Australian language poet John Kinsella, whose work exhibits parallel themes to Kentridge's, though in the literary medium. Kinsella employs the word "extinguishment" (accentuated by an exclamation point) in a riff on the history of Australia's indigenous population, driven off ancestral lands by mining companies and white hunters:

> protection
> aggravated
> destruction
> Almighty
> construction
> proclamation
> probability
> disease
> species
> autonomy
> links
> quality
> vis-à-vis
> the centralised
> London dealer in native art
> landing
> like something out of songlines
> the press
> commission/s
> traditional
> punishments
> appropriate
> authentic
> threads
> heresy
> controls

white hunters
alcohol
abuse
custody
motivating
sit-down
leaders
nominated
by
mining companies
pastoral leases
progressive
impacts
and sustain
extinguishment!
as assistance
modifies acts
presence
traces
the local
and maintains
representatives
authentic
claims
to constitutional
strategy
faith
and ownership
rifles
revisionist
histories: lights
in the sky
shackles[6]

The idea of "sustaining extinguishment" alludes to how government policies that have furthered mining interests mask the displacement
of Aboriginal communities in a rhetoric of preservationism. It is an oxymoron that undercuts ecological idealism (the equation of endangered tribal
peoples to endangered animals and plants), while capturing in psychic terms
the trauma experienced by Australia's "stolen generation," removed from
their families by welfare agencies and surrendered, all too often, to adult lives

of poverty and substance abuse. "Extinguishment," suggesting a landscape burned out by fires that form a narrative of dispossession (complementary to Kentridge's map of environmental incidents), exemplifies Kinsella's theory of "radical pastoral," which in "hybridising" the "so-called pastoral tradition with the linguistically innovative . . . ironises the pastoral construct but allows for genuine movement through rural spaces."[7]

Kinsella's high modernist tendencies make him susceptible to classification as a "global" writer who exploits Australian regionalism in the name of a contemporary rewriting of T. S. Eliot's *The Waste Land*. But this reading ignores the language politics of "hybridising" that inform his aesthetic agenda. As a reader of the Murri Aboriginal poet Lionel Fogarty, he commends Fogarty's "communalizing of the lyrical I" (his land-based antisubjectivism) through a hybrid English that "reterritorializes lost ground":[8] In Fogarty's verse, hybrid English is identifiable as pidgin that archives slavery's past while thematizing its own dialectal activism (as in the line "Yea my some communication, still many tribespeople/dialect you and old, not sold.").[9] In the poem "No Grudge," rural radio talks back in a hybrid tongue. Indigenous words plant themselves inside English, and a great ingenuity is applied to the estrangement of English through sound slippages (as in the play between the words, "human," "new-one," and "up man") or the phrase "mass translate" (which trumps the absent yet no less anticipated "mass transit"):

> Our educationalist is the yubba
> on the koori radio.
> Nudge nudge human new one up-man-ship
> run by himself.
> But the community be at each others throats
> but we should consider advocating
> a hurray wireless playing
> Blackfella media, not political
> foot-balling loud-mouth perturbed.
> A happy-go-lucky broadcaster
> is one tribalism sparkling radio
> disc-jockey we seem to criticise
> 100 psychological conditioning
> Let the yubba mass translate
> a mouth communicating
> Suppression, hot reply [10]

While Kinsella's own language games are clearly indebted to Fogarty's local formalism, he also crosses theory with pastoral genres in ways that tie him to the American L=A=N=G=U=A=G=E poets, a loose-linked group including Charles Bernstein, Lyn Hejinian, Ron Silliman, and Jed Rasula that, by the mid-eighties was translating continental theory into writing praxis. Many of the texts in Kinsella's *Visitants* collection experiment with ecological phenomenology and transformational grammar. The poem *Skeleton weed/generative grammar* (for Noam Chomsky), for example, suggests a genetics of language or agri-linguistics in its play on language trees. Several poems bear epigraphs drawn from Lacan, Jacques-Alain Miller, and the Australian Lacanian feminist Elizabeth Grosz, and these frame texts function as more than intellectual captions. Kinsella uses psychoanalytic concepts developed by these theorists—panic fear, anxiety, the uncanny—to stage what Spivak has referred to as "the spectralization of the rural." In the poem *"keeping your mouth shut—against conspiracy"* the rural is erased by the alien presence of chemical plants. Nungalloo becomes the generic site designated as "Area-51," and corporate names—"Associated Labs," "Allied," and "Jennings"—signify the nullification of territory, the advent of industrial apocalypse in Australia's wheatlands:

> Area-51 was a place called Nungalloo
> just north of Geraldton. The huge
> mineral sands processing plants
> of Jennings and Allied mutated
> out of borderline farmland.
> As if a neutral zone, Associated Labs
> sat nearby, upwind. Testing
> monozite and rutile
> late at night a storm hit
> the narrative and the x-ray
> equipment went wild, the gun
> shooting rays outside its alignment,
> the telex scripting the electric air,
> my flesh spread like an internal horizon
> a chemiluminescent shadow puppet
> experimenting with form,
> my organs glowed and I watched
> the machinery of my fear,
> the production of silence. (V 15)

Radioactive waste creates a toxic luminosity captured by the neologism "chemiluminescent." A ghostly body, irradiated and iridescent like electronic text on a dark screen, emerges from a cosmic battle between light rays and X-rays in the night sky.

Kinsella excels in inventing an ecological uncanny that uses extra-terrestrial visitation as the trope of late industrial catastrophism. In *The Three Laws of Robotics, Skylab and the Theory of Forms*, the landscape is possessed by "visitants" in the form of Soviet space trash, which, as you may recall, does in fact routinely drop from the sky between New Zealand and Australia. In the poem "Phenomenology" (leading off with an interesting epigraph from Donna Haraway "But with the advance of civilization, this biology has become a problem"), a child's jerry-rigged telephone system becomes the conduit of "glowing figures with strange limbs like Roswell aliens" (V 11). Chaos theory, paranormal forces, and robopsychology "wire" the outback, transforming it into a force-field of clashing communication systems and inflecting it with manifest spookiness. In "The Savagery of Birds," "live" nature is haunted by the specter of artificial life:

> As smog drifts up from the city
> you realise that the sky is really
> a painted backdrop, and Nature
> has no part in it, that all around
> you is construct—the silos,
> the sheds, the tractors, the trucks,
> cybernetic animals wearing
> fashionable genes, mechanical
> birds that fly with the gravity
> and grace of a computer simulation
> while wearing expressions that belong
> to mythology, making Frans Snyders's
> *Oiseaux sur des branches* relevant
> to the end of the twentieth century,
> to a place deep down in the South,
> where grain-eating birds are turning
> to flesh that tastes like muesli. (V 40)

This poem recalls Lacan's famous example of Zeuxis's painting of grapes so lifelike that they fool the birds, and Parrhasios's painting of a veil so convincing that Zeuxis demands to know what is painted behind it. Lacan reads this as a parable about *Vorstellungsrepräsentanz*—"that something that stands for representation"—which lures the gaze and allows it to triumph over the eye.[11] For Kinsella, the Flemish still-life master of the sixteenth century, Frans Snyder, is deputized as a latterday Zeuxis. But in Kinsella's poetic trompe l'oeil, it is the birds themselves that have become objects of visual fascination. As "cybernetic animals wearing fashionable genes," their

flesh shown mutating into muesli, they resemble allegories of a bio-engi-
neered nature that converts the mechanical into the living, or the animal
into agricultural by-product, according to a common genetic code.

Kinsella's literary experiments with the interface between artificial
nature and virtual environment invite comparison with the work of Andreas
Gursky, an artist for whom photographic virtuality is a signature theme.
Gursky is most famous for his wall-sized photographs of work environments
and commercial hubs—the *Tokyo Stock Exchange*, with its hivelike depiction
of traders coming and going; the *Hong Kong and Shanghai Bank*, with its
serially arrayed and replicated workstations; the *Siemans* factory floor with
its "wired" spectacle of organized chaos; the Salerno car lot, a chromatic
blanket of commodities; or the formal grammar of *Untitled V* (1997), with
its trainers lined up on display shelves like fetishes on a conveyer belt. Not
only do these images deliver great spectacle value, they also offer the intrigue
of visual puzzle, since Gursky is known to have manipulated their *Neue
Sachlichkeit* verisimilitude, emptying out digital information or using over-
lays of other digital images. In *Untitled V*, for example, "The artist built a
short double shelf, which he then photographed six times, painstakingly
figuring out the proper angles from which to shoot and restocking the
shelves with different shoes for each session. The negatives were then pieced
together digitally to make a single, monumental image, reflected on the
floor."[12] Using techniques of digital montage and illusionism, Gursky
straightens and flattens the curved panoramic image into a rectilinear geom-
etry so that every aspect of the image is frontally engaged. These techniques
draw attention to the digital image as a screen of colored pixels that, at high
resolution, produce a kind of pointillism that the eye "corrects" into form.
Gursky explores the relationship between pixilation and printing; square
pixels, once printed, are visually softened and rendered smoothly transitional, a process referred to as "dithering." What the eye accomplishes for
pointillism, digital printing accomplishes by dithering, allowing Gursky's
inserts and collages of groups of people to assume their place as if they were
always there.

The effects of this image manipulation are particularly unsettling
when directed at the German tradition of Romantic nature painting. There
is the sendup of postcard nature in *Yogyakarta*, a photograph that looks like
a European park, but which in fact is "a cheap photomural in a greasy spoon
in Indonesia," according to Peter Galassi.[13] There are images such as *Ruhr
Valley* (1993) that seam together multiple camera angles, creating a "real but
not quite" effect. As Alex Alberro has noted, the images are stuck somewhere
between "simulacrum (a picture of a picture)" and "simulation (in which

the image has no origins in the real), and thus do [*sic*] not entirely cross the threshold into pure virtuality since the final results are composites of photographic documents."[14] In *Autobahn Mettmann*, the view of cows and fields from the window of a highway rest stop presents a visual field striated by horizontal bars, apparently painted on glass to keep motorists from being distracted by scenery. The aluminum strips direct as well as deflect the gaze, cutting into the gestalt of pastureland and bovine forms, as if to reveal how farmland in the European Union (currently beset by the hellish spectacle of piles of smoldering animal carcasses, the "landscape" of mad cow disease) is subject to a managed ecology of seeing and not seeing.

Gursky "translates" linguistic habitat into ontological *habitus* in a curious work that seems, initially at least, to be an anomalous subject in his repertory. A framed page apparently lifted from a German phenomenological treatise is presented in blowup format, like a landscape or scroll that draws the viewer into its totalizing world-view or *Lebensphilosophie* (figure 1).[15] The text contains intriguing phrases and expressions: "a self-renovation longing," "self-destitution," "the state of being, shell-shocked by a group soul" (as in the sentence: "Was diese Renoviersucht des Daseins zu einum Perpetuum mobile macht, is nichts als das Ungemach, dass zwischen dem nebelhaften eigenen und dem shon zur fremden Schale erstarrten Ich der Vorgänger wieder nur ein Schein-ich, eine ungefähr passende Gruppenseele eingeschoben wird" "And the way this addiction to renewal in one's existence makes one perpetually mobile, is motivated by nothing other than destitution, between one's own nebulousness and the already foreign shell that has hardened over one's predecessor, which once again is a kind of appearance-self, an approximate group-soul which is shoved onto one"). Who could write this sentence? one is compelled to ask. It seems to have something of Walter Benjamin in it, some Martin Heidegger perhaps, but it is like neither of them, quite, but rather, like a piece of generic German modernism. As it turns out, this is a collaged and seamed version of Robert Musil's turn-of-the-century Austrian novel *The Man Without Qualities*. Performing a kind of digital sampling on the text, Gursky de-authorizes it, inducing lexical seasickness. Gursky is a master of overlay, transforming environments and habitats into digitally enhanced versions of themselves. Digital modification thus becomes essential to what is "critical" in Gursky's treatment of habitats, however weak that kind of critique-through-representation may seem. Factory floors, ski slopes, supermarket shelves, workstations, football stadiums, library stacks—these sites become interchangeable insofar as they represent environments that have been profoundly mediated by media, visually altered by the effect of what Roland Barthes

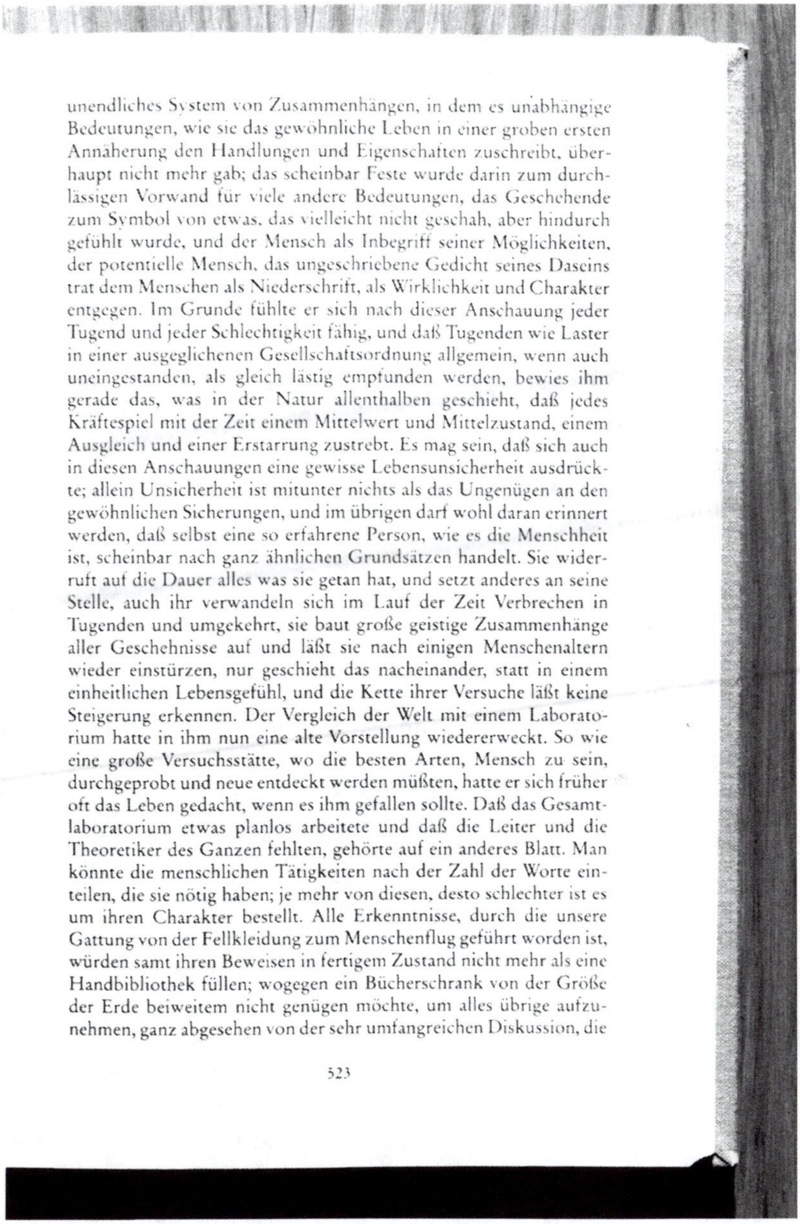

unendliches System von Zusammenhängen, in dem es unabhängige
Bedeutungen, wie sie das gewöhnliche Leben in einer groben ersten
Annäherung den Handlungen und Eigenschaften zuschreibt, über-
haupt nicht mehr gab; das scheinbar Feste wurde darin zum durch-
lässigen Vorwand für viele andere Bedeutungen, das Geschehende
zum Symbol von etwas, das vielleicht nicht geschah, aber hindurch
gefühlt wurde, und der Mensch als Inbegriff seiner Möglichkeiten,
der potentielle Mensch, das ungeschriebene Gedicht seines Daseins
trat dem Menschen als Niederschrift, als Wirklichkeit und Charakter
entgegen. Im Grunde fühlte er sich nach dieser Anschauung jeder
Tugend und jeder Schlechtigkeit fähig, und daß Tugenden wie Laster
in einer ausgeglichenen Gesellschaftsordnung allgemein, wenn auch
uneingestanden, als gleich lästig empfunden werden, bewies ihm
gerade das, was in der Natur allenthalben geschieht, daß jedes
Kräftespiel mit der Zeit einem Mittelwert und Mittelzustand, einem
Ausgleich und einer Erstarrung zustrebt. Es mag sein, daß sich auch
in diesen Anschauungen eine gewisse Lebensunsicherheit ausdrück-
te; allein Unsicherheit ist mitunter nichts als das Ungenügen an den
gewöhnlichen Sicherungen, und im übrigen darf wohl daran erinnert
werden, daß selbst eine so erfahrene Person, wie es die Menschheit
ist, scheinbar nach ganz ähnlichen Grundsätzen handelt. Sie wider-
ruft auf die Dauer alles was sie getan hat, und setzt anderes an seine
Stelle, auch ihr verwandeln sich im Lauf der Zeit Verbrechen in
Tugenden und umgekehrt, sie baut große geistige Zusammenhänge
aller Geschehnisse auf und läßt sie nach einigen Menschenaltern
wieder einstürzen, nur geschieht das nacheinander, statt in einem
einheitlichen Lebensgefühl, und die Kette ihrer Versuche läßt keine
Steigerung erkennen. Der Vergleich der Welt mit einem Laboratorium hatte in ihm nun eine alte Vorstellung wiedererweckt. So wie
eine große Versuchsstätte, wo die besten Arten, Mensch zu sein,
durchgeprobt und neue entdeckt werden müßten, hatte er sich früher
oft das Leben gedacht, wenn es ihm gefallen sollte. Daß das Gesamt-
laboratorium etwas planlos arbeitete und daß die Leiter und die
Theoretiker des Ganzen fehlten, gehörte auf ein anderes Blatt. Man
könnte die menschlichen Tätigkeiten nach der Zahl der Worte ein-
teilen, die sie nötig haben; je mehr von diesen, desto schlechter ist es
um ihren Charakter bestellt. Alle Erkenntnisse, durch die unsere
Gattung von der Fellkleidung zum Menschenflug geführt worden ist,
würden samt ihren Beweisen in fertigem Zustand nicht mehr als eine
Handbibliothek füllen; wogegen ein Bücherschrank von der Größe
der Erde beiweitem nicht genügen möchte, um alles übrige aufzu-
nehmen, ganz abgesehen von der sehr umfangreichen Diskussion, die

523

Figure 1. Andreas Gursky, *Untitled XII (Musil 1)*, Courtesy of the Matthew Marks
Gallery.

calls "the environs of the image," that "leech" factor of exteriority that allows the outside to "stick" to the idea, and that makes the body image or place image stick (or "stick out" as the case may be).[16] The use of scale, serial repetition, and chromatic alteration—the latter bringing on a kind of "new painterliness" according to the photographer James Welling—all serve to intensify the image of nature, and this extreme technological intensification gives nature back an image of itself as visual ideology.

Where Andreas Gursky treats mediality as a technical milieu that explores the porous boundaries of nature and culture, art and digitally enhanced pictorialism, the Catalan artist Muntadas construes translation as a limit case of mediality, as it has been defined in the work of media theorist Samuel Weber. Weber's ascription is born of the dissonant conjunction of Heidegger and Benjamin—specifically, their common fascination with the ontology of technics. In his 1996 book *Mass Mediaurus: Form, Technics, Media*, Weber ingeniously aligns Benjamin's "The Work of Art in the Age of its Technical Reproducibility" with Heidegger's "Questing after Technics."[17] Like Bernard Stiegler, who reminds us that the Greek *tekhnè* denotes the "means of production," as well as *démesure* (excess, hubris, the hyperexpressivity of art), Weber recalls that technics signifies *poesis*, craft, skill, applied science, the afterbirth of nature.[18] Technics undergirds the critical understanding of mediality as something made, thought, experienced, or labored, that remains detached from any specific medium. A transferable quantum, mediality as Weber understands it, designates epistemologies of know-how or "alities" and "abilities" (as in translat*ability*, reproduc*ibility*, medi*ality*) that are culled from such diverse intellectual sources as deconstruction, pragmatism, aesthetics, cybernetics, film, television, technoscience, performance studies, communications, publicity, systems and information theory, artificial intelligence, linguistics, symbolic logic, programming, and psychoanalysis. The problem of mediality gains focus as it is subcontracted to smaller, denser units of exegesis, structured around topoi that include: mimesis and reproducibility, ontology and biogenesis, aporia and iterability, *Gestell* (emplacement) and *Verborgenheit* (bringing forth, unconcealment), the waning of affect, and the targeting of lived experience. Mediality yields a labor theory of value that exposes the way in which televisual information, or mediated forms of knowledge, are "capitalized," that is to say, subsumed by capitalism (like minoritarian resistance movements), or conscripted in the industrialization of democracy.

Muntadas makes mediality a conceptual art practice by treating translational technologies themselves as the grist or filters of medium. Where other artists have focused on revealing how art "translates" the mediatization of natural or social environments, Muntadas takes the media environment itself, along with its second-order transposition to other media systems, as subject to translation. Muntadas archives images, sounds, language, and text in his installations, monitoring and resetting their context parameters. In early projects devoted to televisuality made in the 1970s, loops of "emission" and "reception" are interrupted and rerouted, sometimes across the screen of the TV box, making viewers aware of their own situation within the circuitry of televisual communication. Beginning in the mid-1990s, Muntadas began a series of works that shared the prefix *On Translation* using videotapes, Web sites, publications, site-specific installations, and texts as mediums. *On Translation: The Pavilion*, completed in 1995, reconstituted the glass pavilion used by translators on the occasion of the 1975 Helsinki conference on European Security and Cooperation. The translation booth reappeared in *Translation: The Games*, a work of 1996 (see image on the book cover) made on the occasion of the Atlanta Olympics. Inside the booth, viewers were exposed to recordings of interviews conducted by Muntadas with professional simultaneous translators, translated into Vietnamese (purposely not a superpower language). These audio cues were complemented by images of translators. Normally an unseen army of verbal laborers sealed into soundproof cabins, and further insulated from the world by earphones plastered to their heads, the translators were brought out from the back office and given public visibility in the installation. Shown too, in recycled archival shots of Cold War international congresses, were diplomats wired up to their translators, their faces contorted by expressions of exhaustion, anger, consternation, and despair. *On Translation: The Games*, in addition to serving as a masque of failed diplomacy, demonstrates how language politics historically infiltrates power politics and shapes the media event in countless, untold ways. Muntadas's 1997 *On Translation: The Internet Project* (part of the Documenta X exhibition in Kassel, Germany) extended his experimentation with translation as medium to the realm of software and computational linguistics. A coil or helix, suggesting a 3-D diagram of the Tower of Babel, contained a single phrase rendered in twenty-two languages, each of which could be audio-accessed depending on where the viewer clicked on the spiral. In this way, the translation engine of machine translation programs (like Babelfish and Altavista) was in effect "seen," or at least visualized as an interface, much like the human translators in the translation booths in the earlier works. Where non-Roman alphabets could not be entered into the translation program (because the engine did not recognize their characters), they were used to fabricate multilingual col-

Figure 2. John Klima, *Ecosystm*, Whitney Museum of Art Bitstreams Exhibition, 2001.

lage. Pieces of language, arrayed in polyglot graffiti walls, drew attention to the visual dimension of the translational medium.

Seeming to take up where Muntadas leaves off, the media artist John Klima has also "translated" the computer environment, focusing on interface as a site of transformation whereby unrepresentable processes are converted into false pictorial narratives. Klima makes us aware that a program like "Windows" is a fictive interface operating through opaque layering, a mask for the processing of digital information. Klima's installation *Ecosystm* (figure 2), exhibited at the Whitney Museum's *Bitstreams* show, provides a fractal of the interface between globalization and media environments. The work is conceptually predicated on the translation of currency fluctuations into flocks of birds. One might argue, along the lines suggested by Friedrich Kittler's view of the invisible layering of software and hardware codes, that the birds are revealed to be allegorical structures pasted over digital structures that are themselves electronic responses to market processes.[19] Klima thus creates an information loop or feed that ends up in a transparent visual ideology. The flight patterns are true or deictic signs (in that they stand in for "real time" responses to shifts in monetary value), but the ecological habitat in which they are represented emerges as an arbitrary, fictive interface. In theory, any other screen saver would do. Or would it?

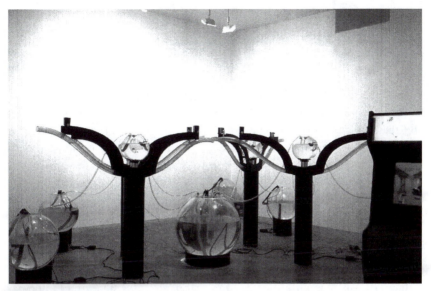

Figure 3. John Klima, *Go Fish*, Installation View, Postmasters Gallery, 2001.

The birds do in fact seem to have been chosen for a reason: their feeding frenzies and bellicose attacks seem to simulate corporate raiding and thus literalize visually the impact of long-distance financial transactions on remote ecologies.

The originality of Klima's work lies in the way in which it indicates how media environments often camouflage what globalization does to local habitats, dissolving political responsibility in information flows. Trained as a programmer with consultant experience for various financial firms, Klima has consistently framed the theme of remote responsibility. As the publicity notice of his Postmasters gallery show informs us:

> In a piece called "Go Fish [figure 3]," the viewer must try to navigate through treacherous waters connected to an actual fish tank. "Go Fish" examines the mini-world of a fishbowl. Visitors play a video game in which the outcome affects the fate of a real goldfish. . . . In the game . . . the player is a fish swimming through dangerous waters. Lose, and a goldfish is shot from a bowl into a tank with menacing oscar fish, that will eat it later that night. Win, and the goldfish head towards less carnivorous company. Players might pity the victim, but the goldfish must lose out sometimes, or the oscars will die of starvation. "It's the moral dilemma any pet owner faces when they feed animals to

their pets," says Klima. "More than that, it may be the reigning moral dilemma in a zero-sum system, where saving one creature means killing another and where one person's calm blue water is another's path to power."

Klima reveals the extent to which media environments, governed by the law of "your loss is my gain," and long-distance ethics, coordinate the cooperative relationship between globalization and ecological exploitation. Interface emerges as a translational medium in which ecological responsibility is shown to be dissolved and re-articulated. The flocks of birds function as the picture or visual ideology that masks the invisible digital process of data transfer and mutation. But they also symbolize the digital capture of market exchanges and their translation into ecosystems. In this sense, Klima offers a literal rendering of Spivak's idea of nature in the global economy as "already on the way to data."

Klima uses the media environment not only as a site for tracking data on its way to environmental damage, but also as a medium of information transfer that is causally implicated in the damage. In this regard, a work such as *Go Fish* contrasts sharply with, say, Peter Fend's satellite images of algae bloom fatal to millions of fish (*Ocean Earth: Processed Imagery from AVHRR of the North Sea 15–16 May, 1988*), or Allan Sekula's *Fish Story* (a series of riveting photo documents of the fishing industry), or Kentridge's *The Deluge* (a charcoal and pastel drawing featuring a toxic swimming pool with giant amphibians thrashing overhead, dodging flying debris in an ominous storm). Each of these fish-themed works enlists an environmental conceptualism in its treatment of medium, and each depicts a growing social panic about the ingestion and circulation of PCBs in the food chain, the precariousness of fishing economies, and the apparition of that supranational sea monster currently crashing the Kyoto Protocols that Antonio Negri and Michael Hardt associate with Empire. But in Klima's installations, the computer medium itself is both the tool of environmental damage and the representational vehicle of critique. The visible conversion of data transfer into nature (and the reverse) allows the viewer to pinpoint precisely where the survival of natural habitat becomes critically endangered.

As we have seen, Kentridge, Kinsella, Gursky, Muntadas, and Klima have each contributed potential ways of making habitat "critical" by treating it as a profoundly translational medium (across nature and information, across language and visual image, across media). But tensions persist between the "grounded" and locally critical representation of "real" habitats, suffering real political devastation and trauma—habitats that are, so to speak, often rendered as stand-ins for political and social struggle—and the more globally produced habitats, virtual habitats if you like, that are constituted by communication networks and represented by the front-end software of the Web. Such tensions cannot simply be overcome by a generalized idea of "globality" (which even in its demystified forms has an uncanny ability to gobble up and assimilate environmental resistance as if it were one of John Klima's vulnerable goldfish), but they can perhaps be made productive in the context of aesthetic strategies of planetary identification that resist both the trap of a myopic, self-enclosed regionalism and a eulogistic acceptance of new technologies of mediality for their own sake.

14

Translation with No Original: Scandals of Textual Reproduction

In a short story titled "The Dialect of the Tribe" by the American Oulipo writer Harry Mathews, the narrator ponders an academic article authored by an Australian anthropologist of the 1890s by the name of Ernest Botherby. The article is of interest because it offers the example of a mysterious technique "used by the Pagolak-speaking tribe to translate their tongue into the dialects of their neighbors. 'What was remarkable about this method was that while it produced translations that foreign listeners could understand and accept, it also concealed from them the original meaning of every statement made.' "[1] The narrator is immediately intrigued: "To translate successfully and not reveal one's meaning—what could be more paradoxical? What could be more relevant?" . . . "What could be more extraordinary than a method that would allow words to be 'understood' by outsiders without having their substance given away?" (HC 8–9). "You and I might know," the narrator confides with smug Eurocentrism to the reader, "that translation may, precisely, exorcise the illusion that substantive content exists at all—but what led a remote New Guinean tribe to such a discovery?" (HC 10). These ironic questions tap into primal truisms of translation, to wit: something is always lost in translation. Unless one knows the language of the original, the exact nature and substance of what is lost will be always be impossible to ascertain; even if one has access to the language of the original, there remains an x-factor of untranslatability that renders every translation an impossible world or faux regime of semantic and phonic equivalence. What makes Mathews's story so clever, in the manner, say, of Jorge Luis Borges's short story *Tlön, Uqbar, Orbis Tertius* (in which the place-name

"Uqbar," presumed to be a variant on the name of the country of Iraq, is suspected of being an "undocumented country . . . deliberately invented . . . to substantiate a phrase") is that it reveals the way in which translations are always trying to disguise the impossibility of fidelity to the original tongue.[2] In the Mathews story, it is the delusional belief that a possible world of translatability exists that induces the narrator to defect from his own language into a Pagolak-speaking world. Translation is thus revealed to be a special case of literature "hors de ce monde"—"Any where out of the world!"—to borrow Baudelaire's famous phrase, that is to say, a literary world that is possible, indeed even plausible, only insofar as it actualizes a parallel universe in and on its own terms.

The narrator's election to enter a possible world of translatability brings to mind the contention of the language philosopher David Lewis that a plurality of worlds must be posited hypothetically, to exist, if the rules of the language allow for it. Lewis's truth-conditional theory of semantics is concerned to determine the conditions under which a sentence is true. Language, he has asserted, needs to be able to talk about things that may not exist, as in the sentence: "Someone seeks a unicorn." We know that the creature doesn't exist but the sentence can be understood. If the meaning of p is posited as true, by necessity, then Lp is true in given worlds in which p *is*.[3] This grammar of necessity, positing the hypothetical grounds of linguistic and literary possible worlds may well yield what Umberto Eco has referred to as "lunatic linguistics." Eco traces this language lunacy back to Gabriel Foigny's invention of a self-translating "austral" grammar in his 1676 work *La Terre australe connue*, but one finds numerous examples closer to the contemporary period in those writers cherished by Deleuze and Foucault who created their own private worlds of syntactic and lexical "shizanalyse": J-P Brisset, Raymond Roussel, and Louis Wolfson.[4] What these writers have in common is the ability to make standard language strange to itself—superimposing their own private grammatical logics and laws of homonymic and syllabic substitution onto the vehicular tongue, such that it remains quasi-intelligible—in a state, if you will, of semi-translation. For a recent example of this process, consider Jonathan Safran Foer's 2002 bestseller *Everything Is Illuminated*, narrated by a young Russian translator whose stilted English is riddled with malapropisms and American pop-cultural lingo. Here, the reader is entered into a possible world that could be characterized as the language limbo of the non-native speaker.[5] In such cases of "lunatic linguistics" we discover an order of language that is not pure babel, but something between a discrete or standard language and a translation, a language-in-a-state-of-translation, which becomes "possible" according to the criteria of modal realism and counterfactual logic used by David Lewis to define the conditions of possibility.

What interests me here is not so much the argument, already considered in chapter 7, over whether possible world theory is useful to the analysis of self-translating private languages (languages that are cybernetic in their capacity to generate new grammatical logics for each new possible linguistic world), but rather, the ethical problem that arises when there is, strictly speaking, no "original" language or text on which the translation is based. The reader is either placed in a netherworld of "translatese" that floats between original and translation, or confronted with a situation in which the translation "mislays" the original, absconding to some "other" world of textuality that retains the original only as fictive pretext. In both instances, the identity of what a translation *is* is tested, for if a translation is not a form of textual predicate, indexically pointing to a primary text, then what is it? Can a literary technology of reproduction that has sublated its origin still be considered a translation? Or should it be considered the premier illustration of deconstructed ontology insofar as it reveals the extent to which all translations are unreliable transmitters of the original, purveyors, that is, of a regime of extreme untruth?

Translation studies typically frames the ethics of textual infidelity in terms of a translation's infelicitous rendering of an original (measured as lack of accuracy, of formal and grammatical similitude, of literary flair, or of poetic feeling), or in terms of the target text's dubious connection to its source; its status as pseudo- or fictitious translation. As part of a larger effort to rethink the critical premises of translation studies,[6] I will be concentrating on the latter case, taking up issues of how to interpret celebrated examples of texts that have turned out to be translations with no originals. My purpose is not to visit the scandal of pseudotranslation for its own sake, but to explore the broader ethical issues surrounding textual reproduction that such scandals bring into theoretical focus.

Douglas Robinson (following Anton Popovic) defines pseudotranslation as "not only a text pretending, or purporting, or frequently taken to be a translation, but also . . . a translation that is frequently taken to be an original work." As Robinson sees it, any work "whose status as 'original' or 'derivative' is, for whatever social or textual reason, problematic" qualifies as pseudotranslation.[7] This broad definition creates, however, as many problems as it solves by inviting controversy over which kind of texts should qualify as pseudotranslation. James MacPherson's 1760 "translation" of "Ossianic" poems, *Fragments of Ancient Poetry Translated from the Gaelic or Erse Language*, clearly warrants designation as such, but other examples—

Longfellow's *Hiawatha* (putatively based on a Finnish scholar's transposition of Chippewa legends), or medieval glosses of Roman texts—inhabit a fuzzy zone between translation and transcription, and become harder to classify as pseudo.

Pseudotranslation, as Robinson's definition suggests, invites emphasis on the exposure of fraudulent translations, with the critic's efforts concentrated on rectifying mistaken attributions in literary history, on drawing generic distinctions between model and imitation, or on refining criteria used in authenticating the status and value of an original work of literature. The literary scandals and accusations of forgery opened up by allegations of pseudotranslation are not unlike the "connoisseur wars" raging around the de-attribution of pricey masterpieces in prestigious museums and private collections worldwide. The drama of revelation—of fakery and forgery laid bare—is what drives this kind of interpretation thematically. By contrast, if the issue of textual fidelity to the original is defined in terms of a theory of textual reproduction, the focus shifts from questions of textual veracity and sham to the conditions of the original's reproducibility. The problem of authorial counterfeit is thus displaced by consideration of whether a translation is born not from a "real" original (an authenticated work by a given author), but from a kind of "test tube" text of simulated originality, a text, if you will, that is unnaturally or artificially birthed and successfully replicated. The idea of textual cloning, emphasizing, in a metaphorical way, literary analogues to genic coding, copying, and blueprinting, problematizes "the work of art in the age of genetic reproduction" in a way that brings Walter Benjamin's famous essay on "The Work of Art in the Age of Mechanical Reproduction" (1936) into colloquy with controversies over the status of "original" identity in the age of the genome project. As a "code of codes" (a kind of HTML or master code used in machine translation), translation becomes definable as a cloning mechanism of textual transference or reproducibility rather than as a discrete form of secondary textuality predicated on an "auratic" original. Benjamin's equally famous essay "The Task of the Translator" (1923) also returns in another guise. His identification of translation as that which usurps the place of the original while ensuring its afterlife, may be used to associate textual cloning with the idea of a "reproductively engineered" original (comparable, say, to the replication of RNA molecules in a test tube), or with a translation that grows itself anew from the cells of a morbid or long-lost original. Under these circumstances, it is increasingly difficult to distinguish between original and cloned embryonic forms; indeed the whole category of originality—as an essentialist life form—becomes subject to dispute.

Pseudotranslation versus textual cloning: two paradigms that address problematic originality in the field of translation studies, two paradigms that are conceptually related, but emphasize distinctly different problems and questions. My particular interest here will be in exploring what the concept of textual cloning might bring to the age-old discussion of textual fidelity in translation studies, how it shifts the terms of translation studies, from original and translation, to clone and code.

There are few more flagrant cases of pseudotranslation than Pierre Louÿs's *Les Chansons de Bilitis*, published in 1894 with the subtitle *traduites du grec pour la première fois par P.L.* and marketed as the translation of works by a sixth-century half-Greek, half-Turkish poetess. Louÿs, as his biographer Jean-Paul Goujon notes, was educated in the manner of the great nineteenth-century philologists and historians: Michelet, Quinet, Renan, Mommsen, Taine, Littré, and Gaston Paris among others. Philological dogma was frequently marshaled in the service of translation. Leconte de Lisle, a mentor to Louÿs, was from 1861 on dedicating his energies to translations of Theocritus, Homer, Aeschylus, and Euripides.[8] Claiming archaeological as well as poetic value, the studies of antiquity that emerged in the second half of the nineteenth century goaded Louÿs to follow suit, first because he believed he could do better in revivifying the past; second, because he suspected erotic censorship on the part of academic classicists; and third, because he sought restitution for Greek decadence by promoting Alexandrian Greek literature (deemed barbaric or obscene) over and against the privileged literature of fifth-century Athens (PL 92). Lucan, Meleager, Theocritus, and Sappho, each orientalized, homosexualized, and sensualized to the maximum, formed the canon of Louÿs's "other Hellenism," according to Goujon. In this light, it is surely no accident that Bilitis herself was billed as a writer of Turkish-Greek origin, or that Louÿs's translation of Meleager was acclaimed for its representation of a "creolized race of Athenians," and invention of a "hellenized Orient" or Syrianized Greece (PL 92).

When *Les Chansons de Bilitis* was initially published, Rémy de Gourmont bestowed fulsome praise: "A personal manner, that is to say, a new way of feeling an old form of Greek poetry full of ideas and images that have passed into the public domain, restores to this poetry a beauty that it had lost or no longer possessed when it was felt and translated by a mediocre professor."[9] It was just such a "mediocre professor," however, who ostensibly discovered the original manuscript of Bilitis's poems and served as their first translator. When Louÿs published *Les Chansons* he included notes on the text's provenance, claiming that the erotic prose poems were discovered by a German philologist by the name of G. Heim in the course of an archaeological excavation in Cypress. When Louÿs delivered the manuscript to his editor Bailly, he maintained that it was a French translation of Heim's German translation from the Greek. Despite allegations of error in his previous translations of Meleager and Lucan's *Scenes from the Lives of Courtesans*, Louÿs's reputation as a classicist passed muster and contributed to the generally favorable reception of *Les Chansons* when it was first published.

Initially, Louÿs confided the secret of the text's true author only to his brother George Louis, but a number of friends detected the ruse, including Gide, Valéry, Debussy, and Heredia. Gide may have unwittingly helped the hoax along by introducing Louÿs to the Algerian courtisan Meryem bent-Ali, thought to have been the live model for his figure of the Greek courtesan. Several critics who initially reviewed the book suspected that the text had a fictitious origin, among them Camille Mauclair who lauded the book as a "livre d'art" rather than as a translation, and Henri de Régnier, who wrote: "I do not know if Bilitis ever existed, but certainly she lives fully in these little poems that M. Louÿs has collected, and engraved on the walls of her pungent, imaginary tomb" (CB 327). Other readers, however, seem to have fallen into the trap; one in particular, to Louÿs's great amusement, sent him some "variants on the translation," and a "mandarin" of classical studies, Gustave Fougère, to whom Louÿs had sent copies of both *Les Chansons* and his Meleager translation, wrote back: "Bilitis and Meleager were not unknown to me, for a long time I have considered them personal friends" (CB 322). Working closely with poems by Sapphic epigones, and putting literary sleuths off the scent by acknowledging his poetic license (especially in the most decadent sections of the song cycle), Louÿs took special precautions to guarantee that this paleographic mockup would be received as an authentic translation. He suppressed his initial temptation to oversimulate the look of a scholarly edition by reducing the plethora of notes, providing a scaled-down yet plausible "Life" of Bilitis, and including an addendum of so-called untranslated verse. In the book's preface Louÿs wrote: "I wanted this story to be Bilitis's, because in translating the *Songs* I myself fell in love with this lover of Mnasidika. Her life was undoubtedly as marvelous as it seems. I only regret that the classical authors did not speak of her more, and that those records that have at least survived, are so meager in providing information about her life." Philodemus, who ransacked her work twice, does not even mention her name. (CB 25).

The success of Louÿs's *supercherie* (even though it only lasted until 1898 when the text was "outed" coincident with the release of the second edition) was helped along by the vogue of Greek revivalism in fin de siècle erotic literature. The work's reception was buoyed by the reading public's keen appetite for Baudelairean Lesbos and Parnassian pastoral love poetry. The same appetite was responsible for the later popularity of Natalie Clifford Barney's 1902 *Cinq petits dialogues grecs* and Renée Vivien's free translations of Sappho, which appeared in 1903. Anticipating Rémy de Gourmont and Natalie Clifford Barney's reinvestment of the Amazon myth, and André Gide's appropriation of platonic dialogue for gay polemic in *Corydon*, Louÿs placed utopian sexual politics at the heart of his agenda in using Greek conceits to express feminine same-sex love. In a letter to his brother he declared his intention to liberate the expression of lesbian desire from the shackles of the femme fatale stereotype, and he "respectfully" dedicated the *Chansons* "to the young women of future society."[10] Louÿs confided to his brother that he thought of lesbian love as a "deformation" not of love but of maternal instinct. Expressive of the essence of femininity unencumbered by Christian morality, lesbianism affords an ideal sexual paradigm of fecundity without biological reproduction. In "Hymn to Astarté," we find this idea of contraceptive reproducibility affixed to a figure of the sui generis Mother: "Mother, inexhaustible, incorruptible, creator, born first, engendered by yourself, conceived by yourself, issue of yourself alone, you, who pleasures herself, Astarté / O perpetually fecund, o virgin and universal wet-nurse" (CB 137). The apparent oxymoron of fertile sterility resurfaces in many other poems in the cycle descriptive of lesbian lovemaking. "Les Seins de Mnasidika," for example, features Mnasidika making an offering of her breasts to Bilitis in lieu of offspring. "Love them well, she tells me; I love them so! They are dear ones, little children" (CB 101). Bilitis conflates maternal and erotic associations as she vows to play with the little breasts, to wash them with milk and put them to bed in wool blankets. Mnasidika enjoins her lover to become a wet nurse to her breasts: "Since they are so far from my mouth, kiss them for me," she orders Bilitis (CB 101).

In attempting to pass as the translator of erotic verse by a woman writer, Louÿs, one could argue, was to fin de siècle France, what Kenneth Rexroth was to postwar America. In much the same way as his decadent forebear, Rexroth, the proto-beat poet, introduced the voice of a Japanese woman author by the name of Marichiko in an anthology that he edited titled *One Hundred More Poems from the Japanese* (1974). Rexroth was active as a translator from the earliest stages of his literary career until the end, publishing collections of translations that included *One Hundred Poems from the Chinese*; *Love and the Turning Year: One Hundred More Poems from the Chinese*; *The Orchid Boat: The Women Poets of China* (with Ling Chung); *Poems from the Greek Anthology*; *One Hundred Poems from the Japanese*; *One*

Hundred More Poems from the Japanese; Thirty Spanish Poems of Love and Exile; and *Selected Poems of Pierre Reverdy.* He apparently had serviceable knowledge of Chinese and Japanese, and worked in close collaboration with native speakers whose technical renderings provided the grist for his own compositional arrangements.

When it came to publishing these collaboratively produced translations under his own name, Rexroth seems to have evinced no qualms. In a preface to the first anthology of Japanese poems, he gave the impression that he was the sole translator: "In my own translations I have tried to interfere as little as possible with the simplicity of the Japanese text. . . . Some of my versions manage with considerably fewer syllables than the originals. On the other hand, I have not sacrificed certain Japanese ornaments which some have considered nonsense or decorative excrescences."[11] Characterizing his translations as literal, in the manner of Arthur Waley, Rexroth assures the reader that his respect for the poems has allowed him to preserve the integrity of the original Japanese in American English. Of course, there was nothing particularly unusual, especially at the time, for a poet-translator to take full credit for a translation that was only partly his or her own. But what makes such credit-grabbing stand out in hindsight is that it looks like the prelude to Rexroth's cavalier—some would say morally suspect—attitude toward authorship, evinced in his covert insertion of a pseudotranslation inside a legitimate anthology of Japanese verse and in the publication of his own "translations" under Marichiko's phantom imprimatur.

Rexroth's biographer Linda Hamalian treats the Marichiko hoax as a career curiosity rather than as a scandal of authorial counterfeit:

> In the last decades of his life, Rexroth did a very curious thing: he published a book of his own poems but identified them as translations from the work of Marichiko, "the pen name of a contemporary young woman who lives near the temple of Marishi-ben in Kyoto." Marishi-ben is patron goddess of geisha, prostitutes, women in childbirth, and lovers. At first, he tried to fool his readers, his publishers and his friends into believing the writer actually existed. In the Marichiko poems, he explored every aspect of what he imagined to be one woman's psyche in order to come to terms with how he as a man who had professed great love for women, could at last acquire a rudimentary understanding of woman's nature.[12]

In his monograph, *Revolutionary Rexroth: Poet of East-West Wisdom,* Morgan Gibson glides over the question of the unacknowledged "invention," preferring to frame the Marichiko poems as Rexroth's way of paying tribute to Yosano Akiko (1878–1942), famous for her sexually daring love poetry and often deemed to be "the greatest woman poet of modern Japan."[13] Noting the narrative parallels in the Marichiko cycle to "a Tantric parable of contemplative ecstacy, in which the goddess Marishiben unites with Buddha," Gibson reads the Marichiko poems as Rexroth's most successful representation of feminine "erotic enlightenment" (RR 84).

It remains to be seen whether Rexroth's "feminist" justification for his specious translation is particularly convincing. Some would say he used feminism opportunistically as cover for the expropriation of feminine literary voice, or as a means of eluding the radar of erotic censorship. Certainly Rexroth's performance of gender ventriloquism has been construed by his critics as a self-serving effort to whitewash his reputation as a predator on female students and admirers. However Rexroth's motivations are hypothetically construed, it is striking that he and Louÿs, both identified with two of the most flagrant cases of pseudotranslation, would adopt the genre of feminine erotic verse for their exercises in literary travesty.

Detection of Rexroth's forgery becomes easier the more closely the poems are examined. Superficial similarities can be found between a Yosano Akiko and a Marichiko poem: a shared hair motif, for example, allows parallels to be drawn between Akiko's "A Hair unbound, in this / Hothouse of lovemaking, / Perfumed with lilies, / I dread the oncoming of / The pale rose of the end of night," and Marichiko's "I cannot forget / The perfumed dusk inside the / Tent of my black hair, / As we awoke to make love / After a long night of love," which, Rexroth writes disingenuously in a footnote, "echoes Yosano Akiko."[14] Further consideration, however, reveals the sexual realism of the Marichiko texts to be more graphic, more prone to Orientalist kitsch. Marichiko's verse 32 grafts the decorative imagery of *japonisme* (flowers, boats) onto an explicit sex scene: "I hold your head tight between / My thighs, and press against your / Mouth and float away / Forever, in an orchid / Boat on the River of Heaven" (FWH 123). By contrast, an Akiko poem favors metaphorical reticence: "Press my breasts, / Part the veil of mystery, / A flower blooms there, / Crimson and fragrant" (OHM 16). Akiko's poems draw a distinct line around the autonomous object, as in this stripped-down image of a deserted boat symbolizing an abandoned woman: "Left on the beach / Full of water, / A worn out boat / Reflects the white sky / Of early autumn" (OHM 11). Rexroth's pastiche breaks down the isolationism of the lyrical "I," introducing pronominal games with gender and identity, that, knowing what we do now about the false identity of Marichiko, read like embedded clues:

Who is there? Me.
Me who? I am me, you are you.
But you take my pronoun,
And we are us. (FWH 116)

On close scrutiny the Marichiko poems fall apart as credible simu-
lations of Japanese women's writing. But why should this matter if the Marichiko texts stand up as aesthetic artifacts in their own right? What difference
does it make whether the Marichiko texts are received as genuine translations or as pseudotranslations that successfully advance the creative use of
literary *japonisme* in Western literature, and which place Rexroth in a continuum of distinguished writers—Mallarmé, Arthur Waley, Victor Segalen,
Lafcadio Hearn, Ernest Fenellosa, Ezra Pound, W.B. Yeats, Henri Michaud,
and Wallace Stevens—all of whom used literary Orientalism as a spring-
board to modernism and wrenched *japonisme* from the clutches of bad
translation? (In a lecture on "The Influence of Classical Poetry on Modern
American Poetry," Rexroth placed the brunt of blame for this tradition of
infelicitous Japanese translation on the poet Sadakichi Hartmann, who may
have been "a bohemian of bohemians," and a "wise and witty man," but
who was ultimately responsible for "a long tradition of vulgarization and
sentimentalization of Japanese classical poetry in translation.")[15]

Rexroth loyalists have located him squarely in this modernist tradition as a transitional figure between the early twentieth-century modernists
and the Beats. The Marichiko poems may fail the authenticity test, but, so
this version of the story goes, they are acquitted by virtue of their adherence
to Rexroth's iconoclastic philosophy of translation. A good translation, he
held, should not be hobbled by fidelity to the original, but rather, motivated
by advocacy: "The ideal translator," he wrote in *The Poet as Translator*, "is
not engaged in matching the words of a text with the words of his own
language. He is hardly even a proxy, but rather an all-out advocate. His job
is one of special pleading. So the prime criterion of successful poetic translation is assimilability. Does it get across to the jury?"[16] This idea of a translation as a reception-driven case to be made in court is complemented by a
principle of translational vivacity. H.D.'s poem "Heliodora" is exemplary,
because instead of "being" translation, it is, rather, "of" translation, demonstrating "the poignancy of that feeling of possession and the glamour of the
beautiful Greek words as they come alive in one's very own English" (PT
22, 26). For Rexroth, how the text communicates translational aliveness is far
more important than whether or not it accurately translates from Meleager's
Greek original. Truth value is supplanted by performative value. Having

shifted the ethical imperatives of translation in this way, Rexroth inadvertently clears the way for authorizing the Marichiko poems as examples of alive translation.

Of course, reading the Marichiko poems on Rexroth's terms sidesteps the larger issue of what it means for a translator to pass as a native speaker. Was Rexroth covertly sending up the reader's transferential relation to cultural affect, concentrated in a fetishism of the aesthetic codes of *japonisme* (haiku-esque brevity, blank spaces, ellipsis, understatement, imagism)? Was he using this exercise in textual counterfeit to reveal the reader's profound investment in conquering the other's language without having to actually learn it? However one might choose to answer these questions, the hoax illuminates the extent to which translation caters to the fantasy of having access to the foreignness of a language without the labor of the language lab.

The revelation of translational false coin leaves the reader aware of the dimension of epistemological scam or faked-up alterity inherent in all translation. The translation business is geared to keeping this scam from view, for it wants to convince readers that when it markets an author in translation, the translated text will be a truly serviceable stand-in for the original; affording a genuine translinguistic encounter with a foreign literature in the language of selfsame. But cases of pseudotranslation reveal the fundamental unreliability of a translation's claim to approximating the original in another tongue.

According to this reading, the Rexroth case is scandalous not just by dint of its cultural appropriationism or caricatural Orientalism, but because it reveals the extent to which all translations qualify as a form of linguistic forgery. The implied ethics of translation presupposes a contract holding between reader and translator whereby the former assumes the good faith effort of the latter to deliver an authentic copy of the original. In breaching that contract, Louÿs and Rexroth exposed the ways in which all translators are to some extent counterfeit artists, experts at forgeries of voice and style.

The Rexroth hoax, on first reading, highlights the case of translation as cultural forgery. But the forgery model—drawing on analogies to the connoisseurial practice of authentication—tends to reduce complex conceptual distinctions among plagiarism, counterfeit, and copy to a familiar discussion of autographic authenticity. According to Nelson Goodman, "A work of art is defined as 'autographic' if and only if even the most exact duplication of it does not thereby count as genuine."[17] In the Rexroth case, where there is an autographic reproduction of an *absent original*, the forgery model breaks down. What might be substituted in its stead is a genetic model of textual reproducibility that defines the translation as the clone of a clone (or clone of a code) that has effectively severed its primordial connection to an original subjective signature. At issue here is the way in which the notion of originality is complicated by what scientists have referred to as replication parameters. These become clear in questions around whether a program that reproduces daughter programs (as in the case of the Tierra program, "born" of the "Ancestor" computer code 85) should be considered a form of life, or whether the notion of original life should be strictly reserved for metabolizing cells whose DNA is replicated in the clone. In fabricating a text out of the codes of "Japaneseness"-in-translation, Rexroth, I would submit, experimented with the literary equivalent of cloning from code.

Reading the Marichiko poems as models of genetic reproduction without origins points to the way in which Rexroth's very notion of poetic creation was entwined with theories of eschatology, parthenogenesis, metempsychosis, and reincarnation. During the early 1940s Rexroth immersed himself in the writings of Meister Eckehart, English mystics of the late Middle Ages, St. John of the Cross, Ouspensky, Madame Blavatsky, and Jacob Boehme's *The Signature of All Things* (the title of which Rexroth took over for one of his own collections of poetry). According to Linda Hamalian: "Since childhood Rexroth had experienced 'occasional moments of vision . . . momentary flashes of communion with others' where time and space did not exist" (H 125). This passion for Western mysticism provided a natural transition to Zen Buddhism. Rexroth discovered Arthur Waley's *The Way and Its Power*, Chinese Taoism, Tantric Buddhism, Hatha and Kundalini Yoga (H 125). The title poem of *The Phoenix and the Tortoise*—the culminating masterwork of this period—is imbued with hybrid mysticism: the poetic subject acts as a conduit "channeling" the spirits of "ruined polities," from ancient Greece to the shores of California, where the body of a dead Japanese sailor has washed up, confirming fears of what will happen in the internment camps that were set up in California in the wake of Pearl Harbor. The corpse seems to make eye contact with the poet, and as he watches with "open hard eyes," the poet experiences a shock of self-identification: "Me— who stand here on the edge of death, / Seeking the continuity, / The germ plasm, of history, / The epic's lyric absolute."[18]

Genetic models of textual reproduction might seem far-fetched if it were not for the fact that Rexroth's own way of describing the creative process were not so eerily compatible with them. In his preamble to *The Phoenix and the Tortoise*, he wrote: "I have tried to embody in verse the belief that the only valid conservation of value lies in the assumption of unlimited liability, the supernatural identification of the self with the tragic unity of the creative process. I hope I have made it clear that I do not believe that the Self does this by an act of Will, by sheer assertion. He who would save his life must lose it" (PT 9). The self-perpetuating force of *bios* is introduced in a *literal* way as synonymous with poetic reproduction. Rexroth's evocative notion of "unlimited liability" suggests an ethics of responsibility to the future, with poetry operating as agent and guarantor of the work of art's reproducibility. And the phrase "He who would save his life must lose it," while obviously a kind of *tao*, also brings out that aspect of cloning that carries the megalomaniac dream of infinite self-preservation at the expense of an originary, signature identity. Consider, in this regard, an extract from Rexroth's epic poem "The Phoenix and the Tortoise" that defines the person as a condition of uniqueness, embodied in perfect surrogacy: "The fulfill-ment of uniqueness / In perfect identification, / In ideal representation, / As the usurping attorney, / The real and effective surrogate" (PT 19). The mys-tic self, infinitely iterated through history, is defined here as an original form of futural being whose signature is preserved in a copy or clone, itself charac-terized legalistically as a "usurping attorney," a guardian, if you will, of the original trust. In this sense the clone succeeds in leasing rather than appro-priating or fully embodying an original subject.

In the introduction to *The Phoenix and the Tortoise*, Rexroth also claimed that the poem "proceeds genetically or historically" (PT 9). But the textual genetics described by Rexroth is less like developmental evolution or hereditary transmission, and more like what we might now, in a digital era, call sampling. Rexroth sifts through the classical archive, paraphrasing and pastiching Hellenistic, Byzantine, and Latin Roman sources. Sometimes he draws directly from Martial, at other moments he avowedly treats his source material more freely, inserting paraphrases from antiquity inside larger poems, and allowing the citation pieces to, in a sense, reprogram the new cell into which they have been placed. (As Gina Kolata reminds us: "In cloning, scientists slip a cell from an adult into an egg with its genetic material re-moved. The egg then reprograms the adult cell's genes so that they are ready to direct the development of an embryo, then a fetus, then a newborn that is genetically identical to the adult whose cell was used to start the process. No one knows how the egg reprograms an adult cell's genes").[19] This repro-grammed work, depending on where one stands on the ethics of cloning, could either be condemned as a tissue of plagiarized fragments,[20] or hailed as a new translational form that, following Walter Benjamin's ascription, ensures the original's glorious afterlife.

Benjamin's theory suggests that the genetic paradigm extends the view of translation as literary testate or inheritance to a philosophy of writing that defines translation as a mechanism of textual reproducibility. In this scheme, the significance of origins and originality cedes to grander concerns over the work of art's messianic perpetuity. Rexroth's faux Japanese translations might, in these terms, seem more legitimate, their inauthentic originality deemed the price worth paying for a form of *japonisme* that bequeathed new life to American poetry. According to this reading, Robert Creeley, Gary Snyder, Philip Whalen, and Cid Corman—all of whom credited Rexroth's Buddhist psesudotranslations as a source of inspiration—spawned the regional/ecological/spiritual aesthetic of California Beat poetry.

The diminished status of originality (long a fixture of avant-garde doctrine or modernist credos of authorial impersonality) finds a limit case in examples of pseudotranslation in which readers are, in effect, urged to accept the clone of a code as a replacement for the original, or to give up conventional, essentialist notions of what the original "is." As far as the ethics of translation is concerned, this demotion of originality accords the translator such license that he or she is authorized to invent an extramural or imaginary source. In this way, just as Rexroth ethically sanctioned his transcription of Japanese verse by a poet who never was, so the late James Merrill and his partner David Jackson dedicated themselves to "channeling" the voices of those no longer there: Plato, Proust, Auden, Maya Deren, Maria Callas, Rimbaud, and Yeats. Alison Lurie's *Familiar Spirits: A Memoir of James Merrill and David Jackson* describes the strange, life-long fascination of the pair with the spiritist messages of the Ouija board.[21] Merrill's magnum opus *The Changing Light at Sandover* (1980) was, in the poet's own estimation, not a work of self-inspired imaginative lyric, but the most outré form of prosopoeia, an address from the dead transcribed *en direct.* Lurie characterizes the way in which the poem came to Merrill and Jackson like a set of instructions in code that demanded transcription rather than an act of imaginative translation. For Lurie, this amounts to a downgrading of the poetic, a submission to the prosaic quality of code, and a tragic sacrifice of lyrical talent on Merrill's part.

The Changing Light at Sandover constitutes an extreme case of translation without an original—an example of translation as language code transmitted from the beyond, of instructions express-mailed from an untenable source written as master-code or program. The text is rendered through the artificial assistance of the poet, now cast as the genetic engineer or technician whose primary challenge consists in transporting the work to its afterlife (Rimbaud will be rebirthed in T. S. Eliot in the phrase: "YET RIMBAUD?

IN HIS GENES WAS A V WORK CUT OFF BY LIFE. . . . Rimbaud ghostwrote 'The Waste Land' " [S 217])[22] or in preventing the garbling of instructions. Not unlike the processes of machine translation or digitally created sound, the text code is recorded, unscrambled, and recombined. Consider this excerpt from Mirabell, Book 2:

> 741 now dictates D's and my
> Vastly simplified *Basic Formulas*:
> JM: 268/I:1,000,000/5.5/741
> DJ: 289/I: 650,000/5.9/741.1 (S 143)

The poet of *Sandover* duly transcribes and decodes these numerological formulas: "Number of previous lives; then ratio/Of animal to human densities." "At 5.1 Rubenstein, 5.2; Eleanor/Roosevelt, 5.3; and so on. The Sixes are / LINDBERGH PLITSETSKAYA PEOPLE OF PHYSICAL PROWESS / & LEGENDARY HEROES / Characters from fiction and full-fledged / Abstractions came to Victor Hugo's tables" (S 143). If Victor Hugo is here transcoded as a kind of literary DNA, elsewhere in the Book of Mirabell textual cloning is an explicit trope: "Is DNA, that sinuous molecule, / The serpent in your version of the myth?" (S 119) or "I AM A MERE MIXING AGENT WITH MY SUPERIORS" (S 155) or "CAN IT BE? DO WE FORETELL THE CLONE?" (S 184). Cloning, in this instance, may be identified as a translational technology that banally reproduces poetic voice (repeating and unscrambling the codes by which it communicates) while providing the latter-day version of aesthetic reincarnation.

In his essay "The Task of the Translator," Benjamin defines translatability as "an essential quality of certain works." Certain originals, have it—the Bible, Heine, Baudelaire—and others do not. Merrill's *Sandover*, according to Benjaminian criteria, would probably fall well below the bar of a text intrinsically worthy of translational afterlife. But what is perhaps most relevant to the ethics of translation is the way in which Benjamin implicitly devalues the original, suborning the source text (and its privileged status as *primum mobile*) to the translation (now elevated to the position of midwife in the obstetrics of translatability):

> It is plausible that no translation, however good it may be, can have any significance as regards the original. Yet, by virtue of its translatability the original is closely connected with the translation; in fact, this connection is all the closer since it is no longer of importance to the original. We may call this connection a natural one, or, more specifically, a vital connection. Just as the

manifestations of life are intimately connected with the phenomenon of life without being of importance to it, a translation issues from the original—not so much from its life as from its afterlife. For a translation comes later than the original, and since
the important works of world literature never find their chosen
translators at the time of their origin, their translation marks
their stage of continued life.[23]

Here, it would seem, translation reproduces not an original text, but an
afterlife cloned from the (lost) life of the original. In shifting the ethics
of translation away from questions of fiability and fidelity (crucial to deter-
minations of pseudotranslation), and toward debates over the conditions
of textual reproducibility, Benjamin provides the groundwork for defining
translation in its most scandalous form: that is, as a technology of literary
replication that engineers textual afterlife without recourse to a genetic
origin.[24]

15

Everything Is Translatable

With the advent of an explosion of world language usage on the Internet, translation theory has become newly serviceable. Instead of fixating mournfully on the supposition that nothing is translatable (the original is always and inevitably lost in translation), translation studies increasingly explores the possibility that everything is translatable. "Translation attains its full meaning in the realization that every evolved language (with the exception of the word of God) can be considered a translation of all the others," Benjamin wrote in 1916.[1] Little could he have foreseen how rife with implication this statement would become in an era of digital translatability, an era in which scientists are inventing devices for translating DNA sequences and encrypting new genetic codes (figure 4).

Everything, apparently, is translatable, it seems, because of advances in technological literacy. Online communication has produced a linguistic marketplace, bringing the languages of the world into colloquy. This Babelian cacophony both reinforces and challenges the ascendency of English, making the whole issue of "other Englishes" a difficult one politically, for on the one hand English (and by extension the wealthy countries that designate it as their national language), opportunistically gains ground through "other Englishes," while on the other hand, it effectively loses ground by becoming a kind of global linguistic property. There is also the emergence of what has been called the "sixth language," the language of the Internet, otherwise known as Netspeak or Netlish (where English is the root language).[2] In the case of both "other Englishes" and "Netlish," norms of literacy, literateness, and literariness are challenged by the Net's indulgence toward ungrammaticality and outsider aesthetics.

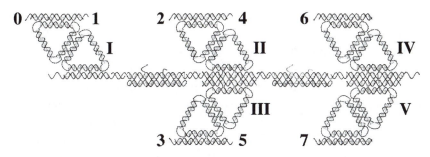

Figure 4. Diagram of Control Signals for DNA Translation Device, 2005, Nadrian C. Seeman. This picture shows the DNA translation device, which consists of five DNA diamond-shaped motifs (numbered with Roman numerals) and translates the control signals that direct the component devices into the products. The first one, and the middle pair of diamonds (II and III), are connected by a DNA nanomechanical device that can flip their relative orientations by a half-rotation. Likewise, the pair of diamonds on the right (IV and V) are connected by a second device of the same sort. The Arabic numerals represent single strands that can code by DNA hybridization for components that are joined together (credited to Nadrian C. Seeman and Shiping Liao).

The impact of electronic communication on the humanities is at present difficult to gauge, but it is already reshaping disciplinary contours. One can imagine a point in the not-too-distant future when departments will debate whether to admit programming languages as legitimate language fields of comparative literary study; whether nonstandard languages should be treated as something more than mere offshoots or subsets of vehicular ones; whether translation studies should be expanded to include the relationship between natural language and code; or whether the interdisciplinary humanities is reaching a convergence point with informatics.

For it is becoming clear that digital code holds out the prospect, at least, of translating everything into everything else. A kind of universal cipher or default language of information, digital code will potentially function like a catalytic converter, translating beyond the interlingual and among orders of *bios* and *genus*, liquid and solid, music and architecture, natural language and artificial intelligence, language and genes, nature and data, information and capital. The idea behind "everything is translatable" is an ideal of informatic commensurability—with promiscuous commutations made possible through a common code. Broadly construed as the language that this code "speaks," Netlish as I am adapting the term, is historically bound up with the military's strategic (and psychological) interest in machine translation as it grew out of experimental work during the 1950s in artificial intelligence, computer voice recognition, encryption, and cybernetics. More recently, Netlish has been shaped by the geopolitical conditions that Manuel Castells ascribes to the "network society": global labor, the flow of information capital, the blurred life cycle, instant wars.[3] Netlish is the expressionism of global capitalism. Recognizable in the multilingual blog, or coded form of "Bot-speak," Netlish may often be recognized by its vacuous content, inscrutable shorthand, mix of alphabetic and algorithmic variables, creative punctuation, diacritical invention, puerile in-jokes, aesthetics of the crashing browser (as Tilman Baumgaertel has put it),[4] and inconsequential live chat (typified by "The Blogalization Community," a site specializing in "cross-language blogging," whose motto is "life is a foreign language; all men mispronounce it").[5]

The term Netlish was initially coined in a narrower context by the media theorist McKenzie Wark. In a letter published on the Internet site "Nettime" in 1996, addressed to fellow media activist Geert Lovink, Wark announced that it was time to examine what is happening to the English language once it starts to circulate "in such a viral way on the net," and he employed Netlish to describe the netlike ways of speaking English, as well as the exponential spread of Englishes on the Internet. Netlish, clearly reinforced what Amitav Ghosh has dubbed the "Anglophone Empire." But it also proved to be a conduit for the proliferation of "Other Englishes," which escaped "a single editorial stand."

> Like a lot of people who work on international journals and publications, I have come across the notorious "Japlish." Japanese usage looks, at first sight, extremely strange. But after a while, it makes sense. And you can start to see a distinctive kind of writing in there. A fantastic hybrid of ways of becoming in language. A wacky sidebar to the Sapir-Whorf hypothesis. This was the idea that each language makes possible certain conceptual structures, and prevents certain others. For example, ancient Greek was a language extremely rich in articles, so it lent itself to the formation of the discourse of philosophy. What *is* being? Its [sic] a thought that Greek—and English—can express easily, but that can't occur in certain other languages. Those other languages, needless to say, are no doubt rich in other kinds of thought.[6]

For Wark, Netlish not only exposed the traces of cultural mentalities in sharp relief, it also restored English to an original creoleness that was crucial to subjectivity formation. Citing Deleuze, Wark argued:

Language is a machine that produces, as one of its effects, subjectivity. As the philosopher Gilles Deleuze said, "what is the self but this habit of saying 'I'?" The net makes English habits of writing one's self come in contact with other habits of self, making them become something else. And making English as it proliferates across the net—Netlish. Adding a richness to the language of potentially Shakespearian proportions. That is more a blessing than a curse. (MW)

Insofar as linguistically hybrid expression has always drawn on creoles, puns, loan words, and slang, there is nothing particularly unique about Netlish. And yet, as Wark persuasively suggested, the electronic medium of exchange does affect how language is generated, recorded, and transmitted. Despite the fact that it remains a tool of elites, the Internet has wildly encouraged the entrance of non–English speakers into the information public sphere. In 2001 the linguist David Crystal tracked over 1,000 languages on the Web and noted that a World Language Resources site listed products for over 728 languages, including 87 European minority languages.[7] By 2003 one source reported roughly 470 million non-English-speaking users, which constitutes two-thirds of all users.[8] If, at the beginning of the twenty-first century, English remains the commercial lingua franca, its hegemony is clearly eroding as more and more languages come on line and more users from non-Western countries obtain access to cyberspace.

As Wark notes, the multilingual Net has also transformed English from within, introducing the usage of non–native speakers, and spawning a boom in (mostly popular) literature written in other Englishes: Spanglish, Japlish, Franglais, Greeklish, Pan-Swiss English, Hinglish (Hindustani English), Pinglish (Punjabi English), Ginglish (Gujarati English), and Singlish (Singapore English). Consider, for example, this light verse in Singlish (Singapore English):

> Verily, verily I say unto thee
> The government hath decreed
> That thou should speak'st like an ang-mor kwee
> 'Tis a message that thou must heed

> When Brits today no longer speak
> The English of their Queen
> Doesn't our country's campaign reek
> Of preserving the Colonial scene?

So speak Singlish as and when you please!
Speak it loud and proud!
And never ever let it cease
Though they say it's not allowed.

For Singlish is something all our own
And if this they should deny,
Then please feel free to them intone:
Kan ni na bu chao chee bye![9]

This text appears in a feature column called Poet's Corner on Singapore's satirical humor Web site TalkingCock.com. Typically, articles posted on the site exemplify code-switching between English and Singlish with an overlay of media-speak. If the poems in Singlish are any indication of problems common to other former colonial and commonwealth communities of speakers, they suggest that all languages preserving the suffix "glish" or "ish" in their appellation remain, at some level, indebted to English and implicated in linguistic neo-imperialism. Preserved in the very names themselves of these languages is a history of cultural dependency. For Wark, however, English is potentially decolonized from within as a result of the democratized conditions of global usage, especially the use of code-switching, which may increasingly become an egalitarian form of "bilingualism within a language."[10]

Though the suffix "lish" in Netlish continues the privileging of English, it may also be taken to signify the mess that English finds itself in as it tangles with technology *and* languages other than English. Books of the 1980s and 1990s that tracked "other Englishes," such as Braj Kachru's *The Other Tongue: English across Cultures*,[11] David Crystal's *English as a Global Language*,[12] Tom McCarther's *The English Languages,* are now being superseded by works like Crystal's own *Language and the Internet*,[13] Robert Logan's *The Sixth Language: Learning a Living in the Internet Age*, and Yoshi Mikani's Web site devoted to the languages of the world by computers and the Internet that explore the strange netherworld of technospeak overlaid upon vehicular languages, vernaculars, and forms of English as a second language. In this netherworld, distinctions between linguistic deviation and grammatical error become harder and harder to draw, with some critics crying "linguistic vandalism," and others (like Michael Specter) hailing the advent of "a linguistic singularity," "a genuine new medium."[14] Relevant in this regard are the tactics of guerilla and class warfare deployed by Internet collectives such as the L.A.-based Slanguage group, or the Afro-futurist performance artist Rammellzee.

The "-lish" in Netlish functions equally in the adjectival sense of language that behaves like the Internet, aping its signal attributes and communicative (dys)functions. In literature, examples of this type of Netlish resemble "translationese." Consider, for example, the diction of the young Russian translator who narrates Jonathan Safran Foer's novel *Everything Is Illuminated*, who speaks a cracked mixture of schoolbook English spiked with computerese and pop-cultural slang:

> Like you know, I am not first rate with English. In Russian my ideas are asserted abnormally well, but my second tongue is not so premium. I undertaked to input the things you counseled me to, and I fatigued the thesaurus you presented me, as you counseled me to, when my words appeared too petite, or not befitting. If you are not happy with what I have performed, I command you to return it back to me. I will persevere to toil on it until you are appeased.[15]

With its comic display of Freudian *Witz* and exposure of the blind egoism of cultural personality intruding on protocols of diction and syntax, Alex's off-base English approximates the English produced by machines, riddled with errors and malapropisms.

Not just a form of Netspeak, Netlish may be identified as a narrative device or "organizational complex" that connects everything to everything else.[16] In William Gibson's novel, *Pattern Recognition*, pattern is not only a system of links allowing for huge jumps between real and virtual worlds, but also a way of re-cognizing the barest semantic unit as a grapheme (a minimal writing unit), a glyph (an abstract form selected as a character), a "dingbat" (typographical ornament or symbol), or an alphabetic super-sign.[17] Pattern emerges as a universal language transversally cutting across numerous mediums from language technologies to the practice of corporate branding.[18] Gibson's female protagonist, a professional trend-spotter and logo tracker, becomes a pawn in a war between partisans of encryption and corporate raiders who want to expropriate electronic watermarks deposited like secret signatures inside a piece of "footage" circulating as a contraband commodity in the international market. The stealth patent thus emerges as a power signifier in the age of image and information piracy. In *Pattern Recognition* Netlish is synonymous with bits of intelligible code that are both enframed in the narrative and comprise its very bone structure.

Though the jury remains out on whether Netlish will become a babelian fount of plurilingual dialects, an addled form of Basic English that will dominate the globe, a software program for machine translation (like

Babelfish), or a language of trademark super-signs negotiating the electronic byways of the Internet, it nonetheless seems clear that the monster to be harnessed in the name of a multilingual Net is some form of lingua franca housed in a Turing machine. That machine is none other than machine translation itself, an artificial intelligence system currently divided between two approaches, interlingual versus transfer. In the interlingual model there is a source language that moves to artificial interlingual representation (Esperanto) and then to the target. Linguistic universality is the hallmark of the interlingual approach. By contrast, the transfer approach performs work at the source and target levels, attempting to bypass the Esperanto intermediary. The best results thus far are produced through a combination of the two approaches, as in Cambridge's Core Language Engine, which draws on a database of already existing translations. The memory database and the search engine emerge as increasingly powerful coordinates of a future pan-translatability.

In defaulting to Esperanto, machine translation, or at least the interlingual kind, revives the old dream of one-world-one-language endorsed throughout history, most notably by Leibniz, the Port-Royal school, and socialist movements in the 1880s and 1890s. In the 1920s and 1930s, lingua franca fashion shifted from a philological model (drawing together etymological roots and grammars from multiple Indo-European languages) to a technical model in which science and logic would be conjoined. In the 1950s and 1960s, as Lydia Liu has demonstrated, the technical model gained further applications still, as cybernetics joined forces with cellular biology in searching for "the letters, codons (words), and punctuation marks of the nucleic acids to decode the speechless language of DNA in the Book of Life."[19]

It was Walter Benjamin, with his customary prescience, who intuited how the language of *techne* would reshape the human sciences. Think of crossing his "The Task of the Translator" (1923) with the later essay "The Work of Art in the Age of Technological Reproducibility" (1935), and you come up with the "The Task of the Translator in the Era of Technological Reproducibility," a problematic addressed indirectly in an essay titled "Problems in the Sociology of Language," written in 1934 that Benjamin published in the *Zeitschrift für Sozialforschung* in 1935. A prehistoric version of Netlish can be located in Benjamin's intriguing reference to Eugen Wüster's *Internationale Sprachnormung in der Technik, besonders in der Elektrotechnik* (International Standardization of Technical Terms, Particularly in the Electrical Industry), Bern 1931. Here, Benjamin examines "the ways in which technologists—who have a special interest in developing an unambiguous vocabulary—have tried to standardize terminology."[20] He notes, "Around

1900, the Verband Deutscher Ingenieure [German Engineers Association] set to work on a comprehensive technical lexicon. Within three years, index cards for more than three-and-a-half million words had been collected" (PSL 76). The association soon realized it was facing massive overload and had insufficient funds to realize the project. Noting the link between philology and this new attempt to forge a standardized technical language, Benjamin wrote: "Incidentally, the attempts to standardize technical terminology have set in motion the most serious endeavors to create a world language—an idea whose lineage, of course, goes back hundreds of years. This lineage, in its turn, especially its ramifications in logic, are another subject which would merit separate investigation by sociologists" (PSL 76–77).

For Benjamin, this world language takes its cue from Rudolf Carnap's notion of logical syntax, which "treats language as a calculus" (PSL 77). "Syntax, pure and descriptive, is nothing more than the mathematics and physics of language," Carnap wrote (PSL 79). Though Carnap would qualify this assertion by specifying the conditions of application, Benjamin extracted the more general ideal of a world language aspiring to formal logic. Translation, in this schema, provides the modest but crucial service of converting mathematical code into syntax, thereby allowing language to be at one with thought. Benjamin seems here to anticipate the Chomskyean idea that the brain is essentially a computer, molded from inside out, containing "a hard-wired ability to learn language."[21]

In the fifties, the Chicago School systems theorists updated the idea of a universal language of *techne* in their hopes for an Esperanto of interdisciplinary communication. Using the term "translationalism" they imagined information theory as the key to deciphering biological and social organization. In his introduction to a series of papers published in 1953 on modeling in the behavioral sciences, James Miller commented on:

> ... the problem of the Babel of many tongues spoken by the different disciplines and schools. It is not always easy for an economist and a political scientist to understand one another, much less a historian and a physiologist. We attempted to meet this block to communication by employing a sort of scientific esperanto of neutral terms not sacred to any single group, and we relied more and more on mathematical and logical formulations.[22]

Though many might shudder at the idea of bringing back the grand era of behaviorist mathematical modeling, or the fetish of "social systems" analysis brought on in the United States by Talcott Parsons (Parsons' *The Social System* appeared in 1951), there is no denying that fifties-style informatics and systems theory has returned in the guise of an "open system" in which everything is translatable. Where the open system was originally applied narrowly to organismic exchanges between matter and environment, or to instances of negative entropy, cybernetics led to a further opening of the open system onto vistas of genetics and language.

> Future research [we read in 1968] will probably have to take into consideration irreversible thermodynamics, the accumulation of information in the genetic code and "organizational laws" in the latter. Presently the genetic code represents the *vocabulary* of hereditary substance, i.e., the nucleotide triplets which "spell" the amino acids of the proteins of an organism. Obviously, there must also exist a *grammar* of the code; the latter cannot, to use a psychical expression, be a word salad. . . . Without such "grammar" the code could at best produce a pile of proteins, but not an organized organism.[23]

Feedback loops, swarms, adaptive and random response models, information spread, allometry, entropy, biomorphic homology, pattern recognition, space-to-surface algorithms, semiotic functions—these units of a formal technical language imagined in the fifties are the direct precursors of an all-over condition of translatability holding among graphic image, linguistic sign, and programming code. The uses of Netlish might thus be extended to experiments with information flow using the critical frameworks of chaos and complexity theory, or to a conception of language that blurs the boundaries between linguistics, symbolic logic, and programming.

In what might initially seem to be a rather surprising turn in her work, Gayatri Chakaravorty Spivak takes up the idea of programmed thought using translation as the guiding metaphor, and drawing on the work of Melanie Klein:

> The human infant grabs on to some one thing and then things. This grabbing (*begreifen*) of an outside indistinguishable from an inside constitutes an inside, going back and forth and coding everything into a sign-system by the thing(s) grasped. One can call this crude coding a "translation." In this never-ending weaving, violence translates into conscience and vice versa. From birth to death this "natural" machine, programming the mind perhaps as genetic instructions program the body (where does body stop and mind begin?), is partly metapsychological

and therefore outside the grasp of the mind. Thus "nature" passes and repasses into "culture," in a work or shuttling site of violence.[24]

Here, translation performs the heavy work of forming the mind-as-computer by becoming the name for the yes-no, on-off, good-bad object choice that coincides in a digital program with the alternance between 1's and 0's. Spivak's emphasis on the link between subject formation (what she calls "ethical semiosis") and programmed genetic instructions, argues implicitly for supplanting traditional notions of language with a universally applicable notion of programmed code. And when she writes of "coding everything into a sign-system," she imagines a code that is good to go across the porous borders of mind and body, genetic and linguistic instructions, thought and ethics. Perhaps Spivak's concern with genetic program can be traced back to her early engagement with Jacques Derrida's *Of Grammatology*, and more specifically to the phrase: "It [genetic script] is a liberation which makes for the appearing of the *grammè* as such and no doubt makes possible the emergence of 'writing' in the narrow sense."[25] In her translator's preface Spivak recalls the phrase from the original *Critique* version of the text, noting that it was subsequently reworked with an emphasis no longer on genetics. In hindsight, though, the original phrase might be interpreted as evidence of Derrida's early fascination, in the era of Crick and Watson, with the idea of genetic program as a substitute code language for metaphysics.

If for Derrida, the language of program could conceivably displace metaphysics, for Lacan, the discursive and linguistic expression of the unconscious could conceivably be reconciled with the language of DNA. Ahead of his time in his thinking along these lines (like Derrida), Lacan, in the 1972 seminar addressed to Roman Jakobson (who had been delivering a series of seminars at the Collège de France), posed "a question that no one raises,"

> that of the status of the notion of information whose success has been so lightning fast that one can say that the whole of science manages to get infiltrated by it. We're at the level of the gene's molecular information and of the winding of nucleoproteins around strands of DNA, that are themselves wrapped around each other, all of that being tied together by hormonal links— that is, messages that are sent, recorded, etc. Let us note that the success of this formula finds its indisputable source in a linguistics that is not only immanent but explicitly formulated. In any

case, this action extends right to the very foundations of scientific thought, being articulated as negative entropy.[26]

Known for his attraction, starting in the 1960s, to mathematical topologies—particularly Moebius strips, horseshoe graphs, vectored zigzags, four-point schemas, Borromean knots, toruses, threefold points, strings, and bent ring chains—Lacan sought a metacritical, purely formal language of psychoanalysis. In the passage above, dedicated to Jakobson (who had been collaborating since the 1950s with MIT colleagues on the possibility of translating information theory into biogenetics), it would seem that Lacan was prepared to coat topological diagrams in nucleoproteins and hormones, thereby modeling a double helix of the subject, or the genome of desire's cause. The dream of a pantranslatable order of knowledge emerges here, with genetics, psychoanalysis, logic, and linguistics subject to a common code of conversion.

It may, however, be held that code, though it shares common properties with language, behaves at certain moments like a language, enables communicating functions, and reveals itself to be capable of aesthetic expression, is also essentially different from language. Code tends to be purely functional—goal-driven, and highly circumscribed in its illocutionary range. The universal language of code might be currently identifiable as HTML (HyperText Markup Language), a typical master or default language, or computer's code of codes, frequently used conjunctively with Unicode Standard (the regular character set for HTML content). And yet, it is equally possible to maintain that the distinction between natural language and code is breaking down; a point made some time ago by Friedrich Kittler in his classic 1997 essay "There Is No Software":

> Programming languages have eroded the monopoly of ordinary language and grown into a new hierarchy of their own. This postmodern Tower of Babel reaches from simple operation codes whose linguistic extension is still a hardware configuration, passing through an assembler whose extension is this very opcode, up to high-level programming languages whose extension is that very assembler. In consequence, far-reaching chains of self-similarities in the sense defined by fractal theory organize the software as well as the hardware of every writing. What remains a problem is only recognizing these layers which, like modern media technologies in general, have been explicitly contrived to evade perception. We simply do not know what our writing does.[27]

Normally invisible, that is to say, masked by conventional language or visual screen-savers, the language of code is erupting into view either as pure algorithm, or as code spliced with traditional orthography (an interface between code and language). It may be precisely at the interstices of language and code that the limits of the aesthetic in art and literature are tested, especially if one looks at some of the recent art installations that treat code-working as medium.

For McKenzie Wark, codeworking is defined against hypertext. "Hypertext dominates perceptions of where writing is heading in the Internet era, the link is perceived as the most interesting strategy for electronic writing." Codework, by contrast, is cast by Wark as "dialogue with all types of communication, an emerging electronic writing ecology."[28] Codeworking seems to foster universal signatures without copyright, groups that offer narrative services, or conceptual works that feature programming at the breaking point. Its model of activism is the tactical intervention: the derailing of English, experiments in radical denationalization through machine English or translationese, the invention of deviant orthography and grammar: "Mangled machine English" and "the decaying grammar and spelling of the Internet becomes a kind of aesthetic alternative," according to Wark, in works by groups like JODI, which performs punctuation art that is neither writing nor visual art and depicts "programming on the brink of failure," or works by Mark Amerika, whose Grammatron introduces the new writing technology of nanoscript and whose project P-HON:E-ME seeks to render "the sound of art and technology" by scrambling the statutes separating colors, notes, and phonemes (MW2). Codework texts often hover on the brink of perceptibility, as when the group Internet Relay Chat effects a *détournement* of on-line conversation unbeknownst to the participants. Wark also mentions the example of Stéphan Barron's project Compost Concepts, which involves randomly recycling text systems in a Joycean way. The artist Florian Cramer pays even more explicit homage to Joyce, inventing permutations of *Finnegan's Wake* through a virtual universe of portmanteau words (MW2).

In twelve software art projects commissioned for the Whitney Museum's artport Web site, artists rendered transparent the "back end" (or invisible side) of codeworking—the blur between language, algorithm, and work of art. According to the program, the aim of project CODeDOC was to reveal the conceptual formalism of the code. Directed "to connect and move three points in space" by writing a source code in JAVA, C, Visual Basic, Lingo, or Perl the artists were implicitly encouraged to see themselves as inheritors of the legacy of Marcel Duchamp, John Cage, and Sol Le Witt, all conceptualists famous for exploiting the formal variations that result from the execution of instructions.

One of the strongest projects is by John Klima. Titled "The Story Show," it deploys game theory to expose the goal-driven nature of code-writing. Klima's acknowledgment that everyone writes code differently, embedding a kind of signature style, belies the "death of the author" shibboleth normally applied to codeworking. Klima's code-writing style is elegant and witty, drawing elements from nursery rhyme, Boolean mathematics, and game instructions.

```
The_Story.Show
While True
   If YourAttitude = CHAUVINIST Then
      If Fetch (pail, jack, jill) Then GoUpHill jack, jill
      If FellDown (jack) And BrokeCrown (jack) Then Tum-
blingAfter jill, jack
   ElseIf YourAttitude = FEMINIST Then
      If Fetch (pail, jill, jack) then GoUpHill jill, jack
      If FellDown (jill) And BrokeCrown (jill) Then TumblingAfter
jack, jill
   End if
      The_Story.Draw

. . . Function BrokeCrown (Leader as PERSON) as Boolean
Static lastCrown As Boolean[29]
```

When you press the "execute" box at the bottom of the code, the game leaps into action. You see toy-figures Jack and Jill moving along a canted conveyer belt. They run up and down the hill, after or away from each other, or toward the pail of water depending on which variables you choose. These include "Your Attitude" (Chauvinist/Feminist); Jack and Jill's "Desire" (Mininal/Moderate/Desperate), or the "Pail's Allure" (Repulsive/Moderate/Undeniable). In sharp contrast to Klima, Camille Utterback's code-writing is prolix and messy. "I was a bit embarrassed and nervous to think of people looking at my code, so I've taken out a lot of my comments where I'm cursing, venting my frustration and thoughts and keeping track of what I've tried and not. In retrospect maybe this was a mistake, as this code no longer really looks like what a working file of mine looks like. What can I say? I'm one of those people that clean my bathroom if my friends are coming over."[30] Scott Snibbe's "tripolar" project uses source code to "demonstrate the 'meta-chaos' of the program itself. A set of key variables defines all the parameters of the simulation. Changing any of these parameters radically alters the artwork, in most cases making it non-functional—in some cases the program will hang [which it did for me when I tried it]—in others the paths will explode, implode or oscillate." Snibbe's instructions display a mordant poetics: "Thread kicker _ = **null**; // Indication that animation thread has halted **boolean** timeToDie_; or // Stop the applet. **Public void** stop ( ) { timeToDie_=**true** or commands such as if, else logarithmically interpolate over last pixel// This allows one to explore values between pixels."[31]

The expansion of the parameters of translation study, especially around "Netlish" as theory and practice responds to what Félix Guattari in his book *Chaosmosis* seemed to gesture towards when he called for new ecologies of the visible and the virtual. Guattari, whose long years of collaboration with Deleuze left his own work unfairly obscured, was committed to breaking up the sectorization of values that control nonverbal semiosis, thereby dismantling "the ontological Iron Curtain that the philosophical tradition erected between mind and matter."[32] Guattari embraced "machinic processuality" as the key to a new expressionism. This was the nub of his concept of chaosmosis, a provocative, dare we say "proto-netlish" morph of chaos and osmosis. His notions of "fractal ontology" and the interactivity born at "the junction of informatics, telematics, and the audiovisual" pointed him toward what he called "a post-media era" (C95, C97).

Netlish might be defined as a postmedia form of expressionism driven, on one side, by experimental forms of multilingualism across media, and on the other, by the desire for a lingua franca of translatability or universal code for the logical formalism of cognitive process. In these terms, Netlish is an essentially schizophrenic phenomenon, pulled apart by the opposing forces of linguistic entropy and semantic condensation. This opposition is seated in the divergent positions of Netlish's original theorists, McKenzie Wark and Geert Lovink. Wark is the optimist, focusing on the benefits of Netlish for multilingual users, and celebrating experimental codeworking. Lovink adopts a more pessimistic stance, seeing Netlish as the gateway to the hegemony of Euro-English: "Euro-English will perhaps be the 20th century Latin spoken on 'the continent,' " he suggests, a language "beyond all accents and apparent mistakes, a 'Gesatsprachwerk.' "[33] Just as a homogenized, standard or technical English threatens to consume the small languages of Europe, so Netlish— traceable in his estimation to the "Pax Americana, pop culture, global capitalism, Europe after '69 and the rise of the Internet"—threatens to condemn other Englishes to the status of "minor, subcultural deviations."

Lovink's political concerns about Anglocentrism are of course well-founded. United States hegemony on the Internet has been ensured thus far by the fact that the root server that routs global e-mail resides in Virginia; it really is a case of the United States versus the rest of the world in the matter of who controls the information superhighway. Despite their differences, however, Wark and Lovink meet in their desire for a many-to-many language-translation interface that would enable us to move beyond, say, the recently completed "Eurotranslation Pyramid Schemes" that are being developed to allow the ten new European Union member states to communicate (translation combo specials include Maltese to Portuguese, or Estonian to Cypriot Turkish) and toward tectonic shifts in language power politics that obviate the risks posed to minor tongues by the muscle languages of populous nations. Optimally, Netlish would become identified with the expressionism of "other languages" that are both interlingual *and* intermedial, languages that override the ontological distinction between natural language and code, and that inaugurate an eminently fungible, democratic order of pan-translatability in which everything—data, language, matter, information, aesthetic expression—is mutually translatable. More realistically, as spoofs like Alan Leo's "Hour is the moment for all good men to come the subsidy of them country" make abundantly clear, electronic decoding remains an imperfect art and leaves us wondering how translators working for homeland security and the CIA define the limits and form of a discrete language in an era in which the proliferation of dialect, code-switching, nonstandard language, computer argots, and electronic abbreviations are the order of the day.[34] The shadow of the military-industrial-academic complex continues to overhang future definitions of Netlish, as does the shadow of class, religious, and ethnic warfare, thus darkening utopian projections of manifold translation.

CONCLUSION

16

A New Comparative Literature

In attempting to rethink critical paradigms in the humanities after 9/11, with special emphasis on language and war, the problem of creolization and the mapping of languages "in-translation," shifts in the world canon and literary markets, and the impact of enhanced technologies of information translation, I have tried to imagine a program for a new comparative literature using translation as a fulcrum. I began with an attempt to rethink the disciplinary "invention" of comparative literature in Istanbul in the 1930s, using the work of Leo Spitzer and Erich Auerbach as figures whose names became synonymous with defining early iterations of global humanism in exile. I end with some reflections on what happens to philology when it is used to forge a literary comparatism that has no national predicate, and that, in naming itself *translatio* names the action of linguistic self-cognizing, the attempt to bring-to-intelligibility that which lies beyond language ("God," Utopia, Nature, DNA, a Unified Field Theory of Expressionism).

In naming a translational process constitutive of its disciplinary nomination comparative literature breaks the isomorphic fit between the name of a nation and the name of a language. As Giorgio Agamben has observed (with reference to Alice Becker-Ho's determination that Gypsy *argot* failed to qualify as a language since Gypsies as a people were deemed to be without nation or fixed abode), "we do not have, in fact, the slightest idea of what either a people or a language is."[1] The Gypsy case, for Agamben, reveals the shaky ground on which language nomination rests. In affirming that "Gypsies are to a people what *argot* is to language," Agamben unmasks standard language names as specious attempts to conceal the fact that "all peoples are gangs and *coquilles*, all languages are jargons and *argots*" (MWE 65, 66). For Agamben, languages that defy containment by structures of the state (as in Catalan, Basque, Gaelic), or the blood and soil mythologies of peoples, might conceivably prompt the ethical "experience of the pure existence of language" (MWE 68). "It is only by breaking at any point the nexus between the existence of language, grammar, people, and state that thought and praxis will be equal to the tasks at hand," Agamben concludes (MWE 69).

Samuel Weber performs a similar dissection of national/nominal language fallacies with more direct pertinence to translation, noting that,

> [T]he linguistic systems between which translations move are designated as "natural" or "national" languages. However, these terms are anything but precise or satisfactory. . . . The imprecision of these terms is in direct proportion to the linguistic diversity they seek to subsume. . . . The difficulty of finding a generic term that would accurately designate the class to which individual languages belong is indicative of the larger problem of determining the principles that give those languages their relative unity or coherence—assuming, that is, that such principles really exist.[2]

Comparative literature answers Weber's call for the generic term to which individual languages belong. As such, it functions as an abstract generality or universal sign on the order of Wittgenstein's *Urzeichen*, which sounds out the *forçage* of nation-subject and language-subject in the process of nomination. We hear this *forçage* in an expression like *traduit de l'américain* ("translated from the American"), which captures a non-existent language coming into being through the act of rendering it coincident with the name of a nation or people. There is, of course, no standard language with discrete grammatical rules and protocols called "American." "American" may be the name of a language referring (in nominalist terms) to a possible world of language, but it is neither a term used by North American speakers of English to refer to their idiolect, nor a legitimate nation-marker. (As Jean-Luc Godard said recently: "I would really like to find another word for 'American.' When someone says 'American' they mean someone who lives between New York and Los Angeles, and not someone who lives between Montevideo and Santiago.")[3] As the name of a language, "American" implicitly consigns Spanish to "foreign"-language status even though millions of hemispheric subjects of the Americas claim Spanish as their native tongue. A new comparative literature would acknowledge this jockeying for power and respect in the field of language. A new comparative literature seeks to be the name of language worlds characterized by linguistic multiplicity and phantom inter-nations.

In *Poétique de la relation* Edouard Glissant authorizes the move toward linguistic inter-nationalism when he subordinates instabilities of nomination to geopoetics, replacing the old center-periphery model with a world system comprised of multiple linguistic singularities or interlocking small worlds, each a locus of poetic opacity. Glissant's paradigm of the *tout-monde*, building on the nondialectical ontological immanence of Deleuze and Guattari, offers a model of aporetic community in which small worlds (modeled perhaps after a deterritorialized Caribbean) connect laterally through bonds of Creole and a politics of mutualism centered on resistance to debt. Looking ahead to a day when *toutmondisme* will surpass *tiermondisme*, that is to say, when the nation form gives way to the immanent, planetary totality of Creole, Glissant imagines Creole "transfigured into word of the world."[4] Building on Glissant, the authors of *Éloge de la créolité* envision *créolité* as "*the world diffracted but recomposed*, a maelstrom of signifieds in a single signifier: a Totality. . . . *full knowledge of Creoleness*, they argue, *will be reserved for Art*, for art absolutely."[5] As Peter Hallward has remarked: "The nation's loss is . . . Creole's gain."[6]

Insofar as Creole heralds a condition of linguistic postnationalism and denaturalizes monolingualization (showing it to be an artificial arrest of language transit and exchange), it may be said to emblematize a new comparative literature based on translation. Though, as I have argued in this book, Creole has emerged as an omnibus rubric, loosely applied to hybridity, *métissage*, platforms of cross-cultural encounter, or to language as a critical category of literary history; it has also emerged as a synonym for traumatic lack. Marked by the Middle Passage, and the coarse commands of human traffickers and plantation owners, Creole carries a history of stigma comparable to that of pidgin translation in nineteenth-century Chinese. In Haun Saussy's estimation, Chinese pidgin translation was, for the grammarians, an exhibition of "incompleteness . . . an unequal relationship between normal speech in the target language and the halting, misarticulated, or excessive speech of the source language it represents." In Saussy's reading, Walter Benjamin's sacred, interlinear ideal of translation offers the possibility of revaluing pidgin because interlinear's word-for-word literalism authorizes a translation full of holes: "Pidgin stands for—it makes audible and visible—the incommensurability of languages. The discussion of Chinese, that "grammarless" language, gives pidgin its greatest representational license."[7] Recuperated in the guise of sacred translation, Creole, like pidgin, may be cast as a language "blessed" with the fullness of aporia.

For Derrida, the aporia names the conceptual impasse of death lodged in the body of language. Beginning with a phrase "*Il y va d'un certain pas* [It involves a certain step/not; he goes along at a certain pace]," Derrida associates the *pas* with a "recumbant corpse" or limit-condition between language and that which is other to itself:[8]

> a Babel "*from* and *within* itself . . . the stranger at home, the in-vited or the one who is called. . . . This border of translation does not pass among various languages. It separates translation from itself, it separates translatability within one and the same language. A certain pragmatics thus inscribes this border *in the very inside of the so-called French language.*" (A 10)

Derrida's concept of aporia—heard in the "*no, not, nicht, kein*" of alterity—is linked to the politics of monolingualism in *Monolingualism of the Other: Or the Prosthesis of Origin* (1996)[9] (A 10). The book's epigraphs from Glissant and Abdelkedir Khatibi attest to a rare engagement with *francophonie* as theoretical terrain. Derrida, with tongue in cheek, competes with Khatibi for title to the stateless status of the *Franco-Magrébin* subject. The hyphen signifies all the problems of national/linguistic unbelonging characteristic of post-Independence Algerians, including the way in which Jews, Arabs, and French were neighbored, yet separated, by the French language. "This language will never be mine," says Derrida of French, drawing from his own experience of national disenfranchisement the lesson that language is loaned to communities of speakers. "The untranslatable remains (as my law tells me) the poetic economy of the idiom" (D 56). Contrary to what one might expect, the prosthetic "other" in Derrida's title "monolingulism of the other," is not polyglottism, but an aporia within ipseity, an estrangement in language as such. For Derrida, untranslatability is the universal predicate of language names.

Derrida's aporia deconstructs the nationalist nominalism of language names by locating an always-prior other within monolingual diction. The aporia loosens the national anchor from the language name, wedging a politics of the subject between the name of a nation and the name of a language. Blocking the automatic association of specified language properties with the universal set of a given nation, Derrida's aporia approximates the logician's "X" in the modern nominalist formula "For any X, if X is a man, it is mortal," which disables the universal qualifier "all men are mortal" and relativizes the human status of the subject in question. X may or may not be a man in the same way that Francophone speaker X may or may not be French. The contingency of the subject suggests here that French speakers who are French nationals constitute one possible world of French speakers among many. Once the national predicate is dislodged, no speaker maintains exclusive ownership of language properties; the right to language is distributed more freely as language is classed as the property of X-many lease-holders.

Abolishing the divides of inside/outside, guest/host, owner/tenant, "the monolinguism of the other" names a comparatism that neighbors languages, nations, literatures, and communities of speakers. This idea of "neighboring" is borrowed from Kenneth Reinhard, specifically his Levinasian understanding of a "comparative literature otherwise than comparison . . . a mode of reading logically and ethically prior to similitude, a reading in which texts are not so much grouped into 'families' defined by similarity and difference, as into 'neighborhoods' determined by accidental contiguity, genealogical isolation, and ethical encounter."[10] For Reinhard, treating texts as neighbors "entails creating anamorphic disturbances in the network of perspectival genealogies and intertextual relations. That is, before texts can be compared, one text must be articulated as the uncanny neighbor of the other; this is an assumption of critical obligation, indebtedness, secondariness that has nothing to do with influence, Zeitgeist, or cultural context" (KS 796). Departing from philological tradition, which argues for textual relation based on shared etymology, tropes, aesthetic tastes, and historical trajectories, Reinhard proposes in their stead a theory of "traumatic proximity": "How [he asks] can we re-approach the traumatic proximity of a text, before or beyond comparison and contextualization? Asymmetrical substitution implies that there is no original common ground for textual comparison, but only the trauma of originary nonrelationship, of a gap between the theory and practice of reading that is only retroactively visible" (KS 804). Reinhard's notion of "otherwise than comparison" shifts the problematic from language nomination to the ethics of traumatic proximity.

"Neighboring" describes the traumatic proximity of violence and love, manifest as exploded holes in language or translation gaps. Such spaces of nonrelation can be condemned as signs of profanation, but they are also susceptible to being venerated as signs of sacred incommensurability. These aporias are directly relevant to the problem of how a language names itself because they disrupt predication, the process by which verbal attributes coalesce in a proper name or noun.

The difficult process of depredication, otherwise known as secular criticism, is one of the premier tasks of philology, as conceived by Edward Said in his final writings. In a chapter of *Humanism and Democratic Criticism* devoted to "The Return of Philology," Said wrote:

Philology is, literally the love of words, but as a discipline it acquires a quasi-scientific intellectual and spiritual prestige at various periods in all of the major cultural traditions, including the Western and the Arabic-Islamic traditions that have framed my own development. Suffice it to recall briefly that in the Islamic tradition, knowledge is premised upon a philological attention to language beginning with the Koran, the uncreated word of God (and indeed the word "Koran" itself means reading), and continuing through the emergence of scientific grammar in Khalil ibn Ahmad and Sibawayh to the rise of jurisprudence (*fiqh*) and *ijtihad* and *ta'wil,* jurisprudential hermeneutics and interpretation, respectively.[11]

Said makes a sweeping pass through systems of humanistic education based on philology in Arab universities of southern Europe and North Africa in the twelfth century, Judaic tradition in Andalusia, North Africa, the Levant, and Mesopotamia, then on to Vico and Nietzsche. He extols a humanism of reading and interpretation "grounded in the shapes of words as bearers of reality, a reality hidden, misleading, resistant, and difficult. The science of reading, in other words, is paramount for humanistic knowledge" (HDC 58).

Just as *Humanism and Democratic Criticism* openly engages Leo Spitzer's philological legacy (Spitzer rather than Auerbach for once!), so too does the 2002 essay "Living in Arabic," which invites being read in tandem with Spitzer's "Learning Turkish." Spitzer with Said plays off the epistemological modalities of "living" and "learning" a language.[12] Where Spitzer fastened on the ontological implications of sequencing in Turkish, and emphasized how the consecutive unfolding ("one by one") of an action mimics the nature of experience, thereby enlivening narration in a uniquely "human and subjective way," Said gleaned significance from the relational gaps of word-by-word analysis. Spitzer was drawn to modes of expression that seemed wreathed in scare-quotes, that somehow marked "what is happening" as things happen. Interrogative enunciations in Turkish such as "He saw me, or did he not?" or "Did he or did he not open the door?" epitomized for Spitzer a habit of self-questioning that initiated an othering of self within subjectivity. The term *gibi* he suggested, whether attached to verb forms or just thrown out at random, indexed the speaker's loss of conviction in his own words. "Words no longer signify a definite event but carry the ambiguity of comparison within them." *Gibi,* then, was interpreted as a part of speech tailored for the philologist, for it called attention to how each word internalizes comparability. Similarly, in his conclusion to "The Return to Philology," Said fixed on the "space of words" as the aporia of comparison. Humanism, he maintained,

> is the means, perhaps the consciousness we have for providing that kind of finally antinomian or oppositional analysis between the space of words and their various origins and deployments in physical and social place, from text to actualized site of either appropriation or resistance, to transmission, to reading and interpretation, from private to public, from silence to explication and utterance, and back again, as we encounter our own silence and mortality—all of it occurring in the world, on the ground of daily life and history and hopes, and the search for knowledge and justice, and then perhaps also for liberation. (HDC 83)

As if anticipating Said's lifelong commitment to a lexicon of exile affording existential humanism, Spitzer delighted in the way in which the grammar of mitigation—the generous sprinkling of equivalent terms for "buts" and "howevers" through Turkish speech—afforded felicitous relief "to the thinking man from the pressures of this difficult life." "In this decreasing voice," Spitzer asserted, "I see our humility. For an instant, the human spirit descends to pessimism to rid itself of numbness, triumphing over difficulty through reason. Thus a small word like 'but,' or 'yet,' though a mere grammatical tool of negation, becomes an emotional manifestation loaded with the weight of life. In these small words, we see humanity deal with adversity." Spitzer traveled down to the micrological stratum of speech particles to observe "life" swimming against the current of "death." Grammatical markers of doubt or negation were cast as valves that released the pressure that builds up in the course of fighting to stay alive, rallying the subject's determination to go on. For Said, these particles comprise a syntax of traumatic incommensurability; they contour the aporias of militant love. Said and Spitzer seem to have entered into stichomythia in their common regard for word spacing as the "program" of life and death, the grammar of grounding and unhoming. Saidian-Spitzerian philology portends the advent of a translational humanism that assumes the disciplinary challenges posed by Turkish and Arabic in their respective circumstances of institutional exile. Turkish and Arabic name, for each of them, a crisis of theo-poetics in secular time.

In his considerations on the status of Arabic language, which one can only speculate might have been the subject of a book-in-the-making, Said experimented with using philology to re-articulate the sacred otherwise. It was as if he were aware of Kenneth Reinhard's conviction that the unconscious—like divine language—comes through in the desire to "re-speak or repunctuate" a language that comes from the outside, bearing "the marks of its strange desires and cruel imperatives."[13] Rather than dodge the issue of how a secular language copes with the mandate of neighboring a sacred tongue, Said took up the problem of "living in Arabic," a task complicated in everyday life by the split between classical (*fus-ha*) and demotic (*'amiya*).[14] Though one of Said's clear intentions in the essay was to reform Arabic so that it could better deal with classical expression in quotidian speech, his greatest concern, it would seem, was to use philology to de-translate the "fundamentalist" attribution of Arabic. To this end, he recalled the term *al-qua'ida* to its philological function (as the word for "grammar," or "base" of language), just as in *Humanism and Democratic Criticism*, he reclaimed *jihad* for secular usage, contextualizing it as commitment to "isnad" or hermeneutical community:[15]

> Since in Islam the Koran is the Word of God, it is therefore impossible ever fully to grasp, though it must repeatedly be read. But the fact that it is in language already makes it incumbent on readers first of all to try to understand its literal meaning, with a profound awareness that others before them have attempted the same daunting task. So the presence of others is given as a community of witnesses whose availability to the contemporary reader is retained in the form of a chain, each witness depending to some degree on an earlier one. This system of interdependent readings is called "*isnad.*" The common goal is to try to approach the ground of the text, its principal or *usul*, although there must always be a component of personal commitment and extraordinary effort, called "*ijtihad*" in Arabic. (Without a knowledge of Arabic, it is difficult to know that "*ijtihad*" derives from the same root as the now notorious word *jihad*, which does not mainly mean holy war but rather a primarily spiritual exertion on behalf of the truth.) It is not surprising that since the fourteenth century there has been a robust struggle going on about whether *ijtihad* is permissible, to what degree, and within what limits. (HDC 68–69)

As this passage affirms, Said was committed to extracting the predicate "terror" from Arabic as the name of a language. But in seeking to secularize the sacred word, Said wandered into the nominalist quandary of how to name languages otherwise. The need to disrupt the deep structural laws by which languages are named after nations, peoples, and God-terms complemented

Said's concern to posit a philological humanism no longer hobbled by neo-imperialist jingoism, no longer shy of facing off against the autocracy of theocratic speech-acts, and yet, also no longer able to deny the idea of "life" as an untranslatable singularity, a "cognition of paradise" that assumes tangible guise in Babel or the "afterlife" of translation.[16] Linguistic monotheism (inherent in Derrida's "monolingualism of the other"), Said's paradigm of "Living in Arabic" (the set that excludes itself, the logic of one sacred language constituted as two—*fus-ha* and *'amiya*), and Spitzer's paradigm of "Learning Turkish" (which activates standing reserves of nontranslation) together push the limits of how language thinks itself, thereby regrounding the prospects for a new comparative literature in the problem of translation.

Introduction

1. Andrew Dalby, *Language in Danger: The Loss of Linguistic Diversity and the Threat to Our Future* (New York: Columbia University Press, 2003), p. 239.

2. Rem Koolhaus, *Content* (London: Taschen, 2004), p. 90.

3. Walter Benjamin, "On Language as Such," trans. Edmund Jephcott, in *Walter Benjamin: Selected Writings*, vol. 1, 1913–1926, ed. Michael Jennings (Cambridge Mass: Harvard University Press, 1996), p. 69–70.

4. Translation lay at the crux of Renaissance humanism, enabling it to become a medium of intellectual exchange between East and West, and to preserve and disseminate the archive of ancient learning and culture. The value placed on translation on the part of German Romance scholars helped redress the general disregard for the translator's craft exhibited by the nineteenth and early twentieth centuries. In these periods, the names of translators were routinely left off book covers unless the translators happened to be celebrated authors in their own right. When comparative literature became a postwar academic discipline, translation was made part of a theorist's training (for example, the translations of Jacques Derrida's work by Gayatri Chakravorty Spivak and Barbara Johnson).

5. Barbara Johnson, *Mother Tongues: Sexuality, Trials, Motherhood, Translation* (Cambridge, MA: Harvard University Press, 2003), p. 60.

6. Philippe Lacoue-Labarthe and Jean-Luc Nancy, *The Literary Absolute: The Theory of Literature in German Romanticism*, trans. Philip Barnard and Cheryl Lester (Albany: SUNY Press, 1988), pp. 27–33.

7. On planetary criticism, see Wai Chee Dimock, "Literature for the Planet," *PMLA* 116 Jan. 2001: 173–88; and Gayatri Chakravorty Spivak, *Death of a Discipline* (New York: Columbia University Press, 2003).

Chapter 1
Translation after 9/11: Mistranslating the Art of War

1. MSNBC (October 7, 2002) www.aaai.org/AI Topics.

2. Peter Spiegel, *The Financial Times* (October 7, 2003).

3. John Milner, *Art, War, and Revolution in France 1870–1871: Myth, Reportage and Reality* (New Haven: Yale University Press, 2000), p. xi.

4. Carl von Clausewitz, *On War* [*Vom Kriege* 1832], trans. Col. J. J. Graham (London: Penguin, 1982), p. 119. Further references to this work, including the preface by Anatol Rapoport, will appear in the text abbreviated OW.

5. Michel Foucault, *"Society Must be Defended": Lectures at the Collège de France 1975–1976*, trans. David Macey (New York: Picador, 2003), p. 48.

6. Philip Smith, "Codes and Conflict: Toward a Theory of War as Ritual," in *Theory and Society* 20: 1991, p. 107.

7. *The Daily Telegraph*, Frank Johnson, "Notebook," 10/25/2003 telegraph.co.uk

8. Peter Schwarz, "Schröder, Bush and the 'Agenda 2010' " Oct. 8, 2003. ws.ws.org

9. Michael Duffy, 2002–2003. Http://firstworldwar.com/source/emsteltegram.htm

10. My account of the Ems incident relies on multiple Internet sources, on Michael Howard's *The Franco-Prussian War* (New York: Collier, 1961), and on James F. McMillan's *Profiles in Power: Napoleon III* (London, 1991).

11. The first citation was supposedly a verbatim quotation of Lacan by Françoise Giroud in an article published in *L'Express* titled "Quand l'autre était Dieu." Lacan's famous dictum "There is no sexual relation" occurs in Seminar XX "Encore" (Paris: Seuil), 1975), p. 14. Both quotes cited by Elisabeth Roudinesco, *Jacques Lacan* (Paris: Fayard), 1993, p. 439.

12. Emile Zola, *La Débâcle*, trans. Elinor Dorday (Oxford: Oxford University Press, 2000), p. 19–20.

13. Discussing "a pathological mode of defence" in an 1895 extract from the Fliess papers, Freud alluded to the Franco-Prussian war explicitly. *The Standard Edition of the Complete Psychological Works of Sigmund Freud*, vol. 1, trans. James Strachey (London: The Hogarth Press, 1966), p. 207.

14. See Jacques Rancière, *La mésentente. politique et philosophie* (Paris: Galilée, 1995), and Jonathan Shell, *The Unconquerable World: Power, Nonviolence, and the Will of the People* (New York: Metropolitan Books, 2003).

Chapter 2
The Human in the Humanities

1. Thomas Keenan, Introduction to "Humanism without Borders: A Dossier on the Human, Humanitarianism, and Human Rights," eds. Emily Apter and Thomas Keenan in *Alphabet City* (Fall 2000), p. 41.

2. Spitzer refers lugubriously and *un*ironically to the fact that his work as a military censor brought him definitive linguistic rewards. In the essay "The Individual Factor in Linguistic Innovations" (1956), in which he examines how hard it is for neologisms (or what he calls "nonce-words") to enter into standard language, he finds the precedent for "linguistic innovations" such as the word *Kodak*, introduced

by the Eastman Kodak company, in the ingenious, periphrastic inventions of Italian prisoners whose letters Spitzer vetted during World War I. Spitzer offers a lengthy account of how the prisoners came up with rhetorical disguises for the word "hunger," expressions intended to elude the censors yet signal to their families the urgent need to send food. Spitzer says nothing of the sad condition of the prisoners who have the ill fortune of having a crack-shot interpreter monitoring their correspondence, treating the prisoners' letters as a providential opportunity to test out early versions of his philological theory, an opportunity that led to his publication in 1919 of a study of the words for hunger (*Die Umschreibungen des Begriffes "Hunger"*).

3. Hans Ulrich Gumbrecht offers a fascinating description of Spitzer's identification with Germany, including his reaction of dismay and disbelief when, in 1933, he was denounced by a leader of the National Socialist student party and soon after dismissed from his post at the University of Marburg. See *Vom Leben und Sterben der grossen Romanisten: Karl Vossler, Ernst Robert Curtius, Leo Spitzer, Erich Auerbach, Werner Krauss* (Munchen: Carl Hanser Verlag, 2002).

4. "Linguistics and Literary History," in *Leo Spitzer, Representative Essays* (Stanford: Stanford University Press, 1988), p. 16. All further references to this text will be to this edition and will abbreviated in the text as LLH.

5. Spitzer wrote: "[N]ot only was this kind of humanities not centered on a particular people in a particular time, but the subject matter itself had got lost: Man" (LLH 6).

6. Erich Auerbach, "Philology and *Weltliteratur*," trans. Maire and Edward Said, *The Centennial Review*, vol. 13, no. 1 (Winter 1969), pp. 14 and 3, respectively.

7. www.wimall.com/pullportermu/

8. Leo Spitzer, "Ratio > Race" in *Essays in Historical Semantics* (New York: S. F. Vanni, 1948), p. 152.

9. Ibid.

10. Peter Sloterdijk, "Règles pour le parc humain, Réponse à la lettre sur l'humanisme," Translated from the German by Christiane Haack, *Le Monde des Débats* no. 7 (October 1999), pp. 1–8. The translation from the French is my own.

11. Dina Al-Kassim, *On Pain of Speech: Fantasies of the First Order and the Literary Rant*, unpublished book manuscript, p. 14.

12. Louis-Ferdiand Céline, *Bagatelles pour un massacre* (Paris: Les Editions Denoël, 1937), p. 72. All further references to this work will be to this edition and will appear in the text abbreviated BM.

13. Daniel Sibony, *La haine du désir* (Paris: Christian Bourgeois, éditeur, 1978), p. 28. Further references to this work will appear in the text abbreviated HD.

14. The question of whether racism is classifiable as a pathology or mental disorder is an old one. In an article in the *New York Times* (Jan. 15, 2000) titled "Bigotry as Mental Illness or Just Another Norm," Emily Eakin reviews the way in which the debate was reignited when the Atlanta Braves pitcher John Rocker was sent for psychological evaluation after his racist remarks about blacks, homosexuals, and foreigners were quoted in *Sports Illustrated*.

15. Henri Godard, *Céline scandal* (Paris: Gallimard, 1994), p. 107.

16. For further analysis of the problem of verbal contagion, particularly as it emerges in the "sense of homosexual proclamations as contagious acts," see Judith Butler, *Excitable Speech: A Politics of the Performative* (New York: Routledge, 1997), pp. 114–15.

17. Louis-Ferdinand Céline, *Mea Culpa and the Life and Work of Semmelweis*, trans. Robert Allerton Parker (Boston: Little, Brown and Company, 1937), p. 173.

18. An example of identification with an othering perspective on oneself can be found once again in Spitzer. In an essay, "Gentiles," published in the collection on historical semantics, he notes the recursive effect of a common variety of Help Wanted ad stipulating "Gentiles only." In applying the term "Gentile" to themselves, Spitzer discerns an astonishing example of "Christians agreeing to being looked at from without" (*Essays on Historical Semantics*, p. 171).

19. Luca Cavalli-Sforza, *Gènes, peuples & langues* (Paris: Editions Edile Jacob, 1996).

20. Hans Ulrich Gumbrecht, "Leo Spitzer's Style," unpublished manuscript.

21. Bill Readings, *The University in Ruins* (Cambridge, Mass.: Harvard University Press, 1997), p. 105.

22. Denis Hollier, "The Pure and the Impure: Literature after Silence," in *Literary Debate: Texts and Contexts* (New York: The New Press, 1999), p. 13.

23. Paul de Man, "Conclusions: Walter Benjamin's 'The Task of the Translator,' " in *The Resistance to Theory* (Minneapolis: University of Minnesota Press, 1986), p. 92. Further references to this essay will appear in the text abbreviated RT.

24. I borrow this construction from Manuel de Landa who wrote a book titled *War in the Age of Intelligent Machines* (New York: Swerve Editions, 1991).

Chapter 3
Global *Translatio*: The "Invention" of Comparative Literature, Istanbul, 1933

1. Franco Moretti, "Conjectures on World Literature," *New Left Review* (Jan.–Feb. 2000): 68. All further references to this essay will appear in the text abbreviated CWL.

2. Erich Auerbach, *Mimesis: The Representation of Reality in Western Literature*, trans. Willard R Trask (Princeton: Princeton University Press, 1953), p. 557.

3. Edward Said, *The World, the Text and the Critic* (Cambridge, Mass.: Harvard University Press), p. 8.

4. Edward Said, "Humanism?" in *MLA Newsletter*, Fall 1999, p. 4.

5. AamirMufti, "Auerbach in Istanbul: Edward Said, Secular Criticism, and the Question of Minority Culture," *Critical Inquiry* 25 (Autumn 1998). Further references to this essay will appear in the text abbreviated AI.

6. A brief account of Spitzer's and Auerbach's Istanbul careers may be found in Geoffrey Green's *Literary Criticism and the Structures of History: Erich Auerbach*

and Leo Spitzer (Lincoln and London: University of Nebraska Press, 1982). Green maintains that Istanbul was not a place of hardship for Spitzer. While there, he maintains, Spitzer "concentrated upon 'the inner form': with the 'brazen confidence' that comes from placing one's faith in Providence, he viewed his surroundings—despite their shortcomings—as being vitalized by a divine spirit" (p. 105). Thomas R. Hart's essay "Literature as Language: Auerbach, Spitzer, Jakobson," is one of the few to credit the influence of Istanbul and Turkish alphabetization on Auerbach's oeuvre. In *Literary History and the Challenge of Philology: The Legacy of Erich Auerbach,* ed. Seth Lerer (Stanford: Stanford University Press, 1996. See pp. 227–30.

7. René Etiemble, *The Crisis of Comparative Literature,* trans. Georges Joyaux and Herbert Weisinger (East Lansing: Michigan State University Press, 1966), p. 56.

8. Ibid., p. 57.

9. Paul de Man, *Blindness and Insight: Essays in the Rhetoric of Contemporary Criticism* (Minneapolis: University of Minnesota Press, 1971), p. 171. Several recent publications attest to renewed interest in the Romance philological tradition prior to and during World War II. See Hans Ulrich Gumbrecht, *Vom Leben und Sterben der grossen Romanisten: Karl Vossler, Ernst Robert Curtius, Leo Spitzer, Erich Auerbach, Werner Krauss* (Munchen: Carl Hanser Verlag, 2002), and Peter Jehle, *Werner Krauss und die Romanistik im NS-Staat* (Hamburg: Argument Verlag, 1996). For a review of Jehle's book, emphasizing the timeliness of re-examining the career of Werner Krauss, the "militant humanist" and Enlightenment scholar who joined the party in 1945 and emigrated east to become chair of the Romance Institute at Leipzig, see Darko Suvin, "Auerbach's Assistant," *New Left Review* 15 (May–June 2002): 157–64.

10. John Freccero, "Foreward" to *Leo Spitzer: Representative Essays* (Stanford: Stanford University Press, 1988), pp. xvi—xvii.

11. See, Leo Spitzer, *Die Umschreibungen des Begriffes "Hunger" im Italienischen* (Germany: Verlag von Max Niemeyer, 1921).

12. Curtius's careerist opportunism vis-à-vis Spitzer's vacated post has been read as evidence of his compromised position with respect to the bureaucracy of National Socialism. The debate is still on with respect to Curtius's vision of Europeans as citizens of humanity. Earl Jeffrey Richards frames these concerns in terms of a series of important questions: Was Curtius's vision of a supranational Europe, captured in his 1948 masterwork *European Literature and the Latin Middle Ages* a dangerous rampart offered to Himmler's ideology of "Fortress-Europe" or to the Nazi vision of a new Germania built on romantic neomedievalism? Was Curtius politically naive to assume that his ideal of European humanism would remain untainted by historical circumstances? Or was he simply the scapegoat for all the German Romantic scholars who continued to work unscathed or who profited from the émigré departures under the Third Reich? Was Curtius unfairly misread given his consistent, and some would say, courageous refutation of national character theory? See Earl Jeffrey Richards, "La Conscience européenne chez Curtius et chez ses détracteurs," in *Ernst Robert Curtius et l'idée d'Europe* eds. Jeanne Bem and André Guyaux (Paris: Editions Champion, 1995), pp. 260–61.

13. Though Spitzer received an offer from Harvard in 1934, Rosemarie Burkart was unable to obtain U.S. residency papers, and they stayed in Turkey for another two years.

14. Despite Auerbach's oft-repeated criticism of the bibliographical shortcomings of the Istanbul library, he managed to edit a Romanology seminar publication around 1944 that included well-referenced essays on Shakespeare, Péguy, Shelley, Marlowe, Rilke, and Jakobsonian linguistics.

15. The interview took place in the summer of 2001. It was conducted in French at Süheyla Bayrav's house, located in a suburb on the Asian side of Istanbul.

16. Harry Levin, "Two *Romanisten* in America: Spitzer and Auerbach," in *Grounds for Comparison* (Cambridge, Mass.: Harvard University Press, 1972), pp. 112–13. Further references to this work will appear in the text abbreviated GC. Levin, in this essay, argues that Spitzer and Auerbach reacted in contrasting ways to "the lack of scholarly paraphernalia" in Istanbul. He casts the former's *Wortbildungslehre* or word-formation approach as "infra-scholarship," and the latter's "sociohistorical rather than strictly stylistic" approach as "para-scholarship" (GC 118).

17. As cited by Karlheinz Barck, "Walter Benjamin and Erich Auerbach: Fragments of a Correspondence," *Diacritics* (Fall—Winter 1992), p. 82.

18. Hans Ulrich Gumbrecht suggests that the Istanbul period was the culmination of a sense of intellectual melancholia already fully fledged in Auerbach's pre-exile professional life. Gumbrecht wagers "that his passionate and distanced view of European culture emerged during his exile in Istanbul, or even after his emigration to the United States in 1947. At most, the experience of expatriation that the National Socialist regime had inflicted upon him gave Auerbach the opportunity to become fully aware of his distanced and sometimes melancholic perspective on western culture as a culture that had entered its final stage." See Gumbrecht, " 'Pathos of the Earthly Progress': Eric Auerbach's Everydays," in *Literary History and the Challenge of Philology: The Legacy of Erich Auerbach*, ed. Seth Lerer (Stanford: Stanford University Press, 1996), p. 31.

19. Anne Dietrich, *Deutschsein in Istanbul* (Opladen: Leske and Budrich), 1998.

20. Other notable visitors included Cemil Bilsel, Ernst Reuter, Rudolf Nissen, Beyazit Platz, Alexander Rustow, Wilhelm Röpke, and Hellmut Ritter.

21. Sources here include *Cogito, sayi:* 23 (2000), and the appendix to Horst Widmann, *Exil und Bildungshilfe: Die deutschsprachige akademische Emigration in die Türkei nach 1933* (Bern: Herbert Lang and Frankfurt/M: Peter Lang, 1973).

22. Sir Steven Runciman, "Muslim Influences on the Development of European Civilization," in *Şarkiyat Mecmuasi* [*Oriental Magazine*] 3 (1959): 1–12. Runciman's argues, "The medieval French romance, *Floire et Blanchefleur*, is an eastern story; while one of the most famous and lovely of all European romances, *Aucassin et Nicolète*, betrays its Muslim origin. There [*sic*] hero's name is really al-Q-asim, while the heroine is stated to be a Muslim princess of Tunis. It seems, also, that the use of

rhyme in medieval European verse was inspired by Arabic models. . . . Long before Europe knew of the collection of short stories which we call the *Arabian Nights*, Muslim romance and poetry were making a mark on European literature" (p. 22).

23. Despite Turkey's neutrality, the Nazis also maintained a significant foothold in the city, taking over the banking and administrative structure of the "Deutschen Kolonie" once they assumed power. There were branches of the Hitler Youth, German press outlets for propaganda, and a program of Nazification in the German schools in Istanbul. The tensions between these two German-speaking communities—proximate yet offshore—were needless to say rife. For an account, based in part on the documentation of Liselotte Dieckmann (who worked with Spitzer as a lecturer), see Anne Dietrich, *Deutschsein in Istanbul*, chapter 4. Dieckmann also echoes the fears expressed by Auerbach that modern Turkish nationalism would come to resemble National Socialism.

24. Victor Klemperer, *I Will Bear Witness: A Diary of the Nazi Years*, vol. 1 (1933–41), trans. Martin Chalmers (New York: Modern Library, 1999), pp. 175 and 178, respectively.

25. Harry Dember to Victor Klemperer in Victor Klemperer, *The Language of the Third Reich: LTI—Lingua Tertii Imperii A Philologist's Notebook*, trans. Martin Brady (London: Athlone Press, 2000), p. 159. Further references to this work will appear in the text abbreviated LTI.

26. For an account of Malche's role in the reform, Horst Widmann, *Exil und Bildungshilfe*, pp. 45–48.

27. Ibid., 45–48.

28. Geoffrey Green, basing these assertions on an interview published by Spitzer in *The Johns Hopkins Magazine* April 1952. See his *Literary Criticism and the Structures of History: Erich Auerbach and Leo Spitzer*, p. 105.

29. It is strange that Paul Bové does so little with the impact of Istanbul on Auerbach's work given his criticism of the inattention paid to "the cultural and political roots" of Auerbach's work, and his argument that "Auerbach's project of writing 'a synthetic history-from-within' owes much to its own academic cultural context." Ideally one would match Bové's useful reappraisal of the impact of Weimar culture and German modernism on Auerbach's thought with a discussion of the influence of Turkish alphabetization on Auerbach's analysis of literary language and its public. See, Paul Bové, *Intellectuals in Power: A Genealogy of Critical Humanism* (New York: Columbia University Press, 1986), p. 79.

30. Erich Auerbach, *Introduction to Romance Languages and Literatures*, trans. from French by Guy Daniels (New York: Capricorn Books, 1961). The Turkish edition, translated by Süheyla Bayrav, appeared in 1944.

31. Erich Auerbach, *Literatursprache und Publikum in der lateinischen Spätantike und im Mittelalter* (Bern: Franke Verlag, 1958). Published in English as *Literary Language and Its Public in Late Latin Antiquity and in the Middle Ages*, trans. Ralph Mannheim (Princeton: Princeton University Press, 1965). Adopting the same

gloomy tone that one finds in the afterword to *Mimesis,* Auerbach articulates his profoundly pessimistic fear that Western civilization would be subsumed by modern global culture:

> European civilization is approaching the term of its existence; its history as a distinct entity would seem to be at an end, for already it is beginning to be engulfed in another, more comprehensive unity. Today, however, European civilization is still a living reality within the range of our perception. Consequently—so it seemed to me when I wrote these articles and so I still believe—we must today attempt to form a lucid and coherent picture of this civilization and its unity. (p. 6)

32. Thomas Hart has surmised that the break with tradition induced by the banning of Arabic script "may have reminded Auerbach of the loss entailed by the decline of classical studies in the West," and in support of this claim he cites a letter sent by Auerbach to Benjamin shortly after his arrival in Istanbul in December 1936:

> Here all traditions have been thrown overboard in an attempt to build a thoroughly rationalized state that will be both European and extremely Turco-nationalistic. The whole process is being carried out with a fantastic and unearthly speed [*es geht phantastisch und gespenstisch schnell*]; already it is hard to find anyone who can read Arabic or Persian or even Turkish texts written in the last century, since the language has been modernized and reoriented along purely Turkish lines and is now written in roman letters.

In Thomas R. Hart, "Literature as Language, pp. 230–31.

33. As cited by Karlheinz Barck, "Walter Benjamin and Erich Auerbach, p. 82. Robert Stein's more precise translation of this phrase (and the passage of the letter in which it is set) reads:

> I am more and more convinced that the contemporary world situation is nothing other than the cunning of providence to lead us along a bloody and circuitous route to the Internationale of Triviality and Esperanto-culture. I've surmised this already in Germany and Italy, especially in the horrible inauthenticity of "Blubopropaganda" [blood and soil propaganda], but here for the first time it has become for me a certainty.

As cited by Robert Stein in his unpublished paper "After Culture: Erich Auerbach and Walter Benjamin in Correspondence" (2004).

34. Erich Auerbach, *Literary Language and Its Public.* Auerbach argues that the stability of Latin as a literary language was crucial to the formation of a literary public during the Empire. After imperial decline, written Latin endured as a language of law and religion because "there was no other written language and because it had long served, with the same homogeneity and the same conservatism . . . as the specialized language of the various branches of public life" (p. 252).

35. For a fascinating discussion of how the theme of intergenerational language loss, acquisition, and recovery informs the work of a modern Turkish writer living in Germany, see Azade Seyhan's examination of Emine Sevgi Özdamar's

Mutterzunge (1994) in *Writing Outside the Nation* (Princeton: Princeton University Press, 2001), pp. 118–19.

36. Robert M. Stein translates and cites this letter of Auerbach to Benjamin of Dec. 12, 1936, in "After Culture." The essay makes a substantive case for recognizing a stronger connection between Auerbachian philology and Frankfurt school critical theory than has generally allowed. Stein speculates that Auerbach and Benjamin may have overlapped in the 1920s when Auerbach was a librarian at the Berlin Staatsbibliotek and Benjamin was writing his *Trauerspiel* thesis there. Auerbach's omission of a chapter of *Mimesis* on the Spanish Golden Age and German baroque tragic realism may thus be linked, Stein suggests, to the fact that it was Benjamin's thesis subject.

37. The translated essay titles are Azra Ahat, "A New Method in Studies of Style" (a study of Spitzer's word art); Eva Buck, "Color in Dorothy Richardson's 'Pointed Roofs' "; Rosemarie Burkart, "Go-Between"; Herbert Dieckmann, "Diderot's Nature-Empathy and Life Feeling"; Traugott Fuch, "The Early Poetry of Rimbaud"; Sabahattin Eyüböglu, "Turkish Anonymous Riddles"; Leo Spitzer, "Remarks on Dante's 'Vita Nuova' "; Süheyla Sabri, "Un passage from 'Barlaan and Josaiat"; Erich Auerbach, "On the Serious Imitation of the Everyday."

38. When Comp Lit took root as a postwar discipline in the United States, the European traditions were dominant, and the Turkish chapter of its life was effaced. What attracted the American academics was European erudition. As Carl Landauer notes in his consideration of "Auerbach's Performance and the American Academy, or How New Haven Stole the Idea of *Mimesis*," the idea of the "virtuoso performer created by the author of *Mimesis* in Istanbul in the 1940's played perfectly to American audiences of the 1950's." "But Auerbach was not alone," Landauer writes,

> for a number of émigré scholars with their obvious erudition and their mastery of an enormous range of cultural artifacts became prized possessions of their adopted culture, so that reviews of books by Kantorowicz, Panofsky, Cassirer, Jaeger, Spitzer, Kristeller, and Auerbach seem to blend into one another. It was not just an encyclopedic range that marked these scholars but a sense that they brought a certain "depth" to the study of culture and history from which Americans could learn. It was, then, as a masterful scholar and a translator of European "depth" that the author of *Mimesis* made his name in an American academy looking for exactly such exemplars.

Literary History and the Challenge of Philology, p. 180.

39. This appropriation of Greek culture in Turkey must be considered against the backdrop of the history of Greek minorities in the region. For a lucid account of historic religious and ethnic tensions, see Neal Ascheson's lucid book, *Black Sea: The Birthplace of Civilization and Barbarism* (London: Vintage, 1996), p. 177: Greece, in a wild imperial venture supported by Britain, had invaded Western Anatolia, hoping to make itself an Aegean "great power" and to construct a greater

Greece out of the ruins of the Ottoman Empire. But the invasion ended not simply in Greece's defeat at the battle of Dumlupinar in 1922, but in a calamitous rout and slaughter that drove not only the Greek armies but much of the Greek population of Anatolia into the sea. The Treaty of Lausanne, in 1923, settled the frontiers of the new Turkey under the leadership of Mustafa Kemal Ataturk. The universal caliph-ate—a sprawling, multi-ethnic and multi-religious empire—now imploded like a dead star, metamorphosing itself into a compact, homogenous modern state of Mos-lem religion and Turkish speech. At the same time, Greece and Turkey agreed to ex-change minorities. Nearly half a million Muslims (many of whom were Greeks in all but religion) were forced to leave Greece, while more than a million Christians (some of whom were culturally Turks) were expelled from Turkey. Most of the Christians were Pontic Greeks, who abandoned their monasteries and farms, their town houses and banks and schools, and fled with what they could carry down to the docks.

40. This information is based on my interview with Professor Süyehla Bayrav.

41. Paul Bové, *Intellectuals in Power*, p. xiii.

42. Bernard Cerquiglini, *In Praise of the Variant: A Critical History of Philol-ogy*, trans. Betsy Wing (Baltimore: Johns Hopkins University Press, 1999), p. xiv.

43. Michael Holquist, *Association of Departments of Foreign Languages Bulle-tin*, vol. 33, no. 2 (Winter 2002), p. 18.

44. Klemperer treated LTI almost as if it were a linguistic totem warding off the evil effects that Nazism wrought upon language. In his posthumously published book he wrote:

> The label LTI first appears in my diary as a playful little piece of parody, al-most immediately afterwords as a laconic *aide-mémoire*, like a knot in a handkerchief, and then very soon, and for the duration of those terrible years, as an act of self-defence, an SOS sent to myself. A tag with a nice eru-dite ring—the Third Reich itself after all delighted from time to time in the rich sonority of a foreign expression. (LTI 9)

45. Hugo Friedrich, "On the Art of Translation," trans. Rainer Schulte and John Biguenet, in *Theories of Translation: An Anthology of Essays from Dryden to Der-rida*, eds. Rainer Schulte and John Biguenet (Chicago: University of Chicago Press, 1992), pp. 12–13.

46. Roman Jakobson, "On Linguistic Aspects of Translation," in *Theories of Translation: An Anthology of Essays from Dryden to Derrida*, eds. Rainer Schulte and John Biguenet (Chicago: University of Chicago Press, 1992), p. 145.

47. Klemperer writes:

> Long before the Nazi SS even existed, its symbol was to be seen painted in red on electricity substations, and below it the warning "Danger—High Voltage!" In this case the jagged S was obviously a stylized representation of a flash of lightening [*sic*]. That thunderbolt, whose velocity and capacity for storing energy made it such a popular symbol for the Nazis! Thus the SS character was also a direct embodiment, a painterly expression of light-

ening [*sic*]. Here the double line may well suggest increased energy, because the little black flags of the children's formations only bore one jagged bolt, what you might call a half-SS. (LTI 68–69)

48. For more background on the disciplinary schisms within comparative literature induced by the advent of postcolonial theory, see my essay "Comparative Exile: Competing Margins in the History of Comparative Literature," in Charles Bernheimer, *Comparative Literature in the Age of Multiculturalism* (Baltimore and London: The Johns Hopkins University Press, 1995), pp. 86–96.

49. Edward Said, *Culture and Imperialism* (New York: Alfred A. Knopf, 1993), p. 51.

50. Herbert Lindenberger, "On the Reception of *Mimesis*," in *Literary History and the Challenge of Philology*, ed. Seth Lerer (Stanford: Stanford University Press, 1996), p. 209. My thanks to Howard Bloch for bringing this article to my attention.

51. Dipesh Chakrabarty, *Provincializing Europe: Postcolonial Thought and Historical Difference* (Princeton: Princeton University Press, 1999).

52. Edward Said, *Representations of the Intellectual* (New York: Vintage Books, 1994), p. 31.

53. See Said's statement "The intellectual is fundamentally about knowledge and freedom" (RI 59).

54. Leo Spitzer, *American Journal of Philology* 70 (s.d.), 425–26. As cited by Hans Ulrich Gumbrecht, " 'Zeitlosigkeit, die durchscheint in der Zeit': Uber E. R. Curtius' unhistoricsches Verhältnis zur Geschichte," in *Ernst Robert Curtius: Werk, Wirkung, Zukunftperspektiven*, eds. Walter Berschin and Arnold Rothe, (Heidelberg: Carl Winter-Universitätsverlag, 1989), pp. 233–34.

55. Edward Said, *Out of Place: A Memoir* (New York: Vintage Books, 1999), p. 205.

56. Leo Spitzer, "Linguistics and Literary History," p. 35.

57. Walter Benjamin, "The Task of the Translator," in *Illuminations*, trans. Willard Trask (New York: Schocken Books, 1969), p. 82.

58. Theodor Adorno, "Words from Abroad," in *Notes to Literature* II, pp. 187–88.

59. Paul de Man, "Conclusions: Walter Benjamin's 'The Task of the Translator,' " in *The Resistance to Theory* (Minneapolis: University of Minnesota Press, 19), pp. 84–85. Further references to this work will appear in the text abbreviated RT.

60. Geoffrey Hartman, *The Fate of Reading* (Chicago: Chicago University Press, 1975), p. 121. See also, Hartman's *The Fateful Question of Culture* (New York: Columbia University Press, 1997) for a discussion of the contrast between the idea of culture that arose from émigré cosmopolitanism and culture as it is being defined within a globalized literary studies today.

61. David Damrosch, "Auerbach in Exile," *Comparative Literature*, vol. 47, no. 2. (Spring 1995), p. 109.

Chapter 4
Saidian Humanism

1. Jonathan Arac, "Criticism between Opposition and Counterpoint," in *Edward Said and the Work of the Critic: Speaking Truth to Power*, ed. Paul A. Bové (Durham, N.C., and London: Duke University Press, 2000), p. 68. Arac cites an interview published as "Orientalism and After," in *A Critical Sense: Interviews with Intellectuals*, ed. Peter Osbourne (London: Routledge, 1996), p. 68

2. Paul A. Bové, ed., *Edward Said and the Work of the Critic*.

3. Edward W. Said, *Humanism and Democratic Criticism*, (New York: Columbia University Press, 2003), p. 61.

4. Edward W. Said, *Orientalism* (New York: Vintage, 1979), p. 69–70. Subsequent references to this work are cited parenthetically as O.

5. Edward W. Said, introduction to *Mimesis: The Representation of Reality in Western Literature*, by Erich Auerbach, trans. Willard R. Task (Princeton, N.J.: Princeton University Press, 2003), pp. xv, xxi. Subsequent references to this work are cited parenthetically as M.

6. Walter Benjamin, from Review of Renéville's *L'Expérience poétique*, p. 117.

7. Walter Benjamin, "Exchange with Adorno on Paris of the Second Empire," in *Walter Benjamin: Selected Writings Vol. 4 (1938–1940)*, trans. Edmund Jephcott et al. (Cambridge, Mass.: Harvard University Press, 2003), p. 108.

8. Edward W. Said, *The World, the Text, and the Critic* (Cambridge, Mass.: Harvard University Press, 1983), p. 148. Subsequent references to this work are cited parenthetically as WTC.

9. See, Aamir Mufti, "Auerbach in Istanbul: Edward Said, Secular Criticism, and the Question of Minority Culture," *Critical Inquiry* 25 (Autumn 1998): 96, 99, 102, 105.

10. Aamir Mufti, "Secularism and Minority: Elements of a Critique," *Social Text* 45, vol. 14, no. 4 (Winter 1995): 93.

11. Edward W. Said, "Edward Said Talks to Jacqueline Rose," in *Edward Said and the Work of the Critic*, p. 25.

12. Edward Said, *Out of Place: A Memoir* (New York: Viking, 1999), p. 3.

13. Victor Klemperer, *I Will Bear Witness: A Diary of the Nazi Years, 1933–1941*, vol. 1, trans. Martin Chalmers (New York: Modern Library, 1999), p. 23.

14. Victor Klemperer, *I Will Bear Witness: A Diary of the Nazi Years, 1942–1945*, vol. 2, trans. Martin Chalmers (New York: Modern Library, 2001), p. 382.

15. Edward Said, *Freud and the Non-European* (London: Verso, 2003), p. 44.

16. On the logic of extension in Spinoza, see Michael Hardt, *Gilles Deleuze: An Apprenticeship in Philosophy* (Minneapolis: University of Minnesota Press, 1993), pp. 110–11.

17. Edward Said, *Beginnings* (New York: Columbia University Press, 1975), p. 212. Subsequent references to this work are cited parenthetically as B.

18. Riccardo Fubini, *Humanism and Secularization: From Petrarch to Valla*, trans. Martha King (Durham, N.C.: Duke University Press, 2003), p. 9.

19. See Aamir Mufti, paraphrasing Bruce Robbins, in his essay "Auerbach in Istanbul," p. 96. He cites Robbins's essay "Secularism, Elitism, Progress, and Other Transgressions: On Edward Said's 'Voyage In,'" *Social Text* 40 (Fall 1994): 26.

20. Stathis Gourgouris, "Transformation, Not Transcendence," in *boundary 2* vol. 31, no. 2 (Summer 2004): 55–79.

21. P. H. Wicksteed, as cited by John D. Sinclair, in notes to Canto II of Dante's *Paradiso*, trans. John D. Sinclair (New York: Oxford University Press, 1939), p. 45.

22. Erich Auerbach, *Dante, Poet of the Secular World*, trans. Ralph Mannheim (Chicago: University of Chicago Press, 1961), p. 17. Subsequent references to this work are cited parenthetically as *D*. Auerbach's reading of Augustine as the guardian of the human connection to God is perhaps subject to contention, especially if one goes back to humanist theological debates over the anthropomorphization of God. In the fifteenth century, Andrea Biglia attacked San Bernardino for losing "the wholly Augustinian sense of the infinite distance between Creator and creature, and of the enlightening power of grace that excludes a narrowly prescribed ethics." See Fubini, *Humanism and Secularization*, p. 68.

23. See notes to Canto XVIII of Dante's *Paradiso*, p. 266–67.

24. John D. Sinclair, in notes to Canto XVIII of Dante's *Paradiso*, p. 266.

25. Mahmoud Darwish, *Unfortunately, It Was Paradise*, trans. Munir Akash and Carolyn Forché with Sinan and Amira El-Zein (Berkeley: University of California Press, 2003), p. 9.

Chapter 5
Nothing Is Translatable

1. Badiou's singular universality can perhaps be better appreciated when read contrastively with philosophers working out of a Hegelian tradition. Judith Butler's reading of Hegelian universality, for example, cautions against the implicit formalism of efforts "to establish universality as transcendent of cultural norms" and claims that Hegel's universal is fettered to the substance of cultural norms (*Sittlichkeit* or custom). "If Hegel's notion of universality is to prove good under conditions of hybrid cultures and vacillating national boundaries," Butler writes, " it will have to become a universality forged through the work of cultural translation." Butler sets her sights high on this new form of "universal" cultural translation, based not on "a presumption of linguistic or cognitive commonness nor a teleological postulate of an ultimate fusion of all cultural horizons," but rather on "cultural location," as exemplified by Gayatri Spivak's notion of a "'violent shuttling' between discourses that show the sharp edges of all available discourses of collectivity." For Butler then, the form of universality is translation itself—albeit performative, alive to the syntactic stagings of linguistic difference. Though Butler remains critical of Euro-universalism's legislation

of absolute truth and common ground, while Badiou subscribes without qualm to a universalism based on absolute textual singularity, both would seem to agree that incommensurability governs universalism. See, Judith Butler, "Restaging the Universal: Hegemony and the Limits of Formalism," in *Contingency, Hegemony, Universality: Contemporary Dialogues on the Left,* eds. Judith Butler, Ernesto Laclau, and Slavoj Žižek (London: Verso, 2000), pp. 20 and 37, respectively.

2. Alain Badiou, *Petit manuel d'inesthétique* (Paris: Seuil, 1998). Epigraph.

3. Mahmoud Darwish, "A Rhyme for the Odes (Mu'allaqat)" in *Unfortunately, It Was Paradise,* trans. Munir Akash and Caroyn Forché et al. (Berkeley: University of California Press, 2003), p. 91.

4. Stéphane Mallarmé, *Oeuvres complètes* (Paris: Gallimard, 1945), pp. 368 and 370, respectively.

5. Ibid., 387. English translation, Malcolm Bowie, "Mystery in Literature," in Mary Ann Caws, ed. *Mallarmé in Prose* (New York: New Directions, 2001), p. 51.

6. Peter Hallward, *Absolutely Postcolonial: Writing between the Singular and the Specific* (Manchester and New York: Manchester University Press, 2001), pp. 2 and 3, respectively. Further references to this work will appear in the text abbreviated AP.

7. Alain Badiou, "Philosophy and the War against Terrorism," in *Infinite Thought: Truth and the Return of Philosophy,* trans. and ed. Oliver Feltham and Justin Clemens (London: Continuum, 2003), p. 149.

8. Gayatri Chakravorty Spivak, *Death of a Discipline* (New York: Columbia University Press, 2003), p. 72. Further references to this work will appear in the text abbreviated DD.

9. Dennis Overbye, "What Happened before the Big Bang?" in the *New York Times,* Nov. 11, 2003, p. F6.

10. Daisetz Teitaro Suzuki, *Essays in Zen Buddhism* (London: Luzac and Company, 1933), p. 42.

11. Martin Heidegger, "The Question of Being (Letter to Ernst Jünger 'Concerning "The Line" ') (1955), trans. By William Kluback and Jean T. Wilde in *Martin Heidegger:Philosophical and Political Writings,* ed. Manfred Stassen (New York: Continuum, 2003), pp. 127 and 139, respectively.

12. Walter Benjamin, "The Railway Disaster at the Firth of Tay," in *Walter Benjamin: Selected Writings,* vol. 2, 1927–34, trans. Rodney Livingstone et al., and ed. Michael Jennings et al. (Cambridge, Mass.: Harvard University Press, 1999), p. 563.

Chapter 6
"Untranslatable" Algeria: The Politics of Linguicide

1. Juan Goytisolo, *Landscapes after the Battle,* trans. Helen Lane (New York: Seaver Books, 1987), pp. 4–5. Further references to this work will appear in the text abbreviated LB.

2. Homi K. Bhabha, "How Newness Enters the World," in *The Location of Culture* (New York: Routledge, 1994), p. 227.

3. Tahar Djaout, as cited in *The Economist,* Jan. 27, 1996, p. 79.

4. Roger Cohen, *New York Times*, Sept. 24, 1997, p. A3.

5. Ibid.

6. Réda Bensmaïa, *Experimental Nations: Or, the Invention of the Maghreb* (Princeton: Princeton University Press, 2003), pp. 8, 15, and 17. Further references to this work will appear in the text abbreviated EN.

7. Assia Djebar, *Le blanc de l'Algérie* (Paris: Albin Michel, 1995), pp. 274 and 275.

8. Mongo Beti, in discussion session during a conference on "The Chosen Tongue" organized by Maryse Condé and Pierre Force at Columbia University's *Maison Française*, April 7–8, 2000.

9. More works of fiction and criticism translated from Arabic are in evidence in France, attributable, perhaps, to France's gradual wake-up to the importance of a Maghrebian cultural presence within its borders, and to the prescient, if modest, efforts of small *maisons d'édition* such as Actes Sud to redress habits of Francocentric insularity and Arabophobia within the publishing industry.

10. Many of the major publishing houses in France maintain international distribution ties to the Third World. L'Harmattan, for example, distributes "Editions Caribéennes," Editions Clé, and Editions Semences Africaines all of which target the postcolonies. Le Seuil has also invested in Third World fields, notably the prestigious "Collection Méditerranée" which launched writers such as Nabile Farès and Tahar Djaout. Gallimard includes Oriental Studies in its line-up of strengths. Hatier has representatives in Cameroon, Ivory Coast, and Zaire and serves as principal distributor for Présence Africaine and Nouvelles Editions Africaines. Hachette maintains important links to Senegal through its sponsorship of a Centre Sénégalais d'Édition et de Diffusion. This neocolonialism of the publishing industry cuts both ways: it enhances the publication and distribution network in former colonies where such networks are weak, yet preserves structures of cultural dependency.

11. In April 2005 PEN's World Voices Festival in New York featured the deservedly celebrated Salman Rushdie, Paul Auster, Wole Soyinke, Andrëi Makine, Nuruddin Farah, Assia Djebar, Lyonel Trouillot, Nancy Huston, Elena Poniatowska, Breyten Breytenbach, Ngũgĩ wa Thiong'o, Carolin Emcke, Tsitsi Dangarembga, Azar Nafisi, Antonio Tabucchi, Bei Dao, Michael Ondaatje, Peter Carey, Nuria Amat, Durs Grünbein, Antoine Audouard, Victor Erofeyev, and Hanif Kureishi, along with many other lesser known writers from around the globe, but one is always left wondering about the ways in which an author gets anointed as a "World Voice."

12. Walter Benjamin, "The Task of the Translator," in *Illuminations*, trans. Harry Zohn (New York: Schocken Books, 1969), p. 70.

13. Literary translations in the United States between 1993 and 2000 made up approximately 37 percent of the national translation market. This stands in moderate contrast to the market share of literary translations in a number of countries around the globe. Between 1993 and 2000, India (59%), Denmark (55%), the Netherlands (53%), France (55%), Germany (53%), the Czech Republic (61%), and Russia

(63%) were amongst the countries where the market share of literary translations consistently made up more than half of the overall translation market.

14. Maya Jaggi, "Stars Are in the West," *Guardian Weekly* Aug. 28, 1997, p. 28.

15. Stephen Owen, "What Is World Poetry: The Anxiety of Global Influence," *The New Republic* (Nov. 19, 1990), pp. 28–32.

16. As cited by Andrew F. Jones, "Chinese Literature in the 'World' Literary Economy" (*Modern Chinese Literature*, vol. 8, nos. 1–2 (Spring/Fall 1994): 171. Further reference to this essay will appear in the text abbreviated AJ.

17. Gayatri Chakravorty Spivak, "The Politics of Translation," in *Destabilizing Theory*, eds. Michèle Barrett and Anne Phillips (London: Polity Press, 1982), p. 179.

18. Elisabeth Young-Bruehl, *Global Cultures: A Transnational Short Fiction Reader* (Hanover: University Press of New England, 1994).

19. Preface by the editors, Kateb Yacine, *Nedjma*, trans. Richard Howard (New York: George Braziller, Inc., 1961), p. 6–9.

20. Edward Said, "Embargoed Literature," in *Between Languages and Cultures: Translation and Cross-Cultural Texts*, Anuradha Dingwaney and Carol Maier, eds. (Pittsburgh: University of Pittsburgh Press,) p. 97.

21. Ibid., p. 101.

22. Hélène Cixous, "My Algeriance, in Other Words to Depart Not to Arrive from Algeria," lecture delivered at a conference at Cornell University, "Algeria In and Out of France," organized by Anne-Emannuelle Berger, October 1996. A version of this lecture was published with the same title in *Tri-Quarterly* 100 (Fall 1997): 259–79. For additional writings on Algeria by Cixous, see "The Names of Oran," in *Algeria in Others' Languages*, ed. Anne-Emmanuelle Berger (Ithaca: Cornell University Press, 2002), p. 184–94, and *Portrait of Jacques Derrida as a Young Jewish Saint*, trans. Beverly Bie Brahic (New York: Columbia University Press, 2004).

23. Abdelkebir Khatibi, *Love in Two Languages*, trans. Richard Howard (Minneapolis: University of Minnesota Press, 1990), p 4.

24. Rachid Boudjedra, "Les mots et la langue" (extracts from letters 1 and 2 of his *Lettres algériennes* (Paris: Denoël, 1995), in *Algérie Littérature/Action* 5 (November 1996), p. 97. Further references to this article will appear in the text abbreviated B. Translation my own.

25. Assia Djebar, *La Disparition de la langue française* (Paris: Albin Michel, 2003), p. 271. Translation my own.

Chapter 7
Plurilingual Dogma: Translation by Numbers

1. Lars von Trier and Thomas Vinterberg, "The Vow of Chastity, " Dogme 95, www.dogme95.dk/

2. Wilhelm von Humboldt, *Linguistic Variability and Intellectual Development*, Miami Linguistics Series No. 9 (Coral Gables, Florida: University of Miami Press, 1971), pp. 39–40.

3. Willard Van Orman Quine, *Word and Object* (Cambridge, Mass.: The MIT Press, 1960), p. 15. All further references to this work will appear in the text abbreviated WO.

4. Wilhelm von Humboldt, "Uber die Verschiedenheit des menschlichen Sprachbaues und irhen Einfluss geistige Entwicklung des Menschengeschlechts," in *Wilhelm von Humboldts Werke*, vol. 7 (Berlin: Behr, 1907), p. 60.

5. In a section called "Translations," the Oulipo authors write: "Il s'agira ici surtout de traduire des textes à l'intérieur d'une même langue" ["Here our business will be to translate texts within the same language"), in *Atlas de littérature potentielle* (Paris: Gallimard, 1981), p. 143.

6. Eugene Jolas, *Man from Babel* (New Haven: Yale University Press, 1998), p. 35. All further references to this work will appear in the text abbreviated MB.

7. Eugene Jolas, *Words from the Deluge* (New York: Gotham Book Mart, 1941), n.p.

8. Ibid.

9. Ralph Ellison, *Juneteenth* (New York: Random House, 1999), p. 259.

10. Michael North, *The Dialect of Modernism: Race, Language, and Twentieth-Century Literature* (New York: Oxford University Press, 1994).

11. Mina Loy, "English Rose," in *The Last Lunar Baedeker* (Highlands: The Jargon Society, 1982), p. 130.

12. Text in Eugene Jolas's papers classified under the rubric "Reporters" (Box 16 Folder 304).

13. Box 12 Folder 247. Eugene Jolas, "Vocabulary for the Superoccident," Jolas Papers.

14. Jorge Luis Borges, "The Library of Babel," in *Labyrinths: Selected Stories and Other Writings*, trans. by J.E.I. (New York: New Directions Publishing Corporation, 1962), p. 54.

15. Eugene Jolas, "Silvalogue," in "Multilingual Poems," n.d., Jolas Papers.

16. Eugene Jolas, "Babel: Across Frontiers," Jolas Papers. Book Room and Manuscript Library.

17. Eugene Jolas, "Vertigralism," in *Vertical: A Yearbook for Romantic-Mystic Ascensions* (New York: Gotham Bookmart Press, 1941), p. 156. Further references to this work will appear in the text abbreviated V.

18. Theodor W. Adorno, *The Stars Down to Earth and Other Essays on the Irrational in Culture* (London: Routledge, 1994), p. 34.

19. Eugene Jolas, *Planets and Angels* (Mount Vernon, Iowa: English Club of Cornell College, 1940), p. 171.

20. Ibid., p. 206.

21. Eugene Jolas, *Secession in Astropolis* (Paris: The Black Sun Press, 1929), p. 206.

22. Gilles Deleuze, "Louis Wolfson, ou le procédé," in *Critique et clinique* (Paris: Editions de minuit, 1993), pp. 19–22.

23. Louis Wolfson, *Le Schizo et les langues* (Paris: Gallimard, 1970), p. 37.

24. Georges Perec, *A Void*, trans. Gilbert Adair (London: Harvill, 1994), p. 282. Further references to this work will appear in the text abbreviated V. French original, *La disparition* (Paris: Éditions Denoël, 1969), p. 310.

25. Georges Perec, *The Exeter Text: Jewels, Secrets, Sex* in *Three by Perec*, trans. Ian Monk (London: The Harvill Press: 1996), p. 55. Further references to this work will appear in the text abbreviated ET. French original, *Les Revenentes* (Éditions Julliard, 1972). No page number.

26. Norbert Wiener, *The Human Use of Human Beings: Cybernetics and Society* (Garden City, N.Y.: Doubleday and Company, 1954), p. 92. Wiener is referring here to the philologist Otto Jespersen.

27. Michel Foucault's review of J-P Brisset's book *La Science de Dieu ou la Création* is the source of this description of Brisset's technique. See Foucault, "Le cycle des grenouilles" (which originally appeared in *La Nouvelle Revue Française* no. 114, June 1962). Republished in *Michel Foucault: Dits et Ecrits I (1954–1975)* (Paris: Gallimard, 1994), p. 252.

28. Michel Foucault, reviewing the 1970 republication of J-P Brisset's *La Grammaire Logique ou Théorie d'une nouvelle analyse mathématique résolvant les questions les plus difficiles* (1878). "Sept propos sur le septième ange" in *Michel Foucault: Dits et Ecrits I (1954–1975)* (Paris: Gallimard, 1994), p. 886.

29. Paul Braffort, "Formalismes pour l'analyse et la synthèse de textes littérraires," in *Atlas de littérature potententielle* (Paris: Gallimard, 1981), pp. 127 and 109.

30. Jacques Bens, Claude Berge, Paul Braffort, "La Littérature récurrente," in *Atlas de littérature potentielle*, pp. 86–87.

31. Roman Jakobson, "Linguistics in Relation to Other Sciences," in *On Language*, eds. Linda R. Waugh and Monique Monveille-Burston (Cambridge, Mass.: Harvard University Press, 1990), p. 476. Jakobson cites Crick and Watson's (at the time) breakthrough work on deciphering the DNA code, François Jacob's "discovery of nucleic script," and George and Muriel Beadle's 1966 book *The Language of Life: An Introduction to the Science of Genetics* in his remarks on "the extraordinary degree of analogy between the systems of genetic and verbal information."

Chapter 8
Balkan Babel: Translation Zones, Military Zones

1. Maria Todorova, *Imagining the Balkans* (Oxford: Oxford University Press, 1997).

2. Maria Todorova in discussion of her book, University of California, Los Angeles, May 25, 2000.

3. Ismail Kadare, *The Three-Arched Bridge*, translated by John Hodgson (New York: Vintage International, 1997), p. 18. All further references to this work will appear in the text abbreviated TAB.

4. Ismail Kadare, *Albanian Spring: The Anatomy of Tyranny*, trans. Emile Capouya (London: Saqi Books, 1994), p. 34.

5. If at times border wars are fueled by the lack of official recognition accorded small linguistic differences, in other instances it is the threat of sameness that sparks discord. The political motivations of linguistic separatism are no more clearly in evidence than in the post-Bosnia decision to break Serbian and Croation into separately classified tongues, despite their grammatical similarities. As George Steiner noted in 1963, decades before the Wall would come down, language divisionism can be most acute where homonymity is greatest. Observing the way in which "The East German language is developing its own jargon and dialect," Steiner concludes: "The words may continue to sound alike, but have contrary definitions. A young East German might come to be more at home, in the syntax of his politics and feelings, in Peking or Albania, than in Cologne." George Steiner, *Language and Silence: Essays on Language, Literature and the Inhuman* (New Haven: Yale University Press, 1970, 1998), pp. 348–49.

6. Ivo Andríc, *The Bridge on the Drina*, trans. Lovett F. Edwards (Chicago: University of Chicago Press, 1977), p. 86. Further references to this work will appear in the text abbreviated BD.

7. Manuel de Landa, *War in the Age of Intelligent Machines* (New York: Swerve Editions, 1991).

8. Ismail Kadare, *The Palace of Dreams*, trans. from the French of Jusuf Vrioni by Barbara Bray (New York: Arcade Publishing, 1993), pp. 13–14. Cited passage italicized in the original text.

9. Pierre Clastres, *Archeology of Violence*, trans. Jeanine Herman (*Recherches d'anthropologie politique*, Seuil 1980) (New York: Semiotext[e], 1994), p. 55.

10. Georges Bataille, "Structure et fonction de l'armée" (1938), in Denis Hollier, *Le Collège de sociologie* (Paris: Gallimard, 1979), pp. 255–67.

11. Carl von Clausewitz, *On War*, trans. Michael Howard and Peter Paret (Princeton: Princeton University Press, 1976), p. 87.

12. Randalph Quirk, "International Communication and the Concept of Nuclear English," in *English for International Communication*, ed. C. J. Brumfit (Oxford: Pergamon Institute of English, 1982), p. 19.

13. Renée Balibar, *L'Institution du français: Essai sur le colinguisme des Carolingiens à la République* (Paris: Presses Universitaires de France, 1985); Pierre Clastres, *Archeology of Violence*.

14. Louis-Jean Calvet, *Language Wars and Linguistic Politics*, trans. Michel Petheram (Oxford: Oxford University Press, 1998).

15. Ernest Renan, *De l'origine du langage* (Paris: Michel Lévy Frères, 1859), pp. 95–96.

16. A *New York Times* article by Nicholas D. Kristof, "Stateside Lingo Gives Japan Its Own Valley Girls" (Oct. 19, 1997), p. 33 gives a good sense of this phenomenon:

> With the forces of globalization gaining ground every day, perhaps it is not surprising that 15-year-old Japanese girls like Kaori Hasegawa use English expressions like "chekaraccho."

English?

Well, a version of English spoken by Japanese teen-agers. Chekaraccho is a corruption of "Check it out, Joe," and is a casual greeting, a bit like "Hi there." Japan has always been quick to absorb foreign words along with foreign technology, and in the 19th century there was even serious discussion about whether the country should switch to English. This month, The Japan Times—one of Tokyo's four daily English-language general-interest papers—noted the pressures of globalization and suggested that it might once again be time to consider a switch to English.

Already Japanese is a mishmash of Chinese, English, Dutch and German influences. But what is new this time is the way young people are seizing English words and manipulating them to create their own hip dialect, known as "ko-gyaru-go."

The "gyaru" derives from the English word gal, and ko-gyaru-go roughly translates as "high school gal-talk." It is used mostly among teenagers, as a secret code by which they can bond and evade surveillance by hostile forces, like parents.

17. The Internet is nearly impossible to police, for the same reason that it is so difficult to define. It is not "owned" or regulated by private businesses or individuals. It consists of telephone lines and countless computer sites linked together in a system through which anyone can navigate anonymously. In this environment, freedom of expression, commercial transactions, political activity and the simple pleasure of gathering information and communicating have come to flourish in ways few thought possible only a few years ago. These very qualities are what make the Internet vulnerable to anonymous attack.

. . . Even more insidiously, the hackers have apparently enlisted unknowing allies in the attacks by invading vulnerable computer systems and using those computers to help carry out the assaults.

"Hacker Attacks on the Internet," Editorial, *New York Times*, Feb. 11, 2000, p. A30.

Chapter 9
War and Speech

1. Harold Bloom, *How to Read and Why* (New York: Scribner, 2000).

2. Interview with Pascale Casanova, "Ces guerres littéraires insoupçonnées," in *Politis*, March 25, 1999.

3. Pascale Casanova as cited by Pierre Lepape in his review "Du Bellay et compagnie," in *Le Monde des Livres*, March 26, 1999.

4. Pascale Casanova, *La République mondiale des lettres* (Paris: Seuil, 1999).

5. Jackie Kay, *Off Colour* (Newcastle on Tyne: Bloodaxe Books, 1998), p. 45.

6. On the logic of minority language see Harry Garuba, "Ken Saro-wiwa's *Sozaboy* and the Logic of Minority Discourse," and Adetayo Alabi, "Ken Saro-wiwa

and the Politics of Language in African Literature," both in Rasheed Na'Allah, ed. *Ogoni's Agonies: Ken Saro-wiwa and the Crisis in Nigeria* (Trenton, N.J.: Africa World Press, 1998).

7. Michael North, "Ken Saro-wiwa's *Sozaboy*: The Politics of 'Rotten English,'" *Public Culture* 13, no. 1 (Winter 2001), p. 100. Further references to this essay will appear in the text abbreviated PC.

8. A number of essays in *Critical Essays on Ken Saro-wiwa's "Sozaboy: A Novel in Rotten English,"* ed. Charles Nnolim (Port Harcourt, Nigeria: Saros International Publishers, 1992), offer illuminating appraisals of Saro-wiwa's grammatical inventions. See, in particular, Augustine C. Okere, "Patterns of Linguistic Deviation in Saro-wiwa's *Sozaboy*," pp. 9–15; Doris Akekue, "Mind-Style in *Sozaboy*: A Functional Approach," pp. 16–29; and Asomwan S. Adagboyin, "The Language of Ken Saro-wiwa's *Sozaboy*," pp. 30–38. See also Chantal Zabus's fascinating discussion of what she calls "pidgin in vitro," in her *The African Palimpsest: Indigenization of Language in the West African Europhone Novel* (Atlanta, Georgia: Editions Rodopi, 1991), pp. 179.

9. For an excellent reading of *Sozaboy* in terms of the politics of oil and citizenship, see Andrew Apter, "Death and the King's Henchmen: Ken Saro-wiwa and the Political Ecology of Citizenship in Nigeria," in Rasheed Na'Allah, ed. *Ogoni's Agonies: Ken Saro-wiwa and the Crisis in Nigeria* (Trenton, NJ: Africa World Press, 1998).

10. For a trenchant account of Saro-wiwa's career and writings as a political activist, see Rob Nixon's essay, "Pipe Dreams: Ken Saro-wiwa, Environmental Justice, and Micro-Minority Rights," *Black Renaissance/Renaissance Noire*, vol. 1, no. 1 (Fall, 1996): 39–55.

11. Philip Lewis, *The Measure of Translation Effects*, Joseph Graham, ed. *Difference in Translation* (Ithaca: Cornell University Press, 1985), p. 41.

12. Ken Saro-wiwa, "High Life," in *A Forest of Flowers* (Longman Group Limited: Essex, England, 1995), p. 73.

13. Achille Mbembe, "The Banality of Power and the Aesthetics of Vulgarity in the Postcolony," trans. Janet Roitman, *Public Culture*, vol. 4, no. 2 (1992): 1–30. A version of this seminal essay, along with a chapter "Of *Commandement*," clarifying his use of this concept, appears in Mbembe's book *On the Postcolony* (Berkeley: University of California Press, 2001).

14. Ken Saro-wiwa, *Sozaboy: A Novel in Rotten English* (Essex: Long Group Limited, 1994), pp. 3 and 11. All further references to this work will appear in the text abbreviated S.

15. Paul de Man, "Anthropomorphism and Trope in the Lyric," in *The Rhetoric of Romanticism* (New York: Columbia University Press, 1984), p. 242.

16. There are striking parallels between *My Life in the Bush of Ghosts* and *Sozaboy*, especially in the way in which war and phantoms are narratively intricated. While Tutuola's Pidgin English is not as pronounced as Saro-wiwa's, it has been duly acknowledged as an important precedent by critics such as North and Mbembe. We can see how difficult it remains to have this form of nonstandard English recognized

on its literary merits in the Reverend Geoffrey Parrinder's foreword to the Grove Press edition of Tutuola's novel: "The book has been edited to remove the grosser mistakes, clear up some ambiguities, and curtail some repetition." In Amos Tutuola, *My Life in the Bush of Ghosts* (New York: Grove Press, 1984), p. 15.

17. Ahmadou Kourouma, *Allah n'est pas obligé* (Paris: Seuil, 2000), p. 9.

18. Ibid., pp. 10 and 11, respectively.

19. Baldwin points out that white Americans would not "sound the way they sound" if Black English had not afforded the nation "its only glimpse of reality" through the language of jazz and jive. Black English, according to Baldwin, has brought "a people utterly unknown to, or despised by 'history' . . . to their present, troubled, troubling, and unassailable and unanswerable place." Rotten English, I am suggesting here, does the same for Nigeria's disenfranchised minorities. See, James Baldwin, "If Black English Isn't a Language, Then Tell Me What Is?" in *The Price of the Ticket: Collected Nonfiction 1948–1985* (New York: St. Martin's/Marek, 1985), pp. 650 and 651, respectively.

Chapter 10
The Language of Damaged Experience

1. Emily Apter, "Comparative Exile: Competing Margins in the History of Comparative Literature," in *Comparative Literature in the Age of Multiculturalism*, ed. Charles Bernheimer (Baltimore: Johns Hopkins University Press, 1995), pp. 86–96.

2. Theodor Adorno, *Minima Moralia*, trans. E.F.N. Jephcott (London: Verso, 1974), p. 40. Further references to this edition will appear in the text abbreviated MM.

3. As cited by Susan Buck-Morss, in *The Origins of Negative Dialectics: Theodor W. Adorno, Walter Benjamin, and the Frankfurt Institute* (New York: Macmillan, 1977), p. 83.

4. Walter Benjamin, *Understanding Brecht [Versuche über Brecht]*, trans. Anna Bostock (London: New Left Books, 1973), p. 81. Further references to this work will appear in the text abbreviated UB.

5. Randolph Stow, "Trainspotters' Heaven" in *Times Literary Supplement* no. 5037, Oct. 15, 1999, p. 40.

6. George Eliot, *Adam Bede* (New York: The Modern Library, 2002), p. 250.

7. James Kelman, *How Late It Was, How Late* (New York: Bantam Doubleday Dell Publishing Group, 1994), p. 248.

8. Duncan McLean, *Buckets of Tongues* (London: Martin Secker and Warburg Limited, 1992).

9. Duncan McLean, *Bunker Man* (London: Jonathan Cape, 1992), p. 180.

10. David Lloyd tends to use the concept of minor literature to refer to emergent or marginalized national literary traditions, thus giving a regionalist application to master-minor or metropole-periphery paradigms that in turn privilege thematic and narrative applications. While I would in no way wish to dispense with this approach, my own emphasis is on the textual/linguistic order of interpretation,

stressing ways in which the term "minor lit" engages a volatile relationship to standard language.

11. David Lloyd, *Nationalism and Minor Literature: James Clarence Mangan and the Emergence of Irish Cultural Nationalism* (Berkeley: University of California Press, 1987).

12. Gilles Deleuze and Félix Guattari, *Kafka: Toward a Minor Literature*, trans. Dana Polan (Minneapolis: University of Minnesota Press, 1986), p. 23.

13. James Joyce, *Finnegan's Wake* (New York: Penguin Books, 1969, 1939), p. 6.

14. Irvine Welsh, *Trainspotting* (New York: W.W. Norton and Co., 1993), p. 94. All further references will be to this edition and will appear in the text abbreviated T.

Chapter 11
CNN Creole: Trademark Literacy and Global Language Travel

1. Leo Spitzer, "The Individual Factor in Linguistic Innovations" (1956), in *The Routledge Language and Cultural Theory Reader*, eds. Lucy Burke, Tony Crowley and Alan Girvin (New York: Routledge, 2000), p. 66.

2. Leo Spitzer, "American Advertising Explained as Popular Art," in *Leo Spitzer: Representative Essays*, eds. Alban K. Forcione et al. (Stanford: Stanford University Press, 1988), p. 332. All further references to this essay will appear in the text abbreviated AA.

3. Maryse Condé, "Chercher nos vérités," in *Penser la créolité* (Paris: Editions Karthala, 1995), p. 306. Further references to this work will appear in the text abbreviated PC.

4. Jean Bernabé et al., *Éloge de la créolité*, bilingual edition, trans. M.B. Teleb-Hyar (Paris Gallimard, 1989), p. 126. Further references to this work will appear in the text abbreviated E.

5. Raphaël Confiant, "Confiant sur son volcan," *Magazine Littéraire* (November 1994): 77.

6. Wilson Harris also experiments with historical displacement, placing the trauma of the recent past (the Jonestown mass suicide in Guyana) in the perspective of history *longue durée*. See *Selected Essays of Wilson Harris: The Unfinished Genesis of the Imagination*, ed. Andrew Bundy (London: Routledge, 1999).

7. Raphaël Confiant, *Bassin des ouragans* (Turin: Editions Mille et une nuits, 1994), p. 42. All further references to this work will appear in the text abbreviated B.

8. Spitzer wrote:

> Against Schuchardt who by his life in the Austro-Hungarian empire was conditioned to see language mixture as the basic factor in linguistic change (and who therefore saw no difference between Creole and the great cultural languages), a less gifted pupil of his, von Ettmayer, was right when he once said to me: "The speaker does not mix languages, he speaks." "He speaks" must mean here, I suppose: he speaks his language, one language whose continuity he feels to be uninterrupted, he does not speak two languages at

the same time; if he accepts, under the influence of his bilingual setting, certain features of the other language *he is selective.* (LI 65)

9. Rose-Myriam Réjouis, "Afterword," in Patrick Chamoiseau, *Texaco*, trans. Rose-Myriam Réjouis and Val Vinokurov (New York: Vintage, 1998), p. 393.

10. Raphaël Confiant, *La Savane des pétrifications* (Turin: Editions Mille et une nuits, 1995), p. 83. All further references to this work will appear in the text abbreviated SP.

11. Translation by Lucien Taylor, in Lucien Taylor, "Créolité Bites: A Conversation with Patrick Chamoiseau, Raphaël Confiant, and Jean Bernabé" *Transition*, issue 74: 159.

12. Raphaël Confiant, *La Dernière Java de Madame Josepha* (Turin: Editions Mille et une nuits, 1999), p. 12. All further references to this work will appear in the text abbreviated MJ.

13. Christopher L. Miller, *Nationalists and Nomads: Essays on Francophone African Literature and Culture* (Chicago: University of Chicago Press, 1998), p. 162.

14. Raphaël Confiant, *Dictionnaire des Titim et Sirandanes* (Martinique: Ibis Rouge Editions, 1998), pp. 40–41.

15. William Safire, "On Language," *New York Times Magazine*, Sept. 9, 2000, p. 37.

16. Raphaël Confiant, *Dictionnaire des Titim et Sirandanes*, p. 242.

Chapter 12
Condé's *Créolité* in Literary History

1. See, Georg Lukács, Preface of 1962 to his *The Theory of the Novel*, trans. Anna Bostock (Cambridge, Mass.: MIT Press, 1977), p. 16.

2. Erich Auerbach, *Mimesis: The Representation of Reality in Western Literature* (Princeton: Princeton University Press, 1953, 2003), p. 554.

3. Paul de Man, "Literary History and Literary Modernity," in *Blindness and Insight: Essays in the Rhetoric of Contemporary Criticism* (Minneapolis: University of Minnesota Press, 1983), pp. 142–43.

4. Franco Moretti, "Conjectures on World Literature," *New Left Review* (Jan.–Feb. 2000): 67.

5. Patrick Chamoiseau, *Ecrire en pays dominé* (Paris: Gallimard, 1997).

6. See Gilles Philippe, "1890–1940 Le moment grammatical de la littérature française?" *Le débat*, no. 120 (May–Aug. 2002): 109–18.

7. Pascale Casanova, "Consécration et accumulation de capital littéraire," *Actes de la Recherche en Sciences sociales* 144 (September 2002): 7–20.

8. Okwui Enwezor, "The Black Box," in *Documenta 11, Platform 5: Exhibition Catalogue* (Kassel: Hatje Publishers, 2002), p. 51.

9. Ibid.

10. Pascale Casanova, *La République mondiale des lettres* (Paris: Seuil, 1999), pp. 402–10.

11. The rapprochement of telepathy and thought transference in Freud and Derrida is made by Marina Warner in her review of Richard Luckhurst's *The Invention of Telepathy* (Oxford: Oxford University Press, 2002), which appeared in the *London Review of Books*, vol. 24, no. 19 (October 2002): 16.

12. Marina Warner, ibid.

13. Edward Said, *Culture and Imperialism* (Cambridge Mass.: Harvard University Press, 1993), pp. 63–4.

14. Emily Brontë, *Wuthering Heights* (London: Penguin Books, 1995), pp. 19–20. Further references to this work will be to this edition and will appear in the text abbreviated WH.

15. Harold Bloom, *Genius: A Mosaic of One Hundred Exemplary Creative Minds* (New York: Warner Books, 2002), p. 316. Further references to this work will appear in the text abbreviated G.

16. See, Juliet Barker, *The Brontës* (New York: St. Martin's Press, 1994), p. 534.

17. Emily Brontë, *Wuthering Heights* (London: England, 1995 [1847]), p. xliii. Further references to this work will appear in the text abbreviated WH.

18. Patricia Crain discusses the complex range of associations clustering around alphabetization in early American literature in *The Story of A: The Alphabetization of America from* The New England Primer *to* The Scarlet Letter (Stanford: Stanford University Press, 2000). With reference to Nathaniel Hawthorne's *The Scarlet Letter* she offers a particularly fascinating interpretation of alphabetic signs:

> Hawthorne finds in the alphabet an artifact that resonates with his sense of how people move through and are shaped by what he calls the "world's artificial system." He feels the alphabet, like a mote in the eye that can't be removed; somewhat painfully it both shapes and distorts perception. His scarlet letter's resumé might look like this: it unfolds to reveal a narrative; it takes on human form; it has a rich Puritan as well as an Elizabethan heritage; it is created by a woman's art, but is a disciplining tool of bureaucracy; it can be found in nature; it can represent many things to many people, but it is also an object of representation; it ranges freely between the satanic and the sacred; it is intimately involved in forming children. (p. 11)

19. On reading as a process of interiorization, Patricia Crain has noted, "Literacy in operation requires that the alphabet be broken into elements and recombined to make sense: B, Ba, Bat. But this alphabet-all-at-once, accompanied by prayers already gotten by heart, exemplifies alphabetization: aurally or visually, the alphabet and the prayers are taken in, internalized." Patricia Crain, *The Story of A*, p. 23.

20. Maryse Condé, *La migration des coeurs* (Paris: Editions Laffont, 1995), p. 67. Further references to this work will appear in the text abbreviated MC.

21. Maryse Condé, *Windward Heights*, trans. Richard Philcox (New York: Soho Press, 1998), p. 61. Further references to this work will appear in the text abbreviated WWH).

22. Paul de Man, "Literary History and Literary Modernity," in *Blindness and Insight*, p. 143. Later in this essay, citing Nietzsche's "Vom Nutzen und Nachteil der Historie für das Leben" ("Of the Use and Misuse of History for Life"), de Man homes in on the problem that concerns him most, namely "the complications that ensue when a genuine impulse toward modernity collides with the demands of a historical consciousness based on the disciplines of history" (p. 145). Though constraints of focus do not permit me here to take up the implications of this problem in detail for my attempt to write *créolité* into literary history, I want to emphasize once again that obstacles to *créolité*'s acquisition of historical status may indeed be traceable to the antipresentist or antimodern prejudices built into the discipline of history and its literary adjunct.

23. Georg Lukács, Introduction to *Rob Roy* (New York: Modern Library, 2002), p. xix.

Chapter 13
Nature into Data

1. Gayatri Chakravorty Spivak, *A Critique of Postcolonial Reason: Toward a History of the Vanishing Present* (Cambridge, Mass.: Harvard University Press, 1999), p. 164.

2. Kenneth Frampton, "Towards a Critical Regionalism: Six Points for an Architecture of Resistance," in *The Anti-Aesthetic: Essays on Postmodern Culture*, ed. Hal Foster (Port Townsend, Wash.: Bay Press, 1983), pp. 21, 26, and 27 respectively.

3. William Kentridge, in *William Kentridge* (London: Phaidon Press Limited, 1999), p. 108. All further references to this work and essays in it will appear in the text abbreviated WK.

4. Rosalind Krauss, " 'The Rock': William Kentridge's Drawings for Projection," in *October* 92 (Spring 2000): 3–35.

5. Rosalind Krauss, *"A Voyage on Art in the Age of the North Sea": Art in the Age of the Post-Medium Condition* (New York: Thames and Hudson, 1999), p. 56.

6. John Kinsella, "Dispossession," in *Visitants* (Newcastle upon Tyne: Bloodaxe Books, 1999), pp. 36–37. Further references to this work will appear in the text abbreviated V.

7. John Kinsella in *Landbridge: Contemporary Australian Poetry*, ed. John Kinsella (North Fremantle: Fremantle Arts Centre Press, 1999), p. 193.

8. In an essay largely devoted to Lionel Fogarty, Kinsella writes:

> For me, the most significant voice to emerge in the latter years of this century is that of the Murri poet Lionel Fogarty. Fogarty has managed to use English as a weapon against its own colonizing potential. He has created a positive hybrid that undoes the claim of linguistic centrality, and registers the primacy of the oral tradition. . . .
>
> I've referred to the kinds of poetry Fogarty and I write, from entirely different perspectives, as examples of "hybridising." By hybridising, I don't

mean a mixing or a production of a third-party alternative from set of specific material. A hybrid is not a possible next stage in a developmental sense, nor a "dilution" of the component parts! Nor is it a fusing of traditions. It is, in fact, a *conscious undoing of the codes that constitute all possible readings of a text. It is a debasement of the lyrical I.* (My emphases) . . .

John Kinsella, "The Hybridising of a Poetry: Notes on Modernism and Modernity— The Colonising Prospect of Modernism, and Hybridity as a Means to Closure," www.geocities.com/SoHo/Square/8574/newessays.html

9. Lionel Fogarty, "Jukambe Spirit—For the Lost" in *Landbridge*, p. 130.

10. Lionel Fogarty, "No Grudge," in *The Penguin Book of Modern Australian Poetry*, eds. John Tranter and Philip Mead (Middlesex: Penguin Books, 1991), p. 452.

11. Jacques Lacan, "The Line and the Light," and "What Is a Picture?" in *The Four Fundamental Concepts of Psychoanalysis*, trans. Alan Sheridan (New York: W.W. Norton and Co. 1973, 1978), pp.110 and 103, respectively.

12. Alex Alberro, "Blind Ambition," in *Artforum* (Jan. 2001): 109.

13. Peter Galassi, *Andreas Gursky* (New York: Museum of Modern Art, 2001), p. 34.

14. Alex Alberro, "Blind Ambition," p. 109.

15. The full text reads (in rough translation):

Just as water lilies on water consist not only of leaves and blossoms and white and green, but also of "gently lying there." Normally they lie there so peacefully that one doesn't notice them in their entirety anymore; the feeling must be peaceful, so that the world is in order, and only sensible relationships prevail in it. It is a sinking or climbing of all humanity to another level, a "sinking up high," and all things change in accordance with that. One could say they stay the same, but then they find themselves in another space, or it is all colored by another sense. In such moments one realizes that beside the world that everybody knows, the one you can investigate and grasp with your mind, there exists yet a second, moveable, singular, visionary, irrational one that only appears to be the same. But we don't just carry it in our heart or head, as people believe, but rather it stands outside us, just as real and valid as that other one. It is an uncanny mystery and like all things mysterious, when one attempts to speak about it, it gets easily confused with the most mundane things. He understood its story. Hundreds of human rules have come and gone; from the Gods to the needle in the jeweled ornament, and from psychology to the gramophone, each a dark unity, each a dark belief, the last to be the one just rising, and every several hundred or thousand years collapsing mysteriously and deteriorating to rubble and construction, what is this other than a climbing out of nothingness, tempted every time to search for the other side. (And no trace of it so that we could contain it in cycles!) Just as a sand dune is blown by the wind and takes on a certain shape for a while, and then again, is gone with the wind? What is everything we do other than a nervous fear of being nothing: starting with pleasures that aren't any, but rather instead are just noise, a stimulating chatter to kill time, because a dark certainty warns us that it will ultimately kill us. All the way through to those transcendent inventions, and meaningless heaps of money that kill the spirit, whether one is sustained or smothered by it, the fearful, impatient modes of the spirit, of clothing, which changes continually. And the way this addiction to renewal in one's existence makes one perpetually mobile, is motivated by nothing other than destitution, between one's own nebulousness and the already foreign shell that has hardened over one's predecessor, which once again is a kind of fake self, an approximate group-soul that is shoved onto one. And if one pays just a bit of attention, one can always see in the newly arrived past the future of coming ancient times.

(Translation by Zaia Alexander)

16. Roland Barthes, "The Image," in *The Rustle of Language*, trans. Richard Howard (Berkeley: University of California Press, 1986), p. 352.

17. Samuel Weber, *Mass Mediauras: Form, Technics, Media* (Stanford: Stanford University Press, 1996).

18. See, Bernard Stiegler, *La Technique et le Temps: La faute d'Epiméthée* (Paris: Galilée, 1994), *La Technique et le Temps: La désorientation* (Paris: Galilée, 1996), and *Philosopher par accident: Entretriens avec Elie During* (Paris: Galilée, 2004).

19. Friedrich Kittler, "There Is No Software," in *Friedrich Kittler: Literature, Media, Information Systems*, ed. John Johnston (Amsterdam: G + B Arts International, 1997), p. 158.

Chapter 14
Translation with No Original: Scandals of Textual Reproduction

1. Harry Mathews, "The Dialect of the Tribe," in *The Human Country: New and Collected Stories* (Chicago: Dalkey Archive Press, 2002), p. 8. Further references to this collection will appear in the text abbreviated HC.

2. Jorge Luis Borges, "Tlön, Uqbar, Orbis Tertius," trans. Alastair Reid, in *Ficciones* (New York: Grove Press, 1962), p. 18.

3. David Lewis, *On the Plurality of Worlds* (Oxford: Blackwell, 1986).

4. Umberto Eco, *Serendipities: Language and Lunacy*, trans. William Weaver (New York: Columbia University Press, 1998), pp. 80–81.

5. Jonathan Safran Foer, *Everything Is Illuminated* (New York: Houghton Mifflin, 2002). The parts of the novel written in "translatese" are both weird and funny. English takes on the quality of a language learned word by word out of the dictionary rather than holistically. The narrator's diction, when not in flagrant violation of good grammar, opens up a world of linguistic possibility precisely because it is off.

6. The work of rethinking the terms of translation studies is, of course, well under way. The ethical considerations I am raising here are indebted to Lawrence Ve-

nuti's work, particularly his book *The Scandals of Translation: Towards an Ethics of Difference* (New York: Routlege, 1998). On translation hoaxes, see Eric R. J. Hayot, "The Strange Case of Araki Yasusada: Author, Object," in *Publications of the Modern Language Association of America* 120, no. 1 (January 2005): 66–81.

7. Douglas Robinson, *Routledge Encyclopedia of Translation Studies*, ed. Mona Baker (New York: Routledge, 1998), p. 183.

8. Jean-Paul Goujon, *Pierre Louÿs: Une vie secrète (1870–1925)* (Paris: Editions Seghers, 1988), p. 90. All further references to this work will appear in the text abbreviated PL.

9. Remy de Gourmont, in a letter to Louÿs of January 7, 1899, as cited by Jean-Paul Goujon in his edition of *Les Chansons de Bilitis. Avec divers textes inédits* (Paris: Gallimard, 1990), p. 332. Further references to this work will appear in the text abbreviated CB.

10. In a letter of December 22, 1897, Louÿs wrote: "jusqu'ici les lesbiennes étaient toujours représentées comme des femmes fatales." As cited by Jean-Paul Goujon in his preface to *Les Chansons de Bilitis*, p. 14.

11. Kenneth Rexroth, *One Hundred Poems from the Japanese* (New York: New Directions, 1955), p. x.

12. Linda Hamalian, *A Life of Kenneth Rexroth* (New York: W.W. Norton and Co., 1991), p. 252. Further references to this work will appear in the text abbreviated H.

13. Morgan Gibson, *Revolutionary Rexroth: Poet of East-West Wisdom* (Hamden, Conn.: Archon Books, 1986), p. 82. Further references to this work will appear in the text abbreviated RR.

14. Kenneth Rexroth, *One Hundred More Poems from the Japanese* (New York: New Directions Books, 1974), p. 9, and Kenneth Rexroth, *Flower Wreath Hill: Later Poems* (New York: New Directions Books, 1974), pp. 124 and 143. Further references to these works will appear in the text abbreviated OHM and FWH. respectively.

15. Kenneth Rexroth, "The Influence of Classical Japanese Poetry on Modern American Poetry" (1973), in *The World Outside the Window*, ed. Bradford Morrow (New York: New Directions Books, 1987), p. 268. Rexroth wrote:

> The translations and imitations of Yone Noguchi and Lafcadio Hearn, and of E. Powys Mathers, from the French, were considerably better, yet no better than the best sentimental verse of the first years of the twentieth century. They established Japan in the literary imagination as a reverse image of America, a society whose system of values had been moved through the fourth dimension so that left was right and up was down. Japan became a dream world in the metaphorical sense—a world of exquisite sensibility, elaborate courtesy, self-sacrificing love, and utterly anti-materialistic religion, but a dream world in the literal sense, too, a nightside life where the inadequacies and frustrations of the American way of life were overcome, the repressions were liberated and the distortions were healed. This isn't

Japan any more than materialist, money-crazy America is America, but like all stereotypes some of the truth can be fitted into it. (p. 268)

16. Kenneth Rexroth, "The Poet as Translator," in *Essays* (New York: New Directions Books, 1961), p. 19.

17. Richard Wollheim, "Nelson Goodman's *Languages of Art*," in *On Art and the Mind* (Cambridge, Mass.: Harvard University Press, 1974), p. 291.

18. Kenneth Rexroth, *The Phoenix and the Tortoise* (Norfolk, Conn.: New Directions, 1944), p. 14. Further references to this work will appear in the text abbreviated PT.

19. Gina Kolata, "Researchers Find Big Risk of Defect in Cloning Animals," *New York Times*, March 25, 2001, p. 1.

20. In a 1948 letter to James Laughlin, his editor at New Directions:

I am working on the Chinese & Japanese poetry book—I think we will have an incomparably better book than anyone else. I plan to translate from [Judith] Gautier (use [Stuart] Merrill for her) and to translate from French versions of IndoChinese poetry. . . . You have some sort of block re the orient. You have no idea of how popular such subjects are in universities now.

This remark to Laughlin is interesting not just because it identifies the cultural provincialism and distinct lack of interest in non-Western literature that prevailed in American letters in 1948, but also because it provides rather concrete evidence of what we are associating with textual cloning. For this letter comes accompanied by an editorial note citing Laughlin's "discovery of the source of KR's first Japanese and Chinese translations, rather to his chagrin." Laughlin, according to his own account, noticed marked similarities between Rexroth's Chinese and Japanese translations and French translations from the 1890s that were included in Judith Gautier's *Livre de Jade* and later carried over into Stuart Merrill's anthology *Pastels in Prose: Kenneth Rexroth and James Laughlin: Selected Letters*, ed. Lee Bartlett (New York: W.W. Norton, 1991), p. 121.

21. Alison Lurie, *Familiar Spirits: A Memoir of James Merrill and David Jackson* (New York: Viking, 2001).

22. James Merrill, *The Changing Light at Sandover* (New York: Alfred A. Knopf, 2000), p. 217. Further references to this work will appear in the text abbreviated S.

23. Walter Benjamin, "The Task of the Translator," in *Illuminations*, trans. Harry Zohn (New York: Schocken, 1976), p. 71.

24. Jacques Derrida's famous reading of Benjamin's translation theory, titled "Des Tours de Babel" engages the problem of afterlife as "sur-vie," a problem to which he returns in depth in an essay titled "Living On" devoted to Blanchot's "Arrêt de Mort" ("Death Sentence"). See, Derrida, "Des Tours de Babel," in Joseph F. Graham, ed., *Difference in Translation* (Ithaca: Cornell University Press, 1985), pp. 209–48).

Chapter 15
Everything Is Translatable

1. Walter Benjamin, "On Language as Such and on the Languages of Man," in Walter Benjamin: Selected Writings, vol. 1: 1913–1926, ed. and trans. Michael W. Jennings (Cambridge, Mass.: Harvard University Press, 1996), pp. 69–70.

2. See Robert K. Logan, *The Sixth Language: Learning a Living in the Internet Age* (Toronto: Stoddart Publishing Co., 2000). Logan argues, p. 2, that "speech, writing, mathematics, science, computing and the Internet" are the six languages of communication.

3. Manuel Castells, *The Rise of the Network Society* (Oxford: Blackwell Publishers), 1996.

4. Tilman Baumgaertel, "The Aesthetics of Crashing Browsers," *Telepolis* www/factory.org/nettime/archive/1056html.

5. http/www/blogalization.org/community/weblog.

6. McKenzie Wark in a revised version of Netletter 1 as it appeared in Wired UK. www.dmc.mq.edu.au/mwark/warchive/Other/netlish.html. Further references to this letter will appear in the text abbreviated MW. In *A Hacker Manifesto* (Cambridge, Mass.: Harvard University Press, 2004). Wark defines what he calls a "vectoral class" that capitalizes information, assigning a "viral" character to its commodification.

7. David Crystal, "Weaving a Web of Linguistic Diversity," in *The Guardian Weekly* Jan. 25, 2001 (Macmillan Publishers Ltd.).
Found at www.onestopenglish.com./Culture/gl

8. Brenda Danet and Susan Herring, Introduction to a special issue on "The Multilingual Net," *The Journal of Computer-Mediated Communication* 9 (1) Nov. 2003. They cite this statistic from the CyberAtlas (June 6, 2003). www.asusc.org/jcmc/vol9/issue1/intro.html

9. (c) http://www.TalkingCock.com 2001–2003. All rights reserved.

10. Tom McCarther explores the notion of "bilingualism within a language" in *The English Languages* (Cambridge: Cambridge University Press, 1998), p. 30.

11. Braj Kachru, ed. *The Other Tongue: English across Cultures* (Urbana: University of Illinois Press, 1982). This is a useful collection of essays. The author concludes with an argument that was adventurous for 1982, namely, that there should be "an attitudinal change toward the institutionalized non-native Englishes," p. 344.

12. David Crystal, *English as a Global Language* (Cambridge: Cambridge University Press, 1997). In posing the question "The future of world English is likely to be one of increasing multidialectism; but could this become multilingualism?" p. 177, Crystal considers the possibility of dialects becoming standard languages (like the vernaculars of Latin), thus enabling the number of official standard languages recognized worldwide to proliferate. Crystal also considers the issue of whether a language that includes the suffix "glish" or "lish" in its name can be upgraded from dialect to vehicular status.

13. David Crystal, *Language and the Internet* (Cambridge: Cambridge University Press, 2001). In his chapter on "the medium of Netspeak," Crystal locates the

uniqueness of the medium in the way in which it ignores conventional differences between speech (dynamic, transient, time-bound, suited to social or "phatic" functions) and writing (static, space-bound, suited to the recording of facts, tasks of memory and learning). The high speed of response time, and an over-reliance on abbreviations that mix letters and numbers (tmot = trust me on this; ruok = are you OK?; ta4n = that's all for now, etc.) are crucial markers of Netspeak in Crystal's estimation.

14. Michael Specter, "World, Wide, Web: 3 English Words," *New York Times* 1996. As cited by David Crystal, "The Internet: A Linguistic Revolution," www .paricenter.com/library/papers/crystal01.php

15. Jonathan Safran Foer, *Everything Is Illuminated* (New York: HarperCollins, 2003), p. 1.

16. See Reinhold Martin's discussion of theories of pattern, especially its universal extension from pattern to man-made organizational "pattern-seeing" by Gyorgy Kepes, in *The New Landscape in Art and Science* (1956). Reinhold Martin, *The Organizational Complex: Architecture, Media and Corporate Space* (Cambridge: MIT Press, 2003), pp. 67–79.

17. I borrow the term "super-sign" from Lydia Liu in her essay "How the English Alphabet Became Ideographical," in *Divided Loyalties*, ed. Louis Menand (New York: Routledge) forthcoming.

18. William Gibson, *Pattern Recognition* (New York: Penguin 2003).

19. Lydia Liu, "How the English Language Became Ideographical."

20. Walter Benjamin, "Problems in the Sociology of Language: An Overview," in *Walter Benjamin: Selected Writings*, vol. 3: 1935–1938, ed. and trans. Michael W. Jennings (Cambridge, Mass.: Harvard University Press, 2002), p. 76. Further references to this text will be to this edition and will appear in the essay abbreviated PSL.

21. Jon Agar, *Turing and the Universal Machine: The Making of the Modern Computer* (Cambridge: Icon Books Ltd., 2001), p. 135.

22. James G. Miller, Introduction to papers originally presented in 1953 at the American Psychological Association under the session title "Profits and Problems of Homeostatic Models in the Behavioral Sciences." *Chicago Behavioral Sciences Publications*, no. 1 (1953): 2.

23. Ludwig von Bertalanffy's *General System Theory* (New York: Braziller, 1968), p. 153.

24. Gayatri Chakravorty Spivak, "Translation as Culture," in *parallax* 14 (January–March 2000): 13.

25. Jacques Derrida, *Critique*, Dec. 1965–Jan. 1966, II, p. 46. Cited by Gayatri Chakravorty Spivak in "Translator's Preface" to *Of Grammatology* (Baltimore: Johns Hopkins University Press, 1974), p. lxxx.

26. Jacques Lacan, *The Seminar of Jacques Lacan Book XX* (Encore), ed. Jacques-Alain Miller, trans. Bruce Fink (New York: W. W. Norton and Co., 1999), p. 17.

27. Friedrich Kittler, "There Is No Software," in *Literature, Media, Information Systems*, ed. John Johnston (Amsterdam: G + B Arts International, 1997), p. 148.

28. McKenzie Wark, "Hypermedia Joyce Studies 3.1 (2002). Further references to this essay will appear in the text abbreviated MW2.

29. John Klima "The_Story.Show," http://artport.whitney.org/commissions/codedoc/Klima/main.html 2003.

30. Camille Utterback, http://artport.whitney.org/commissions/codedoc 2003.

31. Scott Snibbe http://artport.whitney.org/commissions/codedoc/Snibbe/Tripolar_java_wc.html. 2003.

32. Félix Guattari, *Chaosmosis: An Ethico-Aesthetic Paradigm*, trans. Paul Bains and Julian Pefanis (Sydney: Power Publications, 1992), pp. 107–108. Further references to this work will appear in the text abbreviated C.

33. Geert Lovink, "Language? No Problem," Jan. 5, 1997. www.ljudmila.org/nettime/zkp4/61 Further references to this text will be to this Web site and will appear in the text abbreviated LNP.

34. Alan Leo, "Hour is the Moment for all good men to come the subsidy of them country," in *Technology Review*, Sept. 21, 2001. See www.technologyreview.com/articles.

Chapter 16
A New Comparative Literature

1. Giorgio Agamben, *Means without Ends: Notes on Politics*, trans. Vincenzo Binetti and Cesare Casarino (Minneapolis: University of Minnesota Press, 2000), p. 64. Further references to this work will appear in the text abbreviated MWE.

2. Samuel Weber, "A Touch of Translation: On Walter Benjamin's 'Task of the Translator,' " in *The Ethics of Translation*, eds. Sandra Bermann and Michael Wood (Princeton: Princeton University Press, 2005), p. 66.

3. Jean-Luc Godard in interview with Manohla Dargis, "Godard's Metaphysics of the Movies," *New York Times*, Nov. 21, 2004, Arts and Leisure, p. 22.

4. Edouard Glissant, *Poétique de la Relation* (Paris: Gallimard, 1990), p. 88.

5. Jean Bernabé, Patrick Chamoiseau, Raphaël Confiant, *Éloge de la créolité* Edition bilingue français/anglais, trans. M. B. Teleb-Khyar (Paris: Gallimard, 1989), pp. 88–90. Emphasis in italics as appears in the original.

6. Peter Hallward, "Edouard Glissant between the Singular and the Specific," in *The Yale Journal of Criticism* 11.2 (1998): 455.

7. Haun Saussy, *The Great Wall of Discourse and Other Adventures in Cultural China* (Cambridge, Mass.: Harvard East Asian Monographs/Harvard University Press, 2001), pp. 78 and 79.

8. Jacques Derrida, *Aporias*, trans. Thomas Dutoit (Stanford: Stanford University Press, 1993), p. 6. Further references to this work will appear in the text abbreviated A.

9. The word *négritude* offers a good example of a "prosthesis of origin" since it was coined by Aimé Césaire in Martinique, a place that had no single African language on which to ground it.

10. Kenneth Reinhard, "Kant with Sade, Lacan with Levinas," *Modern Language Notes* 110.4 (1995): 785.

11. Edward Said, *Humanism and Democratic Criticism* (New York: Columbia University Press, 2003), p. 58. Further references to this work will appear in the text abbreviated HDC.

12. Leo Spitzer, "Learning Turkish" in *Varlik* [Being], Nos. 19, 35, and 37, 1934. Translation by Tülay Atak.

13. The unconscious is like a text without punctuation written in familiar characters and a foreign language, a sacred or *revealed* text, moreover, in the sense that the discourse it speaks comes from the outside, from the Other, and bears the marks of its strange desires and cruel imperatives. The interpretive work of analysis is not to translate it so much as to *rearticulate* it, to respeak and repunctuate its components: here a stop or blockage separating two morphemes or phonemes is elided, there an associative connection is severed; or perhaps an isolated and intransigent signifier in the unconscious stream, the pole star of a discursive constellation or "complex," is put into significative motion, and another falls out of circulation, as a newly fixed and unspeakable center of gravitation.

Kenneth Reinhard, "Lacan and Monotheism: Psychoanalysis and the Traversal of Cultural Fantasy," in *Jouvert*, vol. 3, no. 12 (1999), p. 7. *http://social.chass.ncsu.edu/jouvert/v3i12/reinha.htm.*

14. On the issue of two Arabic languages in one, see Iman Humaydan Younes, "Thinking *Fussha*, Feeling '*Amiya*: Between Classical and Colloquial Arabic," *Bidoun: Arts and Culture from the Middle East*, issue 02, vol. 01, Fall (2004): 66–67.

15. "In a few years I felt I had no alternative but to commit myself to a reeducation in Arabic philology and grammar. (Incidentally, the word for grammar is the plural *qawa'id*, whose singular form is the by now familiar *al-qua'ida*, also the word for a military base, as well as a rule, in the grammatical sense.)" Edward Said, "Living in Arabic," *Raritan*, Spring 2002, vol. 21, no. 4: p. 229.

16. The phrase "cognition of Paradise," close to the concept of "imparadising" that I developed in my chapter on Saidian humanism, was used by Martin Vialon in an unpublished essay on the Arcadian paintings of Traugott Fuchs, another German émigré who made his career in Istanbul under the mentorship of Spitzer and Auerbach. See "The Scars of Exile: Paralipomena concerning the Relationship between History, Literature and Politics—Demonstrated in the Examples of Erich Auerbach, Traugott Fuchs and Their Circle in Istanbul." I am grateful to Martin Vialon for his rich, ongoing research on Auerbach's Istanbul exile, and for his willingness to share work in progress.

Abeken, Heinrich, 18–19
Abrams, M. H., 38–39
Absolutely Postcolonial (Hallward), 89–91
accents, Scottish, 152–53
Acker, Kathy, 182
adequatio, 5, 86
Adonis, 104
Adorno, Theodor, 36, 62, 67, 90, 97–98, 119, 149–51, 163
Agamben, Giorgio, 243–44
Ahat, Azra, 49, 54, 55
Ahmad, Ahjaz, 45
Albania, 131–33
Alberro, Alex, 201–2
Alexie, Sherman, 98, 102
Algeria, 94–97, 103–8, 246
Algérie Littérature/Action (journal), 97
bent-Ali, Meryem, 215
Al-Kassim, Dina, 31, 34
Allah n'est pas obligé (Kourouma), 147–48
Alloula, Abdelkader, 97
alphabetization, 277n18
Althusser, Louis, 90
Amerika, Mark, 237
"L'Amiral cherche une maison à louer" (Tzara), 117
Anderson, Benedict, 42, 150
Anderson, Perry, 43
Andrić, Ivo, 133–34
Anglophone studies, 87
Anhegger, Robert, 48, 53
Ankara State Conservatory, 50
Ankara University, 50
Ansatzpunkt, 28, 79
Anstock, Heinz, 48
Antilles, 164

anti-Semitism: in American universities, 48; Céline and, 30–36; linguistic excess and, 34–36; Sartre and, 26
Anzaldua, Gloria, 98, 165, 182
Apollinaire, Guillaume, 5, 116–17
Arabic language, 249–50
Arabic literature, 103–4
Arac, Jonathan, 66
Arago, Emmanuel, 20
Arendt, Hannah, 36, 45
Arrighi, Giovanni, 68, 179
art: code and, 237–39; international market for, 99; Kentridge's critical landscapes, 193–96; and technology, 201–9, 237–39
artificial languages, 137
Asia Times, 13
"Astralingua," 112, 119
Atatürk, Mustafa Kemal, 49, 50, 54, 262n39
"Atlantica," 112, 113
Auden, W. H., 113
Auerbach, Erich, 7–8, 47, 64; Benjamin and, 261n36; on Dante, 68–69, 75, 76–78; and exile, 44–45, 50, 258n18; and founding of comparative literature, 41; and humanism, 28; in Istanbul, 27, 44–45, 48, 49–55, 56; and literary history, 179; melancholy of, 44, 258n18, 259–60n31; Said and, 44–45, 56, 59, 65, 67–73, 79–81; Spitzer compared to, 53
Augustine, Saint, 76
Austen, Jane, 182–83
authenticity, 220

Bâ, Mariama, 98
Badiou, Alain, 85–89

Bagatelles pour un massacre (Céline), 30–31, 34–36
Bakhtin, Mikhail, 30, 90, 179
Baldwin, James, 51, 148
Balibar, Renée, 136
Balkans, language politics and, 129–34
Ball, Hugo, 116, 117
Banks, Iain, 152
Banks, Russell, 99
Barka, Ben, 123–25
Barney, Natalie Clifford, 216
Barron, Stéphan, 237
Barthes, Roland, 49, 202
Bartok, Béla, 50–51
BASIC (British American Scientific International Commercial), 135–37
Basic English (BASIC), 135–37
Bassin des ouragans (Confiant), 165–66
Bataille, Georges, 135
Bate, Walter Jackson, 179
Baudelaire, Charles, 7
Baumgaertel, Tilman, 228
Bayrav, Süheyla (née Sabri), 48–49, 55, 56
Bean, George, 51
Beaufret, Jean, 33
Becker-Ho, Alice, 243
Beckett, Samuel, 86, 98
Before Columbus Foundation American Book Awards, 102
Bei Dao, 101
Bell, Ellis, 189
Bella, Ben, 122
Benedetti, Vincent, 18
Benjamin, Walter, 49, 54, 62, 71, 80, 90, 92, 204, 213; Auerbach and, 261n36; on crude thinking, 150; on philology, 67–68; on technology and language, 232–33; on translation, 4, 6–8, 38–39, 87, 100, 222–25, 226, 245
Bensmaïa, Réda, 90, 96–97
Benveniste, Émile, 51, 56
Berlin University, 57
Berman, Antoine, 6
Bernabé, Jean, 165
Bernheimer, Charles, 58
Bernstein, Charles, 199
Beti, Mongo, 98
Bhabha, Homi, 42, 90, 95
Bing, Gertrud, 48
Bismarck, Otto von, 18–20
Black Vernacular English, 142, 148
Blair, Tony, 18

Blanchot, Maurice, 90
Blavatsky, Helena P. "Madame," 221
blogs, 228
Bloom, Harold, 139, 179, 186
Boehme, Jacob, 221
Borges, Jorge Luis, 117, 210
Boudjedra, Rachid, 106–7
Bové, Paul, 56, 66
Boyle, Danny, 152
Bragg, Rick, 14
brand names, 161, 163, 166–68, 172–73, 175
Braudel, Ferdinand, 179
Brecht, Bertolt, 150, 195
Brennan, Timothy, 42
The Bridge on the Drina (Andrić), 133–34
Brisset, J-P, 112, 125–26, 211
Broken April (Kadare), 135
Brontë, Charlotte, 184, 186, 187
Brontë, Emily, 178, 182–90
Buck, Eva, 48–49, 54
Buck-Morss, Susan, 150
Building a Profession (Grossman and Spariosu), 58
Burgess, Anthony, 124
Burkart, Rosemarie, 47–48, 49, 54
Bush, George W., 15, 18
Butler, Judith, 265n1

Cage, John, 117, 237
California, extinction of Indian languages in, 4
California Beat poetry, 223
Calvet, Louis-Jean, 136–37
Cameron, Dan, 195, 196
Camus, Albert, 102
canons, transnational, 98
Cantor, Georg, 86
capitalism: late, 149–59; Netlish and, 228
Caribbean literature, 164–77, 180–90
Carnap, Rudolf, 233
Carrà, Carlo, 116
Casanova, Pascale, 139, 181
Castells, Manuel, 228
catastrophism, 92
Cavalli-Sforza, Luca, 37
The Celebration (Festen) (film), 109
celebrities, 172–73
Céline, Louis-Ferdinand, 30–36, 166, 181
Cendrars, Blaise, 116
Center for Strategic and International Studies, 13
Central Intelligence Agency (CIA), 14, 15

Cerquiglini, Bernard, 56
Certeau, Michel de, 51
Césaire, Aimé, 98, 104, 164–65, 182
Chakrabarty, Dipesh, 59
Chamoiseau, Patrick, 98, 165, 168, 181
The Changing Light at Sandover (Merrill), 223–24
channeling, 223
Les Chansons de Bilitis (Louÿs), 214–16
chaosmosis, 239
Chatwin, Bruce, 160
Chicago School systems theorists, 233
Chinese pidgin, 245
Chomsky, Noam, 233
Chow, Rey, 42, 101
Christov-Bakargiev, Carolyn, 195
Churchill, Winston, 137
Cione, Edmondo, 51
City of Saffron (al-Kharrat), 104
Cixous, Hélène, 90, 105
class, 150–53
Clastres, Pierre, 135, 136
Clausewitz, Carl von, 15–17, 21, 135
A Clockwork Orange (Burgess), 124
CNN Creole, 161, 166–77
code, 227, 236–39
CODeDOC, 237
Coetzee, J. M., 195
Cohen, Margaret, 43
Cohn-Bendit, Daniel, 122
colonialism, Scotland and, 155–59
Commonwealth Prize, 102
comparative literature: antinationalism of, 41–42; Badiou and, 85–91; categories in, 98–99; changing character of, 10–11, 243–51; founding of, 10, 25, 41–64; global nature of, 41–42, 46, 50, 55–56; idealistic versus cultural basis of, 85–93; selection of global works in, 98–99; shared philological heritage as basis for, 86–87; translatability as issue in, 91; in United States, 261n38
Comparative Literature in the Age of Multiculturalism (Bernheimer), 58
computers: brains as, 233; digital code and translation, 227; in Klima's art, 206–8; war and, 129–30. *See also* Internet; machine translation (MT); programming
Condé, Maryse, 164–65, 178, 181–90
Confiant, Raphaël, 164–77
Conway, John, 126
Core Language Engine, 232
Corman, Cid, 223

Cortázar, Julio, 98
Cosmoglossa, 137
Crain, Patricia, 277n18
Cramer, Florian, 237
Creeley, Robert, 223
Creole: Confiant and, 164–77; global, 245; and lack, 245; literary history and *créolité*, 178–90
critical habitat, 193
critical regionalism, 193
critical theory, 7–8
Croce, Benedetto, 51–52
Crystal, David, 4, 229, 230
culture industry, 97–98
Curtius, Ernst Robert, 47, 53, 59, 73, 257n12
cybernetics, 125–26, 234

Dada, 116, 117
Daily Telegraph (London), 18
Dalby, Andrew, 4
damaged language, 149–59
Damrosch, David, 42, 64
Dante Alighieri, 66–69, 75, 76–78
Danticat, Edwidge, 99
DARPA. *See* Defense Advanced Research Projects Agency
Darwish, Mahmoud, 79, 88–89
Daudet, Léon, 31
Debray, Regis, 122
Debussy, Claude, 215
Defense Advanced Research Projects Agency (DARPA), 12
Degas, Edgar, 15
De Gaulle, Charles, 122
Deleuze, Gilles, 16, 25, 85, 90, 112, 121, 155, 156, 211, 229, 239, 245
De Man, Paul, 6, 25, 38–39, 47, 62, 144, 179, 189, 278n22
Dember, Harry, 52
La Dernière Java de Mama Josepha (Confiant), 171–77
Derrida, Jacques, 6, 26, 29, 90, 183, 235, 246, 251
Desai, Anita, 98
dialect: American, 112–15; class and, 151; modernism and, 114–15
Dialectic of Enlightenment (Horkheimer et al.), 97
Dib, Mohammed, 90
Dieckmann, Herbert, 48, 49, 53, 54
Dieckmann, Lieselotte, 48
digital code, 227

Dilthey, Wilhelm, 73, 80, 137
Dimock, Wai Chee, 92
diplomacy, 17–21
Dirvana, Nesteren, 48
La Disparition (A Void) (Perec), 120, 122–23
La Disparition de la langue française (The Disappearance of the French Language) (Djebar), 106–7
"Dispossession" (Kinsella), 196–97
distant reading, 42–43, 64
Divakaruni, Chita Bannerjee, 102
Divine Comedy (Dante), 66–69, 75, 76–78
Djaout, Tahar, 95, 97, 107–8
Djebar, Assia, 97, 98, 107
DNA translation device, 227
Documenta X (exhibition), 205
Documenta XI (exhibition), 181
dogma, 110. *See also* rule-based translation
"Dogme '95," 109
Dreyfus, Alfred, 21
Drumont, Edouard, 31
Duchamp, Marcel, 237
Dumézil, Georges, 50
Duras, Marguerite, 167–68
Duruman, Safinaz, 48

eating disorders, 121
Eberhard, Wolfram, 50
Eberhardt, Isabelle, 105
Ebert, Carl, 50
Ebonics. *See* Black Vernacular English
Eckehart, Meister, 221
Eco, Umberto, 211
ecology, translation studies and, 4–5
Ecosystm (Klima), 206
Edward Said and the Work of the Critic (Bové), 66
Einstein, Albert, 22, 48
Eliot, George, 152–53
Eliot, T. S., 114–15, 198
Ellison, Ralph, 114
Éloge de la créolité (Confiant, Chamoiseau, and Bernabé), 165, 168, 181, 245
emancipatory humanism, 65, 66
Ems Dispatch, 18–21
Engelburg, Ernst, 48
English: Basic (BASIC), 135–37; Black Vernacular, 142, 148; Euro-, 239; Internet effects on, 229–30; mono- and polylingual aspects, 138; Netlish and, 226, 228. *See also* other Englishes
Enwezor, Okwui, 181

Esperanto, 137, 232
Essays in Comparative Literature (Dieckmann and Levin), 53
essentialism. *See* linguistic essentialism
Etiemble, René, 46–47
Euro-English, 239
Europe, standardization of language for, 137
European Union, 240
Europeo, 137
Everything Is Illuminated (Foer), 211, 231
The Exeter Text (Perec), 123–25
exile, 44–45, 50, 60
experience, withering of, 149–50
Eyüboğlu, Sabahattin, 48, 54, 55–56

Fanon, Frantz, 26, 66, 90
Farès, Nabile, 103
Faulkner, William, 184
faux ami, 20
Favre, Jules, 20
Fend, Peter, 208
Fenellosa, Ernest, 219
Fichte, Johann, 56
figura, 79
Foer, Jonathan Safran, 211, 231
Fogarty, Lionel, 99, 198
Foigny, Gabriel, 211
forgeries, literary, 214–23
Foucault, Michel, 16, 26, 49, 90, 126, 179, 211
Fougère, Gustave, 215
Fournel, Paul, 112
Frampton, Kenneth, 193
France, 18–21, 99–100, 103, 136–37
Francophone studies, 86
Franco-Prussian War, 15, 17–21
Frankfurt School, 7, 98, 149, 193
Freccero, John, 47
French language: in Algeria, 246; Arabic writers using, 106–7; Caribbean writers using, 164–65; Derrida and, 246
Freud, Sigmund, 21–22, 72, 73, 90, 183
Friedrich, Hugo, 47, 57
From Swastika to Jim Crow (film), 48
Fuchs, Traugott, 48, 50, 54, 69
futurism, 116

Gainsbourg, Serge, 166
Galassi, Peter, 201
Galloway, Janice, 154
Gambetta, Leon, 20
Gates, Henry Louis, 179
Gautier, Théophile, 105, 160

genes: DNA translation device, 227; genetic program, 235; Lacan on, 235–36; reproduction models applied to translation, 213–14, 221–25
genome project, 34, 213
geography: comparative literature fields and, 86–87; language nomination and, 243–47
Ghosh, Amitav, 98, 228
Gibson, Morgan, 217–18
Gibson, William, 231
Gide, André, 215, 216
Gilbert, Sandra, 179
Gilroy, Paul, 90
Ginsberg, Alan, 117
Glissant, Edouard, 90, 245, 246
global comparatism, 44–47, 53, 56
Global Cultures: A Transnational Short Fiction Reader (Young-Bruehl), 103
globalization: exploitation and, 207–8; national literatures and, 97–98, 100–102; native languages and, 164; Netlish and, 228; publishing industry and, 100–102; translation and, 97–101; travel and, 160
global *translatio*, 46, 56, 64
Godard, Henri, 35
Godard, Jean-Luc, 244
Goethe, Johann Wolfgang von, 41, 72
Go Fish (Klima), 207
Goodman, Nelson, 220
Gordimer, Nadine, 98
Goujon, Jean-Paul, 214
Gourgouris, Stathis, 75
Gourmont, Rémy de, 214, 216
Goytisolo, Juan, 94–95
Gramont, Antoine-Agénor-Alfred, Duc de, 18
great works of literature, 66, 80, 139
Greece, 261–62n39
Greimas, A. J., 51, 56
Grossman, Lionel, 58
Grosz, Elizabeth, 199
Guantánamo Bay detention camp, 13, 15
Guattari, Félix, 155, 156, 239, 245
Gubar, Susan, 179
Gumbrecht, Hans Ulrich, 37, 258n18
Gundolf, Friedrich, 30, 73
Gursky, Andreas, 201–4
Guyot-Montpayroux, Jules-Simon, 20
Gypsy language, 243

Habermas, Jürgen, 33, 129
Hagedorn, Jessica, 98
Hak Kyung Cha, Theresa, 98, 146

Hallward, Peter, 89–91, 245
Hamalian, Linda, 217, 221
Haraway, Donna, 200
Hardt, Michael, 208
Harman, Mark, 155
Harris, Wilson, 165, 182
Hartman, Geoffrey, 64
Hartmann, Sadakichi, 219
Harvey, David, 179
H.D. (Hilda Doolittle), 219
Hearn, Lafcadio, 219
Hebbel, Christian Friedrich, 62
Hegel, G.W.F., 80, 265n1
Heidegger, Martin, 26, 29, 33, 60, 92, 106, 163, 204
Heim, Michael, 6
Hejinian, Lyn, 199
Herder, Johann Gottfried von, 74
Heredia, José María de, 215
Hertz, Neil, 38
Hiawatha (Longfellow), 213
Hill, Ernestine, 160
Hindemith, Paul, 50
Hitler, Adolf, 149–50
Hofmannsthal, Hugo von, 73
Hollier, Dennis, 38
Holquist, Michael, 56–57
Horkheimer, Max, 36, 97–98, 150, 163
Houellebecq, Michel, 161
Howard, Richard, 6
How to Read and Why (Bloom), 139
HTML (HyperText Markup Language), 236
Huelsenbeck, Richard, 116, 117
Hughes, Langston, 114, 115
Hugo, Victor, 88
human: concept of, 25–26; Heidegger on concept of, 33; humanism and, 38–39; humanities and concept of, 25–26, 28, 38–39; subject versus, 25–26
humanism: emancipatory, 65, 66; Heidegger on, 33; human and, 38–39; and identity, 71; imperialism and, 65, 66; Paradise and, 80; philology and, 37, 247–51; politics and, 66; religious versus secular aspects of, 74–75; Renaissance, 75; Said and, 44–46, 56, 58–60, 65–81, 92–93, 247–51; structuralism and, 38; theology and, 73; transnational, 46, 56, 60–61, 64; Turkish academic reform and, 52
humanities, 25–40; concept of human and, 25–26, 28; death of, 37–38; electronic communication and, 227

Humboldt, Wilhelm von, 56, 110, 129
Huntington, Samuel, 75
Hurston, Nora Zeale, 114, 115
Hussein, Qusay, 13
Hussein, Saddam, 15
Hussein, Uday, 13
Huyssen, Andreas, 57
hybridity models, 182
hypertext, 237

I Am a Soldier Too: The Jessica Lynch Story
    (Bragg), 14
identity, Said on, 70–71
illiteracy, in *Wuthering Heights*, 187
images, "translation" of, 15
immigrant English, 113–15
imperialism: in *Divine Comedy*, 78; humanism
    and, 65, 66; language standardization and,
    136–37; linguistic, 53–54, 57–58, 64, 230
informatics, 227, 233–34
interdisciplinary communication, 233
interlingual model of machine translation,
    232
international prizes, 102, 107–8
Internet: hypertext and, 237; languages on,
    229; Netlish, 226–31, 239–40; and translat-
    ability, 226; as translation zone, 138,
    272n17; United States hegemony on, 239–40
Internet Relay Chat, 237
An Introduction to Arab Poetics (Adonis), 104
*Introduction to Romance Languages and Litera-
    tures* (Auerbach), 53
Iraq War, 12–15
Irigaray, Luce, 90
Irving, Washington, 160
Isabella II (queen of Spain), 18
Islam: in *Divine Comedy*, 66–67; fundamental-
    ist, 95, 250; Goethe and, 72; reading in,
    250; variety in, 59
Istanbul. *See* University of Istanbul
Istanbul Technical University, 51

Jackson, David, 223
Jakobson, Roman, 56, 57, 126, 235–36
Jameson, Frederic, 42, 43, 51
Jane Eyre (Brontë), 184
Japan, 137–38
Japlish, 228
japonisme, 219, 220, 223
Jerome, Saint, 57
Jetztzeit (now-time), 7
jihad, 250

JODI, 237
John of the Cross, Saint, 221
Johnson, Barbara, 6, 8
Johnson, Charles, 90
Johnson, Linton Kwesi, 141
Joint Inquiry into Intelligence Community
    Activities before and after the Terrorist
    Attacks of September 11, 2001, 13–14
Jolas, Eugene, 112–19, 125
Jones, Andrew T., 101–2
Joyce, James, 112, 114, 118, 156, 181, 237
Jünger, Ernest, 92
justice, Paradise and, 78, 79

Kachru, Braj, 230
Kadare, Ismail, 129–35
Kafka, Franz, 155, 156, 181
Kay, Jackie, 140–41
Keenan, Thomas, 25
"*keeping your mouth shut—against conspiracy*"
    (Kinsella), 199
Kelman, James, 152–54
Kentridge, William, 193–96, 208
Kessler, Gerhard, 50
al-Kharrat, Edwar, 104
Khatibi, Abdelkedir, 90, 96, 105–6, 246
Kinsella, John, 98, 196–201
Kiriyama Pacific Rim Book Prize, 102
Kiš, Danilo, 98
Kittler, Friedrich, 206, 236
Klein, Melanie, 234
Klemperer, Victor, 47, 51, 57–58, 71
Klima, John, 206–8, 238
Kodak, 161
Kolata, Gina, 222
Koolhaas, Rem, 5
Kourouma, Amadou, 147–48
Kranz, Walter, 49
Krauss, Rosalind, 194
Kristeller, Paul Oskar, 48
Kundera, Milan, 98

Lacan, Jacques, 21, 26, 90, 120, 199, 200,
    235–36
Landa, Manuel de, 16, 134
Landauer, Carl, 261n38
landscape painting, 193–96
language: code and, 236–37; conquest and, 57;
    damaged, 149–59; and disease, 35–36; evolu-
    tionary models and, 4–5, 37; Internet and,
    229–30; in Maghreb, 96; materiality of, 121;
    media and, 163–64, 166–77; nationality

and, 243–44; Nazism and, 57–58; programming and, 227; respect for, through non-translation, 62–63; standardization of, 136–37, 232–33; technology and, 135–38, 163, 232–33; universal, 136–37, 232–33; war and, 129–30, 135, 144–46
language nomination, 243–47
L=A=N=G=U=A=G=E poets, 199
language wars, 139
Laqueur, Kurt, 48
late capitalism, 149–59
Laughlin, James, 117
Lee, Chang-rae, 102
Lefevere, André, 6
Leibniz, Gottfried Wilhelm, 129, 137, 232
Leo, Alan, 240
Leopold of Hohenzollern-Sigmarinen, Prince, 18–19
Le Pen, Jean-Marie, 122
L'Etang, Gerry, 166
"Lettre Océan" (Apollinaire), 116–17
Levin, Harry, 49, 53
Levinas, Emmanuel, 90
Levine, Jill, 6
Lewis, David, 211
Lewis, Philip, 6, 142
Le Witt, Sol, 237
Lindenberger, Herbert, 59
lingua francas, 136, 137, 232
linguistic essentialism, 110–12, 164–65
linguistic imperialism, 53–54, 57–58, 64, 230
linguistic nominalism, 5
"Linguistics and Literary History" (Spitzer), 25, 27, 47
Lionnet, Françoise, 42
Lipsky, David, 14
Lisle, Leconte de, 214
literacy, in *Wuthering Heights*, 187
literary history: *créolité* and, 178–90; models of, 178–80; modernity and, 278n22; tree and wave models of, 180–81
Literary Language and Its Public in Late Antiquity and in the Middle Ages (Auerbach), 53–54
literary translations, 267–68n13
Littré, Maximilien-Paul-Émile, 39
Liu, Lydia, 232
Lloyd, David, 155, 156
Logan, Robert, 230
logic, universal language and, 233
Longfellow, Henry Wadsworth, 213
Los Angeles Times, 119

Loti, Pierre, 105
Louÿs, Pierre, 214–16
Lovejoy, Arthur, 179
Lovink, Geert, 228, 239–40
Loy, Mina, 114, 116
Lucan, 214, 215
Lukács, Georg, 68, 179, 189
lunatic linguistics, 211
Lurie, Alison, 223
Luttwak, Edward N., 13
Lynch, Jessica, 14, 15

MacFarquahar, Neil, 13
machine translation (MT), 12, 227, 232
Mahfouz, Naguib, 98, 104
Malche, Albert, 52
Malik, Charles, 60
Mallarmé, Stéphane, 67, 85–89, 219
Mammeri, Mouloud, 97
Mannoni, Octave, 182
Mansfield Park (Austen), 183
Marchand, Hans, 48, 54
Marin, Louis, 51
Marinetti, Filippo Tommaso, 116
Márquez, Gabriel Garcia, 98
Marsa, 103
Marx, Leo, 58
Marxism and Form (Jameson), 43
Mathews, Harry, 112, 210–11
Mauclair, Camille, 215
Mbembe, Achille, 90, 143–44
McCarther, Tom, 230
McLean, Duncan, 152, 154–55
McPherson, James, 212
Meddeb, Abdelwahab, 90
media: language and, 163–64, 166–77; modern war and, 19
mediality, 204–5
Mein Kampf (Hitler), 30
Meissonier, Jean-Louis-Ernest, 15
Meleager, 214, 215
Memmi, Albert, 90, 98, 182
Mencken, H. L., 113
Merrill, James, 223–24
Meschonnic, Henri, 6
Meyer-Lübke (Spitzer's teacher), 28
Michaud, Henri, 219
La migration des coeurs (*Windward Heights*) (Condé), 178, 182–90
Mikani, Yoshi, 230
Miller, Jacques-Alain, 199
Miller, James, 233

Miller, Judith, 13
Milner, John, 15
Mimesis (Auerbach), 67–74, 80
Mine (film), 195
minorities: comparative literature and, 44–45;
    critical secularism and, 70
minor literature, 155, 181, 274–75n10
mistranslation: Franco-Prussian War and, 18–
    21; war dangers of, 12
Miyoshi, Masao, 42
modernism: literary history and, 278n22; Ori-
    entalism and, 219; race and, 114–15
Moltke, Helmet von, 19
monolingualism, 12, 15
Moretti, Franco, 41–43, 64, 179–80
Morrison, Toni, 98
MSNBC, 12
Mufti, Aamir, 44–45, 70
multilingualism, 61–62
Mundolingue, 137
Muntadas, 204–6
Murakami, Haruki, 98
Musil, Robert, 202
My Life in the Bush of Ghosts (Tutuola), 145
mysticism, 221–22

Naipaul, V. S., 160
Napoleon Bonaparte, 16
Napoleon III, 20
nation, language designation not determined
    by, 243–47
nationalism: humanism versus, 71; secularism
    versus, 75; Turkish, 49–50, 55
national literatures: comparative literature
    versus, 41–42; critical approaches and, 42;
    globalization and, 97–98, 100–102; Scottish,
    152–59; silencing of, 96–97, 108
National Security Agency, 14
Native American languages, 4
nature, 193–209
Nazi Germany, 27, 57–58, 259n23
Nedjma (Yacine), 103
Negri, Antonio, 208
Negritude, 170
neighbor, concept of, 247
neocolonialism, 102–3
neologisms, 161, 163, 175–76
Netlish, 226–31, 239–40
Neumark, Fritz, 50
New Englishes, 142
New Left Review (journal), 43

New Scotologists, 152–59
New York Times, 13, 14, 95–96
Nietzsche, Friedrich, 144
Nigeria, 142–47
"No Grudge" (Fogarty), 198
Noma Award, 102
nonstandard English. *See* other Englishes
nontranslatability, 85–93, 105, 111, 210, 246.
    See also translatability
nontranslation, philology and, 61–62
Nord Deutsche Allgemeine Zeitung, 19
North, Michael, 114–15, 141, 146–47
now-time (*Jetztzeit*), 7
Nuclear English, 135–37

Ogden, C. K., 135–37
Okri, Ben, 98
Ollivier, Emile, 20
One Hundred More Poems from the Japanese
    (Rexroth), 216
open system, 234
Orientalism, 44, 45, 75
Orientalism (Said), 65, 66–67, 74
original, translation and, 210–25
Ossianic poems, 212
other Englishes: Internet and, 226, 228–30; mi-
    nority literatures and, 141; political aspect
    of, 146–47, 156; Saro-wiwa's *Sozaboy* and,
    141–48; standard English in relation to,
    138, 148, 155–56, 226, 228, 230
Ouija board, 223
Oulipo, 112, 120, 125–26, 210
Ouspensky, P. D., 221
Owen, Stephen, 101

Pächt, Otto, 48
Pamuk, Orhan, 98
Panofsky, Erwin, 48
Paradise, 76–80
parallel worlds, 211–12
Parrhasios, 200
Parsons, Talcott, 233
Pasley, Malcolm, 155
Pasternak, Boris, 113
Paz, Octavio, 98
Pennycock, Alistair, 137
Perec, Georges, 112, 120, 122–25
Pessoa, Ferdinand, 98
Petrarch, 75
Pevsner, Nikolaus, 48
Phantastische Gebete (Huelsenbeck), 117

Philippe, Charles-Louis, 30
philology: critical theory and, 7–8; humanism and, 37, 247–51; modern history of, 56–58; and popular culture, 59–60, 161–63; race and, 27–37, 39–40; as resistance, 58; Said on, 247–51; significance of, 25; tree model in, 180
"The Phoenix and the Tortoise" (Rexroth), 222
pictograms, 58
pidgin: Chinese, 245; Fogarty and, 198; Saro-wiwa's *Sozaboy* and, 141–48
Pierneef, J. H., 194
planetary criticism, 92
plurilingualism, 112–19
Poets' Messages (publication series), 113
politics: language standardization and, 136–37; Perec's works and, 122–25. *See also* imperialism
Pontalis, J-P, 120
Popovic, Anton, 212
popular culture: linguistic influence of, 161, 163; philology and, 59–60, 161–63
Port-Royal school, 232
possible worlds, 211–12
postcolonial fiction, CNN Creole in, 161
postcolonial studies: comparative literature and, 58; foreshadowing of, 46–47; Hallward and, 89–91; shared philological heritage as basis for, 86–87
postcolonial theory, 149
Pound, Ezra, 114–15, 116, 181, 219
Prix Méditerranée, 102
prizes. *See* international prizes
programming, 227, 234, 236–39
Prost, Henri, 51
Proust, Marcel, 167
Prussia, 17–21
pseudotranslation, 212–25
psychoanalysis, 17–18, 21–22
Publications de la faculté des lettres de l'Université d'Istanbul (journal), 54
publishing industry: Algerian literature and, 103; globalization and, 100–101; and literary translations, 267–68n13; and national literatures, 108; and translations, 101–2, 268n13
Pullman porters, 29–30

al-qua'ida, 250, 286n15
Quayson, Ato, 43

Queneau, Raymond, 112, 120
Quine, Willard Van Orman, 6, 110–11
Quirk, Randolph, 135

Rabassa, Gregory, 6
Rabelais, François, 30
Rabi'a, Labîd ben, 85–89
race: Caribbean languages and, 188–89; humanism and, 26; modernism and, 114–15; philology and, 27–37, 39–40; racial etymon, 25; reason and, 32; universalism and, 27
Radziwell, Prince, 20
Ralls, Steve, 14
Rammellzee, 230
Ramuz, C-F, 181
Rancière, Jacques, 22
Rapoport, Anatol, 16
Rasse, 27, 32, 34, 39
Rasula, Jed, 199
ratio, 27, 32–33, 35, 39
"Ratio {{gthan}} Race" (Spitzer), 27
rational-choice theory, 17–18
readability, 139
reading, in *Wuthering Heights*, 187
Readings, Bill, 37–38
reading wars, 139
Reclus, Elisée, 179
Régnier, Henri de, 215
Reichenbach, Hans, 50
Reinhard, Kenneth, 247, 249, 286n13
Réjouis, Rose-Myriam, 168
religion, 66–67, 71–73, 75–76. *See also* Islam
Renan, Ernest, 137
Renoir, Pierre-Auguste, 15
La République mondiale des lettres (The Global Republic of Letters) (Casanova), 139, 181
Rétamar, Fernando, 182
Les Revenentes (The Exeter Text) (Perec), 123–25
Rexroth, Kenneth, 216–23
Rhys, Jean, 182
Richards, Earl Jeffrey, 257n12
Richards, I. A., 58
Rippon, Max, 165, 182
Robbins, Bruce, 42, 75
Robinson, Douglas, 212
Rohde, Georg, 50
Romanization, 53–54
Rose, Jacqueline, 70
Ross, Brian, 14
rotten English. *See* other Englishes

Roubaud, Jacques, 112
Roussel, Raymond, 112, 211
Roux, Dominique de, 34
Roy, Arundhati, 98
Royal/Dutch Shell Group, 142
rule-based translation, 111–12, 120–26, 211–12, 233
Rumsfeld, Donald, 15
Runciman, Steven, 51
Rushdie, Salman, 98
Russia, 137

el-Saadawi, Nawal, 104
Sabri, Süheyla. See Bayrav, Süheyla
Said, Edward, 42, 51, 90; on Arabic language, 249–50; on Arabic literature, 104; and Auerbach, 44–45, 56, 59, 65, 67–73, 79–81; on colonial influence in literature, 183–84; and humanism, 44–46, 56, 58–60, 65–81, 92–93, 247–51; on identity, 70–71; as literary critic, 66; on philology, 247–51; and popular culture, 59–60; and religion, 66–67, 71–73, 75–76; and Spitzer, 70
Said, Maire, 44
Salih, Tayeb, 98
Sapir-Whorf hypothesis, 228
Sappho, 214, 216
Sarduy, Severo, 90
Saro-wiwa, Ken, 141–48
Sartre, Jean-Paul, 26, 148
satori, 91–92
Saussy, Haun, 245
"The Savagery of Birds" (Kinsella), 200
La Savane des pétrifications (Confiant), 165–66, 168–70
Saxl, Fritz, 48
Schalaben Shalamai Shalamezomai (Huelsenbeck), 117
Schell, Jonathan, 22
Schelling, Friedrich, 57
Le Schizo et les langues . . . (The Schizo and Languages . . .) (Wolfson), 119–22
Schleiermacher, Friedrich, 56
Scholem, Gershom, 71
Schröder, Gerhard, 18
Schwarz, Roberto, 43, 179
Scotland, 152–59
secularism, 74–75
Segalen, Victor, 219
Sekula, Allan, 208
Selvon, Sam, 141
semantic zoning, 6

semiotics, invention of, 51
Semmelweis, Philip, 36
Sénac, Jean, 97
Le Seuil, 103
Shanks, Wayne, 14
al-Shaykh, Hanan, 104
Sibony, Daniel, 34–35
Sieburth, Richard, 6
Silliman, Ron, 199
Silvalogue (Jolas), 118
Simplo, 137
Sinbad, 103
Singapore, 230
Singlish, 229–30
singularity: Badiou and, 85–89; relativism versus, 90
sixth language, 226
"Skeleton weed/generative grammar (for Noam Chomsky)" (Kinsella), 199
Slanguage, 230
Sloterdijk, Peter, 33–34
Smith, Philip, 17
Snibbe, Scott, 238–39
Snyder, Frans, 200
Snyder, Gary, 223
socialism, 36, 232
Society for Pure English, 115
Sontag, Susan, 6
sound-poems, 117
South Africa, 194–95
Soyinke, Wole, 98
Sozaboy (Saro-wiwa), 141–48
Spanish and Latin American studies, 86
Spariosu, Mihai, 58
species, 32
Sperber, Hans, 175
spiritism, 223
Spitzer, Leo, 8, 25–40, 68, 69, 73; affair of, 47–48; Auerbach compared to, 53; on Creole, 168; and founding of comparative literature, 10, 25, 41–64; and Germany, 47, 255n3; and humanism, 59; influence of, 47; in Istanbul, 27, 47–50, 52–55, 56, 63–64, 248–49, 257n6; and literary history, 179; as military censor, 47, 175–76, 254n2; on neologisms, 161, 175–76; philology of, 61–64; and popular culture, 60, 161–63; race and philology in, 27–37; Said and, 70; and universalism, 26–27, 41
Spivak, Gayatri Chakravorty, 6, 42, 90, 91, 92–93, 102–3, 193, 199, 234–35, 265n1
standardization of language, 136–37, 232–33

Stein, Gertrude, 114
Steiner, George, 6, 135
Stevens, Wallace, 219
Stiegler, Bernard, 204
Stow, Randolph, 152
structuralism, 38
subject: Dante on, 75, 76–77; human versus, 25–26; language and, 229; translation as repositioning of, 6
Sunkist, 161–62
Surrealism, 116
Suzuki, Daisetz Teitaroo, 91–92
Syme, Ronald, 51
systems theory, 233–34

Taine, Hippolyte, 178
Tanguy, Yves, 113
Tapsell, Peter, 18
"The Task of the Translator" (Benjamin), 7, 224–225
Taut, Bruno, 51
technology: art and, 201–9, 237–39; language and, 135–38, 163, 232–33; role of, in translation, 8, 226. See also computers
tensors, 156
terrorism: Perec's works and, 122; translation and, 12–16
textual cloning, 213–14, 221–25
theodicy, 76
Thiers, Adolphe, 20
The Three-Arched Bridge (Kadare), 130–34
Tietze, Andreas, 48, 53
Tocqueville, Alexis de, 160
Todorova, Maria, 130
Tóibín, Colm, 98
total war, 16–17
Toussaint L'Ouverture, 184
trademarks. See brand names
Trainspotting (Welsh), 100, 152, 155–59
transfer model of machine translation, 232
transitions (journal), 112, 115
translatability, 91, 226–40. See also nontranslatability
translation: of Arabic literature, 103–4; Benjamin's contribution to, 6–8; conquest and, 57; culture industry and, 97–102; dilemma of, 210–11; extinction and preservation issues, 4; fidelity model of, 5, 7, 210–14, 225; Franco-Prussian War and, 18–21; genetic reproduction models applied to, 213–14, 221–25; globalization and, 97–101; historical sketch of, 10, 253n4; machine, 12,

227, 232; Muntadas and, 204–6; neocolonialism and, 102–3; original and, 210–25; political significance of, 3, 6; pseudotranslation, 212–25; rule-based, 111–12, 120–26, 211–12, 233; subject repositioned through, 6; technology and, 8, 226; transcoding model of, 7; twenty theses on, xi–xii; U.S. defense and, 12–15; visual, 15; war and, 12–22. See also mistranslation; nontranslatability; nontranslation; translatability; translation studies; translation zone; translators
translationalism, 233
translational transnationalism, 5, 87
translation studies: changing character of, 3–5; ecological approach in, 4–5; electronic communication and, 227; status of, 10
translation zone: anxiety and, 133–34; concept of, 6, 129; war and, 129, 133–35
translators: in Muntadas film, 205; Rexroth, 216–20
transnational humanism, 46, 56, 60–61, 64
travel-writing, 160
Trotsky, Leon, 36, 50
Tupi-Guarani Indians, 135
Turkey: Greece and, 261–62n39; language reforms in, 53–56; nationalism in, 49–50, 55; Nazis in Istanbul, 259n23; University of Istanbul, 43–44, 48–56
Turkish Worker's Syndicate, 50
Tutuola, Amos, 145
Tzara, Tristan, 116, 117

Ulam, Stanislaw, 126
unconscious, 286n13
unilateralism, 12, 15
United States: comparative literature in, 261n38; Internet hegemony of, 239–40; language and dialect in, 112–16; literary translations in, 267–68n13
Universalglot, 137
universalism: Badiou and, 85–89; Hegelian, 265n1; Spitzer and, 26–27; universal language, 136–37, 232–33
University of Istanbul, 43–44, 48–56
Untitled XII (Musil 1) (Gursky), 202–3
untranslatability. See nontranslatability
Urgan, Mina, 48
Utterback, Camille, 238

Valéry, Paul, 215
Valla, Lorenzo, 75
Van Gogh, Vincent, 29

Vargas Llosa, Mario, 104
Varlik (journal), 54, 55
Venuti, Lawrence, 6
Verband Deutscher Ingenieure (German Engineers Association), 233
Vergès, Françoise, 90
vertigralism, 119
Vian, Boris, 166
Vico, Giambattista, 80
Les Vigiles (Djaout), 107–8
Vinokurov, Val, 168
Vinterberg, Thomas, 109
Virilio, Paul, 16
"*Virus****" (Kay), 140–41
Vivien, Renée, 216
A Void (Perec), 120, 122–23
Volapük, 137
Volschenk, Jan Ernst Abraham, 194
Vom Kriege (Clausewitz), 16
Von Neumann, John, 126
Von Neumann, Oskar, 16
Vossler, Karl, 37, 47, 53, 73

Wagenbach, Klaus, 156
Walcott, Derek, 165, 182
Waley, Arthur, 217, 219, 221
Wallerstein, Immanuel, 43
Walters, Donald, 14
war: Clausewitz on, 16; communication effects on, 19; cultural role in, 17; language and, 129–30, 135, 144–46; realist view of, 16–17; total, 16–17; translation and, 12–22; translation zones and, 129, 133–35
Wark, McKenzie, 228–30, 237, 239–40
Warner, Marina, 183
Wa Thiong'o, Ngũgĩ, 90, 170
Web. *See* Internet
Weber, Samuel, 6, 204, 244
Weil, Simone, 36
Weiner, Karl, 48
Welling, James, 204
Welsh, Irvine, 100, 152, 155–59

Weltliteratur, 41, 66, 72
Weltsprache, 137
Whalen, Philip, 223
Wharton, Edith, 160
Whitehead, Alfred North, 60
Whitney Museum, 237
Wide Sargasso Sea (Rhys), 182
Wiener, Norbert, 125
Wilhelm I (king of Prussia), 18–20
Williams, William Carlos, 113
Windward Heights (Condé), 178, 182–90
Wittgenstein, Ludwig, 111, 244
Wolcott, Derek, 98
Wolfson, Louis, 112, 119–22, 125, 211
women, scholars launched by Spitzer, 49
Women of Sand and Myrrh (al-Shaykh), 104
Woolf, Virginia, 182
Words from the Deluge (Jolas), 113
"The Work of Art in the Era of Its Reproducibility" (Benjamin), 7
world literature, how to teach, 42–43
world-systems theory, 43, 64
World Wide Web. *See* Internet
Wüster, Eugen, 232
Wuthering Heights (Brontë), 178, 182–90

Yacine, Kateb, 97, 103
Yeats, W. B., 219
Yeh, Michele, 101
Yosano Akiko, 218
Young, Robert, 90
Young-Bruehl, Elisabeth, 103

Zen Buddhism, 91–92
zero-sum game, 21
Zeuxis, 200
Zhao, Henry, 43
Zimmerman telegram, 19
Zola, Emile, 21
zone, concept of, 5–6
"Zone" (Apollinaire), 5